The Rise and Fall of Catholic Religious Orders

SUNY Series in Religion, Culture, and Society

Wade Clark Roof, Editor

The Rise and Fall of Catholic Religious Orders

A Social Movement Perspective

Patricia Wittberg, S.C.

THE STATE UNIVERSITY OF NEW YORK PRESS

Permissions acknowledgments: Quotation from Burns, AJS 95:5, 1131–32, is reprinted with permission from the University of Chicago Press. Quotation from "Bishops Differ on Exercise of Power," 2:1, 3, reprinted with permission from *Bread Rising.* Three quotations from *Religious Life Review* are reprinted with permission. Quotations from William Hinnebusch, OP, "How the Dominican Order Faced Its Crisis," 32: 1314, 1318; Joseph M. Lackner, "Anomie and Religious Life," 28: 629; Andre Auw, "The Evangelical Counsels," 28: 230; and Vincent Genovesi, "The Faith of Christ," 38: 191–192 are reprinted with permission from *Review for Religious.* Quotations from Joseph G. Mannard, "Maternity of Spirit," 5:4–5, 306-307; Patricia Byrne, "Sisters of St. Joseph," 5:4–5, 267–68 are reprinted with permission from *U.S. Catholic Historian.*

Published by
State University of New York Press, Albany

© 1994 State University of New York

For information address State University of New York Press, State University Plaza, Albany, NY 12246

Production by Laura Starrett
Marketing by Bernadette LaManna

Library of Congress Cataloging in Publication Date

Wittberg, Patricia, 1947–
    The rise and fall of Catholic religious orders : a social movement
perspective / Patricia Wittberg.
        p.   cm. — (SUNY series in religion, culture, and society)
    Includes bibliographical references and index.
    ISBN 0-7914-2229-1 : $59.50 — ISBN 0-7914-2230-5 (pbk.) : $19.95
    1. Monasticism and religious orders—History.   2. Monasticism and
religious orders—History—20th century.   I. Title.   II. Series.
BX2461.2.W58   1994
271'.009'045—dc20   94-1068
                                                                          CIP

10 9 8 7 6 5 4 3 2

Contents

List of Tables

For my parents

Preface

In one sense, I have been preparing to write this book since the fall of 1975, when I read Benjamin Zablocki's *The Joyful Community* as one of the assignments for my first graduate sociology class at the University of Chicago. As a young woman in a Roman Catholic religious community, who had entered the Sisters of Charity less than a decade before and only recently made her final vows, it was disturbing to read Zablocki's contention that the very commitment mechanisms my congregation had discarded (with my enthusiastic endorsement) were utterly necessary for our communal survival. In subsequent years, as the number of women and men in Catholic religious orders declined, my uneasiness grew. For a long while, however, I was unable even to articulate what disturbed me. While the members of Roman Catholic religious communities have acquired an extensive psychological vocabulary that they readily employ to analyze the spiritual and communal aspects of their lives, sociological terminology has remained largely unfamiliar to them. Sociology, if used at all, has been applied to problems in the *ministry*—how better to serve the poor, the sick, the uneducated—and rarely, if ever, to problems in the social groups to which the *ministers* belong. It has taken me a decade to develop a facility in applying the concepts, hypotheses, and research I studied as a graduate student in a secular university to the internal dynamics of Roman Catholic religious orders.

The actual book had its genesis in a stern telephone call I received, in the spring of 1991, from my friend and colleague Helen Rose Ebaugh, who told me that it was not enough to continue writing books and articles on the topic for an audience of religious sisters—that I owed it to the profession and myself to attempt a more in-depth analysis of the decline of religious orders. I believe that the issues raised by this decline have implications, not merely for the functioning of Roman Catholicism in the future, but for the officials and members of every Christian denomination that is faced with the question of how to make provision for the religious virtuosi in their midst. The study of the growth and decline of Catholic religious orders could also benefit sociology, especially the subdisciplines of knowledge formation, communal studies, and social movements, which have not previously investigated these groups. Finally, I believe passionately in religious life and feel that the Catholic Church and Western culture in general will be much poorer if it becomes extinct. If my research helps even one religious community to avoid the mistakes of the past and to survive, I will be more than adequately rewarded.

Along the way, I have received the help of many individuals, without whom this book could never have been completed. My professional colleagues, Barbara Brumleve, S.S.N.D., Sue Steinmetz, Ruth Wallace, Murray Wax, and Bob White, read and commented on all or parts of the manuscript. Mary Ann Donovan, S.C., steered me to indispensible secondary sources in a discipline—Church history—about which I knew very little two years ago. Sisters Elizabeth McDonough, O.P., and Edward Cecile Haefertepe, S.C., read the technical portions of chapter 3 and gave me invaluable feedback on canon law and the economic aspects of religious communities. The present and past heads of the Tri-Conference Retirement Office—Sisters Mary Oliver Hudon, S.S.N.D., Janet Roesener, C.S.J., and Laura Reicks, R.S.M.—provided me with updated information on the retirement fund shortfalls in many religious communities; and the National Association of Treasurers of Religious Institutes sent invaluable data on financial compensation patterns nationwide. Eleace King, I.H.M., and David L. Fleming, S.J., kindly and promptly answered my questions on their publications, providing information vital for chapters 12 and 13. And, finally, some 350 archivists in women's communities around the country not only took the time to fill out my questionnaire, but also inundated me with pamphlets, manuscripts, and published books on their orders' histories. Many of the strengths of this book are due to their assistance; the weaknesses are entirely my own.

Finally, I wish to thank the Sisters of Providence with whom I have lived in Indianapolis these past three years. Even when, at first, I was unable adequately to explain what I was studying (as well as later, when I was only too willing to explain and discuss it ad nauseam), they gave me unfailing support and put up with my often less-than-total presence to them. I hope that they and their community will be able to use this research to grow and flourish in the future.

Chapter 1

The Extent of the Problem

During the past thirty years, profound social and organizational changes have been taking place within American Catholicism. One aspect of these changes has been the sharp membership decline experienced by religious orders, the traditional source of most of the Church's personnel. As recently as the 1960s, religious communities contained over five times as many members as the "secular" clergy staffing Catholicism's parishes and diocesan offices. Even today, there are 94,022 religious sisters, 6,260 religious brothers, and 17,576 religious order priests in the United States— over three times the current number of diocesan priests and bishops.[1] Within the next two decades, however, few if any will remain.

The sharp membership decrease in religious orders has been far more severe than the well-documented drop in Catholicism's diocesan clergy. Whereas the number of diocesan priests has declined by slightly less than 30 percent since 1966, the number of nuns and of nonordained male religious has fallen over 50 percent.[2] Currently, the number of nuns per 10,000 U.S. Catholics is 18.1—lower than at any time since 1860.[3]

The orders' decline is particularly evident in their lack of new members. In the early 1960s, approximately 7,000 young women per year entered religious communities in this country, and these new entrants accounted for about 17 percent of all American nuns. By 1981, however, only 4 percent of the nuns were recent recruits and, in 1990, less than 1 percent were.[4] Fewer than 1,000 Catholic women—out of an expanded Catholic population of over 54 million—entered U.S. religious orders in 1990.[5] Currently, 54 percent of all women's religious communities, 36 percent of the communities of nonordained men, and 22 percent of clerical men's communities have no new members applying at all.[6] The decline in recruits since the 1960s is all the more striking because it has occurred at the precise time when one would have expected the young adults of the baby boom to supply an even larger number of interested applicants than usual.

Another ominous sign is the rising proportion of elderly in religious communities—again, a much more severe problem among these groups than with the diocesan clergy. The 1990 median age of nuns was sixty-five, while that of diocesan priests was fifty-four.[7] According to one estimate, by the year 2000 there will be fewer than 20,000 women in U.S. religious communities who are under the age of sixty.[8] The overwhelming impression left by these figures is that canonical religious communities—especially communities of women, which had once been by far the most numerous—are now experiencing severe difficulties, and may even be facing imminent extinction.[9]

American religious orders are not alone in experiencing declines of this magnitude. The major women's religious communities in Quebec lost 31 percent of their membership between 1966 and 1975 alone.[10] In Ireland, over 57 percent of religious sisters, 47 percent of religious brothers, and 40 percent of religious priests are over sixty years old.[11] In 1970, 300 religious order priests were ordained in Ireland; in 1987, only twenty-five were.[12] Figures from Italy, France, and other Western European countries show similar trends.[13] Such a severe decline in its primary source of personnel obviously has profound implications for the operation of the Roman Catholic Church. And yet far more attention has been paid by organizational researchers to the priest shortage in America and Europe than to the impending collapse of religious orders there.[14]

In contrast to the dismal situation in Europe and North America, religious communities in sub-Saharan Africa and South Asia are experiencing extensive growth. The number of East African sisters increased from 2,839 in 1961 to 10,913 in 1992, matching the almost fivefold increase in the number of Catholics there.[15] Of the 184 novice members who entered the Christian Brothers in 1992, fifty-four were from Africa.[16] The 4,500 U.S. Jesuits had only sixty-six novices in 1992; the Indonesian Jesuits had 340.[17] One source predicts that if present trends continue, India will produce more Jesuits in the twenty-first century than any other country.[18] The number of native-born religious in Brazil, on the other hand, is stable or declining.[19] What factors cause such differences between countries in the receptivity of the Catholics there to entering religious communities?

In addition to their obvious importance for Catholicism, religious orders are significant objects of study in their own right. Such orders are the largest and most widespread representation of the communal religious lifestyle ever to exist in the United States or elsewhere. At their peak in 1965, Roman Catholic religious communities in this country included 181,421 women and 38,478 men. This was over sixty times the highest membership ever achieved by the nineteenth-century Shakers, and almost twice as large as current estimates of the Old Order Amish.[20] However, while even a cursory literature search reveals scores of books on the Shakers and the Amish, few studies exist which analyze the communitarian aspects of Catholic religious orders.[21]

In the dynamics of their growth and decline, religious orders also parallel other religious social movements. Hatch, for example, documents the explosive growth of evangelistic churches on the nineteenth-century American frontier, when the Methodists alone grew from 14,000 menbers to over a million, and when the number of preachers per capita tripled even as the total population was doubling in size.[22] The number of aspirants who were entering Catholic religious orders during the same period is equally impressive. But, whereas America's various Great Awakenings have been intensively studied by historians, political scientists, and sociologists,[23] the periodic revitalizations of Roman Catholic religious orders have not.

The lack of sociological research on Catholic religious communities leaves several important questions unanswered. What forces underlie the current massive decline in American and European religious orders? Why were—and are—so many women and men attracted to this lifestyle at some times and in some places, and why were they comparatively uninterested in it at other times? What implications do the current patterns have for future church staffing, for the success or failure of other religion-based communitarian efforts, or for future movements of religious enthusiasts—Catholic or otherwise—around the world? A sociological analysis of religious orders could provide some insight into these questions.

Toward a Sociological Study of Life Cycles in Religious Orders

Macrolevel: Religious Foundations as Social Movements

In the more than sixteen centuries of their existence within Catholicism, religious orders have experienced recurring expansion periods, when scores of new communities were established and attracted thousands of eager applicants. Inevitably, each such expansion would eventually be followed by stagnation and collapse. These cycles of growth and decline can be considered as recurring social movements of religious virtuosi, comparable to the periodic Great Awakenings that have occurred within American Protestantism.[24] Like the more frequently studied Protestant movements, the waves of enthusiasm for religious life among Catholics were each organized around a particular ideological conception of what the value and content of religious virtuosity should be, with more or less explicitly articulated alterations adapting this ideology to the needs of the time. Whenever one of these adaptations resonated with the currently unchanneled needs of aspiring virtuosi within Roman Catholicism, large numbers of men and women might flock to whichever religious orders had made the new ideology popular. When later cultural changes rendered the ideological base of an order less tenable, it would become less attractive to potential recruits. The frame alignment theories for social movements would, therefore, seem particularly applicable to these situations.

The success of individual orders within the broader virtuoso movement also depended upon their ability to mobilize key resources: support from the hierarchy, a source of livelihood, a dependable supply of new recruits, and so on. Any later environmental changes that reduced the availability of these resources would thus affect the survival chances of religious communities. Resource mobilization theories, therefore, could also be applied to the recurring periods of growth and decay in Roman Catholic religious life.

Microlevel: The Dynamics of Intentional Communities

Concurrent with the general pattern reflected in all of the religious orders during a particular period, there were specific rhythms of growth and decay that affected each individual community. One historian has stated flatly that no religious order ever experienced more than 200 years of growth and expansion at a stretch before declining, no matter how favorable its surrounding environment was.[25] Variants of Benedictine monasticism, for example, declined and were reformed several times during the medieval period. The mendicant orders were even less stable than the monastic ones. Devout Franciscans who felt that their community had lost its original fervor began various reform movements such as the Spirituals (1300s), the Observants (1400s), and the Capuchins (1500s) in an attempt to recapture it. The other mendicant orders were similarly subject to decay and revitalization. Wynne counts at least ten "movements of renewal" among the Carmelites between the fifteenth and eighteenth centuries.[26]

These internal cycles conform fairly accurately to the frequently studied dynamics of other communal groups.[27] The need for commitment mechanisms to maintain member loyalty in an intentional community, the tendency of these mechanisms to usurp the group's original ideological vision, and the different motivations of the second- and third-generation recruits can help to explain the lapses from fervor that regularly afflicted every religious order. The social integration requirements of intentional communities can also explain why nonmonastic orders often tended to adopt communal monastic practices, as well as why the mendicant orders, which refused to do so, remained less stable.

A Research Agenda

So far, these topics have not been analyzed by sociologists. Social movement theories have been applied, for the most part, to waves of political protest, and none of the few studies of religious social movements that do exist have considered Roman Catholic religious communities. Religious orders have been similarly neglected by the sociologists studying intentional communities: not one single work in the literature considers this oldest and longest-lasting communal form.

Until recently, there was also a "dramatic void" in the works of historians with respect to religious life.[28] The major histories of American religions said little if anything about Catholic orders of women, other than a passing mention of their work in parochial schools.[29] Catholic historians, usually male clerics, also neglected to give adequate attention to sisters, even though they comprised between 70 and 80 percent of the Church's entire workforce.[30] As recently as 1987, an edited history of American Catholic parishes barely mentioned women's religious communities.[31] Priests and bishops, however, appeared on almost every page. The few separate treatments of religious orders that did exist were limited to biographies of particular founders or to privately published internal histories of a given community.[32]

During the past decade, however, historians have devoted more attention to the examination of the religious orders in various epochs— both in detailed accounts of the socioeconomic structures that led to their growth and decline and in increasingly sophisticated analyses of the philosophical and theological variations in their spiritual orientations.[33] Religious virgins and hermits in the early Church have been discussed in several works by Brown, as well as in those by Donovan, Kraemer, Fontaine, McNamara, Frazee, and others.[34] Patterns of medieval monasticism, as well as of the various mendicant movements, have been analyzed by Schulenburg, Elkins, Johnson, Lawrence, Little, and Bynum—to name only a few.[35] Rapley's excellent work documents the growth of women's religious orders in seventeenth-century France; Kavanaugh, Luria, and O'Malley discuss religious life in Spain and Italy during the same period.[36] Several comprehensive histories treat of religious orders in nineteenth-century Ireland, Quebec, and France.[37] Kennelly, Misner, Ewens, and Oates, among others, have produced similar historical studies for the United States.[38]

Despite this wealth of data on the growth of religious life in specific historical periods, however, there has been no attempt to discern or analyze the patterns or features they have in common. Tarrow's comment on cycles of political protest movements holds true as well for cycles of religious enthusiasm: "Few have tried to model 'long waves' of collective action as political economists have done for economic cycles."[39]

In part, this neglect is due to the basic focus of historical research, which usually attempts to understand as much as possible about a given event or epoch and strongly resists lumping two or more of such unique phenomena—and all historical phenomena become more obviously unique the more we study them—together in any way. So-called "cycles" of religious enthusiasm "are infrequent, are of unpredictable length and intensity, and appear to involve actors, groups, and modes of activity that differ . . . from each other. History shows that they also *do not* characterize an entire social system in the same way; indeed, they leave large pockets of [the population] uninvolved, produce conflicts between groups of mobilized [followers], and usually awaken a backlash against disorder."[40] Cyclic theorists tend to oversimplify history and to postulate the existence of regular cycles or of a mechanical relationship between movements of religious fervor and large-scale environmental forces—neither of which is empirically justified.[41] Yet, valuable insights can be gained from the comparative analysis of these movements in several different historical periods. What is needed is to look "not for the identical repetition of the same processes in the same form in different epochs, but for . . . successive realizations (in different form) of an identical principle."[42] The application of some underlying principle to separate historical instances of societal mobilization has been the focus of social movement theory.

But social movement theorists have also resisted the study of religious groups, preferring instead to concentrate on political protest movements. This reluctance, Hannigan states, is "primarily ideological in nature."[43] Social movement theorists have traditionally seen religion as a pillar of the status quo, a conservative institution that counselled its adherents to accept their lot and await a heavenly reward. Religiously inspired resistence to social change was precisely what "true" social movements were fighting *against.* Recent research has shown, however, that religious belief and social action are *not* incompatible, that, in fact, they quite frequently accompany each other.[44] Waves of religious fervor such as the periodic foundation of Roman Catholic religious communities *are* social movements. Individuals have participated in them for the same sorts of reasons that activists participate in other types of movements; they grow and decay subject to the same cyclic dynamics. This is not to say, for example, that the waves of men who joined in the mendicant movement in medieval Europe had exactly the same motivations and engaged in exactly the same activities as the 200,000 French women who founded and joined that country's nineteenth-century teaching congregations—or even that all of the mendicants among themselves ascribed to a single mindset or a single plan of action. Cycles of religious fervor, like the cycles of political protest more frequently studied by social movement theorists, "are best seen not as the mood or mentality of an entire epoch, but as aggregates of partly autonomous and partly interdependent episodes of collective action in which new forms of action emerge and evolve, a social movement sector grows and changes in its composition, and new . . . opportunities develop, in part as the result of the actions, themes and outcomes of the early movements in the cycle."[45] Cycles of religious enthusiasm will develop contingently, as individuals and groups interact with each other and choose from the repertoire of behaviors and beliefs available to them from previous cycles—and from the previous participants in their own cycle. Whatever theoretical hypotheses are developed concerning this process, they will apply somewhat differently to each specific instance, and will then be subject to empirical verification by examining consciously selected historical situations in greater detail.[46]

A neglected research opportunity exists: to attempt a sociological analysis of these periodically recurring cycles of Roman Catholic religious life. The theories and research on large-scale social movements and on the internal dynamics of other intentional communities can be applied to the data presented in the historical works on specific periods. By examining the social backgrounds and the motivations (spiritual and material) of those attracted to the burgeoning new movements in each era, the resources (or lack thereof) available to the new communities, the variations in the spirituality and in the organizational functioning of each order, and the mechanisms each group employed to maintain its members' commitment, it should be possible to advance some basic hypotheses about the causes of their growth and decline in the past. Such hypotheses could then be used to analyze empirical regularities within the precarious situation that confronts current religious orders in some countries and to advance some tentative predictions as to their future.[47]

Such is the objective of the present book. Part I presents the necessary theoretical and historical background for the analysis. In chapter 2, some of the sociological literature on social movements, ideology and religious communal groups is used to develop a model that can be applied to the cyclic patterns of growth and decline in Roman Catholic religious life, and a short summary of the cycles themselves is given. For the benefit of readers who are unfamiliar with Catholic religious orders, a brief description of their major constituent aspects and of their relationship to the larger institutional Church is provided in chapter 3. In Part II, the various social movement theories are applied to selected growth periods experienced by religious orders in the past. No claim is made that these particular instances provide the only, or even the most important, examples of such growth movements; they are simply the periods for which the most historical documentation is presently available. Chapters 4 and 5 use resource mobilization theories to analyze the periods during which waves of new religious orders were established. Chapter 4 considers the various benefits the religious communities of a given era could offer potential recruits to induce them to enter, while Chapter 5 examines the resources each order was able to secure from the Church and the larger society. Chapters 6, 7, and 8, on the other hand, use frame alignment theories to consider the definition and content of the various formulations of virtuoso spirituality developed in each movement, and to examine how these formulations functioned as legitimating ideological frameworks for the orders' members. The ninth chapter explores how the orders used their ideological frames as additional resources in their ongoing interactions with other communities, with the Church, and with the society at large.

Part III applies both social movement theory and the sociological research on intentional communities to the inevitable decline phases that followed every period of foundation and growth. Chapter 10 looks at the "resource deprivation" and "frame disalignment" that afflicted earlier monastic, mendicant, and apostolic orders. The degree to which each variant of communal religious life ultimately failed to provide the commitment and control mechanisms essential for their ideological maintenance is analyzed and evaluated in chapter 11.

Part IV applies the analysis of the preceding chapters to the current collapse of religious orders. Chapter 12 gives a brief illustrative summary of the major events impacting U.S. religious orders between 1950 and 1992. Chapters 13 and 14 examine the dissolution of the two most basic elements of the orders' ideological frame—the meaning of the vows and the purpose of religious life—that occurred after 1965. Chapter 14 also applies previous studies of decaying communal commitment mechanisms to analyze the results of similar changes in the sisters' communities. Chapter 15 analyzes the "drying up" of the resources formerly enjoyed by U.S. religious orders. Following this section, a concluding chapter outlines the implications for Roman Catholicism—and other Western denominations—of the collapse of religious orders.

Ideally, this analysis would be done using primary source material. As a nonhistorian, however, I found both my skill and my time inadequate to a project of such scope. I rely, therefore, on secondary sources, chiefly the publications of reputable historians. The validity of my conclusions thus depends "not only on the accuracy of their data but also upon the honesty and correctness of their judgments and interpretations, as well as on the accuracy of my own interpretations of their conclusions."[48] There is some precedent for this approach.[49] I would hope, however, that this study will be supplemented by more methodologically sophisticated sociological and historical research in the future.

The present catastrophic decline and the probable demise of so many Roman Catholic religious communities—of a lifestyle that was once both the largest and the longest-lived exemplar of its type and the source of most of the Church's professional staff—should have profound interest for sociologists. The internal changes currently taking place within the orders themselves offer the opportunity to examine processes of major communal dissolution that formerly had to be examined either in the historical record or in smaller, present-day communes.[50] This should be of great interest to sociologists of intentional communities. The larger patterns of growth and decline in movements of Roman Catholic religious virtuosity also offer the opportunity to apply social movement theories to religious groups—an opportunity which has been too rarely taken in the past. Finally, if religious communities as an internal outlet for virtuoso spirituality are not replaced by other functional analogs within Catholicism, this may affect the total membership figures for the denomination as well—a point of interest to sociologists of religion. This book is but a preliminary study. It is hoped that it will stimulate further research on religious communities and on their interaction with the larger Church. The time remaining to do so is short.

PART ONE

Preliminary Definitions and
Theoretical Background

Chapter 2

Theories of Ideology and
Social Movements

An analysis of the role that religions play in society and in the life of the individual, or of why one social group is more or less inclined than others to emphasize religious beliefs and activities, is beyond the scope of this book. Given, however, that religions *do* exist within at least some cultures and during at least some time periods, certain inescapable consequences follow. One of these consequences is that the members of any religion or religion-based cultural system will vary both in their ability and in their willingness to strive for and to attain the ultimate sacred values of their faith. "The empirical fact . . . that men [sic] are *differently qualified* in a religious way stands at the beginning of the history of religion. . . . The sacred values that have been most cherished, the ecstatic and visionary capacities of shamans, sorcerers, ascetics and pneumatics of all sorts, could not be attained by everyone."[1] Nor, we might add, is everyone equally desirous even of *trying* to attain such spiritual abilities. Thus, states Weber, there is an inevitable tendency toward status stratification between this "heroic" or "virtuoso" religiosity and mass religiosity.[2]

All religions, and especially institutionally organized religions such as Christianity, must therefore deal with the phenomenon of religious virtuosity. Each religion has developed an ordered system or framework of symbols and beliefs that serves as its model for the world and for the individual's relationship to the sacred or divine. This we might call its ideological system.[3] Religious virtuosity must be integrated into this larger ideological framework, and its links to the other symbolic elements must be specified. Is God more pleased by virtuoso than by mass spirituality? Will religious virtuosi achieve higher places in heaven? Are all members called to virtuoso spirituality, or are only a few so chosen? If the latter, who are those few and why were they selected? What are the signs of "true" religious virtuosi, and how can these persons be distinguished from fakers and hypocrites? Who is qualified to decide whether a particular form of virtuoso spirituality is genuinely pleasing to God?

Religions must also deal with virtuoso spirituality organizationally. In some cases, a religion may only recognize as virtuosi the priests or other officials who manage its organizational affairs. If, however, additional *lay* religious virtuosi exist outside of the recognized hierarchy of the church, or if variant forms of lay and clerical virtuosity compete for adherents, then relationships will have to be codified between the "lay" virtuoso and the church government. Certification procedures may need to be established by church officials to distinguish the true religious virtuosi from imposters or to approve those of their spiritual practices that are worthy of being emulated by the masses. Arrangements may have to be made for the economic support of virtuosi, and churches may also have to intervene with state authorities on their behalf. Religious virtuosity, in other words, is impossible for an established or institutionalized religious system to ignore. Defining how a church deals with its religious virtuosi may be a focus of ideological struggle and negotiation for as long as the church exists. Within Roman Catholicism, ideologies of virtuoso spirituality—and the changes that have occurred in these ideologies over the centuries—are some of the causal forces behind the recurring waves of growth and decline in communal religious orders that this book seeks to explain.

Ideological Variations in Religious Virtuosity

Legitimacy and Purpose

The first question that a religion's ideological framework must address is whether *any* form of virtuoso spirituality can have a legitimate role within the church, and, if so, exactly what that role is. For some, the primary purpose of religious virtuosity might be the perfection of the virtuoso's own soul. Alternatively, the religious virtuoso's prayer and penitential practices might be a source of divine favor for his/her family or for the entire church community. Religious virtuosi have also served as spiritual advisers to the masses, who would make long journeys to seek their counsel.

As an alternative to achieving their own spiritual perfection or obtaining graces for others, religious virtuosi might be ideologically defined as prophetic witnesses, denouncing the errors of an audience that had gone astray. At times, prophetic virtuoso spirituality might be a *protest against* the laxity of the larger church or the abuses of authority by the hierarchy.[4] At other times, religious virtuosi *attested to* the holiness of the church vis-à-vis a secular society that was indifferent or hostile to it.[5] Finally, religious virtuosi might be thought useful for instrumental purposes: instructing the young in doctrine and morals, nursing the indigent, and so on. Perhaps the most self-conscious ideology concerning the purpose of religious virtuosity was developed by the nineteenth-century Anglican hierarchy, which promoted the establishment of religious communities in order to keep devout and unmarried Anglican women occupied and to forestall their defection to Methodism or Catholicism.[6]

The ideological systems of most Protestant denominations, however, rejected the very legitimacy of religious virtuosity as a separate calling within the church, and vigorously denied that it could serve any worthwhile purpose at all. The idea that one could achieve greater spiritual perfection through ascetic works was contrary to the Lutheran doctrine of salvation by faith alone.[7] The idea of a "depository" into which religious virtuosi channeled grace and from which the masses could draw indulgences—a popular metaphor of late medieval preaching—was antithetical to the Protestant emphasis on personal responsibility for one's own salvation.[8] According to the Augsburg Confession of 1530, "There are many godless opinions and errors associated with monastic vows: that they justify and render men righteous before God, that they constitute Christian perfection, that they are the means of fulfilling both evangelical counsels and precepts, and that they furnish the works of supererogation which we are not obliged to render to God. Inasmuch as all these things are false, useless and invented, monastic vows are null and void."[9]

In place of a dual system of virtuoso and mass spirituality, many Protestant denominations substituted a "this-worldly asceticism" by which *all* Christians were expected to work out their salvation "*solely* through the ethical quality of [their] conduct in this world. . . . Rationally raised into a vocation, everyday conduct becomes the locus for proving one's state of grace."[10] There was no "better path" of evangelical perfection to which the virtuoso might aspire; all were called equally to holiness.

Denying the legitimacy of virtuoso spirituality, however, did not eliminate it from the Reformation churches. Deprived of an outlet within the state churches of Lutheranism, Calvinism, or Anglicanism, virtuoso Reformers created a plethora of sects—"visible communities of pure saints"[11]—in order to separate themselves from the compromises and the dilution of the Christian message that they felt had infected mainstream Protestantism.[12] These sects served as a functional analog within Protestantism for religious orders within Catholicism: they provided an outlet for unchanneled religious virtuosity.[13]

The Content of Virtuoso Spirituality

In addition to establishing the legitimacy of religious virtuosity and defining its purpose(s), the ideological framework of a religion must also specify what the accepted *content* of this concept might be. What particular behaviors or activities does virtuoso spirituality involve? Should the virtuoso strive for mystical visions and/or ecstatic union with the divine—and, if so, are there special substances one should ingest or fasts one should perform that will facilitate the attainment of this psychic state? Alternatively, the virtuoso might be expected to master a body of abstract theological texts or moral prescriptions and be able to engage in extended debates or discussions about them. Virtuosi may be expected to live as solitary pilgrims or hermits: The early Theodosian Code mandated that "[i]f any persons shall be found in the profession of monks, they shall be ordered to seek out and to inhabit desert places and desolate solitudes."[14] Or they may be required to live communally and forbidden to remain alone. For St. Francis and his followers, poverty was *the* indispensable prerequisite for religious virtuosity; among ascetic Calvinists and Hasidic *rebbes*, on the other hand, wealth could be a sign of high spiritual standing.[15] Even personal salvation might be relegated to second place in some virtuoso spiritualities: "While the pre-eminent objective of the monastic community [was] care for the salvation and perfection of the souls of its own members, the prime task of the Jesuit, though not unmindful of his own soul, is the care and perfection of the souls of others."[16] The wide range of heroic spiritual activities that could be part of religious virtuosity sometimes contributed to the contested existence of several competing virtuoso spiritualities within the same religion.

A given ideology of virtuoso spirituality might also specify which subgroups within the larger population would be the most (or the least) likely to exhibit such heroic religious behaviors. For example, at various times within the history of Christianity, religious virtuosity has been disproportionately expected of one sex rather than of the other. Certain social classes may be almost entirely excluded from the recognized outlets for virtuoso spirituality. Additionally, some geographic areas may yield many religious virtuosi, while others produce few or none. Religious virtuosity may be an entirely urban phenomenon at one period and a rural one during the next. Some historians speak of a "crucible" in Western Europe, within which most Catholic religious orders originated.[17] Geographic and demographic concentrations such as these may be the result of an ideology of religious virtuosity that expects country dwellers, Basques, or Norman French women to be more likely recruits than urbanites, Catalans, or Norman French men. Alternatively, the ideology may prescribe religious virtuosity for all types of people, but it may include behaviors or beliefs that are more appealing to some social groups than to others.

Religious virtuosity as an ideological concept is also bound together with a church's other beliefs and values into constrained belief systems or "schema."[18] The particular constellation of religious beliefs and values assumed to be compatible with virtuoso spirituality in one church, denomination or time period may be thought totally antithetical in another. For example, the religious virtuosi of one era may fervently uphold the powers of the ecclesiastical hierarchy or the truth of orthodox doctrines, while their successors may vigorously challenge such ideas.

Although an ideology of virtuoso spirituality may coexist with the rest of a faith's doctrines without being influenced by them to any discernible extent, the various other components of a religious belief system do sometimes interact with the content of its virtuoso spirituality. As Brown has pointed out, the development of the ideal of sexual continence in early Christianity profoundly affected the type of religious virtuosity that Christians came to value.[19] Similarly, a religion such as Roman Catholicism, where obedience to higher authorities was valued over individual initiative, was less likely to accept a virtuoso spirituality that emphasized the primacy of a soul's solitary spiritual quest.[20]

Religious virtuosity might also be constrained into schema that include a variety of secular beliefs. Kurtz has observed that, in nineteenth-century France, it was considered impossible to be both a republican sympathizer and a good Catholic; a fortiori, a member of a religious order would be even less likely to hold republican sympathies.[21] Nineteenth-century American Catholics, on the other hand, experienced no such contradiction between their democratic instincts and their religion. Accordingly, American religious communities regularly prayed for their civil leaders and strongly supported egalitarian beliefs and practices in their own internal workings.[22] Other interfaces between virtuoso and secular beliefs might also occur. For example, some religious virtuosi have upheld the "God-given" subordination of women, while, at other times, virtuoso movements attracted women precisely because they provideed *more* autonomy and opportunities for personal development than was usual for women in the wider society.[23]

A final ideological component within the content of virtuoso spirituality is the mythic figures or events that lend legitimacy to the virtuoso group and its practices. The symbols, stories, and rituals of a given culture can be "tools" whereby a group of virtuosi constructs and validates its ideology of religious virtuosity.[24] Thus, Christian religious virtuosi may claim to be imitating the preaching life of the seventy-two disciples commissioned by Jesus (Luke 10:1–16), or the communal property holding of the primitive Christians (Acts 4:32–37), or the activities of great saints such as the Virgin Mary, St. Anthony the Abbot, or St. Francis of Assisi. If no scriptural or historical documentation exists to prove that these mythic figures' lives actually did support the practices of the virtuosi, legends may be simply invented. The presentation of the infant Virgin Mary in the temple and her education there as a young girl, or the wanderings of St. Thecla as a participant in the ministry of St. Paul are two examples of these legitimating, but completely unhistorical, legends.[25]

The Church Hierarchy and the Religious Virtuoso

In addition to legitimating the role of religious virtuosity and specifying its content, a religion's ideological system must also define the "proper" relationship between the virtuoso and the larger church. Those religions that are institutionally developed enough to possess a professional clergy will be keenly concerned with whatever manifestations of religious virtuosity appear, and will strongly disapprove of any that cannot be controlled. "[E]very hierocratic and official authority of a 'church'—that is, a community organized by officials into an institution which bestows gifts of grace—fights principally against all virtuoso-religion and against its autonomous development."[26] There are several reasons for this animosity. First of all, religious virtuosi may be trying to "attain grace by their own unaided power" instead of by relying on the sacraments or rituals monopolized by the hierarchy.[27] Lay virtuosi may also threaten the authority and veneration the hierarchy claim for themselves. The messages purportedly received in several nineteenth-century apparitions of the Virgin Mary, for example, included denunciations of unworthy priests.[28] An example of clerical apprehension over the lay virtuoso's potentially competing influence is the opposition expressed by both the local clergy and the Vatican to the popular veneration of twentieth-century mystics such as Alexandrina da Costa and Padre Pio.[29]

An additional source of tension between church officials and religious virtuosi may lie in the kind of spiritual perfection promoted by the latter, especially if the officials themselves are the proponents or the practitioners of an alternate variety. "A decisive influence was everywhere exerted on the character of religion by the relationship between the theological intellectuals, who were the virtuosi of knowledge, and the pious nonintellectuals, who were the virtuosi of religious asceticism and . . . religious contemplation [and] who . . . regarded 'dead knowledge' as of negligible value in the quest for salvation."[30] Still another source of tension might result from the practical difficulties which the virtuoso's activities pose for church officials. "Respectable" churchgoers may be scandalized by some of the practices of the virtuosi: by the Visitation Sisters, who left their cloisters to minister to the poor in public, for example, or by the bedraggled appearance of Francis of Assisi.[31] Additionally, the tendency of some religious virtuosi to show that they consider themselves superior to the ordinary adherents of their religion often causes resentment. Church officials will have to deal with any divisions or scandal that the activities of religious virtuosi may cause within their flocks. Officials also have to buffer potential conflicts between the virtuosi and the larger society. For example, the church may have built up accommodative arrangements with secular authorities that the enthusiasm of the religious virtuosi is in danger of jeopardizing. The objections of the eighteenth-century Spanish and French governments to the "political" activities of the Jesuits is an illustration of this.[32] If virtuosi are allowed to operate unchecked, the church may forfeit valuable political patronage, wealthy funding sources, and social respectability.

The church must, therefore, codify the relationship between its religious virtuosi and the rest of its members. How autonomous are the local virtuosi from the parish priests? From the bishop? Does the spirituality practiced by the virtuosi differ in kind from that practiced by the masses or only in degree? Is the religious virtuoso simply one who prays more than the average adherent, or who fasts more, or who abstains from sex at all times, whereas the average layman prays, fasts, or avoids intercourse only on certain days? If so, the religious virtuosi can be held up to the masses for emulation and can serve as teachers. However, a certain escalation may ultimately develop in virtuoso practices, as the virtuosi strive to keep ahead of their lay imitators.[33] Church officials will then have to deal with any excesses that result from this competition.

On the other hand, virtuoso spirituality may be completely different from mass spirituality, and the lay adherent may be expected simply to reverence the virtuosi from afar and to offer them gifts in exchange for their prayers. Tension may then arise as the church attempts to draw a distinction for the laity between admiring the virtuoso's excesses and imitating them.[34] If the virtuoso's spirituality is completely inimitable, is it holier than the priests' equally inimitable status? If the virtuoso's prayers are perceived as more efficacious than the rituals controlled by the clergy, this may have a negative impact on church finances—unless, of course, some institutionalized collection system is established whereby offerings made to the virtuosi are funneled into the larger church.

The whole question of finances is another aspect that must be resolved, in some fashion, by the church and/or by the virtuosi. According to many theorists, "an essential feature of all virtuoso leadership is its complete separation . . . from direct labor and economic employment."[35] Often lay petitioners support the virtuosi in return for their prayers, thus making the virtuoso dependent upon the selfsame profane employments that their own lifestyle had denigrated as unworthy or sinful.[36] The "parasitic dependence" of the virtuoso upon the labor of the laity or upon the largesse of societal or ecclesiastical elites often leads to other problems.[37] Financially dependent virtuosi may be a drain on ecclesiastical resources. Secular states may attempt to limit citizens' bequests to virtuoso establishments. On the other hand, independent virtuosi who earn their own living and control their own wealth may be an alternative, and unwelcome, locus of power within the church.[38]

An additional complication is posed by the existence of several competing virtuoso ideologies within a single religious system. The ideological variations between these groups do not have to be large. Coser notes that sectarians may exhibit more animosity toward offshoot groups that are quite similar to themselves than they do toward religions that are quite outside the fold.[39] Similar dynamics often exist between related virtuoso communities. As a result, a church such as Catholicism, whose religious virtuosi remain within its bounds, may find itself becoming a battleground between fervently antipathetic groups. The animosities thus engendered may be a source of scandal both within and outside the church, and may also distract the participants from their original missions of preaching or ministering to the poor.

Ideological Interfaces: Religious Virtuosity and the Outside World

The type of virtuoso ideology that develops within a religion is thus profoundly influenced by other elements in that religion's ideological system, by the support or opposition of its hierarchy and by the presence or absence of other virtuoso groups in the church. But outside elements will also have an effect. In some societies, several religions or religious denominations may coexist, with greater or lesser degrees of competition and animosity. If each of these religious systems have their own virtuosi, virtuoso spirituality may become defined in a combative fashion—as the vanguard of the true faith in its struggle with heretics or infidels. At such times, more solitary or mystical variaties of religious virtuosity may be discarded in favor of evangelistic militancy. Alternatively, the virtuosi of one system may be drawn to imitate some of the practices of their competitors, which in turn may make them suspect among their co-religionists.[40] If one religion or denomination accepts the legitimacy of religious virtuosity and the other does not, or if one system allows, for example, women or the working class to become virtuosi while the other excludes them, the latter religion will experience great pressure to change its own virtuoso ideology accordingly. Otherwise, it will risk the loss of its most fervent and committed members to its competitors.[41]

In addition to competing with other ideologies of virtuoso spirituality *within* the church, and with sectarian groups of religious virtuosi *outside of* the church, the adherents of a particular variant of religious virtuosity may also have to contend with the existence of secular analogs of religion in the larger society. To the extent that religions function to define reality[42] or to provide means of grappling with the "ultimate problems of human life,"[43] it can be readily seen that other definitions of reality or other answers to life's problems may appeal to the same audience the religious virtuosi are attempting to reach. Worse, some of these alternative world views may trivialize religion as psychologically neurotic or oppose it as detrimental to the class struggle. "Consider Freud, who managed to characterize religion as a 'neurosis,' an 'illusion,' a 'poison,' an 'intoxicant,' and 'childishness to be overcome,' all on *one* page of his famous book on the subject."[44] Such hostile evaluations of religion by secular world views will, a fortiori, render the virtuoso adherents of these alternative world views (the Freudian psychoanalysts, the Marxist revolutionaries, and so on) extremely antipathetic toward religious virtuosi. The virtuosi, in their turn, may have to devote a portion of their energies to defending themselves from such attacks.

Another point of interface between virtuoso religiosity and secular society stems from the fact that religions often serve as socially integrative forces for a particular group.[45] "Religious ideas and religious mythology provide major vehicles for the expression of social-political protest, especially against secular regimes."[46] When and if it happens that a politically subordinate ethnic group holds to a different religion than that of its rulers, the religious virtuosi within the subordinated group may come to be regarded as the vanguards in the struggle for cultural autonomy or even political freedom. At such times, the ranks of the virtuosi may be greatly augmented by large numbers of nationalist patriots or cultural enthusiasts who, in other circumstances, would have channeled their energies into guerrilla warfare or political protest movements. The rise in entrants to the diocesan priesthood and religious orders in both nineteenth- and twentieth-century Poland would be one example of this process[47]; the ascendency of the ayatollas in Iran would be another. Of course, if religious virtuosi actually gain power in a country, they sometimes lose the appeal they formerly had. The number of applicants to Polish seminaries was recently rumored to have fallen by 20 percent since the elimination of Communism in that country, and a "backlash of anticlericalism" has been observed there.[48]

Conclusion: Ideological Variations in Religious Virtuosity

The previous discussion has outlined some of the ways in which ideologies of religious virtuosity may vary in different cultures, in different churches, or at different periods of time. These variations, however, are not static. Like all ideological components, interpretations of religious virtuosity shift: "Because they are historical products of human activity, all socially constructed universes change. . . . Reality is socially defined, but the definitions are always *embodied*, that is, concrete individuals and groups of individuals serve as definers of reality. To understand the state of the socially constructed universe at any given time, or its changes over time, one must understand the social organization that permits the definers to do their defining."[49] The structural constraints imposed by the political and economic situation within the church and the surrounding society provide both the favorable circumstances that induce the articulation or reformulation of a new ideology of religious virtuosity, and also the limitations that channel that ideology's development in certain directions. The interests various religious groups have in defending or expanding their own autonomy and power vis-à-vis the larger church will lead them to manipulate a vocabulary of concepts, myths, and behaviors drawn from the existing repertoire of virtuoso spirituality—and even to invent new elements when needed.[50] Exactly when and how changes in the surrounding social, cultural, economic, and political environments may lead individuals and groups of religious virtuosi to reconstruct the meaning and content of virtuoso spirituality, and exactly what societal conditions may conduce to the acceptance and spread of these reconstructed ideologies are the focus for a sociology of virtuoso movements that will further illuminate the waves of growth and decline in Roman Catholic religious orders.

Virtuoso Spiritualities as Social Movements

Concerted attempts by religious virtuosi to construct and promulgate new heroic spiritualities might thus be considered a species of revitalization movements—"deliberate, organized, conscious effort[s] . . . to construct a more satisfying culture."[51] The revitalization efforts of communal groups of religious virtuosi are focused on constructing an actual utopia that, depending on the particular ideological formulation of the group involved, may be envisioned as a flight from a doomed secular society, an advance outpost of a future escatological age, or an exemplary witness to convert sinners to the true faith.[52] If "[a] utopia may well be a sensitive indicator of where the sharpest anguish of an age lies," and if the appeal of utopias rises and falls with the level of social discontent in the surrounding culture, then, as changes in the environment produce different loci for that "sharpest anguish," new utopian configurations—new types of religious orders, in this case—will be necessary to deal with them.[53]

The mere presence of some societal strain is not sufficient in itself to produce a new movement of religious virtuosi. The probability that a group of individuals will participate in a movement of virtuoso spirituality depends on the depth of their desire for spiritual activities, on the availability of an ideology to express the new spirituality, and on the perceived costs and benefits of their participation.[54] On the other hand, the existence of such an ideology and its ability to legitimate the new form of virtuoso spirituality and to outline its constituent behaviors is itself contingent upon the interaction of concerned individuals as they mutually define and construct an interpretation of their world.[55] In Wallace's terms, religiously inclined individuals jointly engage in "mazeway reformulation" to create the new model of virtuoso spirituality they need.[56] "Between the structural factors that make it more likely that certain social groups will become the breeding ground for social movements are people and the meanings they attribute to their situation. Consensus mobilization . . . is an essential stage in the formation of a mobilization potential."[57] Thus, reciprocal moments of causation succeed each other in the creation and mobilization of virtuoso spiritualities: The virtuosi whose interaction shapes their nascent ideology are themselves motivated to meet and interact by the ideology they are shaping. While the hegemony of one virtuoso ideology over another is contingent upon the material and political resources its followers can mobilize, the ideology itself is a resource—attracting recruits, donations, and political patronage to the virtuosi who espouse it.

The Mobilization of Virtuoso Groups: Frame Alignment Theories

According to the most recent social movement research, a necessary precondition to individual participation in any collective action—waves of religious virtuosity among them—is the formulation of a common discourse of meaning: a consensus about what is wrong with the present situation, what should be done about it, and who should appropriately undertake the tasks of reform or renewal.[58] Groups thus spend a great deal of their time together "accounting and recounting for their participation; they jointly develop rationales for what they are or are not doing."[59] Even more fundamentally, the individuals must *become* a group—they must mutually negotiate and give meaning to a collective identity for themselves.[60]

From time to time, therefore, religiously inclined individuals within a society may find themselves dissatisfied with the accepted modes of virtuoso spirituality available to them. The current ideology of religious virtuosity may not address their own "sharpest anguish": it may emphasize theological study instead of mystical visions, for example, or contemplation instead of helping the poor. Alternatively, the accepted practice may restrict virtuoso spirituality only to males or to the upper classes, thus "spiritually disenfranchising" whole segments of the population. For whatever reason, dissatisfied individuals may begin in their mutual interaction, through trial and error and constant revision, to grope toward a new framework of spirituality that will be more satisfactory.

Various methods of "frame alignment" exist whereby ideological constructions of virtuoso spirituality can be revised, expanded, and/or extended toward new audiences.[61] The simplest of these is frame bridging, in which a current mode of religious virtuosity is simply introduced to a new population whose orientation is already amenable to it. The most obvious example of frame bridging would be attempts by female virtuosi to adopt a model originally developed by and for men. Another technique, frame amplification, involves the "identification, idealization, and elevation" of a value or belief once essential to virtuoso spirituality that has since been discarded or forgotten.[62]

Other techniques of frame alignment make more fundamental alterations in existing interpretations of religious virtuosity. In frame extension, current concepts of virtuoso spirituality might be expanded to cover concerns or beliefs not present in former articulations. New ministerial foci might be added for religious virtuosi: the mendicants added preaching, for example, and the Daughters of Charity cared for the destitute sick. Other formerly central practices (cloister, for example) might be dropped. Redefining the basic value or role of religious virtuosity within a church (shifting a community's focus from saving the members' own souls to saving others' souls, for example) would also be an example of frame extension.

The widest-ranging form of frame alignment is frame transformation, in which the entire interpretive framework of a culture (or some part of a culture) is altered to such an extent that people reinterpret the meaning of every event of their lives.[63] Several accounts of contemporary cults illustrate this process: "As Krishna explains in the *Bhagavad-Gita*, our lives thus far have been in darkness, in the mode of ignorance. *All our learning up to now has been illusion, garbage.* This is because this past learning we have received does not allow us to know the absolute, Krishna Consciousness."[64] While total transformation in one's world view is a more difficult task than simple frame bridging is, Snow feels that such transformations are most likely to occur in groups with "world transforming" goals that are "greedy" in terms of the commitment they expect of their members: in other words, in precisely the sort of communal religious virtuoso movements we have been discussing here. Frame transformation would occur, for example, when formerly irreligious subsectors of a society become swept with religious fervor, as occurred in the beginning of each of the major cycles of religious community foundation.

Successful religious virtuoso movements are initiated when the interpretive framework that defines the new spirituality "resonates" with the needs or desires of the population at large.[65] When several competing models of religious virtuosity exist, whichever version best fits the experiences of its audience and/or can best be expressed in terms of their stories, myths, and accepted wisdom, will be adopted in preference to the others. Of course, since the personal experiences of different classes or genders may differ, different ideologies of religious virtuosity may appeal to different subgroups. In addition, the followers of previously established (and hence more powerful) modes of religious virtuosity may resist the new formulations, even if the latter offer an ideological framework that is more congruent with contemporary religious needs.

Frame alignment theories can be used to explain not only the rise of movements of religious virtuosity but also their decline and eventual dissipation. Surrounding circumstances—economic changes, the rise of cities, domination by a conquering power—may render the virtuoso spirituality advanced by a former ideological framework less attractive or less feasible and may also create new strains and questions the established ideology does not address.[66] In such times, the number of persons interested in following the established version of religious virtuosity will decrease.

Movements with successful frame alignment techniques may also become victims of their own success. Frame bridging may ultimately oversaturate the market of interested potential virtuosi—a phenomenon that Langlois speculates happened in nineteenth-century France.[67] In such a situation, communities of religious virtuosi will cease to grow, unless and until they are able, through frame extension, to adapt their virtuoso ideology and appeal to a different population. However, frame extension carries its own liabilities. It may dilute and confuse the group's message so that there is less incentive to join, or else it may spark divisive intragroup conficts between the advocates of the different foci.[68]

As the attractiveness of one mode of religious virtuosity decreases, a period of stagnation may set in, especially if no new alternative is available. "Hypothetically, the absence of innovative master frames may account . . . for the failure of mass mobilization when structural conditions seem otherwise ripe."[69] Cycles of mobilization and subsequent stagnation are common in all sorts of social movements.[70] A social movement group whose foundation occurs during one of the cyclic "peaks" would be far more likely to succeed than one which attempts to form in a "trough" period—unless and until its members are able to articulate a variation of the interpretative framework that can begin the cycle anew.[71]

The Mobilization of Virtuoso Groups: Resource Mobilization Theories

An alternative, and somewhat complementary, explanation for the spread of social movements focuses on the resources individual social movement groups are able to tap in order to insure their success. In general, this perspective has rarely been applied to movements of religious virtuosity, since it was formulated largely by theorists specializing in organizational and political sociology. These writers focused primarily on the success or failure of political protest groups and other collective actions with fixed, instrumental goals.[72] Still, resource mobilization theories have been used with some benefit to analyze the organizational aspects of cults and other new religious movements.[73] Movements of Catholic religious virtuosi, and especially of organized groups within these movements such as specific religious orders, could also be analyzed using the concepts of resource mobilization theory. Why do some incipient orders survive while others, founded at the same time, do not? How were some orders able to resist the opposition of the hierarchy? Is it possible to estimate in advance a particular group's chances for survival?

A variety of material and political resources are important for the success of any newly organized community of religious virtuosi. An independent means of securing food, clothing and shelter for the members is the most obvious necessity. The virtuosi may exchange their spiritual services (their prayers, their religious instruction, their literary or artistic endeavors) directly with the consuming public in return for gifts or fees, or they may staff some institution owned by the state or the ecclesiastical hierarchy, which, in turn, provides for their support. In cultures in which almsgiving is a means of securing spiritual merit, virtuoso groups may be able to survive by begging. Some medieval monasteries owned large tracts of land and were self-sufficient.

In addition to securing a reliable source of economic subsistence, successful religious communities may also need to secure the assistance, or at least the neutrality, of ecclesiastical and secular authorities, as well as of other environmental actors. The church hierarchy may help a religious community by acting as its recruiting agents. State officials may be persuaded to enact special tax and inheritance laws or to waive professional certification requirements for the community's members. Already established orders of virtuosi may assist new groups by mentoring their leaders, introducing them to potential sponsors, and even providing them with funds or temporary housing until they are securely established. A key contribution of one branch in resource mobilization theory has been to emphasize the importance of these kinds of outside support in insuring the survival and the success of social movement groups.[74] In contrast, if the church hierarchy is indifferent to or threatened by virtuoso groups, if secular officials are hostile to them, or if established religious communities compete with them for resources and ecclesiastical favor, incipient religious orders may be derailed before they can properly begin.

Another valuable resource for beginning a social movement organization is access to larger networks of like-minded participants, who can share their knowledge and skills. In his study of the Civil Rights movement, McAdam showed how protest tactics such as the lunch counter sit-in were developed and perfected, and then spread to activists in other cities through kin and friendship links.[75] Similarly, the techniques of lay street preaching spread from group to group among virtuosi during the twelfth and thirteenth centuries.[76] In addition to spreading useful skills, pre-existing networks may also act as recruiting devices whereby whole families, guilds, or confraternities can be enlisted at once rather than individual by individual.[77]

If, as is the case in pluralistic societies or during one of the cyclic renewal periods in religious orders, there are several different competing ideologies of virtuoso spirituality, the resources possessed by the adherents of each ideology will determine which framework survives and achieves eventual hegemony over the others. A hegemonic ideology enjoys a significant advantage over upstarts.[78] If the hegemonic framework for religious virtuosity values emotional prayer and discounts serving the poor, or if it constrains virtuoso spirituality into a schema that also includes Biblical literalism, male superiority, and support of the death penalty, then alternate ideologies of virtuoso spirituality will be defined as illogical or illegitimate. Competing religious groups whose virtuoso spirituality includes different elements or is "packaged" differently than the hegemonic standard may have extreme difficulty attracting new members. Whole populations of potential recruits may dismiss the idea of joining a religious community out of hand, not because they dislike the idea of religious virtuosity, but because they disagree with the other ideological components of the dominant framework. Hegemonic ideological frameworks of religious virtuosity thus exert great pressure on subsequent religious communities to conform to them.[79] But since religious orders are normative organizations, their members may strongly resist any fundamental redefinition of their basic purpose and spirituality and may choose organizational death instead.[80]

The first school of resource mobilization theory, therefore, emphasizes the various resources—material, political, social, and ideological—that a social movement organization such as a religious order must be able to tap in order to succeed. A second school focuses more on the factors that motivate individuals, and groups of individuals, to join the movement organization.[81] Prospective virtuosi may come together in the expectation that their participation will help to maintain some *collective good*—the health and welfare of the destitute, for example, or the conversion of heretics, or even the establishment of a utopia of saints on earth that can serve as a beacon to others.[82] However, virtuosi may also join a religious order for more *personal* reasons—perhaps because virginity is more attractive than the perils of childbearing, or because such a choice provides social prestige, or because land inheritances or dowries are not available. Another, and an extremely potent, motivation is the enlargement of one's personal identity that comes from participating in a movement larger than oneself.[83] "Since the motives combine in an additive way, they can compensate for one another. If the collective motive is weak, zero, or negative, other motives can be so strong that a person is willing to participate. If the collective motive is strong, the social motives and/or the reward motives can be negative without making a person unwilling to participate."[84] However, both the collective and the personal motives are vulnerable to changing social conditions. A change in inheritance practices, an expansion of the secular opportunities open to women, or other societal changes can impact dramatically upon the willingness of individuals to join communities of religious virtuosi.

The Support of Ideology: Communal Commitment Mechanisms

The survival and ultimate hegemony of a particular ideological frame for religious virtuosity thus depends both upon the resonance of the ideology and upon the resources the groups ascribing to it can mobilize on its behalf. But other factors are also important. Most notably, the community has to inherit or invent the communal practices that will strengthen its individual members in their *commitment* to the ideology. Without these practices, it eventually becomes difficult, if not impossible, to motivate the members either to devote their energies to the community's work or to submit uncomplainingly to the dictates of communal authority figures.[85] The most effective way to assure continued commitment to a community's ideological frame, therefore, is to reinforce it with practices that assure the development of cathetic ties between the members ("affective commitment"), or that tie specific costs to member defection ("cognitive commitment").[86] Communities have repeatedly reinvented—or stumbled upon—a series of specific commitment mechanisms for these purposes.

Communal Commitment Mechanisms

A primary commitment mechanism is the fostering of a commonality of background and experience in the members.[87] This can be done, first of all, by drawing recruits from the same ethnic group or from a similar socioeconomic background. Communal sharing through living and working together also serves to build up common experiences after entrance.[88] Divisive internal cliques or factions must be eliminated. (Most successful communes even attempted to destroy the dyadic marriage tie by mandating either celibacy or polygamy.[89]) At the same time that communal unity is fostered within the group, ties to the outside must be broken. Movement in and out of the community must be controlled; members' contact with outsiders must be limited.[90] Distinctive dress may be adopted, both to distinguish the members from the rest of society and to foster their sense of group belonging. Even persecution may be helpful if it reinforces the boundary between members and the outside world.

The dual mechanisms of common activity and boundary maintenance serve directly to protect the members' ideological commitment. Constant interaction with like-minded associates makes the group's world view seem more plausible; separation from others who might believe differently prevents the contamination of the ideological frame. But these mechanisms also reinforce the members' commitment indirectly—by assuring that their primary affective ties will be to each other. After several years of isolation from their former associates, the original members may have no remaining friends outside of the community. Any children socialized into the community from birth would be even less exposed to the ideas and friendships available in the outside world. The cathetic bonds fostered by common activity and boundary maintenance may tie members to the community even after their belief in its ideology dims.

Another commitment mechanism is shared sacrifice. Members will be reluctant to believe that any cause for which they have given up significant amounts of money, time, or energy was, in reality, worthless. Hence, sacrifice helps maintain ideological commitment, especially if the personal resources invested are irreversible.[91] Shared sacrifice or struggle also strengthens group solidarity and thus the members' cathetic commitment to each other. Many of the unsuccessful communities studied by Kanter failed, at least in part, because they lacked the bondedness of shared struggle elicited by their members' sacrifices.[92] Finally, cognitive commitment is also enhanced by sacrifice; if a member has surrendered all of his or her property to the group; the fear of impoverishment may be sufficient to discourage leaving.

"Mortification" is an exceptionally potent commitment mechanism. By this process, a person's old identity is stripped away and a new, pure identity is conferred that depends solely upon commitment to the norms of the group.[93] Rituals of confession and mutual criticism, for instance, were common in many successful nineteenth- and twentieth-century religious communes.[94] Various deindividualizing mechanisms such as uniform dress and a lack of personal privacy may also be used by many groups to break down the individual member's ego.[95] According to Hall, the use of mortification techniques such as confession is strongly correlated with a commune's survival.[96]

Not all religious communities were able to initiate the same commitment mechanisms or to utilize them to the same degree. In any age, however, an order's survival and growth depended upon its continued ability to insulate its members from the corrosive influence of competing virtuoso ideologies, whenever such ideologies existed in the surrounding religious or secular environment. Even in solidly Catholic cultures, there were many irreligious persons, whose contaminating beliefs and views were dangerous to the virtuoso ideology.[97] In addition to the influence of competing virtuoso systems or the spiritually lax, the centrifugal ties of family obligations, blood feuds, divisive individualism, and personal ambition also had to be neutralized. Even those orders whose virtuoso ideology was most resonant with their surrounding society still needed strong commitment mechanisms to safeguard it.

But commitment mechanisms also helped attenuate the very ideology they were established to protect. Boundary maintenance could so isolate members that they ultimately remained in the group simply because they no longer felt competent to deal with the outside world. Common ritual and sacrifice might build such strong affective ties among members that friendship, rather than ideological conviction, became the primary binding force. And the more successful the commitment mechanisms were in isolating a community's ideology from the outside world, the less likely it became that even necessary changes would be made to adapt to the surrounding environment. Slowly but inevitably, over several decades or generations, the commitment mechanisms would fossilize an ideological frame, leaving a hollow shell of habit, cliquish exclusivity, and internal factions that leached away the group's original fervor.

Conclusions

The above discussion has attempted to establish a theoretical framework for analyzing the periodic waves of religious virtuosity within Roman Catholicism and the partial channeling of these movements into new forms of religious orders. Emerging ideological frameworks of religious virtuosity are hypothesized to result from a complex combination of struggles and events, both within the Church and in the surrounding environment: economic and political changes, competition from other secular and religious ideologies, and the mobilization of vital material, organizational, and intellectual resources by the adherents of each ideological variant. Subsequent religious orders are then constrained by existing frameworks to develop along certain lines. Some groups may be forced to modify their

original goals and purposes. Others may fail to obtain the material resources or political backing they need to survive. A few manage to coor-
dinate (or to stumble upon) the right combination of ideological,
political, social, and economic factors and to embody them in viable commitment mechanisms. As a result, these orders become the hugely successful models for a new formulation of virtuoso spirituality. Ultimately,
however, even successful orders are fossilized by their own commitment
mechanisms, lose their original fervor, and so become both unwilling and
unable to meet the challenges of later environmental changes. The following section will give a brief overview of how this process played itself
out in the waves of religious orders within the Catholic Church.

Growth and Decay: An Overview of the Historical Pattern

Recurring social movements of religious virtuosi have occurred quite frequently throughout the millenium and a half in which religious orders
have existed within the Church.[98] At the beginning of each period of revitalization, a plethora of new religious communities appeared and underwent extremely rapid expansion. Some of these groups were considered too
radical, and their followers were suppressed as heretics. Others, however,
obtained ecclesiastical approval and entered upon a time of institutionalization and stable growth that lasted as long as several centuries. Nevertheless, most of the religious orders established during a given period
survived only until the end of that period. Of all the religious orders
founded before 1800, 64 percent are now extinct.[99]

The Desert Fathers (and Mothers)

A brief historical description will illustrate the magnitude of each growth
period experienced by religious orders and the depth and extent of each
subsequent collapse. The first cycle, lasting from approximately 200 to
500 C.E., is commonly referred to as the Age of the Desert.[100] With the
waning of the persecutions and the diminishing likelihood of achieving
spiritual perfection through martyrdom, popular Christian writers such as
Origen began to emphasize the possibility of self-transformation through
fasting and sexual abstinence.[101] The "Doctrine of the Two Ways" was developed, which held that a life of perpetual virginity removed from the
world was superior to the daily round of married Christians.[102] Inspired by
such teachings, large numbers of male ascetics left the cities and towns of
the Roman Empire for "dry martyrdom" in the desert or wilderness. By

400 c.e., there were 5000 monks in the Nitria region of Egypt alone, with additional thousands scattered up and down the Nile.[103] Similar activity occurred in eastern Syria, Palestine, and Asia Minor. In remote and desolate areas, considered the last refuge of the devil by the largely urban Christians, the monks hoped to win their interior war against Satan's influence by self-denial and mortification, and thus to attain perfect union with God. For the most part, they lived "alone in their cells, praying and weaving the baskets and mats out of reeds which they sold to support themselves."[104] Perhaps once a week, all of the monks in a particular area would gather for mass and prayer. Many practiced severe penances: eating only a few dates or a crust of bread in an entire day, for example, or passing the nights in sleepless vigils.

The women of this period who desired to follow the "Way of Perfection" did not isolate themselves in the desert. Instead, they achieved a similar withdrawal within the confines of home and local church. Simply by not marrying and by remaining secluded within their houses, these women were believed to obtain great blessings for their families and for the entire community. Linked to loose networks of friends and relations, the virgins and widows attached to a particular church community spent their lives in prayer, study, fasting, and participation at ritual functions. Often wealthy widows or the sisters of clerics would act as patronesses for groups of between fifty and a hundred of these women.[105] The women's form of religious life during this period was even more popular than the men's: fourth-century Egypt, for example, contained an estimated 20,000 celibate religious women as compared to 10,000 monks. The Antioch church in 370 c.e. supported 3000 virgins and widows.[106]

The Monastics

The barbarian and the later Islamic conquests of the fifth through the seventh centuries marked the end of the Desert Period of religious life. Even before that time, however, the fanaticism of many monks, as they strove to outdo each other in ever more rigorous penances, had led religious leaders such as Basil of Caesarea (c.330–379) and Benedict of Nursia (c.480–547) to develop Rules whereby the rugged and unruly desert ascetics could be induced to live truly communal lives.[107] This new form of religious virtuosity was very successful. Although there were wide variations, the accepted definition of Roman Catholic religious life during the Monastic Era (500–1200 c.e.) acquired many of the elements that have characterized it until the present day.[108] Monks began to hold their property in common, and they also prayed, worked, and ate together within the monastery. Personal holiness was achieved, not through the "excessive" personal penances of the Desert Era, but through strict obedience to the Holy Rule of each order and the spiritual direction of the abbot or abbess. The older eremitical ideal did not completely die out, however. Northern Scotland in the eleventh century, for example, contained a large number of male hermits; in medieval England a few centuries later, many female anchoresses lived solitary lives.[109] Some monastic communities attempted to incorporate the solitude, contemplation, and penance of the desert spirituality into their own lifestyle. The Carthusians (1080 c.e.) were the most successful of these. Each Carthusian monk lived as a hermit in his own cell, but the group assembled three times daily to chant the Divine Office together. The Carthusians boasted that, unlike other monastic communities, they had never relaxed strict observance of their original rule.

Other monastic orders did, however, experience internal cycles of decline and revitalization. The Benedictines were reformed several times: at Luxeuil in the seventh century, at Cluny in the tenth century, and at Cîteaux in the twelfth century—to name only the most famous. Even though each of these reforms claimed to be simply a return to the pristine Rule of St. Benedict, they often included subtle alterations either in organizational form or in basic spirituality, alterations of which the reformers themselves may have been unaware.[110] Thus, the centralized administration of the Cluniac monasteries distinguished them from their autonomous Benedictine predecessors. Cistercian spirituality was more communally and affectively oriented than previous monastic spirituality had been, and also offered a form of membership to the peasant classes, which former monasteries on the continent had not done. Each of these subtle variations in the basic monastic pattern resulted in a wave of new entrants to the community that had initiated it.

While men's monasteries flourished throughout the early medieval period, women's monasteries did not. Fewer than 10 percent of the over 3,000 monasteries founded in France, Belgium and Britain between 500 and 1100 c.e. were for women—a stark contrast to the male/female ratio of the Desert Era.[111] The proportion of women's establishments actually declined as the centuries passed: from 25–30 percent during the seventh century to fewer than 5 percent in some localities during the eleventh. "In the tenth and early eleventh centuries . . . few female monasteries were founded, and religious leaders showed little concern for encouraging women's religiosity."[112] In addition, many previously existing women's abbeys were dissolved or given to male groups. The few remaining women's monasteries restricted their membership to the wealthy aristocracy.[113]

That women desired more opportunities to follow religious callings is evidenced by the large female followings of wandering twelfth-century evangelists such as Norbert of Xanten and Robert of Arbrissel. The twelfth-century Cistercians and Premonstratensians found the number of

women's monasteries affiliated with them to be growing at such an "alarming" speed that both groups established strict limits on the number of
women's houses they would be willing to sponsor.[114] Despite these restrictions, women's monasteries continued to grow throughout the twelfth and
thirteenth centuries. One hundred new Benedictine communities of
women were established in Germany alone between 1100 and 1199.
Whereas only ten new monasteries of nuns had been founded in tenth-
century France, the twelfth century saw the erection in that country of at
least forty new Benedictine abbeys and a large number of dependent Cluniac priories. In England, the number of monastic opportunities open to
women increased from twenty in 1130 to over one hundred by 1165.[115]

The Mendicants

By the thirteenth century, a revival of commerce had taken place and a
monetary economy had replaced the "gift economy" of the previous
centuries.[116] The economic changes attendant on profit and commerce
had resulted in growing disparities of wealth and poverty and in the rise of
an increasingly precarious and disaffected urban proletariat.[117] The largely
rural monasteries were ill-equipped to meet the spiritual or material needs
of growing numbers of townsfolk. New, alternate forms of religious life
were therefore invented by the religiously inclined members of the urban
middle classes, who found monastic spirituality less attractive. In place of
the hermit fasting in the desert or the monk chanting vespers in the monastery chapel, the new model of religious life substituted the poor man
who, having given away all of his wealth, followed in the footsteps of
Christ by preaching the gospel to all people. The Mendicant Era (1200–
1500 c.e.) is named after this new ideal. "Male monasticism never recov-
ered from the challenge" of the Mendicant Era, and entered a prolonged
period of decline.[118]

   The new groups achieved startlingly rapid growth in a very short
time. The Humiliati, founded in 1170, were a group of lay cloth merchants, some married, who lived a simple life, ministered to the poor, and
preached the faith in public—a role hitherto forbidden to the nonordained. By 1216, there were 150 convents of Humiliati in Milan alone.[119]
The followers of Peter Waldes, a formerly wealthy merchant from Lyons,
France, achieved similar success. Francis of Assisi attracted his first followers in 1209 and received papal approval in 1210. Eleven years later,
between 3,000 and 5,000 Franciscans attended the Chapter of Mats.[120]
The Dominicans, founded in 1215, had provinces in France, Provence,
Spain, Lombardy, Rome, England, Germany, Hungary, Poland, Scandi-
navia, Greece, and the Holy Land by 1228. There were 13,000 Dominicans by 1256.[121]

Women also attempted to adopt the mendicant form of religious life. Many of the Waldensians, for example, were women, who preached along with the men. Clare of Assisi, a wealthy noblewoman, renounced her wealth in 1212 to follow Francis. For seven years, mendicant Franciscan sisters lived in absolute poverty, working with the equally poor Franciscan brothers among the ill and the destitute. In 1219, however, ecclesiastical authorities forced these women to adopt a variation of the monastic rule, which required them to cease mendicant evangelization and retire to a cloistered life. Unlike their Franciscan sisters, Dominican women were cloistered from the beginning. Their function was not to preach, in the manner of the Waldensian women, but rather to support the preaching work of the male Dominicans by their prayers. The prospect of unchaperoned women roaming the countryside as the friars did was considered dangerous and a source of scandal. The Waldensians were ultimately excommunicated. The orthodox Dominican, Franciscan, and Cistercian women, confined perforce to monasteries, gradually came to outnumber the male monastics. They developed a mystical spirituality that had a profound influence on their male contemporaries and provided "some of the most distinctive aspects of late medieval piety."[122]

An informal, noncloistered form of female religiosity, the Beguines, also developed during the thirteenth and fourteenth centuries. Beguine women took no formal vows and could leave to marry at any time. During the time of their membership, they could live either singly in their own houses or communally in the beguinage. They wore a simple beige dress in lieu of a religious habit, ministered to the sick and poor, and attended daily mass at the local church.[123] Most earned their living in the textile industry. Rubin estimates that the diocese of Liege alone contained 1500 Beguines in 1240.[124] By 1320, the fifty-four Beguine establishments in Cologne contained 15 percent of the city's entire adult female population.[125] Such unorthodox activity for women, however, was frowned upon by Church officials. The Beguines were ultimately suppressed, as the Waldensians (with their female preachers) and the Humiliati had been.

While women's religious communities were forced to adopt monasticism, the male mendicant orders often found themselves drifting in a similar direction, adopting monastic practices, such as communal living and communally chanted prayers, which their founders had never intended for them.[126] Through this gradual "monasticization," the monastic version continued to influence religious communities, even after its displacement by the mendicant and subsequent models.[127]

The Reformation marked the end of the Mendicant Era, and also witnessed a drastic decline in the overall number of men and women in religious orders. In Protestant countries, religious communities were simply disbanded by government fiat: "In 1536 there were over 800 monasteries and religious houses in England and Wales, housing some 10,000 monks, canons, friars and nuns. By April of 1540 there were none. . . . Monastic property was confiscated and secularized. In England, most of the monks and nuns were turned out of their houses and given small pensions; only a few resisted, or tried to carry on their religious lives."[128] In sixteenth-century Germany, 66 percent of the 115 Benedictine and 62 percent of the 220 Cistercian monasteries for women were destroyed.[129] More than half of the Dominican provinces vanished:

> The grandeur of the order is utterly extinct in the most powerful King-dom of England, as in Scandinavia. In the realm of Hungary, scarcely two priories remain in our possession. Of the provinces of Bohemia, Scotland, Ireland, Greece and the Holy Land, would that we could boast of something more than the name. The vastness of our order in that most popular district of upper Germany and Saxony is reduced al-most to insignificance.[130]

Other orders dwindled, as their members were forbidden to receive new novices. Between 1475 and 1575, the number of males in Europe's reli-gious orders declined from 250,000 to under 200,000.[131] Many groups simply became extinct. Even in Catholic countries, there was evidence of much internal decay: religious orders had become lax in spiritual disci-pline, and the perpetual feuds of the Dominicans and Franciscans had be-come a scandal.[132]

The Apostolic Orders

In response to this situation, a new form of communal religious life was invented, which differed in notable aspects from both the mendicant and the monastic models. Instead of the poor, wandering friar of the Mendi-cant Period or the silent monk at prayer of the Monastic Period, men and women religious of the Apostolic Era (1500–1800) were to be "an elite corps of devoted servants ready to aid the Church in its new apos-tolic needs, especially the formidable renewal tasks of the Counter-Reformation."[133] The prototypical male order of the period—and the most successful one—was the Society of Jesus. Perhaps because Ignatius of Loyola (1491–1556) had been a soldier rather than a monk, the life and organization of the Jesuits he founded differed profoundly from that of pre-ceding religious orders. For monastic prayer and silence or for mendicant poverty, the Jesuits substituted the spiritual discipline of ministering "where no one else will."[134] All else was subordinated to the demands of ministry. The Jesuits did not chant the Divine Office in choir as the monks did; many did not even live in a communal residences. An initial "formation" period for new members, lasting several years, was introduced, together with periodic spiritual retreats for all Jesuits. These innovations served to create and maintain such a high level of commitment that Jesuit priests and brothers could be sent alone to the far reaches of Paraguay or among the Huron Indians in Canada and be still trusted to remain true to the service of the Church.[135]

As in the previous periods, the new orders' rapid expansion filled the void left by the demise of former groups. The Jesuits, founded in 1540, numbered 930 by 1556, 3,500 by 1565 and 15,500 by 1629.[136] Other new male orders included the Theatines (1524), the Barnabites (1533), the Clerks Regular of the Mother of God (1583), the Camillians (1591) and the Piarists (1597). "All told, some 17 communities of men were established in the sixteenth century."[137]

Religious life for women experienced a dual renaissance. Traditional cloistered monasteries (the only officially recognized form of religious life for women) showed rapid growth. In the early seventeenth century, for example, Pierre de Berulle induced six cloistered Carmelite nuns from Spain to take up residence in France; during the next forty-five years, fifty-five new Carmelite convents were established in that country.[138] Rheims, which had had only sixty cloistered nuns in 1619, had 400 by 1658. In Troyes, ten new religious houses were established between 1605 and 1641. In one single Paris suburb, three separate convents were founded between 1625 and 1629. One of these had seventy-four inhabitants by 1670, which was more nuns than had existed in all of Paris seventy years earlier.[139] By 1700, there were approximately 2000 cloistered women's monasteries in France alone.

Women also attempted to establish noncloistered, apostolic orders after the models so popular among the men. Initially, this was strongly resisted by the hierarchy. One foundress, Angela Merici (1474–1540), specified that her Ursulines were to wear no habit, take no vows and observe no cloister or common life. Throughout her lifetime, the Ursulines lived at home with their families, attended services in their local parish church, and devoted themselves to educating young girls. After Merici's death, however, church officials forced the group to adopt a habit, cloister, and solemn vows. Similar restrictions were imposed on the Visitation Sisters (1610), the Congregation de Notre Dame (1597), and the "English Ladies" (1609) founded by Mary Ward. Vincent de Paul's Daughters of Charity finally succeeded in avoiding cloister and retaining their original mission of nursing and ministering to the poor by the simple expedient of denying that they were a religious order at all. The Daughters of Charity took vows for one year only and could either leave at the end of that time or else renew their vows for another year. They lived in rented rooms attached to each parish, and wore the dress of French peasant women. Between their founding in 1633 and 1658, the Daughters of Charity grew to

800 women, drawn mostly from the working classes.[140] Their example sparked a wave of similar foundations. In all, eighty-three apostolic congregations of women were founded in France between 1630 and 1720. Some of these groups established as many as 240 separate branches.[141]

The political and philosophical upheavals of the French Revolution marked the end of the Age of Apostolic Orders. "Seldom before . . . had the position of the Church been so critical. Not only was it faced by radical unbelief, the passing of an old social and political order, and the de-Christianization of society, but it had also lost many of its traditional educational, social welfare and other Church-related agencies."[142] In countries directly affected by the revolution, members of religious orders were expelled from their houses and left to fend for themselves. In 1789, "there were approximately 2,000 Benedictine establishments in Europe; by 1815, only 20 were still functioning."[143] The 133,000 Franciscan friars in 1775 had dwindled to 39,000 by 1850. The Jesuits were disbanded by Pope Clement XVI in 1773, in an attempt to win the favor of several national governments that had opposed the order. Among the Dominicans,

> no general chapter convened between 1777 and 1833. Between 1790 and 1819 the houses of France, Belgium and Germany were closed. After 1808, wars of independence destroyed most of the Latin American provinces. Suppression of Spanish and Portuguese priories followed in 1834 and 1837 respectively. Russia gradually smothered the Lithuanian, Russian and Polish houses under its dominion in 1842. After repeated suppression in Italy during the Risorgimento, only 105 of 750 priories survived."[144]

In 1780, there had been forty-five Dominican provinces, containing a total of between 30,000 and 40,000 friars. By 1844, fewer than 5,000 members were left.[145]

Of the more than 300,000 monks, friars, and members of men's apostolic orders in Europe in 1773, fewer than 70,000 remained by 1825. Most of these were "old and shell-shocked," attempting few, if any, new initiatives while they waited for death.[146] Only two of the religious orders of men in existence before 1800—the Christian Brothers and the re-founded Jesuits—ever regained the numerical strength that they had possessed before the French Revolution.[147] Women's orders suffered somewhat less than the men, but the French Revolution caused great disorganization among them: dispersing their members, nationalizing their properties, and temporarily suspending their recruitment. There were 8,000 women in French religious communities in 1790; by 1808 there were only 7,000, a figure that included several new groups founded after the end of the Reign of Terror.[148] Several orders simply became extinct.

The Teaching Congregations

By 1850, however, this decline had been reversed. Over 600 new religious communities were founded in Catholicism worldwide during the nineteenth century, more than had been established in any previous period. In fact, almost 80 percent of the religious communities existing today first began in the nineteenth century.[149] In the United States, six indigenous communities of women were founded between 1810 and 1829, three within a radius of thirty miles from each other.[150] In addition, over 200 European orders sent missionaries to the new country, where their numbers were augmented by recruits from among American Catholics. In 1850, there were 1,344 sisters in nineteen religious congregations throughout the United States; by 1900 there were 40,340—in forty-five congregations. This was four times as many as the number of diocesan priests at that time.[151] By 1900, American sisters ran 3,811 parochial schools, 633 girls' academies, 645 orphanages, and at least 500 hospitals.[152]

Similar growth occurred in other countries. In 1800, there had been only eleven convents in all of Ireland, containing a total of 120 sisters from six different religious orders. One hundred years later, there were 8,000 sisters, living in 368 convents and representing thirty-five orders.[153] The rapid increase in the number of Irish nuns happened in spite of the fact that the country's overall population had drastically fallen during this period. In Quebec, 361 men and 673 women were members of religious orders in 1850; by 1900, there were 2391 men and 9601 women. The number of separate communities operating in French Canada increased from twenty-one to sixty during the latter half of the nineteenth century. In France, 400 new women's communities were founded between 1800 and 1880, and the already existing communities grew at an average rate of 5.5 percent a year. In the first eight decades of the nineteenth century, 200,000 French women entered religious orders, 116,000 of whom remained in France, while the rest established "daughter congregations" in Asia, Africa, and the Americas. By 1880, there were 130,000 women and 30,000 men in religious communities in France. Polish sisterhoods also multiplied in the second half of the century, and, in Russia, the number of Russian Orthodox monks and nuns increased from 10,625 in 1825 to 94,559 in 1914. Elsewhere on the European continent, the Jesuits and the Dominicans were revived, and several new groups, such as the Salesians (1859), were established.

In contrast to the previous models of religious life, the Catholic religious communities founded or reestablished during the nineteenth century were oriented around a specific work or institution. The vast majority—as high as 90 percent in some dioceses—were involved in teaching; hence, the period has been designated by Cada as the Age of the Teaching Congregations.[154] Initially, the women's communities radically modified the traditional monastic model of religious life in order to meet the needs of their new environment: dispensing with cloister, for example, and with solemn vows. In 1917, however, a revision of the Code of Canon Law reimposed many of the monastic restrictions upon these women: "In the 1920s, 1930s, and 1940s, sisters were warned to restrict contact with the outside world as much as possible. Newspapers, radios, libraries and so on were seen as dangerous distractions, as were various kinds of public events and meetings."[155] These restrictions were, for the most part, lifted in the years after the Second Vatican Council, although there have been recent—and largely unsuccessful—attempts to reimpose them.

Summary

Periodically throughout their history, Roman Catholic religious orders have undergone significant periods of growth and decline, often triggered by political or economic changes in secular society. While there have been other growth and decline periods specific to particular countries, the periods mentioned above are the ones most extensively documented in recent historical studies. Table 2.1 summarizes these periods, which will be the focus of subsequent chapters.

In these cycles, we can see the pattern outlined in the theory section of this chapter. At the beginning of each growth period, a new ideological frame was developed to model an innovative form of religious virtuosity. Initially, the followers of the new forms were somewhat suspect because they did not conform to the previously accepted model. The Benedictine monks did not do the heroic works of penance that had characterized desert spirituality. The mendicants did not live in monasteries. The Jesuits did not say prayers in common, and often did not even live together. The Beguines, the Daughters of Charity, and the nineteenth-century teaching and nursing sisters did not take solemn vows or observe cloister. All of these practices made Church officials doubt that the new groups could *really* be considered bona fide expressions of religious life. However, the explosive growth of the new orders usually overcame official reservations. The new religious communities were officially approved, and then continued to grow and spread, sometimes for centuries. Eventually, however, external social and political developments altered the favorable environment that had fostered their version of religious virtuosity. Most of the communities, lulled by their institutionalized commitment mechanisms, were unable to meet the challenges of their new environment, and therefore declined or were disbanded. The teaching congregations originally founded in the nineteenth century are experiencing precisely such a time

Table 2.1 Selected Growth and Decline Periods in Roman Catholic Religious Orders

Variety of Religious Virtuosity	Representative Order(s)	Principal Location(s)	Height	Decline
Desert Monks and Hermits	Pachomian Monks	Egypt Syria Asia Minor	300–400	late 400s
Medieval Monasticism	Benedictines	Luxeuil Cluny Citeaux	700s 1000–1050 1100s	900's 1080– 1200–
Mendicants	Franciscans Dominicans	Italy/Western Europe Spain/France/Western Europe	1200s, late 1300s 1200s	1300s, 1400–1500 1300s
Beguines	—	Holland/Belgium/Western Germany	1200s	1350
Apostolic Orders	Jesuits	Spain/Italy/Europe/other countries	1540–1600s	1700s
	Ursulines Daughters of Charity	Italy/France/other countries France/other countries	1600s 1600s	1700s 1700s
Teaching Congregations	Sisters of Mercy Schools Sisters of Notre Dame Felician Sisters	France/Ireland/U.S./Quebec/Germany/Poland	1850–1950	1965–

of transition today. Chapters 4 through 11 will apply the theoretical model to the previous cycles; chapters 12 through 15 will analyze the current decline. First, however, it may be helpful to describe the primary characteristics and lifestyle of present-day religious communities. It is to this topic that we will turn in chapter 3.

Contemporary Roman Catholic Religious Life: Some Preliminary Definitions

As Ebaugh and Ritterband have observed, Roman Catholic religious orders—especially the contemporary women's communities—have largely been "*terra incognita* to sociologists."[1] Before applying the theoretical framework developed in the previous chapter to the growth and decline cycles of institutional religious virtuosity in the Catholic Church, it will be helpful to define certain key concepts pertaining to religious orders and also to specify the relationship such orders currently have with the Catholic Church as a whole. A glossary is provided at the end of this book, and the reader is encouraged to refer to it for any additional terms or concepts that may remain unclear.

Definitions of Purpose

Religious Orders and Religious Virtuosity in Roman Catholicism

Religious orders are one of the two institutionalized forms of religious virtuosity that exist within Roman Catholicism.[2] The other form, of course, is represented by the "secular," or diocesan, priests who staff the local parish churches, as well as by the bishops, the cardinals, and the pope himself. Throughout the Church's history, the relationship between these two distinct forms of virtuoso spirituality has been subject to periodic renegotiation and redefinition. Religious orders do not participate in the formal government structure of the Church, and have only a limited voice in its official policies.

But if the nonordained men and women in religious communities are considered "lay" in at least some of the Church's official documents, they have traditionally been ranked together with the diocesan clergy in the minds of the other laity. The very term "religious life," when used by Catholics, has come to denote only that particular lifestyle practiced by recognized communities of sisters, brothers, and religious order priests. Such a delimitation of the concept implies that "*the* religious life" was traditionally considered more demanding, more perfect, or "better" than the life of the average lay Catholic, whose own religiosity came to be regarded—both by the religious priest or sister and by the laity themselves—as unspiritual or inferior in comparison.[3]

The scriptural basis cited to legitimate the elevation of religious orders over the rank and file of Catholic laity was Christ's response to the rich young man who had kept all the commandments since his childhood: "If you would be perfect, sell all you have, give the money to the poor and come, follow me" (Mark 10:21). Ordinary "mass religiosity" consisted, therefore, in merely obeying the commandments; the life of religious perfection, on the other hand, took Jesus' words absolutely literally. Not everyone, of course, was called to religious life: Even Mark's rich young man "went away sad." But those who did leave everything to follow Christ were thought to receive a greater reward than their fellow Christians because of their greater sacrifice: "There is no one who has left house, wife, brothers, parents or children for the sake of the Kingdom of God who will not be given repayment many times over in this present time and, in the world to come, eternal life" (Luke 18:30).

Religious Orders and Diocesan Clergy Compared

In theory, at least, the lifestyle practiced by members of religious orders differs from that of the diocesan clergy in several key ways. Diocesan priests do not take a vow of poverty and therefore can own property, inherit money, maintain and manage personal assets, and so on. While priests in the Roman rite are expected to be celibate, this is an administrative requirement that could be revoked by the pope; diocesan priests are not bound by vow to celibacy. Indeed, the priests in several Eastern rite churches affiliated with Roman Catholicism have always been permitted to marry, and several married Episcopalian priests who converted to Catholicism have been permitted to continue their ministries.[4] Diocesan priests are also not expected to live in community with other priests. Members of active religious orders, on the other hand, are bound by their vow of poverty not to own property as individuals or to manage personal assets. Bank accounts are in the name of the congregation or order and the individual members submit any salaries they may earn to their community, retaining only a previously approved amount for their personal needs. Members of religious communities also take public vows of celibacy, which is considered an essential component of their lifestyle. Until recently, members of most religious congregations were also expected to live communally with their fellow members.

In practice, however, the distinction between the lifestyles of religious orders and the secular clergy was often blurred. At various times during the Church's history, the superior prestige of religious communities led the diocesan clergy to adopt many monastic practices, sometimes even to the point of living communally and reciting the monastic Divine Office.[5] The cathedral canons of the Middle Ages are one example of this convergence, but, as recently as the mid-twentieth century, diocesan priests were still expected to say the entire monastic Divine Office in addition to their regular parish duties. Another example of the "monasticization" of the diocesan clergy would be the seminary training of most priests. Seminaries, at least until the mid-1960s, were "total institutions" modeled on monastery life.[6]

On the other hand, the lifestyle of many American religious orders— especially congregations of women—has come more and more to resemble that of diocesan priests.[7] Sisters in many congregations may now live alone, or in groups of two, in rented apartments. They also manage more aspects of their own finances and locate their own jobs.[8] A large proportion of working religious no longer serve with other members of their communities in the schools, hospitals, and other ministries their congregations had formerly staffed, but work as individuals in a wide variety of secular and church occupations.

Religious Life as Subversive or as a Safety Valve

It has been commonly observed that Catholicism has tended to retain its virtuosi within the Church by channeling them into religious orders, whereas Protestant virtuosi tend to split off from their present denominations to form new sects.[9] Religious communities are thus thought to act as safety valves, which keep the Church's most committed and dedicated members within its bounds. The reality, however, is somewhat more complex. There are, first of all, several forms of quasi-religious virtuosity within Catholicism in addition to the established and recognized orders. These "ecclesiolae" range from groups who plan and participate in saints' festivals, Passion plays, pilgrimages, and the like to the devout worshippers at Pentecostal prayer meetings or healing services, and even to quasi-monastic "covenant communities."[10] Since such popular devotions are lay-organized and unofficial, power struggles have often arisen between their participants and the hierarchy over whether and how these activities can be subordinated to "proper" clerical supervision. Often this involves pressuring the lay group to accept official status as members of a religious order, with all of the regulations such a state implies. For example, only when Adele Brice, the nineteenth-century Wisconsin lay preacher and visionary, entered a local Franciscan convent together with her followers was the local hierarchy's threat to excommunicate her defused.[11] More recently, many charismatic covenant communities have been subjected to ecclesiastical investigation, and some have been ordered to disband their own worship services and to reaffiliate themselves with their assigned parishes.[12] Also problematic for the hierarchy is the recent spate of visionaries claiming to have received special messages from the Virgin Mary, "messages that purport to come directly from heaven and therefore sidestep the teaching Magisterium"—the Vatican officials who normally define Church doctrine.[13] Unless carefully controlled, therefore, popular expressions of religious virtuosity are a two-edged sword that can breed "either a sense of attachment to the Church or a feeling of detachment from it."[14] Religious orders, too, have experienced periods in which they were viewed with suspicion by the hierarchy for their uncontrolled and potentially subversive character, rather than being appreciated for their role of providing an outlet for lay religious virtuosity within the Church.

Of course, not every group manifestation of virtuoso religiosity within Catholicism remains within the Church. Many lack the willingness—or the organizational and diplomatic finesse—to work out an accommodation with the hierarchy. For every Franciscan, Dominican, or Jesuit order that managed to wrangle official approval, one can cite groups such as the Humiliati, Waldensians, or Beguines whose failure to do so led to their ultimate expulsion. The line between the religious and the heretic, between the mystic and the witch, is often blurred and contested, as Bynum points out.[15] Boundaries of authority over both internal and ministerial affairs are constantly renegotiated between the hierarchy and the religious order, with the balance of power shifting back and forth between the two camps.

Accepted Variations in Catholic Religious Life

The Contemplative/Active Distinction

As was pointed out in the preceding chapter, the organizational forms and the lifestyles of religious communities have varied widely throughout history. Echoes of these variations continue to exist today. One basic distinction is between the contemplative and the active communities. The former are the descendants of the desert hermits or (more frequently) of the early medieval monastics. Both the men and the women who are members of contemplative communities observe cloister (that is, they strictly limit their contacts with the outside world). Their days are spent primarily in prayer and study, and in working at whatever moneymaking activity has been established to supply the material needs of the group. For most male orders, this is farming and/or the sale of some agricultural product.[16] Many women's groups make the wafers and candles used at mass or sew the ritual vestments worn by the priest during such functions. Both male and female monasteries may derive some income from artistic, musical, or literary endeavors, or from giving spiritual retreats. They also may have investments that provide income. Strictly speaking, only the members of contemplative orders should be called monks or nuns. The 1993 *Official Catholic Directory* listed 153 contemplative communities of women in the United States, averaging between sixteen and seventeen members each. Male contemplative orders could not be readily determined from the *Catholic Directory*, but the 1992 CARA *Formation Directory* lists seventeen such communities, averaging thirty members.[17]

As might be expected from the preceding chapter, the vast majority—well over 95 percent—of the men and women in religious life today are not members of the contemplative communities descending from the desert or monastic periods, but rather of the active congregations which have been established or revived since the beginning of the nineteenth century.[18] Members of active congregations, unless they are ordained, are officially termed "brothers" or "sisters," and their communities are usually known as "congregations" rather than "orders." In everyday use, however, it is customary to use terms such as "nun" and "sister," or "order" and "congregation" interchangeably. Active religious congregations tend to be larger than the contemplative orders: the 1992 CARA *Directory* listed 450 active congregations of women and seventy-two orders of men serving in the United States, with an average of 225 (for the women) and 265 (for the men) members apiece.[19]

The members of active religious congregations customarily devote themselves to charitable works. The most common of these was, traditionally, teaching. In the late 1960s, 58 percent of American sisters were teachers, and another 5.7 percent were grade and high school principals. Among the men, 48 percent of the brothers and 24 percent of the religious order priests were also engaged in education during the 1960s.[20] Figures for Quebec were even higher: 64 percent of male religious and 67 percent of the female taught in the school system.[21] A smaller number of sisters and brothers were involved in health care, parish work, retreats, and social service.

By the mid-1980s, however, the proportions of religious, especially of sisters, who were involved in education had drastically decreased. While the total number of sisters declined 33 percent between 1966 and 1984, the number teaching in Catholic schools decreased by 68 percent.[22] Currently, only about 27 percent of the nonretired sisters and 25 percent of the nonretired priests and brothers are still engaged in teaching.[23] Hospital service also occupies fewer sisters today than formerly: One study found only 1.9 sisters engaged in bedside nursing in the average Catholic hospital.[24] Instead of teaching and nursing, women in religious orders are more likely to work in parish ministry as assistants to the pastor or, increasingly, as the sole administrators of priestless parishes.[25] Others work in catechetics, in diocesan administration, or in the social services.[26]

Charisms

In addition to the contemplative/active distinction, each religious community believes itself to possess a unique "charism," that is, a particular spiritual or ministerial focus developed by the community's founder.[27] The Benedictines, for example, were known for their emphasis on prayer and common life, and the Franciscans for their spirit of poverty. Other groups derived their identity from the specific works in which they engaged: The Dominican Sisters of the Sick Poor, for example, did home health care, while the Daughters of St. Paul ran religious bookstores and did catechetical work. These charisms, whether based on a distinct ministry or on a spiritual focus, were treasured by each community. "It is difficult to explain to the outsider how religious orders each feel they have a peculiar spirit and style which differentiates them from every other group. . . . Religious orders are convinced that each of them has its 'corporate personality' and one who does not see it is kindly forgiven as not being very perceptive."[28]

As will be argued in chapter 7, however, the possession of a distinctive charism by each congregation—especially by each congregation founded in the nineteenth century—is open to question. Moreover, after the adoption of the 1917 Code of Canon Law, much of whatever original distinctiveness the nineteenth-century congregations may have had was "ironed out" in favor of uniform quasi-monastic practices.[29] Additionally, after the Second Vatican Council, many members of religious orders moved into ministries that differed from those traditionally performed by their congregations. This has tended to diminish the ministerial distinctiveness of individual communities. Finally, the decline in new recruits has caused many orders to cooperate by establishing "intercommunity" training programs for the few young men or women who apply each year, rather than maintaining a separate novitiate that emphasizes the distinctiveness of the particular community. As a result of such developments, whatever charism a particular congregation may have had has been attenuated, and often refers simply to a certain "flavor" or esprit de corps possessed by the group. Recent critics have charged that the attenuated "flavor" of many religious orders is no longer the sort of true spiritual focus that can be said really to distinguish one community from the next or to serve as a rallying point for the group's commitment.[30] Both historically and currently, those orders that have retained distinctive charisms based on some particular spiritual emphasis have been the most successful in avoiding the periodic extinctions that have afflicted religious communities.[31]

The Vows

All members of religious communities take some form of vows, by which they bind themselves in solidarity to the order and its ideals. Typically, there are three vows: poverty, by which the individual gives up most forms of private property ownership; chastity (or celibacy), by which he or she renounces all sexual involvement; and obedience to the legitimate superiors of the order or congregation.[32] There are variations in this format, however. The earliest monastic orders, such as the Benedictines, vowed chastity, conversion of manners (which meant adopting the monastic lifestyle and, in practice, included poverty and obedience), and stability—attachment for life to a particular monastery. Contemporary Benedictines continue to use this formula. Other groups add fourth vows: the Jesuits take a special vow of obedience to the pope; Mother Teresa's Missionaries of Charity vow service to the poorest of the poor. Moreover, as we shall see in chapter 7, the meaning of the vows may shift over time, even if their names stay the same.

As chapter 14 will show, there has recently been some confusion among religious men and women on what the vows of poverty and obedience mean. In contrast, there has been little disagreement about the meaning of the vow of celibacy, or about its value and importance for religious life. Many priests and ex-priests among the diocesan clergy may have called for the abolition of celibacy and the permission to marry, but, for the most part, this has been a non-issue among the members of religious orders.[33]

The number, meaning, and content of the vows, therefore, change from community to community and from time to time. There are also other distinctions. Vows may be temporary or permanent ("perpetual"). The Daughters of Charity continue to take vows for only one year at a time, as do the new members (the "temporarily professed") of most communities during the first five or ten years of their membership. After that time, however, most religious communities require permanent vows. Prior to the most recent revision of canon law, vows could also be either simple or solemn. Solemn vows, theoretically at least, could not be later abrogated and required some additional obligations. In general, members of orders took solemn vows and members of congregations took simple ones. The new Code of Canon Law omits this distinction, and most authorities hold that all perpetual vows are solemn.[34]

The Relationship between Religious Communities and the Larger Church

Legal Incorporation

Any group of individuals who wish to become a recognized religious community within the Roman Catholic Church must first apply to the bishop of the diocese in which they reside for official status as a "public association of the faithful." Bishops are initially reluctant to grant such a status and may require the group to live together for a several-year probationary period, to submit to the direction of an appointed diocesan priest or to comply with other requirements. Bishops and parish priests can also take the initiative to establish religious communities within their jurisdictions, and, in previous centuries at least, many did so.

Once it receives its preliminary status, the new community begins to write its official constitution. This document is to spell out the group's mission or purpose, the basic rules or procedures it intends to follow, its governing structure, and so on. The constitution must ultimately be submitted to the Sacred Congregation of Religious and Secular Institutes in the Roman Curia for approval, and guidelines are available to aid the new community in writing the kind of constitution that will be acceptable. During this initial period, the new community may also incorporate civilly as a nonprofit religious organization.

Once established, the religious community may relate to the diocesan hierarchy in one of several ways. Religious *orders* are exempt from episcopal interference; religious *congregations* are not. No new religious orders, however, have been approved by Rome since 1752. This meant that the wave of new groups founded in the nineteenth century all had to be chartered as congregations and subjected to the local bishop. Men's communities resisted this necessity, and a few obtained special exemptions from Rome. The rest organized as "pious societies" rather than as congregations. "Members of a pious society took no special vows, and so the group could not be classified as a true religious institute, although its constitution had to have Church approval. . . . Women, on the other hand, were not permitted to establish pious societies. The only structure for which they could obtain approval was the non-exempt congregation."[35]

There were, and are, two kinds of religious congregations: diocesan and pontifical. In the past, diocesan congregations were subordinated to the local bishop in many ways: The bishop had veto power over their elections, for example, and might also supervise their finances. In addition, diocesan congregations were often restricted to working only within one diocese. Pontifical congregations, on the other hand, were chartered by authorities in Rome. This gave them some, but not complete, autonomy vis-à-vis the local bishops. In former times, therefore, bishops preferred that the religious communities in their dioceses be subject to them, while the communities themselves attempted to obtain pontifical status.[36] For the most part, they succeeded. Of the over 500 women's congregations listed in the 1993 *Official Catholic Directory,* fewer than one hundred are diocesan congregations.

Recently, however, the Vatican has taken a more activist role in attempting to direct the religious congregations directly subjected to it, while the local bishops are often less interested in doing so. Sisters in U.S. pontifical congregations also cite the cultural differences and misunderstandings when a largely Italian (or at least non-American) Vatican committee is expected to approve their constitutional revisions and other community practices. Such difficulties have made many women's communities less eager to obtain, or to keep, their pontifical status.

Financial Relationships

Financially, religious orders or congregations are completely separate entities, independent both of other religious communities and of the diocesan or Vatican ecclesiastical structures. A local bishop usually owns the diocese's churches (and some of the attached grade schools, high schools, and other church property) as "corporation sole."[37] Religious communities are separate civil corporations and own their own central motherhouses, as well as some schools and other property. If involved in health care, they may own the hospitals in which they work, or these may be separately incorporated. Each religious community is totally responsible for its own finances, including educational expenses for the new members and all retirement, insurance, and medical expenses for the elderly ones. The diocese has no financial responsibility for any debts the individual orders may incur.

Formerly, religious communities earned some of the money they needed through the services they provided at their own schools and hospitals. Others of their members were "subcontracted" to work in diocesan-owned institutions, for which their congregation was paid a very small, and relatively fixed, stipend. Between 1905 and 1921, while the per capita expenses in convents rose 43 percent, the sisters' diocesan stipends rose less than 25 percent.[38] As late as the 1940s, the average *annual* stipend per teaching sister was $335.00.[39] The stipends paid religious brothers—at least prior to 1940—were more than twice what was provided to the sisters for the same work.[40] Nevertheless, many religious communities of men still found the stipends for teaching in diocesan schools insufficient and withdrew to teach in their own institutions. Records show that the heads of several nineteenth-century women's communities objected strongly to the unequal salaries received by the sisters and the brothers.[41]

The teaching sisters' stipend was less than what was needed for basic subsistence, and many orders made up the difference by offering private music lessons or by relying on gifts of food or money from individual parishoners.[42] Religious orders that owned and staffed hospitals fared better financially: By the mid-twentieth century, the sisters who were nurses or hospital administrators were beginning to receive salaries closer to those earned by their lay counterparts. This money, paid to the orders, helped to make up the shortfall in the stipends received by the sisters in teaching or social service ministries.

Monetary remuneration for religious has, of course, risen over the last decade, although over three-fourths of all U.S. dioceses still continue to pay stipends rather than salaries that would be equivalent to the market value of the brother's or sister's work. The average annual stipend, for those brothers and sisters who continue to work within diocesan schools and other institutions, was $13,776 in 1992–1993.[43] The range of the stipends varies between $7,100 and $25,000, with midwestern dioceses generally paying the higher amounts and dioceses on the East and West coasts and in the South paying the lower figures. For some of the parish positions, housing and/or transportation may be provided. Dioceses may also contribute additional amounts for health and retirement benefits. In general, these add another $2,000 to $5,000 to the basic stipend.

Today, many members of religious communities work in new ministries outside of Church structures: in colleges, social work agencies, and other institutions. These receive salaries comparable to the other lay employees. If the employing organization is a secular one, the sister or brother must pay Federal, state, and local income taxes, something religious working in church-related institutions do not have to do. Whenever possible, congregations attempt to subsidize the ministry of some of their members, so that they can continue to serve poor populations that are unable to pay them. However, since a large proportion of religious men and women (over 50 percent in some communities) are elderly and retired, the salaries of the working religious are often insufficient even for their order's daily expenses, and little, if any, money is available to subsidize ministry to the poor.

The financial difficulties of religious orders, sparked by an aging membership and the dearth of new entrants, have recently received widespread media attention.[44] In 1991, the aggregate national figures for the unfunded gap between the money the orders had available and the amount they would need to meet their retirement and medical expenses was estimated at $3.5 billion.[45] The gap is unevenly distributed among the orders: 102 communities (approximately 13 percent of the total number of communities) are experiencing no financial difficulties at all. Others have been reduced to selling their own motherhouses and other properties to meet their expenses. In 1988, a special national fund-raising effort was initiated to alleviate the religious orders' financial distress. By 1992, it had raised $123 million of the estimated $3.5 billion needed.[46] Grants from this fund and social security benefits account, on the average, for 24 percent of an order's cost of caring for its retired members. This means that communities must somehow find the remaining 76 percent themselves. Many come nowhere near this figure. The Tri-Conference Retirement Office, which sponsors the current fund-raising campaign, estimates from its data that half of all religious congregations can raise only 28 percent or less—not 76 percent—of their retirement expenses themselves.[47] Many orders are establishing development offices and exploring other ways to meet their projected shortfall. Some may eventually have to apply for Medicaid or other government assistance programs.

Conclusions

Although religious orders are a long-established institution within Roman Catholicism, the financial, juridical, and organizational aspects of their internal functioning, as well as of their relationship with the clergy and hierarchy, have varied substantially over time. The often-contested boundary between autonomy and subordination, between financial self-sufficiency and dependence, is a major factor in the large-scale cyclic movements of growth and decline which have affected religious life, as well as in the fate of individual religious orders. Parts II and III will explore the economic, social, and ideological forces behind the previous growth and decline periods in religious life. Part IV will examine the present collapse of religious orders, and will draw some conclusions for the future.

PART TWO

The Mobilization of Religious Virtuosi in the Catholic Church

Chapter 4

Personal Incentives for Membership

In attempting to disentangle underlying causes for the cyclic movements of religious virtuosi within Roman Catholicism, it is difficult to decide where to begin. If an analyst emphasizes alterations in the basic ideology of virtuoso spirituality—a valid perspective that accurately reflects one dimension of the reality—he or she runs the risk of reifying ideas and divorcing them from their social context. But to focus on the personal incentives that motivated the individual movement participants, or on the material, social, and political resources an incipient religious order could mobilize for its survival and growth, risks the accusation of engaging in an inadequate reductionism.[1] Recent theorists have emphasized that *both* the development, adoption, and elaboration of a motivating ideology, *and* concrete personal incentives and group resources, are necessary for the survival and success of new social movements.[2] These factors reinforce each other: ideological frameworks are developed by interacting individuals as they compare and mutually validate those interpretations that advance their own interests.[3] On the other hand, a new ideological formulation, once articulated, is itself a resource that can contribute to the survival and hegemony of a social movement group.[4]

Despite their independent influence on the initiation and development of social movements, movement ideologies must nevertheless be understood within the historical context of the societies in which they emerge and by which they are fundamentally constrained.[5] Our discussion of the various religious virtuoso movements in Roman Catholicism and of their concretization in new religious orders will, therefore, begin by analyzing the economic, social, and demographic conditions that encouraged individual recruits to join such groups. This personal incentive approach is comparable to the "economic model" of resource mobilization theory.[6] At this initial level of analysis, it will be hypothesized that individual recruits joined religious orders primarily because such a lifestyle provided concrete benefits—both material and nonmaterial—that could not be attained elsewhere. One of the nonmaterial benefits, of course, was the assurance of salvation or spiritual perfection promised by whatever ideology of virtuoso spirituality was current at the time. But the material benefits cannot be discounted.

An alternative approach within resource mobilization theory has been called the "political process model," and focuses more on the outside support an emerging group needs to marshall in order to assure its survival and growth.[7] Accordingly, chapter 5 will examine the resources in the surrounding environment that were available to newly established religious communities at the time of their founding. Financial self-sufficiency and/ or wealthy patrons were an obviously necessary resource, and the support or mentoring of already existing groups of virtuosi was also helpful. A key resource was access to political support—both from the Church hierarchy and from secular authorities. Chapter 5's analysis will therefore discuss the reasons bishops, popes, kings, and governors might have benefitted from supporting new virtuoso groups, as well as the consequences for a given religious community if such support was not forthcoming. Whichever religious orders could marshall these economic and political resources were the ones most likely to survive. And the particular ideology of virtuoso spirituality that the most successful groups professed would then become the standard model to which subsequent religious communities were expected to conform.

A newly developed ideology of religious virtuosity was a valuable resource in and of itself, and served as a powerful incentive in the recruitment of new members, as a motivating force in enlisting support from secular and ecclesiastical elites, and as a hegemonic blueprint for the development of subsequent religious orders. Chapters 6, 7, and 8 will discuss alterations in the dominant ideology of virtuoso spirituality developed by the individuals or groups that had been "spiritually disenfranchised" or ecclesiastically subordinated under the existing system. Struggles between the adherents of competing virtuoso ideologies in each period will be considered in chapter 9, along with the homogenization and standardization of a hegemonic ideology and its imposition upon subsequent religious orders.

The goal, therefore, of our analysis is to uncover common patterns in previous historical periods when a declining model of Roman Catholic religious virtuosity was supplanted by a new and more vigorous one: similarities in the socioeconomic situations of religious orders as they developed, similarities in the social classes most (or least) attracted by either the old- or the new-style communities, necessary resources possessed by all successful groups, ecclesiastical and secular authorities whose good

will and support had to be secured, typical ways in which the most resonant ideologies were developed and elaborated, and common pitfalls that
recurred and had to be avoided. Following this analysis of the mobilization
periods of religious orders, Part III will analyze the recurring decline
phases of these groups, using both social movement theories and recent
sociological research on the deterioration of other types of intentional
communities.

Social, Political and Economic Benefits for Individual Recruits and Their Families

Demographic Pressures

An obvious pattern emerges in any examination of the various historical
periods when large numbers of recruits entered burgeoning new religious
orders. Such a lifestyle usually provided them—and their families—with
either concrete benefits or the solution to vexing problems. A dearth of
suitable spouses or of the financial wherewithall to obtain them, for example, often led men or (more commonly) women to enter religious life.
In the second- and third-century Roman empire, high-status Christian
women had difficulty finding Christian husbands; rather than marry pa-
gans, these women were encouraged to remain consecrated virgins.[8] The
unequal ratio of males to females in medieval Germany was a motivating
force behind the interest of women in religious life during that era. Medieval French convents were useful repositories for handicapped or otherwise unmarriageable girls, and also for a family's excess daughters: 76
percent of the women sent to monastic life in thirteenth-century Lyons
came from families with five or more children. The well-publicized "surplus" of 500,000 women revealed in the 1860 English census was one factor in the rise of various forms of religious virtuoso lifestyles in that
country, both within the Church of England and in Roman Catholicism.
  Men and women, therefore, often entered—or were sent to—
religious communities because of a lack of marriage opportunities. The
women's demographic imbalance was sometimes a result of an actual
shortage of men, due either to wars or to the entrance of large numbers of
males into monastic life.[9] At other times, however, the surplus resulted
from changes in dowry values or inheritance customs, such as occurred
both in nineteenth-century Ireland and in medieval Europe.[10] A related
consideration was the fear many women felt of the rigors of childbearing.
Several authors point out that, in previous centuries, the physical dangers
of childbirth were such that many women preferred celibacy.[11] Or an ex-

pansion of the population may simply have reduced the pressures on young women to marry and produce children. [12] For whatever reason, historical periods in which large numbers of individuals found themselves unable or unwilling to marry often saw a corresponding increase in membership among religious orders.

Opportunities for Personal Fulfillment

Potential recruits to religious orders were often concentrated in social strata whose members felt restricted or limited in their activities. Roman civil marriage laws, for example, required all women to marry and bear children, and also limited the amount of money that they could control. The widespread disregard of these laws is evidence that such restrictions were unpalatable to most women, who were likely to find the life of a consecrated virgin an appealing alternative. Similarly, upper-class medieval women found the monastic or eremitical life attractive when compared to the narrow sphere otherwise allocated to them. In seventeenth-century France, women's religious communities offered opportunities for advancement "during a period that for most other women was characterized by retreat. . . . The great Catholic females of the Counter-Reformation enjoyed opportunities for organizational activity far beyond anything that Protestant women were allowed," and superior as well to the lot of dependent, upper-class wives in arranged marriages. [13]

Women in nineteenth-century Europe also chafed at their limitations. Irish women found their opportunities for economic independence increasingly scarce in the years after the famine, as domestic textile production, dairying, and poultry raising were taken over by English mills and commercialized agriculture. [14] By 1850, twice as many Irish women as men were workhouse inmates. A rural Irish woman's social opportunities were as restricted as her economic prospects: A reputation for "looseness" would doom her already scant marriage prospects in an era when only one daughter in a family could be dowered. By 1880, the only opportunities for social interaction available to such women were within the family and at Sunday church services. This constriction of social spheres affected all levels of Irish society.

> For the middle class young woman of nineteenth century Ireland, adult life was very often a "horrible problem"; many had no real marriage prospects, no prospect of ever moving out of the family home, and faced a future of single idleness or perpetual dependence upon the whims of older relatives. Becoming a nun offered the comfort of the familiar and the challenge of a new way of life, and, in an evangelical age, it apparently ensured salvation. [15]

Joining or founding a religious community was also the only accepted form of collective organization open to nineteenth-century Irish Catholic women who wished to do philanthropic work.[16]

The bleak situation of nineteenth-century Irish women was echoed in other countries. Several commentators have remarked upon the social restrictions that confined middle-class Victorian Englishwomen "to a life of enforced idleness in a parlor."[17] Middle-class women in France also "saw their role limited [to] family, worldly parties, the rearing of children, charitable works and devotions. . . . In the nineteenth century, religious congregations were practically alone in furnishing . . . a variety of feminine employments, and especially employments which demanded a high level of responsibility. Which accounts for their success."[18] A similar situation confronted women in nineteenth-century Poland and Germany.

In times of diminishing secular possibilities, therefore, religious life was attractive because of the opportunities it offered for intellectual challenge, creativity, and the development of one's own talents. In the fourth-century Church, religious life was a way for women to acquire literacy; they needed to be able to read the Bible.[19] The monastic schools of the early Middle Ages were one of the few places where a man or a woman could receive any education at all. The mendicant orders dominated the European universities of the thirteenth and fourteenth centuries to such an extent that the most prominent theologians and biblical scholars were all members of these religious groups. Both the Franciscans and the Dominicans thus did much of their recruiting among ambitious university students. Similar educational advantages have been noted for nuns in Spanish Colonial America, in French Canada from the seventeenth through the early twentieth centuries, and in nineteenth-century England and Poland. Nuns were also "among the most liberated women in nineteenth century America," according to one historian. "They were self-supporting, owned property, were well-educated, held administrative positions, lived in a community of women, and were free from the dominance of husbands and the responsibility of motherhood. Often they were envied by their Protestant sisters for their independence and hailed by businessmen for their acumen."[20] Wealthy, upper-class Protestant women such as Sara Worthington King Peter, the daughter of an Ohio governor, were first attracted to Catholicism because of the opportunities its religious orders offered to women.[21]

Political and Social Advantages

Religious orders offered their members other benefits in addition to being a substitute for marriage or a source of economic security, education, and personal fulfillment. One of these was increased social status. For example, what knowledge we have concerning the social background of the medieval Franciscans indicates that these men came from the rising mercantile classes—"groups that commanded vast material resources but lacked commensurate social prestige and political power."[22] Women, too, might enhance their social status by joining a religious order:

> When women joined [religious] communities, they shed many of the attitudes and much of the behavior of secular women. No longer were they individual females defined primarily through the men to whom they were related or attached, instead, they became brides of Christ who were part of the ecclesiastical establishment. By becoming participants in the Church's liturgy and life, by belonging to the Church more completely than was possible for any secular person—female or male—nuns collectively were empowered by their communal privileges and status to think and act with self-confidence.[23]

Religious life also offered an opportunity for increased social status to Catholics in nineteenth-century Ireland, Quebec, and the United States, where the secular elites were largely Protestant.[24] The increased social standing of nuns was especially attractive to women who had been marginalized in some way: the daughters of impoverished nobility, widows, those in ill health, and those generally facing straitened circumstances for which their former background had left them unprepared.[25]

In cultures where the elevated social status of the nun reflected back upon her family, young girls might also experience a great deal of familial pressure to enter a convent:

> Only too clearly, the interests of the girls themselves were confounded with the piety, or the self-interest, or both, of their families. . . . "One goes," wrote Jean Cordier in 1643, "to the clothing of a girl who has been trained to respond according to the wishes of her father and mother, not her own wishes. They dress her like a little goddess . . . they assemble her relatives, they ask her, My daughter, do you wish to be a religious? Her conscience says no but her mouth, betraying her heart, says yes."[26]

In addition to these social advantages for individuals and their families, political advantages, both secular and ecclesiastical, often motivated the recruits to enter religious life. For fourth-century Egyptian farmers, life as a religious hermit was a way to escape government interference and taxation. The upsurge of vocations to the priesthood and religious life in nineteenth-century Ireland has been linked, at least in part, to resurgent Irish nationalism, while the founding of several Canadian orders was due to a desire to keep French Catholic children out of English-speaking public schools.[27]

Spiritual Power

Entrance into a religious order was also a frequent lay response to the hierarchy's attempts to monopolize spiritual power and prestige within the Church. At the time of the fourth-century desert hermits, for example, the division between the clergy and the laity was becoming more marked, and increased status was being given to priests and bishops both by the state and by church theologians.[28] According to St. John Chrysostom, a priest who handled the Eucharist was greater in dignity than the angels, and certainly far above the lowly layman. By the early fifth century, priests had begun to wear special clothing to mark their separate status. During subsequent centuries, the church roles given to the laity were reduced or eliminated. By the tenth century, the anointing of the sick and the solemnization of marriage, two sacraments lay church members had traditionally administered, were reserved to the clergy.[29] The Gregorian reforms of the 1050s de-emphasized the prayers of monks and nuns and the folk magic practiced by the rural peasantry in favor of the all-important supernatural powers of the Eucharist, which only the priests could perform. Confession of sins by the laity to the priest began to be emphasized in the eleventh century, thus further increasing clerical power. The separation and elevation of the clergy has also been noted for seventeenth-century France, as well as for nineteenth-century Ireland and America.[30]

In the face of increasing clericalism, religious life offered an alternative source of spiritual equality and ecclesiastical power. The writings of Origen, the teaching of Peter Waldes, and the writings of Teresa of Avila each sparked waves of religious virtuosity in their resepctive centuries precisely because they admitted women and other nonclerics to spiritual equality with the ordained.[31] At times the lifestyle of the monk or nun even promised spiritual superiority over the clergy: The religious life often flourished during times of laxity and worldliness on the part of priests.[32] The idea that religious men or women were holier beings was cultivated: Their celibacy and their vows gave them a superior status, especially in eras when the lower clergy were *not* celibate; their prayers were seen as more efficacious; their mystic experiences of receiving the Eucharist independently of priests and their ability to discern unworthy clergy were ways of reasserting their position in the Church at a time when their specifically clerical roles were being diminished or denied.[33] Founding or joining a religious order might also be a way to advance the interests of other constituencies within the Church—Levesque argues that some nineteenth-century French congregations were established to reassert the interests of the rural Church in an increasingly urban-dominated ecclesiastical structure.[34]

In addition to spiritual authority, religious orders might also offer actual decision-making power within the Church. The consecrated virgins of the fourth century were actively involved in local churches and sometimes wielded great influence there. Early medieval abbesses had quasi-episcopal jurisdiction, and could preach, hear their nuns' confessions, handle communion vessels, and preside over semiliturgical rituals.[35] Later in the medieval period, women mystical writers influenced lay spirituality "by supplying a vocabulary and a nomenclature for spiritual experience, which until then was usual only in monastic circles. This was audaciously novel."[36] Nuns in seventeenth-century Quebec developed a theology of evangelization that came close to equating their own missionary endeavors with the priest's sacramental role at mass.[37]

The fact that sisters provided essential services to the Church could at times be an additional source of power. In the nineteenth-century United States:

> Bishops and priests came to have a healthy respect for the power of sisters, and with good reason. The sisters were important influences in the Catholic community and ran most of the Church's charitable institutions. In disagreements, sisters fought for their rights and usually won. Then, too, they could and did vote with their feet, or threatened to, when the occasion warranted it.[38]

In times, therefore, when the average layman—and certainly the average laywoman—had little power or influence over the hierarchical Church, religious orders could offer the only means available to achieve some degree of spiritual and ecclesiastical self-determination.

Summary

Recent historical scholarship thus provides a wealth of evidence to support the personal incentive model as at least one explanation for the periodic mobilization of new religious orders within Roman Catholicism. Table 4.1 attempts to summarize these findings. It is obvious that, in each of the periods when religious communities experienced rapid growth, many social, political and economic factors within the surrounding society were making such a lifestyle option very attractive.

If religious virtuosity expanded at least in part because of the benefits it could provide to its members, it would follow that this lifestyle would be the most attractive to the individuals who felt most in need of these benefits. In this respect, movements of religious virtuosi within Roman Catholicism resemble various political social movements that arose "under conditions where social mobility [was] restricted, and where access to powerful positions [was] closed off."[39] In a given historical period, therefore, the majority of the recruits to religious orders would be drawn from a comparatively specific background. In subsequent waves of virtuoso spirituality, on the other hand, the lifestyle of religious orders might appeal to very different categories of people.

The Social Background of Entrants

What social and economic groups, then, were typically attracted to religious life? In general, the very poorest classes of society were rarely good sources for recruits, perhaps because such individuals were too preoccupied with securing bare subsistence to spare either their time or their children for virtuoso spirituality. Then, too, an order's need for economic self-sufficiency might force it to restrict its recruiting practices to the wealthier classes.[40] The religious virgins of the third century, therefore, were from the middle and upper strata of their society.[41] Prospective entrants to medieval monasteries were expected to bring with them gifts of land or to furnish a dowry sum sufficient to support them for the rest of their lives. Monks in sixth-century Ireland, in seventh-century Gaul and England, and in twelfth-century Italy and France were predominently from the knightly class, with some members who were "middling landowners and better-off townsmen."[42] The women of both the traditional Benedictine and the newer Cistercian and Premonstratensian establishments during the same period were also from the aristocratic classes.

Some monastic communities developed a dual system of membership whereby entrants were assigned to either "choir" or "lay" status. Entry as a choir monk or nun was restricted to the nobility in the eleventh century and only gradually expanded to include the mercantile classes. Lay sisters and brothers, who were generally from poorer backgrounds, did most of the manual labor and housekeeping, thus freeing the choir monks and nuns for prayer, study, and teaching in the monastic school. At times, an aristocratic entrant would bring his or her own servant to enroll as a lay member of the monastic community. The lay/choir distinction thus offered one of the few opportunities available for members of the lower or peasant classes to enter religious life. But, with the exception of the twelfth-century Cistercian monks, whose lay members actually outnumbered the choir, men's and women's monasteries usually contained comparatively few lay sisters and brothers in proportion to the number of choir monks and nuns.

A predominantly aristocratic, or at least an upper-middle-class, background could also be discerned among the members of the cloistered and semicloistered women's orders of later historical periods. The religious orders of seventeenth- and eighteenth-century Quebec recruited their mem-

Table 4.1 Motivations for Entering Religious Life

	Demographic Pressures/ Marital Shortage	Education, Opportunity to Use Talents	Financial Security/ Advantages	Social Status	Spiritual Power	Other Motives
4th c. Egypt/ Syria	Brown 1988: 144	Brown 1988: 276 McNamara: 108 Rausch: 45 Brock & Harvey: 23 Pagels 1988: 88–89	Rausch: 39 McNamara: 45 Pagels 1988: 88	Brown 1985: 320, 431 Pagels 1988: 52	Brown: 119, 143, 175, 266, 276, 382 Donovan: 26 McNamara: 58, 82, Fontaine: 454, 464 Wynne: 62 Hill: 23	Brown 1988: 88 McNamara: 71 (childbirth) Rausch: 39 (political)
Early Monasticism, 500–1000	Turner: 147 Lawrence: 72, 180 Schulenberg: 218	Donovan: 11 Knowles: 306 Lawrence: 57	Turner: 147 Schulenberg: 218 Knowles: 197	Lawrence Johnson: 231	Morris Lerner: 25	
Mendicants, 1200–1500		Little: 173–75 Courtenay: 111 Lawrence: 260	McDonnell: 82		Little: 120	
Beguines, Woman Monastics, 1200–1500	Bynum 1987a: 19 Bynum 1987b: 126 McDonnell: 83 Johnson: 14, 23, 254 Lawrence: 216, 232 Ashley: 45	McDonnell: 85 Lawrence: 233	McDonnell: 82 Johnson: 28	Johnson: 28, 100	Haas: 141 Kieckhefer: 99 Bynum 1987a: 220 Bynum 1987b: 128 Rubin: 120 Johnson: 100	Bynum 1987: 126 (child birth) Johnson: 28 (refuge from danger) Ashley: 45
France, 1600s (women)		Rapley: 5, 11 Taylor: 312	Rapley: 188 Taylor: 423	Rapley: 187, 154	Rapley: 255 Buckley: 28	Taylor:423 (childbirth)
France, 1800s (women)	Langlois: 634	Langlois: 643–44	Langlois: 643	Langlois: 643	Levesque: 179	

Ireland, 1800s (women)	Clear: 136 Nolan: 29–33	Clear: 143 Nolan: 88 Luddy: 1992	Clear: 19 Nolan: 29	Clear: 148, 151		Clear: 135, 140 (nationalism, childbirth)
Quebec, 1800s (women)	Dumont-J. 91	Allen: 80 Dumont-J: 87–88	Dumont-J: 84, 91	Dumont-J: 86 Denault: 54, 101		Jean: 154 (nat.) Dumont-J: 93 (childbirth)
U.S. 1800s (women)		Kenneally: 43, 63 Ewens, 1983: 107 Mannard: 305 Thompson, 1986: 288	Hollermann: 360	Oates 1983: 149 Ewens 1989: 17	Ewens, 1981: 106–7 Deacon: 143, 351–55 Thompson, 1991: 148 Oates, 1985: 185	Thompson, 1986: 287 Kenneally: 78 (childbirth)

bers primarily from the province's elite (35.5 percent) and from wealthy rural landowners (24.3 percent). The artisanal (16.8 percent) and entrepreneurial (15.7 percent) classes were much less well represented.[43] This class imbalance resulted from the French government's imposition of the same dowry standards as existed in France, at a time when the colonials rarely had access to such sums. In seventeenth-century France and nineteenth-century Ireland, too, the majority of the choir postulants were from the comparatively wealthy, or at least middle-class, families of the surrounding area. Replicating medieval practice, the congregations also admitted a smaller number of "lay sisters" to do domestic work. These paid lower dowries and came from more working-class backgrounds.[44]

In contrast to the aristocratic membership of medieval monastic communities, and of the semicloistered women's communities in later periods, the male mendicant orders of the thirteenth and fourteenth centuries and the women's teaching congregations of seventeenth-century France appear to have drawn the majority of their members from the rising merchant and entrepreneurial classes. The first Dominicans and Franciscans were "burghers" from merchant families, as were the Humiliati and the Waldensians.[45] Most commentators agree that the Beguines, too, were from the bourgeoisie, although some poorer women did become members. Even communities explicitly designed to recruit the poor as members seem not always to have done so. Although St. Vincent de Paul, the founder of the seventeenth-century Daughters of Charity, claimed that these women were mostly the children of peasant farmers or artisans, they, in fact, "seem to have included women from all walks of life."[46] In succeeding centuries, the Daughters of Charity became more bourgeois in membership than they had been at their founding, and included comparatively few women of artisanal or peasant background.[47]

In nineteenth-century France, the socioeconomic background of the sisters varied from community to community and from decade to decade. Prior to 1850, the majority of the entrants came from the bourgeois or artisanal classes; after 1850, an increasing number were drawn from the rural peasantry. Few, if any, of the nobility joined the nineteenth-century French religious congregations—a pronounced contrast to the medieval pattern.[48] In Victorian England, it was the middle- and upper-middle-class ladies, rather than the aristocracy, who were "the most vulnerable to the novelty and spiritual allure of the sisterhoods"—both Catholic and Anglican.[49] However, the *foundresses* of the nineteenth-century orders seem to have come from a higher socioeconomic background than did the majority of the members. Several of the French and Irish foundresses were heirs to large fortunes.[50] Comparatively few of the European religious orders, in any century, drew their members from the urban working class.

It is interesting to explore whether the nineteenth-century United States is an exception to this pattern of limited working-class membership. Research on Maryland religious orders in the early nineteenth century indicates that they drew their recruits largely from established Catholic families (31 percent) and wealthy farmers (25 percent). Only 2 percent of those entrants whose family background could be traced had fathers who were unskilled laborers.[51] As to place of birth, over 60 percent of the sisters whose origins were recorded were American-born. During the first half of the nineteenth century, only two communities—the Sisters of Charity of Emmitsburg, Maryland, and the Sisters of Our Lady of Mercy—had more immigrant members than native-born. On the basis of this evidence, Misner states that the early American religious orders, too, first drew their recruits from the middle class.

With the increase of immigration as the century progressed, however, this situation changed somewhat. By the late nineteenth and early twentieth centuries, the vast majority (over 90 percent in some instances) of American Catholic women who entered religious communities were either immigrants themselves or of immigrant parentage.[52] Over half of the nineteenth-century School Sisters of Notre Dame—with 1731 members, the largest religious congregation in the United States at the time—were from working-class backgrounds. Another 38 percent had parents who were farmers. Only about 10 percent of the communities were from what we would today call white-collar families. "Generally," wrote one mother general to an official in Rome, "there are many vocations for the religious life, but they are especially from the class which is less wealthy, since wealth is principally in the hands of Protestants in this country."[53]

But, if most American sisters in the latter half of the nineteenth century came from the immigrant working class, it was from that class's more affluent segment. One study of several communities found that sisters whose fathers were craftsmen were between two and three times as numerous as those whose fathers were laborers.[54] Moreover, orders varied in the classes from which they drew their members. "To put it bluntly, certain congregations traditionally have been regarded as more 'prestigious' or 'important' than others," usually because they operated private academies for wealthier pupils and drew many of their members from this source.[55] Many nineteenth-century religious congregations attempted to open such schools, and experienced a rise in the number of vocations once they had done so.[56] In general, therefore, one can state that nineteenth-century American sisters came from what passed in U.S. Catholicism as a middle class.

The various religious communities thus attracted somewhat different socioeconomic groups at different periods of history. Religious life often provided a means of attaining an education, ecclesiastical power, or social status, and was the only expression of virtuoso spirituality permitted to the nonordained. Thus the most likely recruits to join religious communities were those whose socioeconomic background both deprived them of these key benefits and also sensitized them to their loss. If, however, an order was for some reason unable to achieve financial self-sufficiency—if ecclesiastical pressure forced it to adopt an excessively strict cloister, for example—sheer economic necessity might restrict its recruitment to the wealthier classes, whatever the preferences of other socioeconomic groups might have been. Individuals from the bourgeois or artisanal classes, who may also have felt their lack of spiritual fulfillment, ecclesiastical power, or social status, would then be frustrated in their ability to obtain these benefits. The pent-up desires of these spiritually disenfranchised groups could explain the explosive growth of the new orders, once outside restrictions were removed.[57]

Outside actors, therefore, often had a profound impact on the survival of new religious communities. It was not enough merely to offer material and spiritual incentives to attract likely recruits. A religious order also had to mobilize support from Church officials, civil rulers, and the laity in general. Chapter 5 will explore some of the ways in which religious communities attempted this task.

The Mobilization of Resources by Religious Orders

The personal benefits obtainable by individuals who joined religious orders, while a powerful incentive for membership, were insufficient by themselves to assure the survival and growth of an incipient community. It was also necessary for the new religious order to be able to procure food, clothing and shelter for its recruits once they had joined. The members of the active communities usually furnished these basic necessities for themselves, by offering some service or product for which outsiders were willing to pay. If unable to be self-sufficient in this manner, however, a religious community would either have to limit its recruitment to the aristocracy, or else persuade wealthy individuals in the surrounding society to supply their needs. This was often difficult.

A new religious community also needed to be familiar with certain skills that were essential for approved religious expression and communal survival. Depending on the model of virtuoso spirituality current at the time of the community's foundation, members might need to know the proper rituals for saying the Divine Office, or the techniques of ecstatic prayer, or the correct times and procedures for fasting. The various internal commitment mechanisms which are necessary for the continued functioning of any intentional community also had to be learned or discovered, as did the procedures for making decisions, choosing leaders and organizing the daily life of the group.[1] Such skills were often acquired through a mentoring relationship between the new community and a previously established one. Again, the new order's inexperience and lack of skill meant that outsiders had somehow to be persuaded to assist them.

It was also necessary to forestall the creation of obstacles by various ill-disposed actors within the community's larger environment. If powerful church or state officials refused to recognize the order's legitimate existence, if they confiscated its property or enacted unfavorable tax and inheritance laws, the nascent community often suffered irreparable harm. Previously established orders might also hinder the new group, especially if the latter represented a different model of virtuoso spirituality or if the orders perceived themselves to be in competition for resources, sponsors, or areas of ministerial service.

Individual religious communities can thus be considered as separate social movement organizations and analyzed using the "political process model" of the resource mobilization perspective.[2] Such an analysis would examine how the orders dealt with the various other institutional actors in their environment, either to neutralize their opposition or to enlist their support. The following section will consider the interests of these outside actors and will describe the incentives new religious communities could offer to assure their good will and assistance.

The Church Hierarchy: Types of Support

Ideological and Ministerial Legitimation

Of all the outside actors whose good will was necessary for an incipient religious community, the Church hierarchy was the most important. First of all, the Church provided essential ideological support, validating the legitimacy of the new group's lifestyle and activities. Unless a community was officially certified by the Church hierarchy as a bona fide religious order or congregation, its members would not be eligible for key spiritual and financial benefits. In the Middle Ages, for example, monks and nuns were permitted to attend church services even during times of ecclesiastical interdict when ordinary lay people were denied the sacraments.[3] Special indulgences were given to members of recognized religious orders. Indulgences were also available to the wealthy lay persons who contributed to the erection of monastic churches; it was a coup when the Beguines were officially permitted to offer these indulgences for contributors to *their* churches. Church certification was necessary, not only to attain eligibility for such spiritual favors, but also to confirm the members' status in the surrounding society. Without evidence of their respectable church standing, communities often found it difficult to attract both financial donors and new recruits, especially if they espoused a novel interpretation of religious virtuosity.[4] Hostile bishops and priests might even channel potential recruits *away* from a new community. On the other hand, the public recognition by the hierarchy of a new order's spirituality was a valuable source of new entrants.

The ministerial activities the group intended to perform also required approval by the Church hierarchy. Prior to the thirteenth century, for example, bishops were believed to be the only official preachers and teachers of the Catholic faith.[5] Preaching by Dominican friars or, worse, by lay men and lay women among the Franciscans, the Waldensians, and the Humiliati, went against this assumption and had to be dealt with. Church authorities finally permitted the ordained Dominican priests to give sermons on both doctrine and morality, and allowed the laymen in other mendicant groups to exhort their fellows to moral reform. Similarly, the very idea that women religious might leave their cloister to teach or visit the sick was a scandalous novelty in seventeenth-century France and was legitimated only with great difficulty.[6] In the nineteenth century, religious congregations had to obtain the permission of the local bishop before they could perform ministerial services within his diocese. Refusal of this permission was used to keep recalcitrant communities—and their superiors—in line. The Sisters of St. Joseph of Peace, for example, were forbidden to operate in *any* U.S. diocese until their controversial founder, Margaret Cusack, withdrew from the community.[7]

Finally, it was necessary to obtain the Church's agreement that religious virtuosity was a possible and acceptable practice for the particular social class or gender from which the new community drew its members. In the early Middle Ages, for example, monastic activity was considered antithetical to women's putatively carnal nature. Church authorities were, therefore, extremely reluctant to support the founding of women's monasteries, and even dissolved the ones already in existence in order to award their property to monks. Later in the medieval period, merchants were thought to be condemned by their worldly occupation to spiritual inferiority, and possibly to eternal damnation. Such men, it was thought, could never achieve spiritual perfection in religious life. Again, in late sixteenth-century France, it was women who were thought to be too carnal to achieve "true" spiritual perfection.[8] In each of these examples, and in many others, it was necessary for the new communities to demonstrate to the Church hierarchy that virtuoso spirituality, and religious life, were indeed possible for the members of these formerly despised social groups.

Spiritual and Financial Support

In addition to providing ideological legitimation for a new religious order's lifestyle, ministry and membership, the ordained clergy and hierarchy also provided other services essential to the community. Priests were necessary in order to say mass, hear confessions, and offer spiritual direction to nonordained religious. Since this caused a drain on their time and personnel, dioceses and monasteries of ordained monks were reluctant to take on the responsibility of too many nonordained communities, especially when these communities were unable to offer them any spiritual benefits in return.[9] In addition to their need of spiritual services, the *financial* dependence of women's monasteries—so strictly cloistered that it was impossible for them to earn their own living—made both male monasteries and the hierarchy especially unwilling to sponsor them. Medieval nuns were generally much poorer than medieval monks; Johnson estimates that thirteenth-century Norman nunneries possessed only 15 percent of the mean wealth of the male monasteries.[10] Both the monks and the friars, therefore, attempted repeatedly to avoid any responsibility for the communities of women that sought to affiliate with them. This caused a severe shortage of opportunities for religious virtuosity among women at a time when the virtuoso lifestyle was highly prized and sought after. Jacques de Vitry is said to have complained that, in the Liege area alone, the Cistercian monasteries could have sponsored three times as many convents as they were currently sponsoring and still not be able to accommodate all of the women who wished to join.[11] When they could not avoid responsibility for a women's community, medieval abbots often treated these dependent nunneries "as a carcass to be picked over for tasty tidbits," removing any items of value which they desired for their own establishments, and sometimes even evicting the nuns and taking over the property for their own use.[12] As late as the nineteenth century, many male orders were unwilling to retain sponsorship of women's groups, and would turn them over to diocesan authorities for supervision—whether the sisters wanted this change or not.[13]

Not only might having to support groups of dependent nonordained religious be a drain on ordained monastic personnel and on the diocesan or monastic treasury, it might be a source of bad publicity as well. Several authors mention the disruption that lack of financial solvency in religious orders caused the surrounding societies: Both monks and nuns were often forced to resort to begging, and the nuns might even be driven to prostitution.[14] Of the 2000 women's communities existing in seventeenth-century France, at least 25 percent were "miserably poor."[15] French bishops worried that the many small, financially precarious communities of women in their dioceses would find it hard to survive or carry on their apostolate. There was similar concern in other centuries. "Bishops [of nineteenth-century Ireland] had seen the failure of convents and the consequent plight of members forced to seek refuge with their families."[16] To avoid both the scandal of insolvent convents and also the financial burden of dependent ones, bishops preferred to encourage wealthy lay families to support the sisters and friars, rather than to provide such support themselves.[17] If no such wealthy sponsors were available, convents and monasteries might not be founded.

Although the many spiritual and financial needs of religious orders were galling to the clergy, such dependence also served their interests. Indeed, the hierarchy sometimes deliberately fostered a community's dependent status in order to keep its members from breaking away from the Church altogether. One sixth-century pope, for example, forbade all monks from becoming priests, or priests from becoming monks. This rendered the monks dependent on the clergy for the sacraments that only ordained priests could provide, and thus neutralized their previous hostility toward the institutional church.[18] Similarly, several historians have noted the hierarchy's desire to keep medieval and reformation women from heresy and schism by reinforcing their dependence on the ordained clergy. In the nineteenth century, too, the dependence of women's communities on the clergy for provision of the sacraments was used as a threat to keep them in line.

Political Support

New religious groups had other difficulties in addition to securing ideological legitimation, spiritual services, and financial support from the Church hierarchy. The opposition of other, already existing religious orders also had to be neutralized if a newly organized form of virtuoso spirituality was to succeed. Every period in the history of religious orders can provide examples of these struggles.[19] The cathedral canons of the eleventh and twelfth centuries (quasi-monastic groups of priests who retained their own private property while living in common and engaging in teaching and other ministeries) were opposed both by the secular clergy as being too strict and by the monks as not living "true" monastic lives. The canons argued that they were distinct from, and superior to, the monks; the monks argued otherwise. Both the Cistercians and the canons objected to the activities of the Waldensians. The Cistercians and the Franciscans contended with the Dominicans over the latter's right to supervise the Beguines. In seventeenth-century France, the male Franciscans and Dominicans opposed the arrival of the Ursuline nuns, fearing that this new order would compete with their own female branches for recruits. In nineteenth-century Ireland, the already established Sisters of Charity and Presentation Sisters objected to the foundation of the Sisters of Mercy. In nineteenth-century Quebec, established congregations of sisters had been accustomed to establish auxiliary groups of lay women to help them in their work. Often these "Third Orders" would split off and become new religious communities on their own, to the consternation of the parent congregation that had been deprived of their help.

In addition to their conflicts with already established groups of religious virtuosi, some new orders got caught up in existing factional battles within the larger Church. Thirteenth-century secular clergy who opposed the growing power and influence of the Dominican friars, but who were refrained by the latter's popularity from attacking them directly, attacked the Dominican-supported Beguines instead. This caused the Beguines great difficulty.[20] As another example, the English diocesan clergy were engaged in a rivalry with the Jesuits during the early seventeenth century and refused to support Mary Ward's "English Ladies," whose spirituality and ministry had been modeled on that of the Jesuits. The Jesuits, in their turn, withdrew from the women because of their controversial reputation.[21] Deprived of her ecclesiastical support, Mary Ward was arrested as a heretic in 1630; in 1631, her order was formally suppressed. Some two centuries later, Margaret Cusack, the "nun of Kenmare" who founded the Sisters of St. Joseph of Peace, accidentally became embroiled in an ongoing conflict between the "Americanizing" bishops of the nineteenth-century United States and the more conservative Archbishop Michael Corrigan of New York. As a result, she earned Archbishop Corrigan's undying opposition. In order for her community to survive, she was ultimately forced to leave it and return to England. Eventually, she left Catholicism entirely.[22]

In their conflicts with already established religious orders or with elements of the diocesan clergy, new religious communities needed the active support of powerful ecclesiastical sponsors, whether in the hierarchy or in another religious group. The nineteenth-century Mercy sisters in Ireland, the medieval Franciscans and Dominicans, and other successful groups were finally able to overcome the opposition of their established competitors primarily because of strong papal or episcopal support.[23] Other communities, deprived of this support, collapsed.

Not all established religious orders opposed the arrival of new communities. Many provided them with valuable material assistance, and some even served as their teachers and mentors. Established medieval orders often sent one of their members to a newly founded community to instruct them in prayer and ritual, and sometimes provided the new order with its first superiors.[24] One historian records many examples of mutual help in nineteenth-century Ireland: the Carmelite nuns in Loughrea who gave hospitality to the Sisters of Mercy on their journey to Galway in 1840, for example, or the Sisters of Mercy who regularly invited the Faithful Companions of Jesus to their convent for morning Mass and breakfast and who aided the Little Sisters of the Poor on the latter's fund-raising tour.[25] Similar incidents occurred in the United States.[26] The Mercy convent in nineteenth-century Chicago sent a wagon load of groceries to a recently arrived—and destitute—group of cloistered nuns. The Sisters of Charity at the New York Foundling Home gave money and supplies to

Frances Cabrini's community, as did the Bon Secours sisters. Established nineteenth-century religious congregations often trained the foundresses of new groups. After passing her novitiate at the supporting order's motherhouse, the foundress would return to set up her own community.[27] A final example of intercongregational cooperation occurred in the nineteenth-century United States, where the heads of various congregations of sisters shared information and strategies on how to transfer their communities from diocesan to pontifical status—a necessary step to break the intrusive control of the bishops.[28] This procedure took a great deal of political skill, since it required the endorsements of the very bishops from whose control the sisters were attempting to escape.

In order to survive and prosper, therefore, a new religious order had to enlist the support of the Church's hierarchy and, sometimes, of other religious communities as well. The good offices of the hierarchy were vitally necessary: to give formal legitimation to a community's particular model of virtuoso spirituality, to supply it with the sacraments and other spiritual services, to recommend it to the laity for financial support and new recruits, and to support it against the opposition of already established orders. Communities of women, especially, were utterly dependent upon this ecclesiastical assistance. Jean describes the "rather pathetic" odyssey of the Little Franciscans who, after being abandoned by the priest who had founded them, wandered between Massachusetts and Canada for several years during the late nineteenth century until a parish priest finally accepted them.[29] Fitzgerald contrasts the success of the Sisters of Mercy, who enjoyed Archbishop Hughes's support for their New York ministries, with the struggles of the Good Shepherd Sisters, whose "Magdalene Asylums" for unwed mothers was grudgingly accepted by the archbishop only after years of pleading.[30]

The importance of ecclesiastical support for women's religious orders can also be seen by comparing the fate of the Catholic orders with that of the Anglican sisterhoods and deaconesses in nineteenth-century England. In general, Anglican bishops approved of the *work* of the sisterhoods but were not yet ready to sanction "the kind of community and ritual life that these women were aiming at."[31] As a result, the Anglican bishops did not defend the sisters from Protestant attacks on their legitimacy and readily washed their hands of sisterhoods that became financially precarious or troublesome. This led, some critics argued, to extreme insecurity on the part of the sisterhoods, to clinging to novices and encouraging even those with evident lack of vocation to remain, and to cults of personality centered on the novice director or the mother superior.[32] Anglican deaconesses, too, needed and often did not receive episcopal validation and support. "Hence the failure of the Church to clarify the status of the fe-

male diaconate was particularly cruel. Individual bishops formally institutionalized the female diaconate in their several dioceses; the Anglican
Church as a corporate body did not."[33]

Within Catholicism as well as within Anglicanism, there were deep-
seated reasons why the support of the hierarchy might be withheld from
newly founded religious communities. In many ways, the clergy and bishops embodied an alternate model of virtuoso spirituality that competed
with the model espoused by the religious orders. This meant that episcopal
relationships with both the new and the existing orders were fraught with
potential conflicts. The following sections of this chapter will attempt to
describe the roots of such conflicts, as well as to outline the benefits that
could nevertheless motivate Catholicism's ordained virtuosi to sponsor
groups of lay competitors.

The Church Hierarchy and Religious Orders: Sources of Conflict

Jurisdictional Issues

By formal Church law, the local bishop enjoyed sole jurisdiction over all
religious personnel and their activities within his diocese. To escape from
this control and to retain their autonomy, male orders could apply to the
papacy for formal exemption from episcopal oversight.[34] For the bishop,
the exempt religious orders posed several problems. If such groups contained ordained members, these men could be preaching, saying mass, and
offering spiritual direction within the bishop's diocese and yet be totally
outside of his authority. Exempt orders also exercised greater control over
their own finances and property.

Because of the threat male orders posed to their authority, the bishops
of every period resisted their presence. Fourth-century bishops "regarded
monasticism with reserve, since it had originated outside of the standard
Christian institutions."[35] Seventh- and eighth-century English bishops
contended with the monasteries in their dioceses about who had authority
over whom. The mendicant friars of the Middle Ages were bitterly opposed by the French bishops, who considered them to be hypocrites and
disruptive elements. The friars also exercised significant authority over
communities of nuns in the Middle Ages, "both to oversee convents' affairs, and in general to give spiritual direction to women, cloistered or
not."[36] The bishops regarded this arrangement with suspicion and attempted to curtail it. The nuns, meanwhile, could be caught in the middle of a dispute over whose authority—the bishop's or the friars'—they
would be required to obey.

Episcopal hostility toward religious priests persisted in subsequent centuries. In the seventeenth-century Netherlands, male religious orders and bishops engaged in almost constant conflict.[37] In the nineteenth century, Bishop Amat of Los Angeles engaged in a running feud with the Franciscan priests in his diocese, who had served the Spanish-speaking Catholics there since 1782. The bishop accused the friars of simony (the selling of Church services) and of tolerating a heterodox folk piety among their flocks. In 1858, he withdrew his permission for the Franciscans to serve as priests in his diocese. The friars protested to Rome, and a grudging compromise was finally reached in 1861. Other U.S. bishops felt the same way. As late as the 1890s, "it was said that a Jesuit dared not even change trains in St. Paul [Minnesota]," so great was Archbishop Ireland's antipathy toward them.[38]

Women were less successful than men in achieving exemption from episcopal authority. In most periods, nuns were officially considered minors and were thus wards of the bishop or of his delegate.[39] The bishop was responsible for both their spiritual and financial welfare and would initiate regular inspections of their convent or monastery to assure himself that all was running as it should.[40] He was often entitled to choose which nun would manage the order, or at least to veto the sisters' choice, and he could also dicate what works they would perform and how they would manage their finances.[41] At times a bishop delegated his authority to a parish priest or convent chaplain: In France during the 1600s, it was the local pastor who gave the Sisters of St. Joseph their habit, received their vows, and kept their financial records.[42] Similarly, in nineteenth-century Quebec, it was often the parish priest who defined the need a religious congregation would serve, drew up their Rule and constitution, and permitted the organization of the community.

The sisters, in their turn, were careful to see that their areas of autonomy were officially recorded, so that they could be appealed to, if necessary, in the future. A religious community "learned to establish at the outset of each episcopal reign its freedom from any infringement of its rights, in which effort the nuns received substantial support from all the religious in the city."[43] Although the bishops frequently made visits of inspection to convents, there is evidence that nuns often ignored episcopal reforms.[44]

A primary purpose of this episcopal jurisdiction was to prevent the nuns and monks from falling into error and heresy. Several authors have remarked that women, especially, were attracted to various heretical movements such as the Gnostics, the Cathars, the Waldensians, and the Protestant reformers—perhaps because these groups promised, initially at least, to give their female adherents higher status and more power.[45] As defenders of the "true faith," the bishops were responsible for assuring the doctrinal orthodoxy of the religious communities within their jurisdiction. It was also feared that, if left unsupervised, both women and men in religious communities would degenerate into loose living. St. Jerome, in the fourth century, described a "very inferior and little regarded" kind of monk—men who

> are bound by no rule, but do exactly as they choose . . . They often quarrel because they are unwilling . . . to be subordinated to others. It is true that they compete with each other in fasting; they make what should be a private concern an occasion for a triumph. In everything they study effect; their garb is of the coarsest. They are always sighing, or visiting virgins, or sneering at the clergy; yet, when a holiday comes, they make themselves sick—they eat so much.[46]

In the Middle Ages, "laymen carried the title of abbot and ruled over houses in which they lived with their wives, children, soldiers and dogs. Their morals were corrupt and they squandered monastic revenues."[47] Such behavior reflected a moral laxity that bishops were required to correct.

Still another source of abuse was the admittance of candidates in infancy or as very young children.[48] "These poor children are pushed into these perpetual prisons," wrote Oudart Coquault in seventeenth-century France. "They are put in at ten, eleven and twelve years, clothed at thirteen or fourteen, professed at fifteen at the latest. More than four years later they still don't know what they have done; it is at 22 or 23, 24 and 25 that they begin to realize what sex they belong to."[49] Early recruitment often made for lax or indifferent religious in later life.[50] For this reason Pope Pius IX in 1854 urged that bishops and congregations initiate a three-year period of temporary vows to replace the profession of solemn perpetual vows by candidates as young as sixteen.

In addition to eliminating heresy and laxity within religious orders for their own spiritual welfare, the bishops were also concerned to avoid the scandal that such abuses would cause among the laity. Even legitimate apostolic ministries might be a source of scandal: the Visitation nuns during their early years (1610–1626) were spat upon and reviled by passersby as they left their cloister to visit the sick.[51] Other legitimate groups, such as the medieval Beguines and Beghards, were confused in the popular mind with more radical or heretical groups, and the excesses of the latter were ascribed to them as well. As a result of this confusion, the Beguines and Beghards were first subjected to more rigorous episcopal control and then later disbanded.[52]

The Anticlerical Stance of Religious Orders

The issue of proper episcopal jurisdiction was not the only source of conflict and tension between the Church's hierarchy and religious orders.

Some versions of virtuoso spirituality were essentially hostile to the ordained clergy, having been established at least in part to protest against either the moral laxity or the increasing power of priests and bishops. The generally low level of spiritual life and moral practice among the diocesan clergy was a primary motivating force behind the establishment of the fourth-century eremitical, the early medieval monastic, and the late medieval mendicant models of religious life. Early monastic writers condemned those of their fellows who sought ordination to the priesthood. "Ecclesiastical office was part of that world of secular distinctions the monk had renounced."[53] Later, the evangelical poverty of the mendicants was a protest against "ecclesiastical wealth and the materialism of bourgeois society."[54] The political corruption within the Church, whereby high ecclesiastical offices were awarded to powerful and wealthy candidates rather than to capable and holy ones, was also a target of criticism. Religious virtuosi were not in the least inhibited in their attacks on the abuses within the institutional Church: Arnold of Brescia (1100–1155), for example, urged "that the clergy strip themselves of political and economic power and live on alms alone, going so far as to argue that no monk or cleric who owned property could be saved. In his efforts to eliminate ecclesiastical authority he became involved in two revolutionary communes, first in his native Brescia in 1138 where he led a revolt against the bishop, and later in Rome where he became the leader of a commune . . . which drove Pope Eugenius III from the city."[55] Obviously, such conduct made for strained relations between the church hierarchy and those religious virtuosi who engaged in it.

Lay religious virtuosi also threatened the prerogatives of the ordained clergy and hierarchy by performing for themselves various priestly functions or by appearing able to do without the clergy's services altogether. The desert hermits claimed to have received the Eucharist, and even ordination, directly from the hands of Christ, thus bypassing the mediation of the priests and bishops.[56] Gnostic men and women in the early Church formed study groups in which some among them functioned as spiritual teachers, again angering the clergy who claimed this privilege for themselves. Early Christian women achieved fame as prophets; medieval nuns claimed to be able to discern the state of priests' souls. The Waldensians and the mendicant friars preached, which only bishops and priests were supposed to do. The seventeenth-century French nuns also broke a male clerical monopoly—that of teaching religion to the young. As critics within the hierarchy said of Mary Ward's "Jesuitesses" in 1631:

> They build colleges, erect houses of formation, and have a superior general of their so-called congregation to whom they make vows of poverty, chastity and obedience [instead of making these vows to the local bishop]. . . . They go freely everywhere, without submitting to the laws of cloister, under the pretext of working for the salvation of souls,

and . . . are accustomed to undertake and carry out many other works very little in rapport with the feebleness of their sex and their spirit . . . works which distinguished men of the science of sacred letters only undertake with difficulty and great circumspection.[57]

The relationship between Catholicism's two competing models of religious virtuosity, the ordained priesthood and the religious life, was thus a subject of constant negotiation and struggle. Bishops and priests attempted to assert and defend their power and their sphere of influence over that of monks, nuns, and friars; they also claimed the right and responsibility to monitor the latter for abuses. Members of religious communities, in return, strove for their independence from episcopal and clerical interference, and often assumed an extremely critical stance with regard to the laxity, material wealth, and consolidation of power so often evident among priests and bishops. As table 5.1 indicates, a wide range of reasons existed for bishops and priests to oppose religious communities of men and women. Given the apparently inherent conflict of interests between these groups, how could the Church hierarchy be persuaded even to be neutral toward newly developing religious communities, to say nothing of actively supporting them?

The Church Hierarchy and Religious Orders: Sources of Support and Cooperation

Despite the seemingly intractable conflicts of interest that existed between the Church's hierarchy and its communities of lay virtuosi, priests and bishops not only tolerated religious congregations; they at times even founded them and assumed active responsibility for their growth. The fourth-century Italian clergy strongly encouraged the development of consecrated virginity among wealthy Christian women.[58] Early medieval churchmen "actively recruited women with power and property into the monastic movement."[59] In seventeenth-century France, priests and bishops founded, or helped to found, forty-eight of the ninety-four women's teaching congregations in one study.[60] Even Mary Ward's English Ladies had great support from Bishop Blaine.

But it was the nineteenth-century bishops and priests who were the most actively engaged in fostering the establishment and growth of religious communities. In nineteenth-century Holland, "each pastor [vied] with his neighbor to found his own congregation of sisters."[61] Bishop Ignace Bourget, who governed the diocese of Montreal between 1840 and the mid-1860s, personally founded four different religious communities for women within his diocese, and persuaded an additional ten groups (five

Table 5.1   Motivations of Secular Clergy for Opposing Religious Communities

	Drain on Finances, Usurped Contributions	Source of Scandal	Threat to Power/Role	Threat to Orthodoxy	Anticlerical Stance of Religious
4th c. Egypt/Syria		Donovan: 120 McNamara: 113–15 Brown 1988: 289 Brown 1985: 431	McNamara: 67, 75, 111–12 Hill: 23 Brown: 119, 144 Lawrence: 16 Frazee: 263	McNamara: 68 Pagels: 299 Donovan: 29 Hill: 29	Gannon: 163 McDonnell: 151 Wynne: 62 Hill: 23, 40 Denault: 26
Early monasticism 500–1000	Schulenberg: 225 Lawrence: 195	Schulenberg: 224, 229	McDonnell: 157–58 Lawrence: 136		Gannon: 163
Mendicants, 1200–1500	Lawrence: 261 Hinnebusch: 1309	McDonnell: 485–89	Donovan: 11 McDonnell: 194, 457, 460 Rausch: 67–68 Little: 127–128 Knowles: 57–58, 76 Hinnebusch: 1309	McDonnell: 461	Gannon: 163 McDonnell: 151 Rubin: 323
Beguines, Women Monastics, 1200–1500	Johnson: 219 McDonnell: 442	McDonnell: 121, 409 Lawrence: 224–29, 234 Neel: 257	Bynum 1987a: 220 Rubin: 323 McDonnell: 343, 371, 442 Bynum 1987b: 127 Lawrence: 234 Foley 1991: 14	Neel: 245 Bynum 1987b: 12–27 McDonnell: 121, 136, 442 Bynum 1987a: 17 Rubin: 317–318 Lawrence: 233–34	Donovan: 34 Lawrence: 233–34 McDonnell: 371 Bynum, 1991: 136
France, 1600s (women)	Rapley: 182 Taylor: 531	Rapley: 33, 168 Jean: 21	Rapley: 33, 135–140 Jean 1977: 21 Clear: 47–48 Taylor: 396	Rapley: 11–20	
Ireland, 1800s (women)	Regan/Keiss: 61 Clear: 50–51, 63	Regan/Keiss: 32 Clear: 67–68, 150	Clear: 50, 64–65		
U.S. 1800s (women)		Kenneally: 54–55 Fitzgerald: 49–50 Campbell, 1989: 155	Vidulich: 40, 50 McQuade Deacon: 349, 354, 357–63, 381 Oates: 183 Kenneally: 46–51 Ewens 1981: 106		

men's religious orders and five women's congregations) to send him some of their members from France or Quebec City. Nor was Bishop Bourget unusual. Table 5.2 gives a partial list of the congregations of women founded in, or invited into, various Canadian dioceses by bishops or priests during the nineteenth century. Likewise, in nineteenth-century France, 32 percent of the women's congregations were founded on the sole initiative of a bishop or a priest, and another 26 percent by a cleric and a laywoman acting together.[62]

In the nineteenth-century United States, bishops and priests were similarly involved in founding or recruiting religious communities of sisters. As was the case in Canada, orders invited into the United States were often detached from their European motherhouses by the inviting cleric and then formed into separate communities under his leadership. Thus, Bishop Amat of Los Angeles spent the first two years of his episcopate (1853–1855) touring Europe to invite seminarians and women religious to his new diocese.[63] Abbot Boniface Wimmer brought the first Benedictine sisters to Pennsylvania and a group of Dominicans to New York. Bishop Michael O'Connor invited Ireland's Mercy sisters to his diocese in Pittsburgh; Bishop Simon Brute recruited the Holy Cross sisters and the Sisters of Providence to Indiana. Most of the various branches of the Sisters of St. Joseph trace their orders' arrival in the United States to an invitation of Bishop Rosati of St. Louis. In all, of some 261 U.S. women's communities founded before 1900, fifty-eight were founded by a bishop or a priest: fifteen in America and forty-three in Europe. Another twenty were begun by a male cleric and a woman acting together. Of the communities founded in Europe and invited to this country before 1900, all but three were invited by a bishop, a priest, or the members of a male religious order.[64]

Why have so many bishops and priests throughout the centuries engaged in this activity? One reason undoubtedly was their firm belief in Catholicism as the true faith and their feelings of responsibility for the moral welfare and doctrinal orthodoxy of the souls under their care. Ideological motivations such as these will be discussed in chapter 9. On a more personal and practical level, however, establishing or sponsoring religious congregations offered definite personal advantages to both popes and bishops.

Religious Communities and Clergy Careers: the Papal/Episcopal Power Struggle

One reason why the pope might support a given religious order would be to strengthen his hand in his ongoing competition with the episcopate for dominance within the Church. From the time of Gregory the Great (d.

Table 5.2 A Partial List of Bishops and Priests Who Founded, or Helped Found, Women's Religious Congregations: Canada, 1800–1900

Bishop	Diocese	Religious Community	Date	Role
Bourget	Montreal	Sisters of Charity of St. Hyacinth	1840	invited*
		Religious of Sacred Heart of Jesus	1842	invited
		Sisters of Providence	1843	founded
		Sisters of Holy Names of Jesus/Mary	1843	founded
		Sisters of Charity of Good Shepherd	1844	invited
		Sisters of the Holy Cross	1847	invited
		Sisters of Mercy	1848	founded
		Sisters of Saint Anne	1850	founded
		Little Daughters of St.Joseph	1857	invited
Turgeon	Quebec	Sisters of Charity of Quebec	1849	founded
		Sisters of the Good Shepherd	1850	founded
		Religious of Jesus and Mary	1855	invited
Walsh	Halifax	Sisters of Charity	1849	invited
de Charbonnel	Toronto	Sisters of St. Joseph	1851	invited
Connelly	St.Johns, New Brunswick	Sisters of Charity	1854	invited
de Charbonnel	London	Ursulines	1860	invited
Horan	Kingston	Sisters of Providence	1861	invited
Langevin	Rimouski	Sisters of the Little Schools	1874	founded
		Sisters of Charity	1877	invited
		Sisters of Notre Dame	1877	invited
		Sisters of Jesus and Mary	1877	invited
Prince	St.Hyacinth	Sisters of the Precious Blood	1861	invited
Moreau	St.Hyacinth	Sisters of St. Joseph	1882	founded
O'Connor	Toronto	Sisters of St. Joseph	1890	invited
Labreque	Chicoutimi	Sisters of Good Counsel	1892	founded
Cameron	Antigonish	Sisters of St. Martha	1897	founded
Larocque	Sherbrooke	Sisters of the Holy Family	1896	founded

Priest	Parish	Religious Community	Date	Role
Harper	St.Gregoire	Sisters of the Assumption	1853	founded
Brosseau	Belle Chasse	Sisters of Our Lady of Perpetual Help	1892	founded
Fafard	Baie St Paul	Little Franciscans of Baie St. Paul	1893	founded
Ouelette & Moreau	St.Hyacinth Seminary	Sisters of St. Martha	1883	founded
Mangin	Masson	Third Order Secular of St. Francis	1892	founded
Benoit	Manitoba	Sisters of the Savior	1897	invited

*The majority of the invited congregations later became independent.

Sources: Denault, 1975: 76; Jean, 1977: 78, 90–100, 114–23.

604) on, various popes had attempted to assert their primacy over local bishops.[65] The Cluniac monasteries and, later, the mendicant Franciscans and Dominicans, were able to profit from this situation: By consistently seeking the patronage of popes such as Gregory VII (1073–1085) and Innocent III (1198–1216) and then supporting these popes in their efforts to increase papal power, the orders were able to become exempt from local interference. This was especially necessary for the mendicants, whose mission interfered with the vested interests of powerful local actors. "The revolutionary programme of mendicant preaching, a deadly threat to so many established interests, was turned into a form of orderly internal church reform" through the alliance of the Franciscans and Dominicans with the papacy and against the bishops.[66]

At other times, the bishops—or even local priests—were more likely than the papacy to support the foundation of religious orders. Again, this support occurred most often when it resulted in concrete personal advantages for the sponsoring cleric. "Chanting crowds of virgins" were a status symbol and a source of power for third- and fourth-century bishops, who actively exerted themselves to secure such women—overriding even familial opposition if necessary.[67] Many clergymen, such as Arius and St. Jerome in the early church and, later, the medieval friars, enhanced their reputations and influence by serving as spiritual directors and counselors for groups of religious women.[68] In the Middle Ages, the Eucharistic-centered spirituality of women mystics, both cloistered and Beguine, supported the power of the clergy who monopolized control over this sacrament.[69] The wealth of the consecrated virgins also strengthened the early bishops' hands against secular authorities.[70] Most striking, however, was the relationship between religious congregations and episcopal careers that occurred in the nineteenth century.

Prior to the late nineteenth century, the papacy had little control over episcopal appointments. Most European bishops were either elected by the priests who staffed the local cathedral chapter or else were chosen by the civil authorities.[71] In the United States, "between 1829 and 1884, Rome's authority was mediated by a body of bishops who met regularly in council and recognized the informal primacy of the archbishop of Baltimore. . . . They more or less controlled the appointment of new bishops and secured their own authority over sometimes restive clergy and laity by maintaining a solid front."[72] One furthered one's episcopal career under this system by impressing one's fellow bishops and by cementing alliances with them.[73] And, since the public education, health, and welfare institutions of the United States at this time were perceived as being inimical to Catholics, the surest way to prove to one's fellow bishops that one was a worthy shepherd of one's diocese was to establish and manage an alternative system of Catholic institutions.[74] Priests, too, could become powers in their neighborhoods and in their dioceses by being "brick and mortar" pastors. "Virtually invisible in the early years of the century, the priest-builder image became a dominant one by the mid-nineteenth century. A papal visitor noticed this and remarked quite accurately that 'the most outstanding priest is the one that built the most churches and began the most institutions.' "[75] Communities of sisters were needed to staff these enterprises once they were built.

The development of national churches in American Catholicism also contributed to the growth of Catholic institutions—and of religious communities. The competition that often erupted between the various nationality groups of Catholic immigrants encouraged ethnic pastors to establish or import religious congregations to staff the separate schools and the other institutions which they had developed for their non-English-speaking flocks. By the late nineteenth century, the Irish-controlled "territorial" parishes in many U.S. cities often contained within their borders autonomous Italian, German, and Polish national churches. Each of these maintained their own schools—and staffed them with their own priests and sisters.

The successful careers of the nineteenth-century bishops and the parish clergy therefore required male and (especially) female religious communities to staff the institutions the clerics had established. If no existing order could be enticed to provide sisters (a rational response, since such sisters were often detached from their motherhouse's authority and subjected to the bishop that had invited them), the bishop would himself locate some young women, provide them with living quarters, write them a Rule and constitutions, and establish them as a separate religious congregation under his jurisdiction. The pattern of bishops founding—or causing to be founded—religious communities of women was widespread in the United States, in Canada, in France, and in Germany during the nineteenth century. Sometimes, parish priests also established religious communities. Foundations by parish priests were especially common in nineteenth-century France.[76]

By the end of the nineteenth century, however, this situation had changed. The destruction of powerful European episcopacies by the revolutionaries and by Napoleon, the attacks by secular liberals upon the Church, and the elimination of the papacy's temporal power had the paradoxical effect of increasing Pope Pius IX's autonomy *within* the Church and freeing him to centralize papal control. "Episcopacies no longer institutionally intertwined with the state became more dependent on the Vatican's protection against hostile governments than they did on the state's protection against the papacy. . . . Thus [Pius IX] began the Church's period of greatest centralization, which was to last at least until the second Vatican Council and which, in some respects, still continues."[77] The formerly semi-independent Gallican Catholic Church in France, for example, took on an increasingly ultramontane orientation, adopting the Roman rite for the mass, purging ecclesiastical libraries of Gallican books, and submitting to the supervision of the Roman Curia. "To embrace ultramontanism in this milieu was to stand up for the rightful independence of the church from the state, and to see the pope as the heroic guardian and guarantee of the church's independence and unity."[78] Similarly, in the United States, "after the appointment of the Apostolic Delegate in 1893 and the condemnation of Americanism in 1899, the American Church became a 'states' rights' Church, with each bishop supreme in his diocese, accountable to and dependent upon Rome."[79] One's episcopal career now depended, not on how many institutions one could provide for the needs of one's flock, but rather on one's loyalty to the pope: "A Roman education, along with the faithful implementation of papal encyclicals, became the best assurance for advancement in the hierarchy."[80] A similar change occurred on the local level. Within their dioceses, the bishops now reigned supreme, and the former independence of the early nineteenth-century priest was greatly restricted.[81]

In this new political situation, there were fewer reasons for bishops and priests to found, or to sponsor the founding of, new religous communities. Even if a bishop or a priest wished to do so, daunting new obstacles had been erected that made the project much more difficult. Under Pius X (1903–1914), all new religious congregations, even diocesan ones, now had to be approved by Rome. Vatican approval was often delayed or even withheld: Several French Canadian orders of the early twentieth century experienced extreme difficulty in securing papal certification, even with the active support of their bishops.[82] In most countries, therefore, the rate at which new religious communities were founded by bishops or priests fell off sharply after 1900, even though new entrants continued to swell the membership of the already existing congregations. Bishops shifted their attention from founding new religious congregations to consolidating their control over the groups already founded, since this was one area over which Rome was as yet making no attempts to centralize its authority.[83]

Religious Communities and the Growth of the Church

A second reason why the ordained hierarchy in some eras might support a competing model of virtuoso spirituality such as religious life was because the activities of religious orders helped to secure and increase the overall power of the Church in the larger society—and, consequently, the clergy's own power as well.[84] This was especially true when the Church was being threatened by heretics or by a hostile state. Religious communities in these eras became a sign or witness within the decadent secular environment of the superior holiness of the Church—and, by extension, of the Church's ordained hierarchy, with whom the orders became increasingly identified in the public mind.

Religious communities were also valued by the hierarchy for their role in combatting heresy and for their missionary efforts. Both the monastic communities and the mendicants often served on the margins of Christianity, spreading the faith to as yet unevangelized territories.[85] The Dominicans were also appreciated by medieval popes for their successes against Albigensianism, especially after the failure of bishops and traditional monastic orders such as the Cistercians to counter the spread of this heresy. Similarly, in seventeenth-century France, teaching communities of women were valued for their work in safeguarding young Catholic girls from Protestantism. The Reformation-era Jesuits had a similar function: "When the Catholic hierarchy realized that it was literally fighting for its life, it reasoned that monastic communities . . . were no longer sufficient. The creation of the Jesuit order corresponded to a felt need for shock troops laboring in the World, rather than withdrawing from it, and bringing the message of the Church to the wavering as well as to the infidel."[86] Later, in the nineteenth century, the reconstituted Jesuits served the papacy by spearheading a revival of scholasticism in order to counter the inroads of Kant, Hegel, and other such "atheistic" philosophers.[87]

Within the Church, the presence of religious orders as an accepted form of religious virtuosity also presented an attractive alternative to the lure of heretical groups, thus keeping within the true fold the Church's more enthusiastic and committed members. James of Vitry, for example, portrayed the Beguines as "an orthodox option for women that offered similar advantages in terms of independence from male direction" as were offered by the heretic Cathars of the thirteenth century.[88] Finally, the existence of religious orders sometimes solved certain practical problems for the hierarchy: providing shelter for the wives of men who had decided to enter medieval monasteries, for example, or serving as a link between an immigrant ethnic group in nineteenth-century America and the "old country," or helping to assure the financial solvency of early parish schools by working in them for far lower salaries than lay teachers would accept— and sometimes even for no salary at all.[89]

The Church Hierarchy and Religious Orders: the Perils of Clerical Interest

The Church hierarchy thus derived many compelling advantages from their support of religious communities: advancement of their own ecclesiastical careers, power for the Church vis-à-vis secular authorities and/or threatening heretics, and the practical solution to vexing ministerial problems. In certain eras, these benefits were more than sufficient to outweigh the disincentives posed by the existence of possibly obsteperous religious virtuosi within the boundaries of the Church—virtuosi who were in at least potential competition for the hierarchy's own perquisites. But the juxtaposition of powerful incentives to support religious congregations with equally powerful apprehensions as to the dangers of their "excessive" autonomy led to a new source of conflict: the intense interference by the clergy in the affairs of religious communities, which the communities, in their turn, vigorously resisted.

Episcopal Interference in Religious Communities

Throughout their history, religious orders and congregations have been subjected to a wide range of episcopal—and papal—interference. Popes and bishops regularly attempted to alter the novel lifestyles of the new communities in order to make them conform to older, established models of religious life. As early as 1229, a mere twenty years after their founding, the Franciscans were unhappy with papal attempts to modify St. Francis' original ideal of mendicant poverty in favor of a more monastic type of property holding.[90] Franciscans of subsequent centuries experienced similar confliicts. Women's groups were routinely forced by the hierarchy to adopt strict monastic cloister, even if such practices were contrary to their original founding vision or resulted in extreme financial hardship. The imposition of a more rigorous cloister upon women's orders than was imposed upon men has been documented for the monasteries of the early Middle Ages, for the Premonstratensian women of the twelfth century, for the Franciscans of the thirteenth century, for the Ursulines and the Visitation Sisters of seventeenth-century France, for the Congregation de Notre Dame in eighteenth-century Quebec, and for the American and Irish congregations of the nineteenth century.[91] St. Francis de Sales, who had founded the seventeenth-century Visitation Sisters to minister to the sick in their own homes, saw the imposition of cloister as the defeat of his purposes, and St. Vincent de Paul forbade his Daughters of Charity to identify themselves as a religious community at all, in order to avoid a similar fate.[92]

In addition to imposing cloister, bishops often attempted other forms of interference with the sisters' lifestyles. Elizabeth Seton, the nineteenth-century foundress of the Sisters of Charity at Emmitsburg, Maryland, "waged an intense struggle against her clerical superior, the Frenchman Bishop David, and his plan to structure the community according to the French model of religious life. Seton won this struggle, and for successfully putting up with the harrassment of David and other French male superiors, she deserved canonization!"[93] After Elizabeth Seton's death, however, the French rule was imposed upon her community by its male overseers—which led to the secession of several groups of sisters from the motherhouse in Emmitsburg.[94] Even more drastic lifestyle interference occurred in the Sisters of Loretto, a teaching community in Kentucky:

> Their founder, Charles S. Nerinckx (1761–1824), like most émigré priests a proponent of the European ideal, required the nuns to go barefoot, to sleep on straw or on the floor, to labor in the fields plowing, clearing land, cutting and hauling wood, to maintain silence except for an hour after dinner (a privilege withdrawn during Lent), and to begin their work day at 4:00 AM in the summer and 4:30 in the winter. The rule was so severe that fifteen of sixteen sisters under thirty years of age died of tuberculosis in one year. Their regimens, which hardly suited Kentucky winters, thoroughly drained teaching sisters.[95]

Another area of repeated hierarchical interference was in the governance of the communities. Bishops routinely resisted any attempts by local groups of sisters to consolidate across diocesan lines, since this would have diluted their own episcopal authority over these communities.[96] Barriers to the establishment of a common motherhouse were imposed by various bishops upon the Congregation de Notre Dame in seventeenth-century France, upon the Grey Nuns, the Sisters of St. Joseph, and the Sisters of St. Martha in nineteenth-century Canada, and upon the Sisters of Providence in nineteenth-century France. The Sisters of Notre Dame were forced to move from Amiens, France, to Namur, Belgium, in 1809 in order to retain the centralization of all their houses under one superior general. An attempt to centralize the Sisters of St. Joseph in the United States was thwarted by the bishops. Even seemingly innocuous attempts at simple coordination and networking among the diocesan convents were resisted: the various local communities of Mercy sisters in nineteenth-century Ireland, for example, wanted to meet together and compile a "guidebook" of the ideals and sayings of their foundress Catherine McAuley, since they feared that their lack of a centralized motherhouse would lead to a gradual drift in beliefs and customs. Even this comparatively nonthreatening attempt was opposed by several bishops, who refused to let "their" sisters participate. "The bishop of Elphin, for example, forbade the sisters in his diocese to go . . . on the grounds that he himself intended 'compiling customs' for the sisters, when he could find the time to do so."[97]

Not only did bishops resist attempts at cross-diocesan consolidation by the congregations of sisters under their control, they also actively intervened to detach local convents of sisters from their motherhouses elsewhere and to establish them as separate diocesan congregations.[98] The Irish convents of the Sisters of St. Louis and the Good Shepherd Sisters, both originally French-based, were forced to break ties with their mother-houses. Mother Theresa Gerhardinger had to watch the Bishop of Munich divide her School Sisters of Notre Dame into autonomous houses removed from her authority. Several French, French Canadian, and American congregations were repeatedly subdivided as first one bishop and then another would appropriate their scattered sisters and reconstitute them as a new community. As one Florida bishop wrote to the mother general of the Sisters of St. Joseph in France: "I believe I see a necessity to have only sisters who are entirely diocesan, sisters who obey the Bishop of the Diocese. . . . I repeat, I want sisters who obey me like their Bishop; and who are not in any manner subject to the orders of a superior in another distant country."[99]

Bishops also interfered in the internal governing of the sisters' congregations. They had canonical veto power over whom the sisters could elect to head their community, and they frequently used it.[100] Bishop John Power of Massachusetts appointed all the superiors of the Sisters of Mercy within his diocese. The bishop of Omaha in 1909 deposed the superior of the Mercy community there and appointed his own candidate so that he could better control the sisters. Archbishop William McCloskey (1823–1909) of Louisville intervened in the elections of the School Sisters of Notre Dame, the Sisters of Loretto, and the Ursulines. The bishops of Philadelphia and Michigan banned Mother Theresa Maxis Duchemin "from residence in or even communication with, any of the three mother-houses [of Immaculate Heart sisters] she had founded."[101] Bishop Celestine de la Hailandiere (1798–1880) deposed and excommunicated Mother Theodore Guerin, the founder of the Sisters of Providence in Indiana. Archbishop Kenrick of St. Louis appointed the superior of the Sisters of St. Joseph in his diocese, over the violent protests of the sisters. Upon the death of the bishop of Quebec City, the vicar of the diocese deposed the superior of the Congregation de Notre Dame and installed his own candidate. The bishop of Nottingham, Ireland deposed the foundress of the Little Community of Mary, declaring that he himself would assume the direction of her congregation. As late as 1934, Cardinal O'Connell of Boston attempted to impose a nonelected superior of his own choosing on the Sisters of St. Joseph, "an action without foundation in Canon Law. This brought loud protests from the nuns, who persuaded the apostolic delegate to investigate."[102]

Bishops and priests also attempted to regulate whom the communities could or could not accept as novices (and even, in one case, what religious *names* the novices would be given), whether and when the sisters could leave the convent precincts, and which sisters could be sent to serve in a given assignment.[103] They controlled the communities' finances, often diverting thousands of dollars for their own use.[104] If the sisters had contracted any debts, a bishop could order them to sell their motherhouse and disband the community, even if they had already made arrangements to repay what they owed. The sisters usually had little recourse in such cases, since the bishop would withdraw the provision of mass and the sacraments to them if they refused his demands.

While bishops and priests of every era attempted to interfere in religious communities, the teaching congregations of the nineteenth century were perhaps the most frequently subjected to such treatment.[105] As has been noted, the institutional services provided by the sisters were essential to a bishop's good reputation among his fellow bishops, and hence to his ecclesiastical career. Such a personal investment insured that bishops would take a lively interest in the sisters' congregations—especially in the types of ministerial works they proposed to undertake. The first U.S. bishop, John Carroll, tried in vain to persuade the cloistered Carmelite nuns to open a school.[106] Bishop Hughes of New York wanted the Emmitsburg Sisters of Charity to administer an orphanage for boys and expelled them from his diocese when they refused. Cardinal O'Connell of Boston forced the Sisters of St. Joseph to transfer some of their sisters from teaching into nursing and social work, even though they were already experiencing a shortage of teachers to staff their schools. The bishops' ministerial interference often came at the expense of the congregations' ability to provide for the education of their sisters; Oates cites repeated unsuccessful attempts by the leaders of teaching congregations in nineteenth- and early twentieth-century Boston to retain their young sisters in the novitiate and provide them with professional training before sending them out to teach. Bishops and priests, "indifferent to educational reforms and advances" demanded that the sisters dispense with such frivolity.[107]

Conflicts also occurred between religious communities and the lower clergy. Pastors often clashed with superiors and principals over the staffing of schools.[108] Religious communities established to do housekeeping in diocesan seminaries often found that their priest-employers tried to limit their recruitment to only the number of sisters necessary for that one ministry, and to forbid their acceptance of outside teaching positions. Priests who were appointed as chaplains to convents often felt free to interfere in their internal matters. Newly appointed chaplains might attempt to reverse the policies of the previous chaplain—which at times extended to deposing the superior or impounding the community's finances. The examples of clerical interference are legion. The French Jesuit directors of the Religious of the Cenacle and the Sisters of Charity of St. Joan Antida forced these communities to admit wealthy noblewomen to their orders, and then replaced the original foundresses with their protégés. Boniface Wimmer, the Benedictine abbot who had recruited Benedictine sisters from Bavaria to serve the German immigrants in the United States, assumed the right to countermand the orders of the nuns' superiors, transferring teachers from one school to another, detaching members from one community to begin a second elsewhere, and installing women of his own choosing to head the various communities. Raphael Munos, a Spanish Dominican priest assigned to the Kentucky Dominican sisters, ordered their six-year-old congregation dissolved and refused to provide the community with mass and the sacraments when they refused to disband. The spiritual director of the Milwaukee Franciscan sisters prevented one sister from going to nursing school and, in 1886, appointed his own candidate as superior of the community when the sisters' elected choice displeased him.

An especially fertile field for conflict occurred when a bishop or priest and a laywoman jointly founded a religious community. This was an inherently unequal relationship, since the priest or bishop usually held the post of spiritual director and treasurer, and perhaps was even designated the official superior of the community. "The co-foundress, incapable of supporting this subjugation, either effaces herself or rebels."[109] An especially striking example of this process was that of Jeanne Jugan, who founded the Little Sisters of the Poor in France in 1842, when she was fifty years old. The following year, the Abbe Le Pailleur, a priest who had been assigned to help the new community, deposed her and set up the twenty-three-year-old Marie Jamet as his cosuperior general over the order. "From that time, Le Pailleur managed to create the impression that it was he who was the founder of the institute, with the result that generations of Little Sisters were unaware of Jeanne's role. The last twenty-seven years of her life were spent in the institute's novitiate, with virtually nothing to do—she whose work for the poor had in 1845 won recognition from the prestigious French Academy. It was not until 1902 . . . that Jeanne's role was publicly acknowledged."[110] Another example was that of Mary McKillop, the cofoundress, with Father Julian Woods, of the Australian Sisters of St. Joseph of the Sacred Heart in 1866. When she attempted to secure Roman approval of her congregation and to make some changes in the Rule Father Woods had written, he turned against her. He and the bishop had the Holy See declare her 1881 election as general superior invalid. Not until 1899 was another election held, at which time McKillop was unanimously re-elected and remained superior until she died in 1902. Because of conflicts such as these, joint foundations were usually less likely to succeed than communities established by either a clergyman or a laywoman acting alone.[111]

The Response of the Religious Communities: Techniques for Thwarting Episcopal Domination

In their struggles against the bishops and the priests, religious communities were not totally powerless. Medieval communities of women might simply ignore the directives of the bishop or delay their implementation. Sometimes this delaying tactic could go on for years.[112] Men's religious orders were able to secure exemption from episcopal interference by appealing to the medieval papacy. This technique was also followed by the Franciscan priests who ran afoul of Bishop Amat in nineteenth-century California. Nineteenth-century congregations of women could not obtain such exemptions, but they could escape somewhat from the control of the bishops by applying to change their status from a diocesan to a pontifical congregation.[113] Since the process for doing so required delicate political negotiations with the bishops of every diocese in which a congregation's members were located, the achievement of pontifical status by "dozens" of American congregations "reveals that these women possessed remarkable shrewdness and political savvy, [and] that congregations learned from and co-operated with one another (the sainted Mother Cabrini, whose connections in Rome were unparalleled, was well-known for the skill with which she advised other Superiors General to proceed)."[114] Nineteenth-century religious congregations also cooperated with each other in other ways. Religious superiors would refuse to comply with a bishop's request to open a high school in an area if they thought its presence would hurt another community's school.[115] In Wisconsin, sisters would refuse to replace another community's sisters in a parish until they found out why the first group had left.

If an order or congregation had an officially accepted Rule and constitutions, it could appeal to these documents in its disputes with the bishops and the clergy.[116] The Ursulines of seventeenth-century Nantes were thus able to prevent their bishop's attempt to impose a superior upon their community without an election. The Dominican nuns in Galway used their Rule to resist their bishop's demand that their convent be detached from the mother provincial of all Dominicans in Ireland and subordinated to his authority alone. The Carmelite contemplative nuns in late eighteenth-century Maryland successfully prevented Bishop Carroll's attempt to get them to open a school. The Daughters of Charity in early twentieth-century Boston thwarted Cardinal O'Connell's bid to install himself as head of their two hospitals by appealing to their constitutions. "When a community's constitutions stated its goals narrowly and unambiguously, superiors of pontifical congregations [or of religious orders, such as the Galway Dominicans, the Nantes Ursulines, and the Maryland Carmelites] were relatively successful in resisting requests to undertake unrelated works."[117] But nineteenth-century diocesan congregations often had less success. Since their status was as yet undefined in canon law, "there were no clearly defined limits to the authority that local prelates could exercise" over them.[118] Some bishops refused to write any constitutions at all for the congregations they had established, for, as Bishop England said in 1829, "I do not wish to make my institutions dependent upon superiors over whom I have neither control or influence."[119] Other congregations, even pontifical ones, had constitutions that were so broadly drawn that almost any ministerial service could arguably be asked of them.

Religious communities did have other resources available for resisting the interference of Church authorities. Many U.S. communities incorporated civilly so that they could own property and carry on business in their own name, thus freeing themselves from the possible financial depredations of priests and bishops.[120] Other civil regulations could also be used: Many nineteenth-century French congregations were able to expand beyond their diocese of origin—despite the bishops' opposition—because their state charters did not establish geographic boundaries.

By far the most potent weapon religious communities had was their provision of services that were valued by, and necessary to, the laity, the state, or the bishop—or perhaps to all three. In the earlier eras of the Church, religious orders were often able to defy ecclesiastical domination because their large lay followings valued their prayers even over those of the priests.[121] In later eras, it was the educational and social services of the religious communities that were so valued.[122] The schools established by the seventeenth-century French teaching orders were filled to capacity the moment they opened. The high demand in nineteenth-century Ireland for the sisters' services enabled them to enlist the support of the populace when bishops attempted to interfere with community affairs. At times, the sisters were able to prevail over the bishops because of this lay support.

The services of nuns were equally valued in nineteenth-century America. Most American dioceses were "desperately short of personnel" even before the crest of Catholic immigration in the late nineteenth century.[123] In such situations, the threat by an order or a congregation to withdraw its services was a potent one. There are numerous recorded instances of superiors withdrawing the entire teaching staff from a school because of a disagreement between the pastor and one of the sisters, or because of poor working or living conditions—even in the middle of the school year or against the bishop's will.[124] Since demand for their services exceeded the supply, sisters could, and did, leave dioceses in which they felt unduly restricted, secure in the knowledge that either another bishop or the priests and people of another parish would welcome their arrival. The pastors rarely expelled the sisters for any reason: "At the present time," one priest wrote, "applications being so numerous, it would be impossible to get sisters" to replace them.[125] The provision of needed services enabled some nineteenth-century communities of sisters not only to earn their living but also to accumulate surplus funds, which they promptly invested in education for their members and in property for their schools and hospitals. By the early 1900s, the Wisconsin Dominican sisters owned $600,000 worth of real estate in seven states and the District of Columbia. The LaCrosse (Wisconsin) Franciscans provided over $76,000 in loans to the bishop and priests for diocesan building projects as well.[126]

Conclusions

The support of the Church hierarchy was crucial for the success of a new religious community, more so than perhaps any other factor. A complicated relationship of dependence and resistence, support and conflict, existed between these two accepted, but often very different, forms of religious virtuosity. Over time, the relationship of individual religious orders/congregations with the popes, bishops, and priests of the Church's hierarchy oscillated between several different policies, sometimes combining contradictory poles at once in an uneasy synthesis.

As essential as the Church hierarchy was to the survival and growth of new religious communities, however, the good will and assistance of other environmental actors also played a key role. At times, if a community of religious enjoyed the support of the civil authorities or of the majority of lay Catholics, they could even overcome the active opposition of elements within the ecclesiastical hierarchy. Again, however, such support was not always forthcoming. State officials and the laity had their own agendas and interests, which sometimes favored and sometimes opposed the activities of the new religious communities.

The State: Sources of Support and Opposition

Types of and Reasons for State Assistance

In most eras of history, civil authorities have taken an active interest in the movements of religious virtuosi that have occurred within their jurisdiction. Catholic European rulers throughout the centuries have attempted to make the Church within their borders dependent upon the state, rather than upon Rome. Religious orders were naturally affected by these policies. Secular governments might also exempt religious houses from taxation, they might confiscate the orders' properties, or they might extort heavy "loans" from them that were never repaid. Governments could encourage or forbid religious congregations to enter new ministries and could impose professional certification requirements on their members. Under some regimes, all religious orders had to be officially chartered by the state before they could receive novices or don habits, or age limits might be imposed for entrance.[127] In colonial Quebec, for example, the number of new recruits permitted each convent was strictly limited by Louis XV himself, and the king also fixed the dowries at a sum higher than most of the cash-strapped colonials could afford.

Governments could, however, also provide valuable forms of assistance to new religious orders. In seventeenth-century France, the queen mother Anne d'Autriche was actively involved in insuring that the Daughters of Charity would remain independent of episcopal control after St. Vincent de Paul's death—going so far as to petition the pope personally on this issue.[128] The nineteenth-century French government gave newly founded religious congregations of women some of the old motherhouse buildings that had been seized from other orders during the Revolution, and also provided them with annual monetary grants to pay for the expenses of their novitiates. The government's universal education policies also provided an important source of income for the newly founded French teaching congregations.

Secular governments had pressing reasons to become involved with religious communities. For the eighth- and ninth-century French and German kings, monastic foundations were valuable colonizing and assimilating forces, bringing new fringe territories into the common culture of the kingdom.[129] The Pictish kings of eighth-century Scotland supported the foundation of monasteries in their domains in order to lessen the influence of neighboring Iona and its monks in Pictish affairs. For medieval Spanish monarchs, the Dominicans and Franciscans served as valued preachers in their crusades to win Spanish territory back from the Moslems. Napoleon's active support of nineteenth-century French congregations helped to end his conflict with the pope. Religious orders also furnished a wide variety of social services that benefitted the whole of society.[130] Medieval monasteries provided education and employment for surrounding residents; their charity to the poor and their pensions to retired clerks and soldiers provided rudimentary social service and insurance functions. Later orders provided education and health care for the poor, operated orphanages, settlement houses and asylums, and even nursed on the battlefields of the American Civil War. And, of course, Catholic monarchs, like other lay persons, believed that their financial support of religious orders would secure the salvation of their own souls and divine favor for their kingdoms.[131] Such sentiments made medieval rulers prominent benefactors, both of the early medieval monasteries and of the late medieval mendicant orders.

Reasons for Governmental Opposition

On the other hand, secular rulers often had reason to be wary of religious communities, and especially of the exempt religious orders. Fourth-century monks exercised possibly disruptive influence over the urban population of the late Roman Empire, and also interfered in the workings of the civil courts.[132] Emperor Frederick II considered the mendicant friars to be agents of the pope—at the time, his political enemy. In sixteenth-century England, the friars again came under civil scrutiny: They were considered especially suspect because they were popular preachers and potential political agitators and because "they were members . . . of a fully organized international order pivoted, however loosely, upon the papacy."[133] In later centuries, the Jesuits were suspected of being potential fifth columns in those nations where they served. "Government edicts were issued expelling the Jesuits from France in 1764 and from Spain in 1767. Eventually, in 1773, Pope Clement XVI dissolved the society."[134] Because of these and similar suspicions, international men's orders were often severely restricted by European governments even as these officials courted and valued the women's congregations for their services. In the antebellum United States, on the other hand, women's as well as men's religious congregations were looked upon as the advance guards of papism and aroused considerable Protestant suspicions. "George W. Burnap, lecturing at Harvard College in 1853, considered it a particularly ominous sign that 'a convent had arisen in sight of Harvard Yard.' "[135] The Pennsylvania Know-Nothing Party imposed such strict limitations on the school operated by the Benedictine sisters that they were forced temporarily to suspend this ministry—their only source of income.[136]

Another reason for governmental concern was that the presence of religious communities might have an adverse financial impact upon the surrounding economy. Wealthy consecrated virgins in fourth-century Rome often redirected their money to the Church, to the dismay of secular authorities.[137] Similarly, rulers in the medieval low countries, in sixteenth-century England, and in seventeenth- and nineteenth-century France fretted that religious communities were tying up so much wealth that they imposed a "dead hand" on social progress. Seventeenth-century French towns worried that convents were taking up too much municipal land. State officials also feared the social dislocation that resulted when failed religious orders released their impoverished members to beg in the countryside or to live off their families.[138] And if religious communities such as the Beguines earned their livings independently through the sale of their handicrafts, should they be taxed? Allowed to compete with the medieval guilds? Should the quality and price of their products be regulated in any way? Could the seventeenth-century French congregations, already acting as corporations, be recognized as such in civil law? Under what terms?[139]

Governments of non-Catholic countries might also object to the celibacy practiced in most religious orders, considering it to be detrimental to the social order in and of itself. This was the case in fourth-century Rome, as well as in the nineteenth-century United States:

> The growth of convents in American society profoundly alarmed many Protestants, not simply because nuns were Catholic and often foreign born, but also because their vocation seemed in various ways to challenge the "cult of true womanhood" and the ideal of "Republican Motherhood." By renouncing marriage and motherhood for themselves, by allegedly proselytizing Protestant children and attempting to enlist Protestant daughters into their ranks, nuns appeared to endanger the essential links between family, church and state enunciated in the ideal of domesticity.[140]

Similar objections were raised against both the Catholic and the Anglican sisterhoods in nineteenth-century England.

The good will, or at least the neutrality, of secular authorities was therefore essential to the survival and growth of many newly founded religious communities. The communities could, however, overcome some governmental opposition if they were able to enlist the support of powerful elements within the Church or among lay Catholics. Many religious orders and congregations showed great political sophistication in marshalling allies from all three groups, or in playing on their self-interest and their rivalries with each other.

Lay Society

Financial Support

Religious communities required key forms of support from pious lay church members. The importance of gifts and bequests of money and property has already been mentioned, and is a recurrent theme in many studies.[141] Sympathetic lay men and women might also offer hospitality to wandering friars or intercede for religious at court.[142] One ramification of this support, however, was that wealthy benefactors often felt free to dictate which projects "their" religious congregation could undertake and to intervene in other ways.

> Foundations [by wealthy benefactors] often came with difficult conditions attached, for which the nuns paid heavily through the years. Fre-

quently, the [lay] founders reserved the right to nominate persons to the community. Thus the Ursulines of Boulogne were bequeathed property on condition that two poor girls be received and educated in perpetuity. The Ursulines of Le Havre received a donation of six thousand livres from Denis Barbey "on condition that his daughter Marguerite will be considered as foundress, and received and maintained her whole life long if she wishes to be professed."[143]

Civil inheritance laws provided an additional incentive for familial interference in the convents' ministry and lifestyles: Whereas cloistered nuns officially forfeited their right to inherit their families' wealth, noncloistered sisters did not. Wealthy families of seventeenth-century France thus exerted great pressure on active religious congregations to adopt cloister, lest their daughters return years later and claim a share of their ancestral property.[144]

Why might lay benefactors be willing to provide political and financial support? Historians have noted that, in several different epochs, the presence of a religious community was economically beneficial for a city or town. Villages around medieval monasteries expected to profit from the attraction monastic shrines and relics would have for pilgrims.[145] The city officials—Catholic and Protestant—of nineteenth-century Omaha, Nebraska, Joplin, Missouri, and Yreka, California, welcomed the Sisters of Mercy because they believed that the sisters' acacdemies would enhance the reputation of their town.[146] In fact, when a pastor of Imogene, Iowa had a disagreement with the sisters in 1918 and asked them to leave, the townsfolk left, too. Imogene's reputation as an "up and coming" place was damaged, and it never regained its former population.

Newly wealthy laymen and laywomen might also obtain social status by financially sponsoring the works of religious orders. Seventeenth-century France "was full of newly leisured people anxious to wash away the taint of their bourgeois origins, and the projects of the Saints suggested a way. Bourgeois men and women who commanded wealth but were uncertain how to dispose of it could easily imitate the aristocratic habit of patronizing and participating in religious reform projects. And it was entirely possible that a generous bourgeoise might find herself invited to stand alongside a princess when the institution they both patronized held its next ceremony."[147] Of course, later, when the "fad" of helping religious congregations died out, the congregations might suffer. Later in the seventeenth century, once Louis XIV had made himself "the unique source of patronage and advancement in the kingdom," it was less easy to achieve social status through religious patronage.[148]

As various types of virtuoso spirituality rose and fell in public favor, the individual communities professing that particular type of virtuosity would receive more or fewer gifts. Several historians of tenth-, eleventh-, and twelfth-century Europe record the increasing reluctance of queens and noblewomen to endow women's monasteries as the prestige of monastic life declined in favor of the clergy-controlled Eucharist, and as women's orders began to receive the reputation—largely undeserved—of being spiritually lax. Later in the Middle Ages, and again in seventeenth-century France, benefactors preferred to support officially established cloistered convents rather than informal lay groups of women.[149] Financial concerns were also a factor. Aggrieved heirs in seventeenth-century France often sued to prevent their relatives from endowing a new religious congregation. Langlois mentions the decline in contributions to the nineteenth-century French teaching congregations as the public began to suspect that they controlled too much wealth already.[150]

Recruitment

In addition to financial support, another essential resource provided by the laity was to furnish new recruits to the religious life. Parents in the third and fourth centuries, as well as in the medieval monastic period, often dedicated "surplus" children to religious life at extremely early ages.[151] It was also common for several members of a family to enter the same religious order: St. Bernard of Clairveaux possibly set the record in this regard by arriving at the monastery with thirty relatives and friends, all of whom entered along with him.[152] Familial bonds within many medieval monasteries of women attracted the sisters, aunts, and nieces of the current residents. In seventeenth-century Quebec, 31 percent of the members of the women's religious communities had relatives who were also nuns. The first companions of Mary Ward in seventeenth-century England were cousins and family connections. In nineteenth-century Ireland, 16 percent of the 238 women who entered the Limerick Mercy convent between 1838 and 1900, and 22.8 percent of those who entered the Limerick Good Shepherd convent between 1861 and 1900 had at least one sibling in the same convent. Others had aunts, cousins, or other relatives.[153] Nineteenth-century French communities often counted siblings or other relatives among their founders: Langlois mentions eight such instances on a single page.[154] Two of the first eight Sisters of St. Joseph sent from France to St. Louis, Missouri in 1836 were siblings; their aunt was the mother superior of their home convent in Lyons, and their brother was the chaplain who accompanied them. Eight of the nine women who began a Dominican community in early nineteenth-century Kentucky were related to each other, as were over 25 percent of the 400 women who entered the Franciscan Sisters of Perpetual Adoration in nineteenth-century Wisconsin. Widows often entered with their daughters; "sometimes even three generations were represented among the religious who formed the initial group" in nineteenth-century French congregations.[155] In this, religious orders were similar to the Protestant sects noted by Gerlach and Hine, most of whose members were recruited by relatives.[156] True social isolates tended not to enter Protestant sects— or Catholic religious communities.

Families also supported the teaching congregations by sending their daughters and sons to the schools the communities operated. Many of these students later augmented the communities' membership. In seventeenth-century France and eighteenth-century Quebec, and in nineteenth-century Ireland and America, the majority of a community's entrants were often students from their own schools.[157] Nonteaching orders often received fewer recruits because they lacked this channeling device.[158]

The missionary societies popular in nineteenth-century Germany and France provide still another example of lay assistance to religious congregations. The city of Lyons was the headquarters of the Society of the Propagation of the Faith, a lay organization founded in 1822 at the suggestion of the bishop of New Orleans to help the American missions. Wealthy French laywomen became active in this society, which sponsored the foundation of the Sisters of St. Joseph in the United States and also donated thousands of dollars to other U.S. religious communities.[159] The literature published by the society depicted the United States as a fertile territory for missionary work, with unconverted Indians and uneducated French immigrants longing to be taught the faith. Spurred on by such images, many young Frenchwomen joined the missionary congregations, while others furnished the necessary funds and supplies for their efforts. Similar support was given to German-American congregations by the Ludwig Missionsverein in Bavaria and the Leopoldinen Stiftung in Austria. In 1855, the $1800 grant from the Bavarian society provided almost 25 percent of the operating expenses of the School Sisters of Notre Dame in America. In all, between 1850 and 1866, this one community received $41,000 from the Ludwig Missionsverein.[160] Similar help was given to the Benedictines—men and women—in Pennsylvania. By the turn of the century, these funds had helped these communities establish themselves on sound, and independent, financial footing.

Conclusion

Chapters 4 and 5 have emphasized two categories of reasons for the often explosive growth of new religious communities within Roman Catholicism during certain historical periods. According to the personal incentive model examined in Chapter 4, religious communities were successful because they were able to offer—as few other contemporary institutions were able to offer—opportunities for personal growth, social status, education and ecclesiastical power to individuals who would be otherwise denied such advantages. A second approach was used in Chapter 5 to outline the inducements that could lead powerful outside actors either to support or hinder the growth of individual religious communities. As representatives of the alternative—and dominant—form of religious virtuosity within Roman Catholiciicism, the hierarchy's and the clergy's support was the most crucial for a new religious order or congregation to obtain. Despite an inherent potential for competition and even conflict between the two virtuoso groups, many new communities were able to enlist the hierarchy's own interests in order to secure their support. The good will and assistance of state officials and the laity also had to be sought and obtained.

But to concentrate on the personal interests of the recruits who entered religious communities, or of the bishops, priests, state officials, and laity who supported them, is to present a one-sided picture. The problem with treating these factors separately is that, while such a strategy "successfully specifies the causal dynamics of one factor, it tends to subordinate the roles of other factors." Specifically, we have so far ignored "the autonomous power of ideology" as an equally potent cause behind the establishment and spread of new types of religious life.[161] The following chapters will attempt to redress this imbalance by focusing on the changing ideologies of virtuoso spirituality that underlay each of the cycles of religious virtuosity in the Church.

Chapter 6

Frame Alignment and Religious Virtuosity: Varieties of Legitimation

While internal and environmental *resources* are obviously essential for the survival and the growth of any social movement organization, the group's defining *ideology* is at least equally important.[1] The analyst who wishes to consider the various religious orders that arose within Roman Catholicism's recurring movements of virtuoso spirituality must therefore examine the ideological frames that have supported them. The Catholic culture of a given period provided potential virtuosi with a "tool kit" of "symbols, stories, rituals and world views"—some inherited from previous centuries, some newly articulated—with which a more or less coherent ideological framework for virtuoso spirituality would be constructed.[2] These elements included an overall definition for the legitimacy and purpose of religious life, as well as the various practices that might constitute virtuoso spirituality and the relative importance attached to each one.[3] The myths, metaphors, exemplars, and images that served to justify a particular model of religious virtuosity were also elements of the ideological "frame," as were the "packages" of other theological and secular beliefs with which religious virtuosity became associated.[4] Over time, one or several of these elements might be redefined, altered, expanded, or even discarded in favor of new formulations. At least in part, the changes in these ideological framing elements were the causal factors that initiated and facilitated each of the recurring expansion periods in religious life.[5]

Chief among the changes that will be considered in this chapter are the various frame transformations that have affected religious communities.[6] In global frame transformations, the entire "universe of discourse" was altered among religious virtuosi, leading them to reinterpret their whole lives in new ideological terms. A typical instance of such a transformation would be when the members of some population or social class, which had formerly been uninterested in personally attaining virtuoso spirituality (although they may have reverenced and supported virtuosi drawn from other social or economic groups), suddenly began to aspire after spiritual perfection for themselves. Another such type of frame transformation might be the substitution of one basic definition for another in an effort to articulate a new meaning and purpose for religious life.

A second category of ideological change would include instances of both value and belief amplification.[7] In value amplification, some previously ignored component of virtuoso spirituality (fasting, contemplative prayer, serving the poor, and so on.) might be re-evaluated as central to religious life, while other, formerly emphasized components were subordinated to it. In belief amplification, a group of people might come to re-evaluate their personal salvation as more tenuous—or more achievable—than they had hitherto believed it to be. Their increased insecurity—or their increased hope—might spur them to adopt virtuoso practices they had hitherto dismissed as unnecessary or useless.

Not every combination of elements in a given ideological framework for religious virtuosity was equally successful. "Certain packages have a natural advantage because their ideas and language resonate with larger cultural themes. Resonances increase the appeal of a package; they make it appear natural and familiar."[8] An ideology of virtuoso spirituality was more likely to be accepted when its particular beliefs, values, or interpretations conformed to its followers' personal experiences or to the basic themes of their surrounding culture.[9] A resonant ideological package for religious virtuosity might either affirm or negate the values and beliefs of the larger society. For example, a highly materialistic culture could enshrine material success as the mark of a virtuoso's superior spiritual status or, conversely, it could elevate absolute poverty.[10] But a successful ideological frame had to address the key concerns of a culture in some fashion. Otherwise, it remained peripheral.[11] For example, male Benedictine monasticism languished during the thirteenth century precisely because it did *not* provide a spiritual context in which to fit Europe's newly developing money economy.[12] The construction, testing, and reconstruction of a newly revised ideological framework for virtuoso spirituality, therefore, marked each revival period in the history of religious orders.

As we will be employing it here, the term "ideological frame" will apply to a wider conceptual territory than the traditional Catholic idea of a religious order's charism. The ideological frame includes unarticulated and taken-for-granted assumptions about the purpose and value of religious life, more or less specified definitions of the behaviors a member should exhibit (and the reasons why these behaviors are important), and a set of symbols, mythic figures, and metaphors that both legitimate the lifestyle and serve as conceptual shorthand for its underlying philosophy.

The term "charism," on the other hand, refers to the particular set of beliefs and practices that make a given religious community distinct from its contemporaries and that articulate its reason for existing as a separate entity.[13] Thus, one would speak of a mendicant ideological frame and of the charisms of the Franciscan, Dominican, and Carmelite orders. The two concepts do, however, overlap somewhat. At times, two or three different ideological frames existed simultaneously, each identified with a particular religious order, so that the frame and the charism were coterminous. At other times, the larger ideological frame was attenuated or amalgamated from several previous frames, thus losing its consistency and relevance. In such instances, the specific charisms of the various orders increased in importance, and one or more might even develop into a full-fledged ideological frame to supplant its unsatisfactory predecessor. At still other times, as we shall see in chapter 7, individual charisms for religious communities were almost nonexistent, and the larger ideological frame was applied in a basically invariant manner to all of the individual congregations.

Virtuoso Ideologies and Religious Social Movements: A Reciprocal Relationship

Virtuoso Ideologies as Movement Resources

Ideologies of religious virtuosity were resources in themselves, as essential to a new religious community as its material and political resources were. First of all, an appealing ideological formulation could be a powerful incentive drawing individuals to join religious communities, in addition to whatever material or social advantages they might gain by doing so. This was especially the case when an ideology offered assurance of eternal salvation, or when it provided a collective identity that transcended the individual self.[14] Ideologies could also open up whole new populations within a society to potential recruitment by religious orders. Individuals— women, merchants, peasants—whom the prevailing ideology had barred from virtuoso spirituality were especially attracted to any new ideology that promised to end their spiritual disenfranchisement. A religious order that developed such an ideology often found itself inundated with new recruits, as the medieval Cistercians discovered when they opened up the monastic vocation to formerly excluded peasants, or the mendicants who attracted the merchant class to their ranks.[15] Finally, when the nonvirtuoso members of the surrounding society also believed in the ideology, they were more likely to reverence the religious virtuosi and were thus more easily persuaded to provide them with indispensible financial or political support.

New ideological frameworks for religious virtuosity did not arise spontaneously, however sudden their appearance might seem to be. Like other types of ideologies, they were developed in a continuing, if episodic, dialog between factions and between individuals, and then further shaped and refined through the subsequent decades in the context of larger social or economic conditions.[16] Multiple variations of an ideological framework might coexist for a time, as different groups selectively formulated the version that most suited their needs.[17] "A social movement is not one organization or one particular special interest group. It is more like a cognitive territory, a new conceptual space that is filled by a dynamic interaction between different groups and organizations. It is through tension between different organizations over defining and acting in that conceptual space that the (temporary) identity of a social movement is formed."[18] In the process of developing a new and more useful ideology of virtuoso spirituality that could prevail over competing formulations, religious virtuosi were helped (and hindered) by the conceptual tools and the ideological structures already available to them in their surrounding environment, and also by whatever material, social, or political resources they were able to utilize to advance their views.[19]

Determinants of Ideological Hegemony: the Mobilization of Political, Social, and Material Resources

In their efforts to construct an ideological framework for virtuoso spirituality that would attract needed recruits and sponsors, the members of a religious community had to struggle for the hegemony of their particular version over less desirable contenders.[20] A community's success in this struggle was partly due to the resonance of its ideology, but it also depended upon the group's access to a wide variety of other resources that could be used to present its vision to the outside world. One important resource in the attainment of ideological hegemony was "structural availability": a wide-ranging social network whereby more potential recruits could be reached and converted.[21] "The structural availability principle was especially clear in research on conversion to religious-social movements. Pre-existing and emergent intimate networks both fed and nurtured these movements. Religious sects as ideologically divergent as the Moonies, Mormons, and Nichiren Shoshu Buddhists found most of their new adherents among the relatives, friends, and acquaintances of current members."[22] Religious virtuoso movements that were confined to a small, encapsulated social group usually had difficulty spreading beyond its bounds. Thus, the dispersion of the Dominicans from Toulouse in 1217—at a time when the order contained only twenty men—was considered by Little as a crucial factor in enabling the later expansion of the community.[23]

Still other concrete resources—money, organizational experience, meeting facilities, and the like—are helpful in securing the hegemony of a particular ideological framework. Successful religious orders thus needed to secure the reliable provision of these resources. The support of ecclesiastical or secular elites in the religious community's external environment was also essential. A major reason for the ascendency of the Benedictine model of monasticism, for example, was the support of Pope Gregory the Great.[24] Wealthy benefactors were needed to provide essential financial assistance, and any successful ideology had to appeal to—or at least not to offend—their sensibilities. The eventual hegemony of a particular variant of virtuoso spirituality thus depended, not only on its ideological resonance with the needs, beliefs, and values of a particular group of potential virtuosi, but also on the allies whom these virtuosi could enlist to support their cause.

An additional facilitating factor in the hegemony of a new ideological framework for virtuoso spirituality—and in the consequent success of those incipient religious communities that adopted or developed it—was the weakness or the preoccupation of the secular and religious institutions that had supported the former framework.[25] At times when the ecclesiastical elites were divided into competing factions, for example, a new religious community might be able to secure the support of one of the contending parties. Divisions between Church and state officials, or between secular elites, provided similar opportunities.

Conclusions

In addition to the role played by material, social, and political resources in the rise of new religious orders in the Roman Catholic Church, we must now add the equally essential contribution of ideological resources. Without a coherent and resonant frame that articulates and answers the basic spiritual strains in a culture, that provides a catalogue of behaviors for virtuosi to adopt and the motivating incentives to adopt them, and that induces outsiders to provide key financial and political support, no new virtuoso movement could even begin. So valuable were these ideological frameworks that members of religious orders spent a great deal of their time refining and honing them to reflect and support their own particular interests.[26]

In the struggle to develop new and more resonant ideological frames, however, the other types of resources also played an important part. The rise of new versions of virtuoso spirituality, and their success or failure in being adopted by religious orders, depended on the financial, political, and societal support available to their partisans. The story of the ebb and flow of religious virtuoso movements within Catholicism thus provides valuable opportunities for the integration of frame alignment and resource mobilization theories, as well as for the further cross-fertilization of social movement research and the sociology of religion. An examination of the role material, social, and political resources played in securing ideological hegemony for a particular version of virtuoso spirituality will be the topic of chapter 9. First, however, we must explore the variations that have existed in virtuoso ideologies within the Catholic Church.

Varieties of Frame Articulation and Transformation

Over the fifteen or more centuries of their history, many separate ideological formulations for virtuoso spirituality have been developed in Roman Catholicism. Several different purposes have been advanced to legitimate the very existence of religious life; the emphasis given to each of these fundamental purposes has waxed and waned with each new movement. The specific practices individual virtuosi were expected to perform have also varied, as have their supporting mythic images and metaphors. The remainder of this chapter will outline some of the ideological definitions that have been advanced to legitimate and justify religious virtuosity. Chapter 7 will explore the elements that composed these ideological frames, and will chart how the individual elements varied in meaning and salience over time. Finally, chapter 8 will describe the symbols, myths, and metaphors advanced to support each ideological frame, and will also discuss the implications of the various internal discrepancies that arose in the frames as they developed.

Frame Articulation: The Primary Purpose(s) of Religious Life

The most fundamental and basic aspect of any social movement's ideological frame is the place it postulates for the movement within the larger scheme of things. "It is first and foremost through its cosmology, its world view, that a social movement articulates its historical meaning. The cosmological dimension represents the common world view assumptions that give a social movement its utopian mission."[27] Throughout the centuries of its history, a variety of different meanings have been advanced to legitimate the existence of religious communities in the Roman Catholic Church. At times, religious communities might focus narrowly on a single one of these meanings; at other times, several meanings might be given, with some more or less explicitly subordinated to the others as the means to a higher end.

The earliest ideological meaning or purpose ascribed to religious life was the spiritual perfection of the individual virtuoso. Brown dates this interpretation at least to the writings of Origen (d. 254), who taught that individual Christians could transform themselves through ascetic practices and thus regain the purity of soul once possessed by unfallen humanity in Eden.[28] Although often eclipsed by later formulations or even subordinated to other goals, the ideal of religious life as a "state of perfection" has been implicit in every version of its ideological framework since Origen's time. "I felt called to a higher life," wrote a Dominican sister in nineteenth-century Wisconsin.[29] As late as 1965, a young Canadian sister could remark, "Since religious life was a state of life superior to the others, to enter it was the best way for me to improve myself."[30] The fact that such a large percentage of Catholicism's canonized saints were members or founders of religious orders "merely underlined the growing assumption within high ecclesiastical circles that the religious life was the primary, if not the exclusive, avenue to holiness."[31]

Although spiritual self-perfection may have been the primary goal of religious life, this perfection could mean different things at different times. The desert hermits and the earliest monastics defined self-perfection as mastery of the passions and temptations at war within the soul.[32] This mastery could best be achieved, it was thought, by disciplining the senses in ascetical practices. On the other hand, among the twelfth-century male Cistercians, the thirteenth-century Beguines and female Cistercians, and a host of other religious women in the thirteenth century and later, religious perfection meant primarily achieving union with God in ecstatic mystical experiences.[33] The religious virtuoso's goal thus became mystical contemplation, in which hours were spent in rapt contemplation of the divine.

The introduction of this affective mysticism into the spirituality of Catholicism's religious virtuosi meant a subtle shift of emphasis away from monastic ritual observances such as the communal recitation of the Divine Office (although these prayers were still said by the community) and toward a greater awareness of the interior psychic and spiritual life journey of the individual monk or nun.[34] According to medieval mystics such as Bernard of Clairveaux, the experiences of the heart in its search for the divine were also more important than the arid speculations of theologians. This gave a certain anti-intellectual cast to the mystical version of virtuoso spirituality.[35] In any event, while the primary purpose of twelfth-century religious life remained self-perfection, it had become a perfection defined in more emotional, interpersonal, and ecstatic terms: a complete experiential union with God.

In addition to effecting the spiritual perfection (however defined) of the individual virtuoso, another purpose of monastic or eremitical religious life might be to provide a model for the edification of the rest of the faithful. Sometimes communities of religious virtuosi were supposed to mirror the future eschaton—the coming age when humankind would live "like the angels in heaven," and the "ache of sexual division would be abolished."[36] Alternatively, a religious community might model some *past* golden age—whether of prefallen humanity in Eden, of the early Apostolic Church, or of pre-Reformation or pre-Revolutionary Catholicism.[37] In this way, lay Catholics, and perhaps even heretics and the irreligious, might see in the lives of the religious virtuosi an echo of a vanished time when true religion had held sway over the minds and hearts of all the faithful.

A community of virtuosi might also be established to enact a model of present-day Christian life for the rest of the laity to imitate. Early monastic life was thought to mirror the true Christian family, with the abbot serving as paterfamilias for his children, the monks.[38] Providing a good example to the laity was also one of the goals of the regular canons during the eleventh and twelfth centuries. According to Bynum, the distinguishing characteristic of religious virtuosity as practiced by the canons was "the canon's sense of responsibility to edify his fellowmen both by what he says and what he does."[39]

Self-perfection (whether through asceticism, ritual prayer, or mystical experiences) and serving as a model of some ideal state (whether past, present, or future) were only two of the purposes that have been advanced to legitimate the role of religious life in the Church. Religious virtuosi, especially the early desert hermits and the medieval monks and nuns, also served as sacred mediators between humanity and God. "The great mass of believers were not interested in saints as moral examples, but as spiritual patrons who protected the populace against storms and plagues."[40] This held true for living religious virtuosi as well. The prayers of the fourth-century religious virgins were considered necessary for the well-being both of their families and of the entire Christian community that supported them. Medieval parents sent a daughter or son to a monastery primarily because that child's prayers would then become more powerful and efficacious for the rest of the family's salvation.[41] Often the aristocracy would support the foundation of a monastery connected with the family mausoleum, so that the monks or nuns residing there "could provide perpetual prayers for the 'safety of [the aristocrats'] souls.' "[42] Finally, both monks and nuns in the Middle Ages provided a "vicarious sacrifice for the whole of Christendom," whereby the merit of their prayers and acts of penance was deposited in a heavenly treasury to be bestowed on supplicant faithful in the form of indulgences.[43]

In addition to the superior efficacy of their prayers, medieval nuns were also potent channels of divine power by their very being: "Set apart from the world by intact boundaries, her flesh untouched by ordinary flesh, the virgin (like Christ's mother, the perpetual virgin) was also a bride, destined for higher consummation. She scintillated with fertility and power. Into her body, as into the eucharistic bread on the altar, poured the inspiration of the Spirit and the fullness of the humanity of Christ."[44] The idea of the nun's virginity as a source of spiritual power became especially important as the value of her prayers declined in favor of the superior efficacy of the mass.[45]

Besides releasing souls from purgatory or procuring divine favor for one's family or benefactors, the prayers and ascetical practices of male and female religious virtuosi could be channeled toward other ends. During the seventeenth century, for example, a French convent of Ursuline nuns maintained a perpetual prayer vigil before the Eucharist—twenty-four hours a day, seven days a week, two sisters at a time—on behalf of the Jesuit missionaries to the North American Indians. The Jesuits were aware of the nuns' efforts, and sent them regular reports on the successes which the sisters' prayers had facilitated, as well as on the trials through which they had been upheld by their spiritual benefactors.[46] A similar relationship had also existed between the medieval friars and the holy women whom they directed: "[The friars'] job was to be out doing, [Margaret's] was to make the contacts with God."[47] The idea of the intercessory purpose of religious communities continued in subsequent versions of religious life. The nineteenth-century American Benedictine sisters noted in their constitutions that their special work was "to offer their prayers for the needs of the holy Church, the fatherland, the leaders of the Church and the government, and for the conversion of sinners."[48] The founder of the Sisters of St. Joan of Arc wrote to them in 1915 that it was only because of their prayers that he had retained his good health.[49]

Some groups of religious virtuosi defined themselves as prophets, denouncing by word and example the various abuses within the Church. This was a primary focus of the fourth-century hermits, as well as of both heretical and orthodox religious movements during the twelfth and thirteenth centuries.[50] However, an openly oppositional stance vis-à-vis the hierarchy became more difficult to maintain after the consolidation of papal and episcopal power in the later Middle Ages, and very few subsequent groups were able to define themselves primarily in this manner. Nevertheless, some male religious orders continued to describe their purpose as *reform within* the Church—a somewhat less threatening stance than total opposition. One such group was the Oratorians, a seventeenth-century society of priests, who were founded for the reform of the secular clergy.[51]

Another purpose of religious virtuosity, especially during and after the time of the mendicants, was that of evangelization. Although some monasteries of monks, and even of nuns, had occasionally served as missionaries to as-yet-unchristianized areas during the early Middle Ages, this was not their primary purpose.[52] For the male mendicant and apostolic orders, however, bringing souls to Christ was their first duty. "The inward-searching, self-sufficient world of monachism, nourished on daily devotional exercises, now yielded to the driving impulse to subdue the external world" in the virtuoso spirituality of the Dominicans, Franciscans, and Jesuits.[53] Former virtuoso goals such as self-perfection and mystical union with God were de-emphasized by these groups in favor of their overriding mission to spread the Gospel:

> The monastic orders, though in different degrees, are founded on ascetic premises that are essentially other-worldly and are designed to allow religious virtuosi to reach spiritual perfection. . . . They withdraw from the world in a contemplative quest for sanctification, attempting to discipline and castigate the recalcitrant self and to curb egotistical desires in communion with like-minded religious virtuosi . . .
>
> The Jesuit, in contradistinction, is involved in an essentially *instrumental* activity in which all the resources of the person are systematically disciplined in the pursuit of the apostolic goal of guiding the world to God.[54]

The "vita apostolica," which had been defined in the early Middle Ages as a life in common in the monastery, was redefined in the thirteenth century and thereafter as a life spent preaching the Gospel.

One audience to whom the Gospel might be preached was the non-Catholic world, whether pagan or heretic Christian. The world was full of people yet to be Christianized, and the purpose of the Jesuits, Franciscans, and Dominicans—and even of some women's groups, such as Marguerite Bourgeoys' Congregation de Notre Dame—was to search out these people and convert them.[55] Later groups, such as the nineteenth-century religious congregations, were very conscious of the favorable impression their activities made on non-Catholics, and hoped that this example would lead them back to the true fold. As one Irish sister, some of whose family were Protestants, wrote in describing the formal entrance of a wealthy young woman into the convent: "Our dear and venerated archbishop officiated in the usual impressive and holy manner, which was well, as I don't recall our ever having had so many Protestants" there.[56] The Irish nuns studied by Clear often commented upon the effect their communities were having on Irish Protestants.

Lapsed or lax Catholics comprised a second audience for evangelization attempts, and were targeted by a wide variety of religious communities both in the Middle Ages and later. A common topic of mendicant
preaching was the need for penance by the faithful.[57] The nineteenth-
century Irish sisters and the seventeenth-century French *filles séculières*
were established primarily for the religious and moral reclamation of the
Catholic poor, in order to safeguard them from succumbing to the lure of
Protestantism and thus losing their souls. Whether the audience was non-
Catholic, lapsed Catholic, or endangered Catholic, defining the purpose
of religious life as evangelization was profoundly attractive to a succession
of virtuosi. Religious virtuosity modeled around evangelism seems to have
given adherents "a sense of shared purpose, a definite feeling of being part
of a movement" that could serve as a powerful recruiting device.[58]

For religious communities primarily oriented toward evangelization,
all else was subordinated. Various practices would be retained or discarded
according to how well they served the overriding purpose of leading souls
to God. For example, the learning and study espoused by the Dominicans
was not sought for its own value, but rather to prepare for effective preaching against heretics.[59] The same was true for the extensive intellectual
training of the Jesuits. While Ignatius of Loyola did emphasize that the
goal of study was to develop "the entire man" and allowed his Jesuits to
dispense with some of their prayer schedule if they were studying, this was
not for the sake of learning itself, but rather so that the order could better
serve the evangelization needs of post-Reformation Catholicism.[60] It is
worth noting, as several commentators have pointed out, that Roman Catholicism has rarely considered the intellectual life to be a form of religious
virtuosity in and of itself, but has rather seen it as an instrument in the
service of some other goal.[61]

A related, but subtly different, focus from that of evangelization was
the definition of religious life as one spent in "the service of the Church
and of the people of God."[62] This was an especially common model after
the seventeenth century. At times, this service modeodel was a deeply felt
and consistently articulated ideological frame that served truly to define
the reason for a religious order's existence. The Jesuit priest who founded
the Sisters of St. Joseph in seventeenth-century France envisioned
"our selfless congregation" as striving "to achieve the total double union
of ourselves and our dear neighbor with God" through "all the spiritual
and corporal works of mercy of which woman is capable."[63] The
nineteenth-century Sisters of Mercy seem also to have had a coherent
ideological frame centered on serving Christ in the hungry, sick, and imprisoned. But at other times, service came to be defined more in instrumental than in spiritual terms—as the later definition of the Sisters of St.
Joseph as "a pious and versatile labor force" illustrates.[64] As Hill has

pointed out, a purely instrumental definition of the purpose of religious life had much less appeal to potential recruits.[65] Virtuosi were more likely to enter religious life because they felt called by God—to spiritual perfection, to prophetic witness, or to evangelization—rather than because Church committees or bishops had decided that they were a useful source of cheap labor.

Conclusions

Table 6.1 summarizes the major legitimating purposes advanced for Roman Catholic religious orders in each era, as well as their more subtle variations. The more important motivations—when such existed—are given in italic type; the subordinate ones are listed beneath them. In this context, a frame transformation would be any redefinition of religious life that shifted its primary emphasis to a new legitimating purpose, thus changing the entire definition of what it meant to be a member of a religious community. Often, these new formulations were devised by spiritually disenfranchised virtuosi: "Marginal and disadvantaged groups in a society appropriate[d] that society's dominant symbols and ideas in ways that revise[d] and undercut them," and then rearranged these symbols and ideas into new and empowering versions.[66] As a result, the frame transformation would initiate a significant upsurge of interest in religious life among the laity in general, where before there had been apathy and disinterest. Increased lay interest in religious virtuosity due to frame transformation has been documented for France, Italy, and Belgium during the twelfth and thirteenth centuries, for seventeenth-century France, and for nineteenth-century Ireland, France, and Quebec.[67]

Besides articulating a specific overall purpose for its existence that would resonate with the needs of the surrounding society, however, a religious community also had to develop and/or adopt a wide range of component behaviors through which its members could enact this larger purpose in their daily lives. The various ideological frames for religious life have differed widely along these dimensions as well. It is to an examination of these behavioral components that we now turn in Chapter 7.

Table 6.1 Basic Purposes for Religious Life

4th Century Egypt/Syria	*Spiritualization of self through asceticism*
	Mediating between divine and human
	Obtaining spiritual and material favors for family, petitioners
	Prophetic witness against Church and societal abuses
	Modeling eschatological City of God
Monastics, male and female, 500–1000	*Spiritualization of self through ritual prayer and ascetical obedience*
	Modeling true Christian family relations
	Obtaining spiritual graces for family
	Obtaining graces for all Christians
Cistercians, 12th century	*Spiritualization of self through mystical union with God*
Canons, 11th and 12th centuries	Edification of one's fellow men by word and example
Male Mendicants, 1200–1500	*Evangelization of Christians*
	Evangelization of non-Christians
	Prophetic witness against Church abuses
Beguines, Women Monastics 1200–1500	*Spiritualization of self through asceticism and mystical experiences*
	Obtaining spiritual graces for petitioners
	Obtaining divine assistance for the spread of the faith by the mendicant friars
Male Apostolic Orders, 1500–1700	*Evangelization of non-Christians and heretics*
	Reform of the Church
	Spiritualization of self through obedience
Women Religious, 17th-century France	*Serving the People of God by "all works of which women are capable"*
	Spiritualization of self through service to others
	Religious education of the Catholic poor
	Obtaining divine assistance for the spread of the faith by the male apostolic orders
Teaching Congregations 19th-century France, Ireland, Quebec, U.S.	Service of the poor and uneducated within a specific work
	Religious education of the Catholic poor
	Spiritualization of self through service of others and some monastic practices
	Praying for the spread of the faith and other divine favors
	Model a past golden age of Catholic society

Chapter 7

Elements of Virtuoso Ideologies in Catholic Religious Orders

In addition to defining the basic meaning or purpose for religious life, the ideological framework of a religious order or congregation also contains a variety of practices, values, and beliefs. The specific constellation of these elements, the reasons given for their adoption, and the relative weight given to each one, are additional factors distinguishing each ideological frame.[1] Frames differ from each other, therefore, because each may include a different basic rationale for the existence of religious life as well as a different set of these behavioral components. Frames can also differ in whether they are narrowly focused around a single, clearly delimited purpose and a small range of behaviors or whether they are more diffusely defined. In addition, the elements of an ideological frame may or may not be logically articulated and connected to each other: Some orders spent a great deal of time and intellectual effort in the kind of self-conscious frame construction that would lead to an internally consistent frame, while others managed to muddle along despite some profound ideological inconsistencies. To appreciate the full range of variation in the ideological frameworks of religious orders, therefore, it is necessary to examine the different ways in which their component elements were defined and adapted.

Chastity

Enshrining chastity as *the* chief defining behavior for relegous virtuosi was a novel and threatening concept in the cultures of the second- and third-century Mediterranean world. In late classical, Jewish, and Zoroastrian societies, marriage and sexual intercourse were *social* acts upon which both the solidarity and the perpetuation of the human race depended.[2] Virginity was merely a temporary stage of life that culminated in marriage: the ancient world had no word to denote a permanent spinster or virgin.[3] "To render that one stage permanent was to halt the benign circulation of marriage partners and to deny the solidarity that sprang from such circulation."[4] The insistence of early Christian virtuosi upon remaining lifelong celibates was, therefore, a subversive and completely incomprehensible act.

Reasons for Chastity

The initial reason for such anomalous behavior appears to be that the earliest Christians believed the second coming of Jesus and the end of the world to be imminent.[5] In such a situation, marriage and the production of children were unnecessary distractions. Abstinence from sex (usually practiced by middle-aged couples *within* their marriage) was also thought to be an effective, temporary technique for clarifying one's soul in order to receive the spiritual gift of prophecy.[6] At this early period, therefore, celibacy was not a component of virutoso spirituality per se. The religious virtuosi of the first three Christian centuries were *not* the virgins, but rather the martyrs whose death witnessed for their faith. Later, however, as the prospect both of the second coming and of spiritual self-perfection through martyrdom waned, virginity was redefined and applied to a new—and younger—population. In a conceptual revolution, "continence ceased to be what it had largely been in the Early Church: a postmarital matter for the middle aged" and became a means for male and female Christian youth to attain "the original state in which every body and soul had joined. It was the physical concretization, through the untouched body, of the pre-existing purity of the soul," which would exist again in heaven.[7] By deliberately separating him/herself from the social network of marriage contracts, the young Christian virgin was thus affirming his/her higher citizenship in the kingdom of God.[8] Chastity had become, for the first time, an essential component of religious virtuosity's ideological frame.

The converse of considering celibacy as an exceptionally pure or holy state was that sexual intercourse itself came to be considered as less pure, if not actually evil. Sex began to be seen as a regrettable result of Adam's and Eve's fall from Eden, an act that linked human beings to beasts and by which original sin and death were transmitted to new generations.[9] The carnal nature of men and, especially, of women was thus a source of evil that was best overcome by complete sexual abstinence:

> The general consensus among men in the early Christian church was
> that women were a representation of the carnal side of man's nature and

a living danger to true spirituality. . . . Jerome held that woman was as
different from man as body from soul, but that woman had the option of
attaining spiritual parity with man if she served Christ as a virgin. Peter
of Lombard . . . echoed this in the twelfth century.[10]

Virginity in the third and fourth centuries thus became a form of asceti-
sicm, a purging of base physical appetites.

For most of Catholicism's history, therefore, celibacy has been *the* essential precondition for embarking on any true search for sanctity, as well
as the primary source of the virtuoso's spiritual power.[11] It was vastly superior to marriage: As early as the beginning of the second century, there
is evidence that celibates thought of themselves as superior to married
Christians—superior even to the married bishops and clergy—and as
closest to angels in the heavenly hierarchy.[12] This elevation of virginity
over marriage persisted throughout the Middle Ages, in seventeenth-
century France, and in nineteenth-century Ireland and the United
States.[13] "Virginity was extolled as one of the female's 'most precious trea-
sures,' and the second Plenary Council of Baltimore declared it even more
pleasing to God than the married state. So glorified was celibacy that a
1881 marriage manual incongruously devoted about one third of its nearly
300 pages to praising the single state as superior to married life."[14] As recently as 1954, Pope Pius XII's encyclical, *Sacra Virginitas*, repeated that
celibacy was a higher calling than marriage.

Chaste Behaviors

The reasons given for chastity being an essential component of religious
virtuosity have, therefore, varied—from an attempt to image one's citizenship in the celestial kingdom and freedom from earthly ties, to a valuable ascetic discipline for spiritual perfection, to an avoidance of polluting
and evil sexual activity.[15] The actual behaviors involved in the practice of
chastity have also varied throughout the centuries, although not so
widely, we shall see, as have the behaviors involved in poverty, obedience, and prayer. In the earliest Christian period, for example, sexual
continence was rarely a lifelong commitment made by the young, and was
practiced more by older married couples or widows.[16] By the fourth century, the reverse was true. Some early male celibates had extensive contacts with female disciples; others rigidly avoided any proximity to the
opposite sex.[17] Celibate women of the fourth century were free to make
pilgrimages that lasted several years and to establish wide-ranging networks of friends outside their homes. Celibate women of the early Middle
Ages, on the other hand, were so rigidly cloistered that they found it difficult to survive financially.[18] Not only did the behaviors attached to cel-

ibacy vary over time, they also varied across genders. The practices necessary to safeguard women's presumedly weaker hold on their virginity were generally much more strict than those applied to men. Paradoxically, since women were more supposedly more carnal, their renunciation of sexuality made them holier in the popular mind; living a celibate life was thought to be more difficult for them.[19]

By the nineteenth century, however, the popular culture's view of women had shifted from considering them as more subject to carnal temptations than men were, to denying that the normal woman possessed any sex drive at all.[20] The interpretation of the women's vow of chastity, therefore, underwent a corresponding shift: "Rule books and other guides stressed that chastity entailed a guard on all the carnal appetites. Practical and symbolic safeguards are reflected in the [Sisters of] Mercy *Guide's* treatment of the vow—Time Allotted To Visitors, Political Demonstrations Forbidden, The Sisters' Manner In the Parlour, Seculars Not Admitted To Recreation Or Permitted To Stay In the Convent At Night."[21] What earlier centuries might have considered the core of the vow of chastity—abstaining from sexual intercourse—was buried under a host of rules drawn from secular Victorian customs that governed the minutiae of a sister's behavior in public. It was also in the late nineteenth century that the religious habit—originally simply a plain dress and cap adopted out of practicality and poverty—became cumbersome and elaborated so as to deliberately disguise the shape and sexuality of the female body.[22] Male religious orders of the nineteenth and early twentieth centuries also developed a plethora of minute rules concerning dress and behavior, ostensibly to guard their members' chastity.

The Importance of Chastity

The "staying power" of celibacy as an element of religious virtuosity is partly due to the fact that it was often highly attractive, especially to women. McNamara claims that the virginal life was first developed by women, and "was only fully sanctioned by orthodox writers after the women had made it a practical reality."[23] In every era, abstaining from marriage offered women the freedom of a new social role divorced from their biological one, and perhaps even a superior status to that of married men.[24] Celibacy was also desirable because it enabled women to avoid the dangers of childbirth.[25] But women were not the only ones who were attracted by the idea of celibacy. For men in the late Roman Empire, virility was equated with self-control, and the loss of control during sexual intercourse was looked upon with suspicion. Early Christian men were thus predisposed by their culture to see sexual continence as a manly ideal. Male celibacy as "a form of popular heroism" was also a strong component of Irish and German immigrant subcultures in the nineteenth- and early twentieth-century United States.[26]

Chastity has, therefore, been a basic constitutive behavior of religious virtuosity in Roman Catholicism ever since the development of a separate virtuoso state within the Church. Unlike some of the other behavioral elements, it has not varied in its salience: There has rarely been a recognized religious order for which chastity was not an essential component. There have, however, been some changes in the reasons advanced for sexual continence and in the specific daily activities considered necessary for its practice. As seemingly insignificant as these variations may seem to the twentieth-century reader, they could sometimes be quite controversial. However, it was the variations in the other behavioral elements that more clearly delineated new ideological frameworks for virtuoso spirituality.

Poverty

The Meaning of Poverty

Unlike chastity, the vow of poverty has undergone wide variations in the meanings attributed to it, in the purposes for which it was practiced, in its salience relative to other elements of virtuoso spirituality, and in the specific behaviors it was presumed to entail. For the early hermits, the practice of poverty involved giving away all of one's personal belongings, breaking contact with family and friends, and living on the absolute minimum of food, clothing, and shelter.[27] The medieval mendicants also interpreted poverty as the absolute renunciation of possessions; "they would only wear a simple, worn beggar's robe and would own no property. . . . Franciscans would live solely by begging. . . . Group members were expected to live in caves, abandoned buildings, temporarily 'loaned' rooms, or other expedients."[28] Many of the monasteries of the eleventh and twelfth centuries, on the other hand, were quite wealthy as corporate entities. In contrast to the hermits and the friars, monastic "poverty" meant merely that the monastery's goods were owned in common, and not by the individual monk:

> The Holy Father Benedict says in chapter 33 of the Holy Rule that no one should have anything as his own, anything whatever, even the smallest thing, whether books, tablets, or a slate, a pencil to write—in fact nothing, since they are not allowed even to have free disposal of their own bodies and wills. St. Benedict considers it the greatest evil for one of his disciples to possess property or to act as though he were the owner.[29]

An additional connotation of poverty for medieval monastics was that, by having laid down his knightly arms and renounced violence to enter religious life, the monk lost whatever secular status he may have had and became "poor in spirit."[30]

The definition of poverty continued to change in subsequent centuries. By the nineteeth and twentieth centuries, poverty again resembled the monastic model in so far as it required the surrender of one's property to the religious order upon entering and in forbade any use or lending of property without permission. But the nineteenth-century congregations also adopted some aspects of the mendicant ideal of poverty and— initially at least—practiced "stringent economy measures with regard to food and clothing."[31] As with the vow of chastity, however, the practice of poverty was eventually elaborated into a plethora of minutiae, such as asking permission to use a pencil or a piece of stationery. When some of the nineteenth-century congregations acquired more wealth, the members still considered themselves "poor" because of their adherence to these additional customs.[32]

Reasons for Poverty

The reasons given for the practice of poverty also varied and were usually related to the wider purpose the members ascribed to the entire order. Both the Dominicans and the Franciscans practiced poverty because they wished to imitate the style of itinerant, mendicant preaching prescribed by Christ for the apostles. (See Luke 10:1–12.) Detachment from worldly goods also enabled the friar to be more mobile in following his preaching mission. And for the medieval Dominicans, the practice of poverty defused the criticisms of the Albigensians and Waldensians that Catholic clergy were too worldly.[33]

Other ideological frames, however, gave different reasons for adherence to the vow. Thus monastic religious orders, in addition to having a different basic definition for poverty than did the mendicants, also practiced it for a different purpose: "Benedictine frugality is not conceived as a life goal in itself as with the Franciscans but rather as one ascetical means among others to achieve a type of life conducive to union with God."[34] With the fourth-century hermits, the definition of poverty was similar to that of the mendicants, but their reason for adopting it was closer to that of the Benedictines: "It meant they did not need to concentrate on buying, selling, or efficient production—activities which would bring them into close contact with irreligious persons and disruptive institutions."[35]

The Importance of Poverty

The salience of poverty in the total ideological frame of a religious order's virtuoso spirituality also varied. At one extreme were the Franciscans, whose "refusal to own houses, or to touch money or accumulate any reserves, was not just a missionary expedient or a means to an end. It was in itself the *via salutis*—the literal imitation of the earthly life of Christ, who had nowhere to lay his head."[36] For the Dominicans, Benedictines, and the early hermits, on the other hand, poverty was a useful tool in pursuing the transcendent end or goal of the order. When poverty was *not* useful for the order's goals, it could be drastically de-emphasized. The teaching sisters of seventeenth-century France feared that visible signs of poverty such as coarse clothing or bare feet might drive away their wealthy students. The nuns' style of dress was thus rich and elaborate, as befitted their clientele. Some groups of medieval canons dispensed with the vow of poverty altogether and allowed their members to retain their familial inheritances.[37]

Poverty has had great appeal among potential religious virtuosi, especially at times when rising societal wealth has increased the gap between the rich and the poor.[38] Paradoxically, it was not the destitute who embraced the vow, but rather the wealthy and the rising middle class.[39] Never having experienced personal poverty, the nobles and wealthy merchants were more able to idealize it. They also had a keen vision for the un-Christian implications of having rich aristocrats and hierarchs in the same church as the poor. The vow of poverty offered a way of reducing this cognitive strain.

Obedience

Varieties of Obedience

Like the vow of poverty, obedience has varied in meaning, practice, and salience during each of the periods of Roman Catholic religious life. Some variations were due to the formal governmental structures established for the various communities. Early Benedictine monasteries were small and autonomous, and so each could be ruled by its abbot as a father would a family.[40] The original monastic obedience was thus based less on a written Rule and more on personal loyalty to a known and admired individual. Later, however, the far-flung "empire" of dependent Benedictine houses that became affiliated with eleventh-century Cluny stretched the earlier model of obedience to the breaking point. Despite almost constant traveling, the abbots of Cluny could not continue the level of personal supervision St. Benedict had envisioned. "As time went on, the relationship between the motherhouse and the dependencies lost the intimacy of a filial bond and assumed some of the colour of feudal lordship that existed in the secular world."[41]

The mendicant orders of the later Middle Ages departed both from the early monastic model of autonomous houses with familial authority and from the Cluniac "feudal" pattern. The Dominicans and Franciscans "were international and centralized bodies divided geographically into regional provinces, which elected or appointed their major administrators according to a recognized constitutional system."[42] Still other variations might exist. The Cistercians' innovation was to hold an annual general chapter attended by the abbots of all their houses, at which major policy issues would be decided. The Dominicans and Franciscans later adopted this idea as part of their own governance. The Jesuits, on the other hand, did not incorporate the chapter system into their decision making. The Beguines had a much looser governmental structure, and lacked any hierarchical leadership roles.[43]

In addition to the formal governmental structure—or lack thereof—through which the vow of obedience was channeled, religious orders also differed in the amount of authority given to the superior and in the amount of discretion delegated to the average monk or friar. Initially, Benedictine superiors had wide-ranging authority: "The Benedictine Abbot was the absolute paternal master of a given family of religious and their 'living rule' in all temporal as well as spiritual matters."[44] However, as later monasteries increased in size, a wide variety of subordinate offices were created—several types of priors, the precentor, the cellarer, the almoner, the infirmarian, and so on. Individual monks might also be put in charge of each of an abbey's scattered feudal holdings. By the twelfth century, the majority of the monks were involved in such administrative tasks and ran their offices with minimal interference or supervision. This effectively diluted the abbot's authority over them.[45] Similarly, for the Dominicans, "being given a job meant being given the responsibility for doing it, and priors were not meant to interfere unnecessarily with the way people did their jobs."[46]

Other limitations on the superior's power might be imposed by the community's written charter. The constitution of the Dominicans, with its elected officials and voting by all professed members, was "remarkably democratic," especially when compared the rule of the monastic abbots.[47] Instead of being the patriarch of a family, the Dominican prior was "a minister of the community, with strictly limited rights and functions."[48] Accountability procedures were also established. "At every level, the superiors of the order were not only elected, they were made responsible for the conduct of their office to their constituents."[49] A community's charter might also specify terms of office for its superiors. Benedictine abbots ruled for life, as did the heads of the mendicant orders and the Jesuits. The nineteenth-century teaching congregations, on the other hand, elected superiors only for a specified length of time. Each of these variations affected how the vow of obedience would be conceptualized—and lived.

Women in religious orders had an additional complication in their authority structure since, in addition to the abbess, prioress, or mother superior who was nominally in charge of the community, they might also have to contend with authority figures in the male order to which they were linked, and perhaps with the local bishop as well. While powerful abbesses of sixth- and seventh-century England, Ireland and Gaul were able to rule as virtual matriarchs, later groups were not so lucky and the lines of authority were not always clear.[50] Both in the Middle Ages and in later periods, conflicts occurred over who held the ultimate authority over the sisters.[51] For example, "[t]he two legal documents that provided for the early governance of the Sinsinawa [Wisconsin] Dominicans were diametrically opposed as to who held ultimate authority in the congregation."[52] Their traditional Rule gave only spiritual, not financial, authority to the prioress; their legal incorporation under Wisconsin state law named the prioress and her council the community's executive officers. However, even the prioress's spiritual authority was unclear: Both the community's male Dominican director and the local bishop claimed jurisdiction over her in this matter.

Another variation in the meaning and practice of obedience was the *depth of commitment* it was considered to demand. The obedience of the Benedictines and the Jesuits prescribed not only outward conformity but also the submission of their very wills. "To Ignatius, the simple execution of a command was totally insufficient. Real obedience involved internalized acceptance."[53] For the medieval Dominicans, on the other hand, obedience did *not* involve a surrender of the individual friar's freedom of judgment. Furthermore, unlike the other religious communities, Dominicans were not bound in conscience to obey Dominican law.[54]

In the nineteenth-century men's and women's communities, obedience, like poverty and chastity, was often codified into minute rules governing every aspect of daily life. Among the Jesuits, "the dean's permission was to be obtained, *inter alia*, to practice music, to have more than three library books at a time, to procure books from any but the juniorate library. The rector's permission had to be sought to go to St. Louis and to write letters. Thirty-one items came under the purview of the minister. These included permission to use the telephone, take long walks, play the victrola, and to be dispensed from speaking Latin after supper."[55] Perfect observance of the vow was exemplified by one sister who "was known not to utter a word, finish a word she was writing or a stitch she was sewing after the first sound of the bell calling to prayers, meals or recreation. . . . Obedience entailed fidelity to the rule, and the more unstinting the adherence the nearer perfection the obedience."[56] The meaning of obedience also reflected the values of the surrounding culture: The submissiveness and docility expected of all women in the nineteenth-century United States and Europe, for example, colored the sisters' interpretation of how the vow could best be lived.[57]

The Importance of Obedience

The salience of obedience also varied for the different religious orders. For the Jesuits and the medieval canons regular, obedience was of primary importance, in part because both groups placed less emphasis on the types of communal living that would have insured a certain natural conformity:

> The control of man's willful nature is a relatively easy task in a monastic community where each member is under constant supervision and scrutiny by peers as well as superiors, while, at the same time, all members live together and are physically and geographically removed from outside influence and temptation. But the exacting of total obedience and conformity is a much more demanding task among soldiers in an army . . . where individual supervision may not always be feasible. The Jesuit on mission must, to be sure, give periodical reports of all his activities to his superiors. . . . Yet all such enforcement of conformity of behavior would not suffice were obedience not internalized during the training period so that it becomes, as it were, second nature.[58]

The Jesuits, therefore, enshrined obedience as *the* primary virtue of religious life. For the monastic orders, by way of contrast, obedience was emphasized, not in and of itself, but as a useful tool for developing an ascetic spirit.[59] For other groups, obedience was de-emphasized or even dispensed with altogether. While novice hermits in fourth-century Egypt might submit initially to the guidance of an experienced instructor, this was a temporary discipline. The "intensely individualistic" spirit of these men precluded their prolonged obedience to a common rule.[60]

Unlike poverty and chastity, historians have uncovered little evidence that potential virtuosi were drawn to a religious order because of their attraction to obedience. The almost universal adoption of obedience, in some form or other, by the various types of religious orders, is due more to its indispensible role in maintaining the unity and direction of the group than to its attractiveness to the individual members.[61] Many writers have pointed out, however, that obedience may have been less onerous to young entrants in previous centuries—especially to women—since they had been accustomed from childhood to being strictly subordinate to the authority of their fathers.[62]

The three traditional vows of poverty, chastity, and obedience were thus defined differently, practiced differently, and accorded different levels of importance in different orders. In addition, some orders bound themselves by other vows not in the traditional list. And some "religious societies," such as the seventeenth-century Oratorians, took no vows at all.[63] These variations in interpretation and practice contributed to the accepted ideological frame for each era, as well as to the unique charism of each order. There were, however, other constituent elements in the orders' ideological frameworks besides their interpretations of the vows. Among these were the specific type(s) of prayer to be said by the virtuoso, recommended ascetic practices, and the common life.

Prayer and Spirituality

Variations in Prayer and Spirituality

Like chastity, prayer has been an essential component in every form of religious virtuosity that has existed in Roman Catholicism. But the specific *types* of prayer and the practices thought necessary to foster a prayerful spirit have varied. For the Benedictine monks and nuns of the early Middle Ages, the most important type of prayer was the communal chanting of the psalms, interspersed with readings from the Church fathers, that made up the Divine Office. The monastics esteemed the Office even above the mass; it was the *Opus Dei*, the divine duty to which they had consecrated their entire lives.[64] By the tenth and eleventh centuries, however, the sacrament of the Eucharist had been elevated to a position of supreme importance among all the prayers of the Church, and the priests, who controlled the Eucharist, had begun to be given a higher position than members of religious orders.[65] The celebration of the mass soon came to occupy a central position in the monastic day, usurping to some extent the Divine Office.

With the development of the more affective spirituality practiced by the Cistercians (male and female) and by the Beguines, the ritual round of Office and mass was not enough. "Removed from sacramental trappings and parochial rhythms," the soul longed for unity with God.[66] Even for those who had not yet achieved the heights of affective mysticism, the greater psychological sophistication of the high Middle Ages emphasized the *intention* behind formal prayers, rather than the rote recitation of earlier centuries.[67]

Mystical affectivity was more central to women's virtuoso spirituality than it was to men's.[68] Ordained men had an alternate claim to sanctity in their ability to consecrate the Eucharist and their knowledge of theological matters. Having mystical experiences did not require sacramental mediation, and, furthermore, served as an independent basis for the women's authority. Even the male Franciscans and Dominicans who served as spiritual directors for the medieval female mystics thought that these women had a unique and privileged contact with God—a contact that the men themselves did not possess. Accordingly, women were more likely to display various mystical validations of their prayer—trances, levitations, preternaturally long fasts, stigmata, and the like. Women Cistercians and Beguines were also able to participate vicariously in the new Eucharistic spirituality by cultivating an intense devotion to the body and blood of Christ, and by introducing and popularizing Eucharistic devotions such as the feast of Corpus Christi.[69]

Other differences also existed in the styles of prayer practiced in medieval orders. In their striving for contemplation, some groups advocated the use of inspiring art, music, and poetry; others, such as the Cistercians, scorned such devices as distractions.[70] Some authors spelled out in detail the intermediate steps an individual might expect to traverse in his/her mystical development; other religious virtuosi experienced this state without analyzing it.

By the sixteenth century, the types of prayer practiced by religious virtuosi changed again. St. Ignatius and his Jesuits had developed techniques of structured, private prayer and personal meditation on the truths of faith or the life of Christ.[71] Instead of emphasizing either the communal recitation of the Divine Office or mystical contemplation, therefore, Ignatius ordered that these "Spiritual Exercises" be performed by each individual Jesuit during his annual retreat. The foundation of the Spiritual Exercises was discursive meditation using the "three powers": memory, intellect, and will. The memory recalled some previously chosen topic, the intellect would then reflect on whatever lessons could be drawn from that topic, and the will would make resolutions for future behavior.[72] Making a yearly retreat was another Ignatian innovation.[73]

These new forms of prayer became quite popular, since the Jesuits were widely sought after as spiritual directors both for the laity and for other religious communities. Subsequent groups of religious virtuosi, especially the seventeenth-century French *filles seculieres* and the nineteenth-century women's teaching congregations, were influenced by Jesuit spirituality to adopt meditation and annual retreats as the basis of their own prayer style.[74] The affective mysticism of the twelfth and thirteenth centuries was de-emphasized in favor of structured reflection on preselected "points" or topics. By the nineteenth and early twentieth centuries, it was considered arrogant, dangerous, and possibly heretical for a religious virtuoso to aspire to the kind of mystical, contemplative prayer that Bernard of Clairveaux had recommended as a matter of course seven centuries earlier.[75]

The seventeenth-century filles seculieres and the nineteenth-century teaching congregations also de-emphasized or discarded the monastic Divine Office. This was the case even with some of the women Benedictines, for whom it had formerly been considered essential. The reason given for this change was that the full communal recitation of all the hours of the Office would interfere with the sisters' teaching and nursing duties.[76] In the place of the Office or of mystical contemplation, nineteenth-century congregations substituted a round of devotional prayers—the rosary, novenas, litanies, morning and evening prayers, and the like—which mirrored the explosion of popular devotions current in the larger Catholic culture of the period.

The Importance of Prayer

Not only did the types of prayer practiced by religious orders differ, the salience of prayer itself varied from time to time and from order to order. For the Benedictines of Cluny, chanting a lengthy and elaborate version of the Divine Office in common was the basic foundation of their existence, and supplanted even the manual labor to which Saint Benedict had originally given equal emphasis.[77] On the other hand, although it was never completely absent, prayer was explicitly subordinated to the demands of evangelization by both the Jesuits and the Dominicans.[78] Dominic urged his friars to sing the office "briskly and succinctly lest . . . study be in the least impeded."[79] Dominicans might even dispense with the Office entirely if it interfered with their study and preaching. The Dominicans also subordinated affective, mystical prayer to the demands of their ministry and ridiculed those friars who became "silly through excess of devotion."[80] As a result of their relative de-emphasis of prayer, Tugwell argues, the Dominicans never really developed their own distinctive spirituality, but instead adopted whatever prayer style currently existed—even the Spiritual Exercises of the Jesuits—or else gradually abandoned the effort altogether. "From the time of Jordan of Saxony on, we find prominent Dominicans complaining that they are hardly ever able to pray, so they ask the nuns to pray for them. They do not infer that they ought to abandon their work."[81]

Asceticism

Reasons for Ascetical Practice

According to Weber, one of the primary characteristics of all types of religious virtuosity is asceticism, the "individual observance of rigorous physical and mental methods in pursuit of the goal of perfection."[82] Most

Roman Catholic religious orders were no exception to this. The early hermits, the medieval monastics, and the members of seventeenth and
nineteenth-century congregations all saw in asceticism a kind of athletic
exercise for the soul, preparing it to advance in the love of God and the
renunciation of the devil.[83] Women, who were considered—at least by
male writers—to be "weak natured, wantonly sensual, darkly sexual beings" were in special need of "penance of violent proportions" if they were
to overcome their fallen natures.[84]

Other reasons, however, could exist for asceticism. Bynum argues that
medieval women virtuosi saw in asceticism not so much an athletic exercise for attaining spiritual perfection as a way to imitate, and even to participate in, the sufferings of Christ.[85] Such co-suffering was, first of all,
redemptive—it could be substituted for the torments undergone by fellow
souls in purgatory. Asceticism such as fasting was also a way to gain power,
both by bypassing clerical authority and by exercising control over food—
the only resource available to women.[86] Through extreme asceticism,
women virtuosi "rejected—for a wider, more soaring vision—an institution that made a tidy, moderate, decent, second-rate place for women and
the laity."[87] Finally, the patient bearing of suffering, "without asking
why," was a way to attain "an immeasurable experience of the love of
God."[88] Women virtuosi were, therefore, more likely to suffer extended
illnesses without complaint; male virtuosi were more likely to be miraculously cured.

The Importance of Asceticism

In addition to the various motivations given for asceticism, communities
varied in the salience attributed to it, and in whether they advocated zeal
or moderation in its practice. The Dominican priors could dispense their
friars from fasting if it was necessary to encourage study. The Jesuits de-
emphasized asceticism in favor of the discipline of obedience. As Ignatius
wrote, "We may allow ourselves to be surpassed by other religious orders in
fasts, watchings and other austerities . . . but in the purity and perfection
of obedience together with the true resignation of our wills . . . they who
serve God in this society should be conspicuous."[89] A similar downplaying
of asceticism in favor of obedience was expressed by other male societies
in the sixteenth century, and by the filles seculieres of seventeenth-
century France.[90]

The Common Life

Although the earliest religious virtuosi in Catholicism were isolated hermits, some form of cenobitic, or common, living had developed by the

early fourth century. Initially, the purpose of such a lifestyle was to enable the monks to profit from the physical security and spiritual services that could be provided when several of their kind lived together, as well as to model the true spiritual family.[91] Later, additional reasons were added. The twelfth-century Cistercians held that the companionship and love that could develop in communal living was an essential help for the individual monk's spiritual growth.[92] The Cistercian community was to be a laboratory of brotherly love, through which the individual might learn to feel conpassion and contrition. On the other hand, the thirteenth-century mendicants saw common life primarily as a way of collaborating in their pre-eminent goal of evangelization.[93] The seventeenth-century French teaching sisters found communal living helpful for financial economy and for mentoring each other in their newly developing teaching profession.[94]

As with the other elements that made up the various ideological frameworks for religious life, religious orders not only attributed different purposes and salience to the common life, they also added varying subsidiary practices to it. Whether or not members would live out their entire lives in one house (as the early Benedictines were required to do by their vow of stability) or could move from convent to convent (as did the Dominicans and Franciscans) was one variation.[95] The wide size discrepancies between the houses in various orders—from fewer than five to as many as one thousand under one roof—also had obvious implications for the practice of the common life.

The prospect of a communal lifestyle has been a key attraction for potential recruits to all types of religious communities. This was especially so for women, who were often deprived of other opportunities to associate with each other.[96] In contrast to the lives of their secular sisters, women in monasteries and convents were in contact with an extended family of female relatives and friends. They forged intense friendship networks, taught and counselled each other, cried when the opening of new houses required them to separate.[97] For men's orders, too, there is evidence that the common life was a source of deep personal relationships and a sense of belonging.[98]

Ministerial Works

The Importance of Ministry in Early Virtuoso Ideologies

In comparison to celibacy and prayer, which were present (albeit with variations) in all of Roman Catholicism's many formulations of religious virtuosity, or to poverty, obedience, common life, and asceticism, which were essential components in most versions, the performance of some ministerial work was usually *not* a defining element in the ideological frameworks early religious orders constructed for their lives. Whether or not the early medieval monk or nun, or the fourth-century hermit, engaged in any ministry at all was irrelevant to his/her fundamental goal: personal sanctification through asceticism or prayer. The early hermits supported themselves by basket making or by the freewill offerings of the faithful—and endeavored to live on the bare minimum of necessities so as to have as little to do with these polluting worldly activities as possible.[99] While St. Benedict originally prescribed seven hours of manual labor per day for his monks, this was not performed as a ministry but rather as an ascetic training for the perfection of the monk's own soul.[100] Much of the labor was agricultural work, during which the participants may not have come into contact with nonmonks at all. Later, as the time devoted to liturgical prayer increased, the amount of actual physical labor performed by the monks dwindled to the vanishing point. Such remaining monastic occupations as copying manuscripts were adopted primarily because they did not interfere with the *real* purpose of monastic life: chanting the Divine Office.[101]

Even when monasteries did furnish valuable social services such as sheltering the poor and the aged, Christianizing frontier areas, or educating some of the nobility, these actvities were incidental to their main purpose.[102] Monastic schools, for example, developed primarily because novice monks needed to be literate in order to read their prayers. "Childhood education," reports Taylor, "was not considered a sanctifying activity during the Middle Ages and there was little incentive for people in the tradition of corporate asceticism to devote their time to it. There were no scriptural precedents for childhood education and consequently no external encouragement to incorporate it to the life of perfection."[103] From the twelfth century on, in fact, the monks were convinced that scholastic inquiry and speculation were actually *incompatible* with the monastic goal of self-perfection and union with God, and thus that all learning should be avoided that did not lead to these goals.[104]

For other medieval religious virtuosi, ministerial service was optional. Many Beguine women worked in the textile industry to secure their livelihood, but this was not an essential component of their brand of religious virtuosity. Although some beguinages did sponsor ministerial activities, the participation of the individual members was not required. Some Beguines performed charitable works for the sick and destitute, but others did not, preferring instead to concentrate on prayer and on extremely rigorous ascetical practices.[105] The regular canons of the twelfth century had also added ministerial service to their vision of religious life. As with the

Beguines, however, there was a wide variation in this and many canons did not stress apostolic works.[106]

The medieval Hospitaller orders appear to be an exception to the general tendency of early religious communities not to define themselves by their performance of a ministerial work.

> However, confusion persisted in canon law and Church practice regarding the precise status of the hospitaller orders. It seems—although existing studies are quite inadequate—that medieval authorities simply did not give much thought to the question of whether or not the hospitallers were true religious. The work of the hospitaller was arduous and menial, and hospitallers were undoubtedly recruited from the lower social ranks which also supplied the working lay brothers and sisters of the convents. Thus while the services performed by the hospitallers were recognized to be valuable to society their actual work was disesteemed as vile and degrading; the hospitallers themselves seem to have existed without setting significant precedents or stimulating thoughtful discussion.[107]

In addition to the hospitallers, a few other medieval groups did organize around a specific task. The twelfth-century Knights Templar were established to assist in the reconquest of the Holy Land, while the ministry of the Trinitarians and Mercedarians was to ransom Christian slaves.[108] As Hostie has pointed out, however, medieval orders whose primary purpose was the performance of a specific ministerial work were vulnerable to extinction if societal changes made their focus obsolete.[109] Thus, the Templars vanished from most countries with the end of the crusades; the Trinitarians and Mercedarians survived only by adopting the focus and activities of the mendicants, and hospital orders devoted to a specific disease such as leprosy or the bubonic plague saw their institutions empty out once the ravages of these maladies declined. For the most part, therefore, it was rare for an early religious order to adopt a single specific ministry as the key element in its charism.

The Rise of Ministerial Foci

With the rise of the male mendicants and, later, of the male and female apostolic orders, external ministerial foci became—for the first time—essential components of the dominant frame for religious virtuosity. The mendicants' main purpose was their evangelization ministry; the apostolic orders of the sixteenth and seventeenth centuries had broad service orientations. " 'To do all the good that is possible'—this intention, as enthusiastic as it was imprecise, was typical of the spirit in which women of the early seventeenth century offered their services to the Church."[110] The purpose of the Jesuits was to "minister where no one else will."[111] For

the first time, Roman Catholic religious virtuosity began to join an outward, active focus with its traditional concentration on the individual
monk's, nun's, or hermit's own spiritual perfection. Even so, remnants of
the former tendency to devalue ministry in comparison with the other
purposes for religious life still persisted. As late as the seventeenth century, there is evidence that teaching was not considered as holy an activity
as more traditional monastic practices and was justified primarily as an
ascetic and penitential discipline. "The documents repeat insistently that
teaching is *penible,* a word which carries connotations simultaneously of
painfulness and difficulty. The teaching sisters seem to have taken up their
vocation as a new form of mortification, comparable to but less venerable
than washing the feet of beggars."[112]

Additional Practices

In addition to ministerial works, other incidental practices might be incorporated into an ideological frame. Some groups wore distinctive habits;
others, such as the Beguines, confined themselves to clothes of a particular color. Still others, such as the Jesuits, the first Ursulines, and the
filles seculieres of seventeenth-century France, deliberately renounced
wearing a habit because they did not want to be linked with preceding
forms of religious life.[113] Benedictine monasteries fostered a spirit of silence and the avoidance of conflict; the mendicants thrived on oral
disputation.[114] Some monasteries deliberately limited their size by establishing daughter houses for surplus members; others, such as the Pacho-
mian monasteries of the fourth century, could contain as many as 1000
inhabitants.[115] Specific practices such as these contributed to the particular charism that marked each order's version of whatever overarching
ideological frame for virtuoso spirituality was current in a given era. These
distinctions were noted and sometimes bitterly contested, as each community asserted the superiority of a white habit over a black one, or of
autonomous monasteries over dependent priories. In their concentration
upon the minutiae that divided them, it was often easy for the religius orders of a given period to ignore the commonalities of the larger ideological
frame which they shared.

Summary

In addition to being distinguished by variations in the basic underlying
purpose they postulated for religious life, therefore, the ideological frames
constructed by the various religious orders also differed in the particular
mix of practices each order adopted, in the rationales given for these prac-

tices, and in the relative salience attached to each one. Table 7.1 attempts to outline some of these differences. The assembly of such a montage was difficult and time-consuming, and even the most innovative orders rarely attempted a completely new articulation for reliigous virtuosity. "It is worth noting that in many respects the mid-seventeenth century secular congregations merely recapitualted the long and arduous process of self-definition already achieved by the late medieval semi-monastic communities."[116]

Changes in Ideological Composition

Over time, orders might drift into subtle changes in the mix of practices they had adopted, or might even subtly alter their underlying purpose. Such changes were especially likely when communities were brought into contact with new orders following a different ideological frame. Thus, the Benedictine sisters of post-Reformation Europe, isolated from the sponsorship of male Benedictine groups, supplemented their traditional Benedictine Divine Office with the newer devotions based on Jesuit spirituality.[117] The sisters in U. S. Benedictine congregations elected their superior for a limited term, a "novel departure" from the lifelong terms prescribed for Benedictine abbesses by the original Rule, but quite similar to practices common in contemporary teaching congregations. Religious orders might deliberately borrow elements from one another, as the Beguines did from the female Premonstratensians, the male Franciscans, and the Cistercians.[118]

There were also other variations in religious virtuosity. Thus, religious women in thirteenth-century England tended to be recluses, while their contemporaries in southern Europe stressed active works of charity.[119] The men and women writers of a given period each tended to emphasize different aspects of virtuoso spirituality, even when they were describing the same group or individual. "Male biographers of women between 1200 and 1400 stressed sensationalist and masochistic performance, whereas women writing about themselves or about other women stressed service and the details of ordinary life in the context of cloister or beguinage, private dwelling or civic community."[120]

It was also possible that a religious community, especially a *women's* religious community, might develop *no* distinctive charism of its own. There have been several reasons for this. Sometimes the ideological frame preferred by the community's founder was disregarded by the hierarchy in favor of the imposition of a cloistered monastic model, which was the only accepted form of religious life for women. This happened to St. Clare's Franciscans in the thirteenth century, to St. Angela Merici's Ursulines in

Table 7.1 Alterations in the Ideological Frames for Religious Virtuosity

	Celibacy/Virginity	Poverty	Obedience	Prayer	Asceticism	Common Life	Ministry
Fourth Century Egypt/Syria	V. = Soc/Political Statement V. = Eschatological Witness V. = a manly ideal V. = better than marriage Intercourse as evil No cloister to safeguard V.	Absolute personal poverty P. = an ascetical tool	Master-disciple relationship Individualistic tendencies dilute O.	Sacraments Deemphasized Solitary Prayer Goal: Self-transcendence, union with God	*Chief emphasis* Competitive A. Extremes in A. Goal: Spiritual perfection, preparation for prayer	Initially De-emphasized	None Some manual work for subsistence
Early Monasticism, 500–1000	V. = Source of spiritual power V. = better than marriage Intercourse as evil Women's carnal nature dangerous to male and female spirituality Strict cloister for women	Great wealth held in common P. = "poor in spirit" P. = an ascetical tool	*Chief Emphasis* Internal assent required Elected abbot: absolute authority for life Base: personal loyalty O. = Familial (early Benedictines) O. = Feudal (Cluny) O. = ascetical tool	P. = Chant Divine Office Goal: Intercession, self-transcendence	Moderation in A. Uniformity in A.	*Chief Emphasis* Stability	None prescribed Manual labor for subsistence and asceticism

Table 7.1 Continued

	Celibacy/Virginity	Poverty	Obedience	Prayer	Asceticism	Common Life	Ministry
Male Cistercians, 1100	Women's carnal nature dangerous to male and female spirituality. V. = better than marriage	P. = Emphasize simplicity	Independent houses with visitation. O. = Federal, not feudal. Annual general chapter	More individual emphasis in P. Mystical Prayer. Anti-intellectual. Devotion to Mary. Goal: infused charity	A. = preparation for mysticism	Common life to foster interpersonal relations	None. Reemphasized manual labor as an ascetical practice. Service to others. Not emphasized
Beguines, Cistercian Nuns, 1200s	V. a Source of Spiritual Power. V. better than Marriage. Cloister to Safeguard V. (Cistercians). No cloister (Beguines)	Wealth held in common (Cistercians). Moderate poverty (Beguines)	O. = Loose (Beguines). No common Rule (Beguines)	Divine Office (Cistercians). Eucharistic Mysticism. Erotic metaphors	Severe penances, fasting. A way to imitate Christ	Common life only after 1200 (Beguines)	None (Cistercians). Trade practiced for self-sufficiency (Beguines). Some Ministerial Service (Beguines)
Male Mendicants, 1200–1500	V. = better than marriage. V. = less emphasized than poverty. Fear of women as temptation	*Chief Emphasis:* Absolute communal poverty (Franciscans). P. = end in itself (Franciscans). Poverty useful as aid in preaching (Dominicans)	Elected, based on constitution. Internal assent not required (Dominicans). Discretion given to individual friar	P. = Subordinate to Ministry (Dominicans). Intellectual basis for prayer (Dominicans). No original spirituality (Dominicans). Reject Mysticism (Dominicans)	De-emphasized personal asceticism (Dominicans)	De-emphasized, Common life is a way to collaborate in ministry. No monastic stability	Evangelization as primary ministry. Discarded manual labor

		Mendancy		Support Mysticism (Franciscans) Devotion to crucified Christ (Franciscans)			
Male Apostolic Orders, 1500–1700	All attachments subord. to apostolate V. = better than marriage	De-emphasized P.	O. = *Chief Emphasis* Internal assent required No elected chapter	Both Divine Office and mysticism subordinate to ministry Spiritual Exercises Annual retreat and spiritual direction	A. = De-emphasized	Common Life De-emphasized No monastic stability	Broad focus
Women's Apostolic Congregations, France, 1600s	V. = better than Marriage Attempts to eliminate cloister	De-emphasized P. Mendicancy forbidden	Monastic obedience imposed Each house independent Minute rules	Adoption of Jesuit and other spirituality Divine Office de-emphasized or discarded	A. = de-emphasized Substitute obedience & service	A way to collaborate in ministry No monastic stability	Broad focus, teaching as ascetical practice
Women's Teaching Congregations and Men's Orders 1800s	V. = better than Marriage Minute rules involving V. Habit as safeguarding V. V. = a manly ideal	Initial lack of funds, later common property De-emphasized P. if interfered with cultural mores Minute rules involving P. = ask permission to use articles	O. = Following minute rules Internal assent required Superior general & motherhouse; convents not autonomous Subject to episcopal authority (women) Confusion over lines of authority (women)	Jesuit spirituality widespread Devotions Divine Office de-emphasized or discarded	A. = de-emphasized	A way to collaborate in ministry No monastic stability	Specific works or institutions Teaching Spiritual reclamation of Catholic poor

the sixteenth century, and to St. Francis de Sales' Visitation Sisters and Marguerite Bourgeoys' Congregation de Notre Dame in the seventeenth century.[121] To detach the Franciscan women from the mendicant frame, or the Ursuline and Visitation women from the apostolic frame, resulted in profound alterations of these groups' original visions. After succumbing to such pressures, the women's orders came increasingly to resemble each other. A similar process occurred in the late nineteenth and early twentieth centuries, as women's teaching congregations rewrote their constitutions to conform with the newly promulgated Code of Canon Law. Donovan documents the subtle changes in pre- and post-1917 versions of one community's constitutions, whereby the distinctiveness of its original, noncloistered model was diluted, homogenized, and adapted to a form of limited enclosure.[122]

For some communities, the choice of a charism seems almost to have been an afterthought. In the nineteenth century, for example, groups of pious women organized informally to perform some specific ministry, and adopted a Franciscan or Dominican or Vincentian rule only later, when and if some official status became necessary for the continuation of the work.[123] The work was primary; the rest was more or less secondary. Women's communities might also develop without a distinctive charism if they were founded by bishops or diocesan clerics who were interested primarily in the instrumental services these women could perform. This was especially common in the nineteenth century.[124] "Priests and bishops seemed to see no differences between different types of rules provided that the sisters were useful."[125] Some bishops established different congregations for each ministerial work they felt needed to be addressed. Thus, for example, Bishop Ignace Bourget of Montreal founded four separate religious congregations of women: one to visit the poor, one to educate children, one to work with unwed mothers, and one to do rural work.[126] When a bishop composed the constitution for a group of women whom he was endeavoring to form into a religious community, he was likely to borrow from already written, "generic" constitutions and to make only minor adaptations. As a result, "[t]he constitutions drawn up by the bishops or by the designated chaplains . . . tended to resemble each other, and to imitate those of cloistered orders."[127] Even the names given to nineteenth-century women's congregations often reflected the prevailing fashion rather than any concrete spirituality. At one time, it was fashionable to name communities after saints (Sisters of St. Joseph, Sisters of St. Martha), at other times, after spiritual attributes (Sisters of Charity, Mercy, Providence), and at still other times, after incidents in the lives of Jesus and Mary (Sisters of the Presentation, of the Assumption).[128]

The result of all this was that *many nineteenth-century women's congregations could be distinguished from each other only by the specific ministry they performed, or by very superficial traits.* The distinctiveness of each community was reduced to idiosyncracies of habit or minute variations in the observance of poverty, prayer, or common life.[129] Nineteenth-century American congregations also became segregated by nationality into all Polish, all Irish, or all German communities.[130] Similar ethnic segregation also happened in Canada. Many nineteenth-century congregations can thus be said not to have possessed a true charism at all, but rather an ethnic flavor, a distinctive and often overelaborated habit, and the responsibility for staffing a particular set of institutions. The lack of precision with regard to the communities' charisms was noted and objected to by Rome, even though it was Roman-inspired standardization that had partially contributed to it.[131]

Conclusions

The ideological frames that underlay religious life in its various periods of growth and expansion have varied, not only in the basic purpose or meaning which each postulated for virtuoso spirituality, but also in the specific constellation of practices, values, and beliefs espoused by its adherents. Some frames were focused on a single purpose and a narrow range of behaviors; others included several, often unreconciled, foci. Even the most fundamental marks of Catholic religious virtuosity—chastity and prayer—varied in their meaning and practice.

But there was more to an ideological frame than its definition of a basic purpose for religious life and the combination of beliefs and behaviors it prescribed. A third component of ideologies was the symbol system that supported it. It is to this topic that we will turn in Chapter 8.

Ideological Supports for Religious Virtuosity: Symbols, Myths, and Metaphors

The majority of the virtuosi who joined a religious community modeled on some new ideological framework did not articulate their choice in terms of the abstract elements of this or that ideological frame. Insofar as their new ideology of virtuoso spirituality replicated the old—in postulating the same basic reasons for religious life, for example, or in continuing to require chastity, prayer, or obedience—its elements would simply be taken for granted as normal and natural. Often this meant that the members of the new group may not have been conscious of the subtle ways in which their version of prayer, obedience, or some other element did differ from the older one.[1]

But obviously novel innovations in the ideological frame required some justification, especially since they often appeared to contradict the ways in which religious virtuosity had been expressed in the past—and may have irritated powerful vested interests as well. "It was therefore necessary, wherever innovation was attempted, to give it legitimacy by showing that it was, in fact, a return to old tradition. This could be done by appealing to Church history or—even better—by pointing to a scriptural model. An extensive polemic had to be developed to protect the new congregations from their critics."[2] The creation and the use of mythic elements to support their ideological frame were thus of primary importance to religious communities.[3]

The attempt to get one's symbols, myths, and other justifying metaphors accepted by the society at large was an exercise of power, as Rubin points out.[4] Once a set of such figures was successfully integrated into the culture, however, the survival and growth of the religious orders that subscribed to it were greatly facilitated. Questioners and opponents could be refuted by the simple expedient of citing the accepted myth or symbol. Subsequent groups would be pressured to adopt whatever ideological frame was supported by the dominant myths, and possibly to elaborate on and strengthen these myths with contributions of their own. This constant refinement and reconstruction gave the symbols upholding religous virtuosity "the polysemous, fertile, paradoxical quality that Christian symbols share with all symbols."[5] This chapter will describe some of the manifold ways that symbolic elements were used to uphold the various versions of religious life.

Mythical Figures

Mary, the Mother of Jesus

A readily comprehensible symbol often used to justify an element of religious virtuosity was the life and example of some biblical figure or early saint. The most frequently cited of these was Mary, the mother of Jesus, whose life—real and imagined—was used to validate the elements of several different ideological frames. Tha apocryphal gospels of the second and third centuries, which, McNamara argues, were written to reflect the ideas of the period's consecrated virgins, were the first to advance the doctrine of Mary's perpetual virginity.[6] The earlier canonical Gospels had not been interested in this topic, except to validate the supernatural origins of Jesus himself. The cult of Mary's virginity, once established, served to uphold the superiority of celibacy for the early consecrated virgins, and for every subsequent version of religious life down to and including that of the nineteenth and early twentieth centuries.[7]

Various events in Mary's life were cited to legitimate other aspects of religious virtuosity. The apocryphal third-century *Protoevangelion of James* described an imagined girlhood for Mary as a consecrated virgin in the Jewish temple.[8] This image was seized upon by the seventeenth-century French and French-Canadian sisters. Depending upon each community's own focus, the sisters would emphasize different aspects of Mary's life in the temple: Cloistered nuns focused upon her devotion to prayer and her performance of daily tasks, while the teaching sisters of the new congregations cited Mary's work instructing the younger girls—an exact replica of the instructional ministry these sisters were attempting to establish for themselves. A subsidiary devotion to Mary's mother, St. Anne, arose at the same time, in her role as educator of the child Mary.

The aspect of Mary's life most frequently cited by the seventeenth-century sisters, however, was the Visitation (Luke 1:39–45). The fact that Mary had obviously not been hindered from visiting Elizabeth by any cloister restrictions was used to justify similar activities for the sisters in seventeenth-century France, England, and Quebec.[9] Mary's visitation was seen as a *missionary* activity, bringing Christ (albeit in utero) to those who awaited him. "If the Virgin was a missionary, why could other women not be missionaries too? . . . The idea that women might participate in the apostolate, which was so thoroughly condemned within the Church on the authority of St. Paul, was made respectable on the authority of the Blessed Virgin."[10]

Still other aspects of Mary's life could be emphasized, according to the interests of various groups. Her later life as counselor to the apostles was attractive to the early consecrated virgins, as well as to the seventeenth-century French sisters.[11] Her suffering along with the agonies of her Son was a popular devotion in the late Middle Ages and served to give meaning and nobility to all suffering.[12] Paradoxically, it was the males, rather than the females, in medieval religious life who expressed the most devotion to Mary, seeing in her "the affectivity needed to complement the authority of God the Father."[13] Thus, the cult of Mary served to support the affective spirituality of Cluny and Citeaux. Mary also supported the Cistercian ideology in other ways: The monks had several stories depicting the Blessed Virgin—and St. Anne and St. Mary Magdalen—descending from heaven to wipe the monks' brows as they labored in the fields. This gave celestial validation to the Cistercian reintroduction of manual labor after the liturgical "excesses" of Cluny.[14] A century later, the new mendicant orders used Mary's authority to legitimate their model for religious life: They recounted a vision of Christ who, as he was about to destroy the world for its sins, was deterred by Mary's showing him Dominic and Francis.[15]

Jesus

Rather than citing Mary as a symbol for their way of life, medieval nuns and Beguines were more likely to express a devotion to the human Christ, especially to his infancy and his sufferings.[16] The sufferings of Jesus thus gave meaning and validation to the strong ascetical bent of twelfth- and thirteenth-century religious women. A focus on the suffering Christ was also a primary component of the spirituality practiced by the cloistered nuns of seventeenth-century France.[17] Other virtuoso traditions, however, emphasized different aspects. Christ's virgin birth served to show that, by being conceived without sexual intercourse, Christ had "recaptured the presocial majesty of Adam's first state" and was exempt from human ties or loyalties.[18] This gave divine sanction for the hermits' practice of perpetual virginity "for the sake of the Kingdom of Heaven." The medieval Franciscans, on the other hand, emphasized Christ as a healer and as the wandering preacher who had no place to lay his head.[19]

Biblical Figures and Myths of Saints

In addition to Mary and Jesus, other mythic holy figures could also be used to justify the practices of an era's religious virtuosi. The consecrated virgins of the third and fourth centuries found inspiration in the story of St. Thecla, virgin, pilgrim, and missionary, whom popular tradition had named a companion of St. Paul. Her heroic refusal to marry her fiance was an affirmation that women could be more than merely sexual beings. Her missionary journeys and pilgrimages justified similar activities for other women, and the fact that she baptised herself after St. Paul had refused her the sacrament was an oblique legitimation for a fuller participation of women in the church.[20] Early female virtuosi used the story of Mary Magdalen in a similar way. Third- and fourth-century tradition named her as a special witness to the resurrection and a teacher to the apostles: Peter was depicted as furious at her presumption, but he was rebuked by the other disciples, who invited Mary to teach them.[21] Later ideologies of religious virtuosity also employed the Mary Magdalen figure, but not as the privileged instructor of the apostles. By the Middle Ages, the misidentification of Mary Magdalen with the "woman who was a sinner" had taken place, and the legend had sprung up that she was a former prostitute, converted by Jesus, who spent her later years in solitude and penance. This latter image made her the patron of the medieval Carmelites.[22]

The *vitae* of other early saints also served to inspire various groups of religious virtuosi. Several women had disguised themselves as men and lived lives of heroic asceticism as hermits in the desert; tales of their exploits served to bolster their contemporaries' arguments that such religious virtuosity was indeed possible for women.[23] The Latin version of the *Life of Anthony the Abbot* (384 c.e.) and James de Vitry's life of the Beguine Mary of Oignies (1215 c.e.) moved hundreds of early hermits and medieval women to follow their examples.[24] The regular canons of the Middle Ages looked to St. Augustine for inspiration; subsequent generations of Franciscans embroidered legends about St. Francis.[25] The *vitae* of such saints became models on which subsequent virtuosi patterned their own quest for spiritual perfection; indeed, they were often the *only* definition of sanctity within Roman Catholicism.[26] Entire groups of people might also be held up for imitation: The communal life of the first Christians (Acts 2:44–45), for example, inspired the medieval monks, the regular canons, and the Beguines.[27] The mendicants attempted to pattern their own calling on the missionary journeys of the seventy-two disciples.[28] Subsequent generations of Jesuits found inspiration in the exploits of the early Jesuit martyrs in North America or Elizabethan England. The endurance of these men modeled the "heroic masculinity" of strong soldiers of Christ, capable of withstanding material hardship, torture, and even death without flinching.[29]

Founding Legends

Another powerful source of ideological legitimacy concerned the various stories and legends that each religious community passed down concerning its founding: "the members of religious institutes attributed all of the activities of their founders to direct interventions of God, of Christ, of the Holy Spirit, of saints or of angels. . . . A saint seen in a dream or the voice of the Virgin in a vision definitively sanctions this decision or that behavior."[30] The founding period of a religious order became a mythic archetype in which the members actually enacted in their lives the divinely given mission of their community.[31] The stories of that time would be recounted and ritually repeated by subsequent generations to keep alive the memory of God's dealings with them. Historians have noted a tendency to idealize the founder more in each successive biography and to exalt the status of his/her Rule. Thus, for example, the Rule of Pachomius was later said to have been given to him by an angel.[32] So important were such legends that the medieval Carmelites, who could not trace their origins to a single charismatic figure or to heroic events, felt compelled to invent a legendary founder in the prophet Elijah and a set of early heroes such as the visionary St. Simon Stock. Modern research cannot find any evidence that the latter ever existed.[33] The reluctance of the Dominicans to enshrine St. Dominic as a mythic founder (as the Franciscans had done with St. Francis), meant that later members of the order had no readily codifiable image that could be appealed to when attempting to resolve the inevitable discrepancies between various elements in their community's charism.[34] This ultimately led to serious problems in articulating exactly what the order's basic ideological framework was.

The apotheosis of the founder and the mythologizing of founding events continues in many religious orders to this day. A current Vatican official contends that naming their founder a saint still "means a lot to religious orders." The office "has been beseiged with causes on behalf of founders, most of them women," and he expects that the flood will continue for at least another fifty years.[35]

Metaphors and Images

In addition to their stories of famous saints or founding figures, religious communities were also inspired by certain powerful metaphors for the relationship between the soul and God. Variations in these metaphors served to support new ideologies of religous virtuosity as they rose and fell in popularity throughout the centuries.

"The Bride of Christ"

The most common metaphor was of the soul as "the Bride of Christ." This analogy was used from the third century onward, more commonly among women than among men.[36] In recounting their consecration to religious life, third-century women spoke of receiving marriage with "the true Man" (Jesus), while their male contemporaries interpreted their conversions as receiving knowledge.[37] Similarly, in medieval monasticism, there were two rituals for consecrating new members. "The nun's drew heavily on imagery of marriage; the monk's centered on the idea of the renewal of the whole person."[38] Whereas the spirituality of the monks, friars, and religious clerics of the monastic and later periods was more likely to focus on *maternal* images of Mary, or even on maternal images of Jesus, the women of the period stressed *nuptual* imagery, with strong erotic overtones.[39] References to Christ as the sister's "heavenly Bridegroom" remained common into the nineteenth and even twentieth centuries.[40] The clergy supported this definition because they considered themselves the spiritual representatives of Christ on earth and therefore able to claim "vicarious authority" over his brides.[41]

"The Sacred Heart" and "The Soldier of Christ"

Another metaphor which was quite popular among women religious was that of "the Sacred Heart of Jesus." This image, symbolizing the great love of Christ for human beings, arose in the Middle Ages and was revived in the seventeenth and the nineteenth centuries.[42] By emphasizing Christ's love and the soul's response, devotion to the Sacred Heart implied that one could contact God without the aid of clerical mediators. Another metaphorical image that was popular among men was that of the monk, hermit, mendicant, or Jesuit as a hero in the spiritual war against the devil.[43] This image was especially popular among the fourth-century hermits once their opportunities for martyrdom were dimished, and among medieval monks with their family backgrounds in the knightly class. In the nineteenth century, the image of religious as "prompt and valiant soldiers of Christ" was even applied to nuns. "[Bishop] John Ireland had identified women religious as the Catholic Church's 'regular army.' About this time the title of major superiors moved from Mother to Mother General, and among the School Sisters of Notre Dame to Commissary General."[44]

There were obviously many other symbols, metaphors, and mythic stories developed by the members of various religious communities to legitimate and reinforce both the ideological frame for religious virtuosity current in their age and also their particular charism's interpretation of it. To explore all of these images in the manifold variety of their numerous subtle variations would be a book in itself. It is sufficient here merely to point out the vital role of symbols, myths, and metaphors in every ideological framework for religious virtuosity that has existed in Roman Catholicism, and the correspondingly significant amount of time that the monks, nuns, friars, and sisters devoted to developing, elaborating, and sharing them.

Internal Discrepancies in the Ideological Frame

The ideological framework that supported each of the various models of organized religious virtuosity within Roman Catholicism was thus a composite of specific practices and of the more or less clearly articulated reasons for them, of supporting mythic figures and of metaphoric images, all revolving around some basic understanding of the meaning of religous life and its primary role in the church. These mixtures were not always internally consistent—a circumstance that could eventually cause problems for the community's growth and functioning:

> The ingredients that made up Dominican life were many, and the resulting mixture was not entirely stable. There were . . . tensions between the demands of poverty and study and between the demands of the job and the demands of conventual life. Nor was there an obvious model that could hold the whole mixture together. Whereas the monks and the reformed canons could, without undue difficulty, base themselves on the model of the early Church in Jerusalem as depicted in the Acts of the Apostoles, the chosen Dominican model, Christ the wandering poor preacher, did not suggest any way of holding together itinerant preaching and the conventual life.[45]

As the decades passed, therefore, most religious communities began to experience the cumulative impact of previously unrealized discrepancies in their ideological frames.

Contemplation versus Ministry

The most basic disjuncture, which appeared again and again in the later communities, was between the demands of contemplation and those of ministry.[46] Prior to the thirteenth century, the accepted models of religious life had been oriented almost entirely around the first of these two foci, and conflicts between a life of prayer and one of activism did not exist. The business of the hermit, the monk, or the consecrated virgin was to achieve his/her soul's own perfection (however that perfection was defined and enacted), and to channel divine grace to the lay faithful. Involvement in any worldly affairs—even the tasks of the ordained priesthood—was looked upon as a fall from the higher state of contemplation. With the later mendicant and apostolic orders, however, members were expected to spend all or part of their days in actual work among the laity—preaching, evangelizing, teaching, nursing, and performing a host of other absorbing tasks—which came to usurp the time formerly given to prayer and contemplation. How to strike a balance?

The conflicting pull can be seen most acutely in the medieval Carmelites. These formerly contemplative hermits had come together in Palestine early in the thirteenth century, seeking "a life of prayer . . . silence, solitude in a communal setting, and penance with a special emphasis on an intense relationship to Jesus."[47] There was no initial expectation that the Carmelites would engage in any sort of public ministry. By mid-century, however, the community had begun to migrate to Europe under the pressure of the Muslim reconquest of Palestine, and there they found great difficulties in continuing their original lifestyle. Under the tutelage of the Dominicans, therefore, the male Carmelites adopted the mendicant model.

> The changes in the formula of life . . . set the Carmelites firmly on the road to a mendicant identity. The revisions of 1247 also established the tension that has existed ever since for the Carmelite friars, the paradox of the call to a contemplative attitude and at the same time a call to ministerial service out of the context of communal living.[48]

"The twin tendencies of religious life, retreat from the world and pastoral concern, always caused tension."[49] Later orders, such as the Dominicans and the Jesuits, would attempt to resolve this conflict by emphasizing the demands of the ministry almost exclusively, and de-emphasizing or discarding most of the earlier monastic requirements of contemplation and the common life.[50] Paradoxically, however, an exclusive focus on the active ministry contained its own elements of contradiction and instability. Sometimes, the ministerial focus was itself unclear. Exactly what behaviors did "preaching" require of Dominicans? Speaking at mass and other public gatherings? Teaching in schools? Or simply giving good example by one's life, whatever one did?[51] And the exclusive focus on ministry was often detrimental to the common life. For this reason, as several historians have pointed out, even the most active orders found it necessary to readopt various monastic observances in subsequent centuries.[52]

The conflict between the active and the contemplative life was especially pronounced for women religious. Since Church law prescribed the cloistered contemplative model as the only valid one for women, the seventeenth- and nineteenth-century communities whose members wished to serve in more active ways were subjected to intense pressures to add a full monastic program of prayer to their primary ministry in the classroom or hospital ward.[53] The strain of attempting to meet the requirements of both contemplation and action was a severe liability for many women's communities.

Other Discrepancies

In addition to the basic contemplation/action conundrum, religious orders discovered other inconsistencies in their ideological frames. Benedictine monks often had to make a basic choice between their emphasis on prayer and the practice of monastic poverty. On the one hand, "if monasteries acquired significant wealth, more monks could dedicate more time to performing the Divine Office."[54] On the other hand, such wealth often contributed to laxity and a fall from the contemplative spirit. Other groups, such as the thirteenth-century Dominicans and the seventeenth-century Jesuits, began to experience internal dissension over the relative importance of theological study and affective mysticism.[55] The practical difficulties of combining begging with preaching and study also bedeviled the mendicants. "How could the friars preach and administer the sacraments if they possessed no churches? How could preachers and priests be educated for their task if they had no books and no rooms in which to study? And how could any of these essentials be acquired without funds?"[56] The Dominicans soon modified their practice of poverty in order to meet the demands of teaching and preaching.

Disputes might also arise within a community over the *degree* of poverty, asceticism, or common life that should be expected of the members. The Franciscans experienced several divisive schisms throughout their history over the practice of poverty, and the Carmelites often split over the practice of asceticism. The fifteenth-century Dominicans also "engaged in constant internal struggles" over poverty.[57] At times, too, excessive zeal in the practice of poverty also caused scandal among the laity and opposition from the clergy. Both the seventeenth-century French and the nineteenth-century Irish congregations felt the strain between those values and practices thought essential to poverty and the middle-class respectability esteemed by the surrounding culture.[58] Many of these groups, therefore, redefined poverty in ways that were less repugnant to secular society.

We can see from these examples that the ideological frames that underlay each version of Roman Catholic virtuoso spirituality were not always internally consistent. Nor, in some cases, were they capable of being realized in real-life situations without adaptation and compromise. Divisions and difficulties frequently resulted, however, when the communities attempted to respond to these discrepancies by modifying their practices, their charisms, or even the underlying ideological frames for their mode of religious life. As chapters 9 and 10 will indicate, this creative ferment led sometimes to adaptation and ideological renewal, and sometimes to destructive infighting and the dilution of the original charism, which caused the order to fall into decay.

These adaptations of an order's ideological frame did not happen in a vacuum. Many actors, both within the order and in its surrounding environment, were interested in the outcome. In the following chapter, we will explore how the support of such actors—their money, their patronage, their literary or speaking talents—could be mobilized to assure the development and eventual hegemony of a particular variant of ideological frame for religious virtuosity.

Chapter 9

Determinants of Ideological Change: Internal and External Factors

As several social movement researchers have shown, a movement organization's particular ideology could be a powerful recruitment incentive, as powerful as the various other material and political motivations that had encouraged members to join—and nonmembers to support—the movement.[1] A movement organization's ideological frame also determined which opportunities for growth and expansion its members were able to seize, and which they were liable to neglect or ignore.[2] The exact configuration of a religious order's ideology was thus an important causal factor in its success or failure.

But ideological systems cannot be analyzed solely as independent variables, as necessary resources affecting the development of a religious order. Virtuoso ideologies were also *dependent* variables: Their component ideas, rituals, myths, and symbols were contingent upon the success of the orders—or of the factions within an order—that favored them. The activities of interested outsiders also affected the form and content of a religious community's ideology. Finally, the virtuoso ideology was shaped by the larger ideological frames—both ecclesiastical and secular—of which it was a component part. The ascendency of a given articulation of religious virtuosity, therefore, was not predetermined. It was the result of a series of interacting, hegemonic struggles within the order, as well as between the order and a wide variety of interested actors in its larger environment.[3] The analyst who wishes to understand the development of virtuoso spiritualities must explore the course and outcomes of these struggles.

External Struggles: The Political Opportunity Structure

According to Tarrow, several key aspects of the surrounding environment help determine whether or not a social movement group can mobilize itself and rise to a position of influence.[4] These aspects form the "political opportunity structure" that confronts the group. Newly founded religious communities have faced similar political opportunity structures—civil and ecclesiastical elites whose own interests and belief systems affected the kinds of ideological frameworks the orders were able to develop. Were elites open to the rise of a new type of religious order—and to the possibility of such a group supplanting the more ancient communities with which the elites may have had alliances? Was the order confronted by a united and organized elite or by a set of divided and contending factions that could be pitted against each other? What other belief systems—political, social and economic as well as theological—were current among the elites, and how did these beliefs and values mesh with the new virtuoso ideology? Was some ascendent group among the masses threatening the dominance of the old elite, and could the new religious community ally itself with this rising force? The process by which religious orders negotiated with the external power centers of their particular opportunity structure and crafted—or stumbled upon—an ideology of virtuoso spirituality acceptable to both parties is a fascinating study.

Adapting to Other Ideologies

The Role of Religious Virtuosity in Catholic Theologies

An important determinant of whether or not the Church's hierarchy would be likely to support a new group of religious virtuosi was how that community's ideological frame corresponded with the other aspects of Catholic theology, governance, and practice that the hierarchy espoused. Formulations of virtuoso spirituality often had to be adapted and conformed to some pre-existing belief or teaching of the Church before they could be accepted. With each subsequent change in the larger ecclesiastical and theological setting, the place or role of religious life within that setting might also have to change.

One obvious example of this process is the adaptation of religious communities to the rise in clerical power and prestige that occurred between the tenth and twelfth centuries.[5] The early monks and hermits had avoided any identification with the clergy and with the clerically controlled sacraments: It has been estimated that St. Anthony the Abbot went for years without participating in mass or receiving the Eucharist.[6] In earlier centuries, "there were very strict laws against priests becoming monks and monks becoming priests. When it did happen, the monk had to relinquish all authority in his home monastery and become a true parish priest. A priest who joined a monastery had to give up all Church office and could not say Mass except on the rarest occasions."[7] With the rise to prominence of the Eucharist in later medieval spirituality, however, this situation changed. Instead of asking a monk or a hermit to pray for the souls of their loved ones, the laity became increasingly solicitous that a mass be said for this purpose.[8] In response to the decline in donations for their prayers, the men's lay monastic model began to ordain some or all of their own members. This often entailed a radical departure from the communities' former ideological frame.[9]

Another shift in the Church's large-scale belief system that impacted upon ideologies of religious life was the gradual abandonment of the early medieval concept of satisfaction. It had not been thought enough merely to repent one's sins, one also had to make reparation to the aggrieved party (to God) by performing some penance for a given length of time. If unable to fast or to stand at the door of the church in sackcloth and ashes for several years, however, the penitent could substitute another meritorious act such as founding a monastery and requesting the monks' prayers.[10] In the early Middle Ages, many male and female monasteries were founded for this reason. Later, when the concept of satisfaction became less popular in the larger Church, the incentive to found or support groups of virtuosi for the sole purpose of underwriting their prayers was lost. Religious orders had to revise their ideological frame to incorporate new legitimating reasons for their existence and support.

Church teachings on the role of women and on their relative fitness for religious life obviously had an effect on communities. Opinions regarding women's capacity for true religious virtuosity waxed and waned in the larger Church. At times, contradictory beliefs might even coexist in the same era. Bynum has stated, for example, that the twelfth and thirteenth centuries experienced a "feminization" of religion such that the major models of lay spirituality were all female.[11] On the other hand, a simultaneously prevalent counterbelief held that women were basically carnal and sources of temptation to men. The women had to adapt various elements of their ideological frame in order to reconcile these two somewhat contradictory beliefs.[12]

The opinion that women were sources of temptation and unsuited for virtuoso spirituality persisted into the nineteenth and twentieth centuries. Even when they were not considered completely unsuited for religious life, women were still assumed to be childlike and mentally inferior: "As late as 1931, spiritual directors of women's communities were warned that their charges were emotional beings rather than rational ones, distinguishing the essential from the accidental only with difficulty. Furthermore, it was asserted that they lacked prudence, were shortsighted, and were apt to develop idiosyncracies."[13] Such beliefs obviously affected the kind of virtuoso spirituality the women were permitted to practice. Nevertheless, by not totally closing off the prospect of religous virtuosity, Catholicism offered women a potentially wider scope of religious roles than was available in Protestantism.[14]

In addition to beliefs concerning the superiority of the clergy, satisfaction/reparation for sins, and the proper role of women, still other doctrines existing within the larger theological corpus of Roman Catholicism could influence whatever varieties of religious life were current at the time. Among these were the redefinitions of medieval Christianity that re-emphasized the obligation to love one's neighbor, the revival of biblical study in the fourteenth century, and the rise of Jansenist popular spirituality in eighteenth- and nineteenth-century France.[15] Another extremely important belief was whether salvation was considered possible for those outside Catholicism. Beliefs that heretics—whether third-century Gnostic, twelfth-century Albigensian, or nineteenth-century Protestant— would literally burn in hell for their heresy gave an added spur to the foundation of many religious communities. Every pagan Indian who was converted, every Catholic orphan who was saved from the clutches of Protestant social workers were souls saved from eternal damnation. The noble and exciting work of saving souls was profoundly attractive to devout Catholics, who flocked to join those religious communites that specialized in it.[16] Since bishops and priests also believed that non-Catholics were eternally damned, they were eager to lend their support to new groups that offered prospects of rescuing them. As Bishop John Carroll wrote: "Terrifying is the idea of a young woman being seated down in a hotbed of presbyterianism. . . . No worldly advantage can make compensation" for this mortal danger to her soul.[17] In 1850, U.S. bishops denounced the country's public schools as "both heretical and infidel," and began their push for the foundation of Catholic schools, run by religious orders, where the souls of the faithful would be preserved.[18] Solicitude for the preservation of the faith of Catholics and for the salvation of heathens and heretics was thus a powerful incentive for the bishops to support the foundation of religious communities, and supplemented the political and career benefits that such foundations might also bring them. As chapter 14 will point out, the disappearance of this belief after the mid-twentieth century removed a key motivation for the hierarchy to support religious life.

The Influence of Other Theological Systems

Despite their conviction that individuals seduced by nonorthodox doctrines would forfeit their immortal souls, however, groups of Catholic religious virtuosi often adopted elements of the heretics' teachings into their own ideological frames. The equality offered to women by groups as diverse as the third-century Gnostics, the medieval Albigensians, and some of the sixteenth-century Protestant sects may have spurred the development of new forms of female virtuoso spirituality within Catholicism.[19] The Franciscans borrowed key aspects of mendicant spirituality from the Waldensians and Humiliati; St. Dominic legislated mendicant poverty for his order at least partly because of Cathar austerities.[20] Later, the Protestant emphasis on scripture study, on preaching the Word, and on the individual Christian's responsibility to make an informed assent to his or her faith had a formative impact on the development of the Jesuits, the seventeenth-century Dominicans, and the French filles seculieres. Heretical ideologies could not always be borrowed by religious virtuosi, however. Extremely strong and successful movements such as Protestantism often catalyzed a "siege mentality" in Catholicism that rendered the ecclesiastical authorities suspicious of and resistent to *any* changes. At such times, it was quite difficult for the religious communities whose new ideological frame incorporated suspect "heretical" borrowings to win ecclesiastical approval for their lifestyle.[21]

The above examples are only a sample of the wide variety of theological beliefs and devotional practices which, when current in Catholicism or in other surrounding religions, could have a profound impact upon the types of Catholic religious virtuosity permitted to develop. Communities whose virtuoso spirituality emphasized contemplation in a Church that valued pastoral service, or personal lay asceticism during the ascendancy of the clerically controlled Eucharist, had either to modify their ideological frames or else to face decline and extinction. Still another source of symbols, beliefs, and values that might impact upon an order's ideology, however, was the surrounding secular environment. And the Church's officials might or might not approve of these secular influences.

The Influence of Secular Culture

As several social movement theorists have pointed out, ideological frames are developed and articulated in the context of larger cultural systems. These systems supplied much of the vocabulary and the underlying assumptions with which the virtuosi constructed their own view of the world.[22] And the beliefs, values, and practices current in the surrounding society, by subtly affecting the ways that religious orders lived their virtuoso spirituality in daily life, thus gradually altered their very ideological frame itself.

Several examples, among the many that could be cited, give evidence of this. Religious orders have often duplicated the class structures of the surrounding society. A dual membership—choir and lay—was first adopted on a widespread basis by the twelfth-century Cistercians, as part of their revival of Benedictine manual labor. Gradually, the "ecclesiastical tradition of an inferior class of religious in male and female congregations" arose, even in those religious orders whose ideological frames held no place for them.[23] Thus, the nineteenth- and early twentieth-century Jesuits had a cadre of brothers to do maintenance and cooking in their houses.[24] The nineteenth-century Irish and French congregations also contained lay sisters with second-class status, who wore a different style of habit, were prohibited from voting in community elections and did most of the menial labor. "The reason for having lay sisters was understood by many to have been that servants were essential and that it would have been both harmful to convent discipline and unfair to these servants not to give them the opportunity of taking vows."[25] The class distinction among their membership also served to make the teaching sisters more "respectable" in the eyes of the larger Catholic and Protestant society of seventeenth- and nineteenth-century Europe, and reflected the traditional undervaluation of the cooking, cleaning and sewing work done by women.[26] The Victorian assumption that only "ladies" could properly uplift the poor meant that the sister-teachers and sister-social workers in nineteenth century European congregations had to affirm their middle-class status—which included the use of servant-sisters.

In the American environment, however, with its professed ideals of equality, such class distinctions among the sisters were difficult to maintain. American-born religious even objected to any inegalitarian treatment of hired employees, as Mother Theodore Guerin of the Sisters of Providence in Indiana soon discovered:

> I am not sure whether I told you of the insupportable pride of the Americans. When dinner time came, there was my washerwoman sitting at table with us. I was so indiscreet as to say it would be better for her not to take her dinner with the community. I wish you could have seen the change in the countenances of our American postulants! . . . The mere name of "servant" makes them revolt, and they throw down whatever they have in their hands and start off at once.[27]

If unequal treatment for nonmember employees was difficult for American sisters to accept, the European orders had an even greater difficulty reconciling them to the idea of lay sisters. Such class distinctions were considered un-American by many of the laity and clergy, and there is evidence that potential entrants were put off from entering the communities which had retained these "foreign" practices.[28] Byrne cites several archival entries among the Sisters of St. Joseph that indicate "a rising tide of dissatisfaction with class distinction in the communities as the [nineteenth] century progressed" and as the sisters became more assimilated to American culture:

> Mother Mary John Kieran's diary (1875): "All the professed sisters and novices voted [for the congregation's officers]. All the lay sisters were in a very bad humor all day."
>
> Another American superior (1888): "You know our first lay sister . . . became insane on the subject of her [distinctive] habit and they all hate the [lay sisters'] cap."
>
> In Savannah, Georgia, (1868): "No one wants to be a lay sister."
>
> Also in 1868: "It was feared we should be criticized [for having lay sisters], we are in a country that esteems equality so much."[29]

Gradually, some American branches of European congregations simply dropped the idea of two classes of sisters. Other groups campaigned for decades before finally being allowed to do so. In their 1880 constitution, the formerly German Benedictine sisters of Pennsylvania made no mention of a choir/lay distinction and explicitly stated that all professed sisters would be eligible to participate in the order's chapter. The Wisconsin Dominican sisters, forced by their English male superiors to establish a lay/choir division in 1880, succeeded in abolishing it six years later.[30]

Other aspects of American culture also affected the development of religious life in this country. American ideals of fair play, individualism, independence, and the right to confront one's accusers in a dispute were taken for granted by the women entering the first religious congregations, and led to conflict between the sisters and their superiors—whether the clergy or the European motherhouses—if the latter attempted to disregard them.[31] Still another instance of the influence of secular cultural assumptions on religious life was in the American "ideal of true womanhood." Possibly in order to defend the respectability of Catholicism in the eyes of American Protestants (who looked upon celibate females in convents with great suspicion), nineteenth-century Catholic writers—all male clerics— "defined a feminine ideal that in most essentials was virtually indistinguishable from that of mainstream Protestantism."[32] This ideal was also applied to nuns, whose roles as teachers and nurses were considered "maternity of the spirit." Nuns were expected to be mirrors par excellence of the feminine virtues of self-effacement and submission to authority, and were also required to perform household tasks for priests:

When Father Edward Sorin, the founder of Notre Dame, solicited nuns to come to Indiana to conduct a girls' academy, he took it for granted that they would "look after the laundry and infirmary" of the priests and [male] students—even though the nuns might have to walk six miles [to do so].[33]

Additional instances of societal influence on the ideological elements of religous virtuosity can be cited for other centuries.[34] The development of the early eremitical life was shaped by the "fertile intellectual seedbed" of the Alexandrian Church, with its roots in Platonic philosophical schools. Once the Protestant Reformation had destroyed the Germanic provinces of their order, the sixteenth-century Dominicans lost their former internationalist outlook and became more Latinized. The seventeenth-century French communities were influenced by contemporary Humanist philosophers, who exalted socially useful work and downplayed the supernatural services religious communities had been valued for in previous centuries. The rising nationalism in secular society affected the seventeenth-century Dominicans, whose various provinces began refusing to cooperate with each other in joint ministry endeavors. The nineteenth-century Irish famine and the subsequent changes in inheritance rules resulted in a "cult of male celibacy," which discouraged marriage among Irish males (and, in a "cultural afterlife," among Irish-*American* males), and encouraged large numbers of applicants to the priesthood and religious life. Men in Italy, Spain, and France, where such demographic and cultural conditions did not apply, most emphatically did not idealize celibacy. Vocations among men in these countries were few, and the adherence to their vows among those who did enter was an object of considerable skepticism among the laity. The beliefs and values current in the surrounding culture(s) thus caused corresponding alterations in the ideological frames of religious orders.

The Battleground of Cultural Struggle

Another way in which the larger secular culture might impact upon the ideological frameworks for religious virtuosity was in the opposition that sometimes arose among ecclesiastical officials against it. For example, European church leaders were appalled by the vehement anticlericalism of both the Enlightenment's and the Revolution's intellectuals, and by the rapid growth of nineteenth-century rationalism that attacked "superstitious" church doctrines.[35] In response to these attacks, Catholic traditionalists such as Joseph de Maistre (1753–1821) bagan to argue that only by returning to the absolute authority of the pope could Europe hope to recover from its moral chaos and political devastation.[36] The papacy could and should involve itself in the affairs of temporal governments, de Maistre contended, in order to see that true religion was given primacy over the errors of heretics and atheists.

The results of this conflict for religious communities were several. First of all, repugnance for the antireligious excesses of the Revolution—as well as those of 1830 and 1848—led many French orders to emigrate to the western United States, which they idealized as a pristine wilderness of Indians waiting to be converted and of French-descended settlers longing for the sacraments.[37] In the wilds of Kentucky, Indiana, or Missouri, a new, pure Catholic society could be constructed, uncontaminated by decadent and atheistic European beliefs. The fact that this picture of America had little foundation in reality did not deter communities from sending their members there, nor missionary societies from supporting the endeavor. Many of the earliest teaching communities of sisters in the United States thus had French origins, and French émigré clergy or French bishops wrote their rules. This profoundly influenced the spirituality of these congregations, and provided the base from which their subsequent Americanization had to proceed.

Later, the Vatican's repudiation of Modernism and secular thought affected American religious communities in other, less beneficial ways. As early as 1832, Pope Gregory XVI had publicly condemned such revolutionary doctrines as the separation of Church and State, freedom of the press, and freedom of religion. These were taken-for-granted practices in the United States, however, which contributed to the suspicion among many in the hierarchy that "true" Catholicism was antithetical to the American way of life.[38] The efforts of some American bishops to attempt an integration of American customs with Catholicism came into conflict with an opposing faction, which wanted to protect the newly arrived and uneducated Catholic immigrants from "the wolves of the world."[39] Religious communities could get caught, sometimes disastrously so, in the crossfire.[40]

Meanwhile, in the European church, a sense of siege and a "belligerent antimodernism" had resulted in an "intellectual stasis" that was intensely suspicious of new ideas or lifestyles.[41] The writings of St. Thomas Aquinas were revived and anointed the only true basis for theological speculation. "Neoscholastic manuals were written for seminarians, and so not surprisingly neoscholasticism became a clerical preserve, its method a kind of priestly craft. . . . Seminaries did not encourage research or debate or even much curiosity. Students learned their philosophical and theological lessons mostly by rote, the way law students memorized precedents. Seminary professors seldom pressed their students, nor indeed were they much pressed themselves, to go beyond what the manuals contained."[42] All of the teachers who would be responsible for the intellectual formation of religious order seminarians were required to obtain their own degrees in Rome, studying the approved theological line. Once returned and teaching in their order's seminaries, their lectures and writings often came under surveillance by "spies for orthodoxy," enlisted to insure that they did not subsequently deviate from the official teachings.[43]

The prevailing suspicion of speculative thought had a profound impact upon the ideological frames of religious orders. Even the Dominicans and Jesuits, who had once made study and critical thinking an integral part of their charisms, were affected. For generations of novices in the nineteenth and twentieth centuries, spiritual formation came to mean the memorization of a completed corpus of doctrine, closed to any attempts at further elaboration or refinement.[44] This was a great contrast to the way the early mendicants, for example, had originally approached study and scholarship—as an attempt to construct a completely new theology that would integrate the practices of the burgeoning medieval commercial system into the plan of salvation. It differed as well from the pragmatic syncretism of the early Jesuits, who saw no inherent problem with incorporating American Indian or Chinese beliefs into indigenous variants on Catholicism.[45] The nineteenth-century practices more resembled the monastic rote memorization the mendicant scholars and the Jesuits had originally repudiated.

The crystallization of Catholic theological and social thought into a unified package based upon opposition to the social, economic, and political conditions of nineteenth-century Europe offers a good example of how an ideological frame for religious virtuosity which, objectively speaking, was not necessarily dependent upon some larger schema of beliefs and values, could nevertheless become inextricably attached to it.[46] Rome's suspicion of the way the U.S. Church seemed to be diluting true doctrine culminated in 1898 with Leo XIII's condemnation of "Americanism."[47] Although the American bishops and religious orders contended that what Leo had condemned was a distorted and propagandized version that bore little resemblance to the true state of affairs in the U.S. church, the Americanist controversy made them extremely timid and cautious thereafter.[48] Whenever possible, the hierarchy and the religious orders concentrated on pragmatic projects and tried not to look at doctrine. This further weakened the distinctiveness of the orders' ideological frames.

The ideological frames of religous communities were thus profoundly influenced by the theological assumptions of the larger Catholic church, by "heretical" religious ideologies, and by the secular cultures within which they carried on their activities. Ecclesiastical elites, however, often had strong ideas about exactly which of these influences should be permitted in any accepted model of religious virtuosity. In order to secure the survival of their ideological frame, religious orders had to engage in often complex and intricate negotiations with the Church's hierarchy.

Enlisting the Support of the Church Hierarchy

Types of Ideological Support

Among the types of Church support chapter 5 listed as necessary for new religious communities, the first and most central was its ideological legitimation of their lifestyle and ministry. Without official legitimation, a religious order would find it difficult to attract potential donors and recruits, and might even have trouble persuading clients to use its services. But more important than its role in attracting material resources was the simple fact that ecclesiastical approval was what made the spread and hegemony of the ideology possible in the first place. By mobilizing their power and their far-flung communications networks, Church officials could help promulgate an order's ideological symbols and its basic assumptions about religious virtuosity's purpose in the world.[49]

One key way in which the Church could support a religious community's ideology was for an ecclesiastic to write the life of its founding saint. Athanasius, the bishop of Alexandria, wrote a biography of Anthony the Abbot shortly after that holy ascetic's death in 356. It was widely popular, resulting in a "flood of converts" to the eremitical life, and its depiction of Anthony's solitary struggles with his physical appetites and the demons of the desert greatly influenced how entire generations of subsequent virtuosi would view their own calling.[50] Similarly, it was Pope Gregory the Great's *Life* of St. Benedict that propelled the latter's Rule for monks to preeminence in the West, displacing former versions of monasticism.[51] The *Life* of Mary of Oignies, written by Bishop—and later Cardinal— Jacques de Vitry, greatly influenced the development of Beguine spirituality and was instrumental in the ascendency of the Nivelles-Oignies area as an early center of the movement.[52] Gocelin of St. Bertin, an eleventh-century Flemish monk, wrote lives of famous Anglo-Saxon abbesses that inspired many later nuns to imitate their spiritual and administrative prowess.[53] A number of medieval friars wrote lives of holy women such as Margaret of Cortona, Diana of Andalo, and Christina "The Marvellous," thus popularizing the idea of feminine mysticism as a special channel to the divine.

Church authorities could help spread a particular ideology of religious virtuosity in other ways besides writing the biography of some exemplary virtuoso. A third-century Christian bishop in Asia Minor named Methodius produced the *Symposium of the Ten Virgins*, which extolled the celibate life as superior to marriage. This piece, and other polemical writings by Church officials of the period, strengthened the assumption that virginity was *the* necessary component of virtuoso spirituality.[54] Another way in which the Church could put its stamp of approval on a new virtuoso ideology was for the pope to proclaim its practitioners saints.[55] Throughout the Middle Ages, for example, the proportion of female canonized saints rose, thus validating the model of spirituality these women practiced. Indeed, by the late Middle Ages, the *only* model for lay sanctity was female; all male saints were clerics.[56]

Still other activities by the clergy could help assure the survival of a new religious order—and, therefore, the hegemony of its particular ideological frame. Favorably disposed clerics such as Jacques de Vitry, Cardinal Hugolino, or Vincent de Paul might lobby the papal curia for their protégés.[57] Finally, Church officials could assure the hegemony of a particular ideological frame simply by mandating it for all religious communities, as Rome did in approving Cluny as the only model for monastic reform.[58]

Church support was useful when the new order experienced ideological competition from other religious communities. Competing models of religious virtuosity often advanced quite different definitions of what religious life was about and what behaviors it ought to entail. From their earliest foundations, for example, the monastic orders had opposed the excesses of unsupervised and wandering ascetics, who performed little useful labor and lived parasitically on the donations of the laity. St. Benedict had expressly condemned these "gyrovagues" in his Rule, and Benedictine monastic stability had been developed, at least in part, to curtail such behavior. To thirteenth-century monks, therefore, the preaching activities of the mendicant friars looked suspiciously like the very practices St. Benedict had inveighed against seven hundred years before. Admitting that itinerant preaching was a legitimate form of religious virtuosity would have struck at the very foundations of the monastic way of life.[59] Only by winning the explicit support of ecclesiastical authorities for their version of virtuoso spirituality were the medieval mendicants able to overcome the opposition of the older, more established monasteries. Similarly, many of the seventeenth-century French teaching congregations were opposed by communities following the older contemplative model. Only after they received ecclesiastical approval were these communities able to grow and function freely.[60]

Bargaining for Ideological Support

To enlist the support of the clergy or the hierarchy for their version of religious virtuosity, the participants in a new virtuoso lifestyle had to engage in a subtle process of negotiation.[61] Divisions within the ecclesiastical elite were noted and the members of this or that clerical faction apprised of how the new virtuoso ideology could enhance their side's position. Areas of weakness were exploited with promises of assistance.

Thus, even though the hegemonic establishment of *any* ideological frame-work for lay religious virtuosity posed at least an implicit challenge to the role and prestige of the clergy, active ecclesiastical support could still be enlisted by politically astute virtuosi.

The earliest example of this negotiation process was the acceptance of celibacy/virginity as an essential component of virtuoso spirituality. Several historians have pointed out that the earliest Church authorities were not at all receptive to having a separate caste of virgins in their midst.[62] Ignatius of Antioch (d. 110) "was the first of many moralists to criticize the chaste celibates for their pride and their tendency to boast that they were morally superior to the married bishops over them."[63] Clement of Alexandria (c. 180) spoke for the married clergy and laity in an attempt to keep "radical" celibate groups from taking control of the Church. If the celibate faction won, Clement feared, wealthy married Christians might become alienated and take their donations elsewhere.[64] The priests and bishops also feared the potentially disruptive power of consecrated virgins. "While female virgins held a special place in the community, they were the object of considerable fear and suspicion by the clergy, who could not look at them in their uncontrolled state without deep misgiving. The bishops, in particular, did not want them to join forces with virgin men to form a separate order of Christendom that might challenge their [the bishops'] superiority and authority."[65] This apprehension was justified: Once celibacy had been established as an essential part of virtuoso spirituality, the reputation of the lay men and women who had vowed virginity did come to outrank that of the married priesthood.[66] Eventually, celibacy was imposed upon the secular clergy, at least in part so that the priests could partake of the superior prestige of the monastic life. Early ecclesiastical authorities thus had every reason to oppose this new ideological element that so challenged their hegemony in the Church.

In order to win the approval of the ecclesiastical elites for this threatening ideological innovation, the early celibate virtuosi had to offer them compelling incentives and benefits. Some of these benefits were financial. Several historians have pointed out that competing sects such as the Gnostics and the Encratites were especially attractive to third- and fourth-century Christian women because they offered the tempting possibility of spiritual perfection and equality with men through the practice of sexual continence.[67] Church authorities did not want to lose these women, who controlled much wealth and property. But in order to retain them as members, ecclesiastical officials had to accept and validate their lifestyle. "We can only conclude," states McNamara, that the clergy's acceptance of virginity as a component of religious virtuosity "was the price of a settlement with a portion of [the Church's] membership numerous enough and influential enough to be worth such large concessions. The virgins, the widows, and their supporters imposed their ideology on the church as the price of their adherence to it."[68]

Another example of the ideological bargaining process was the development of a Eucharistic-centered mysticism in the virtuoso spirituality of the Beguines and the medieval women monastics. Church officials were profoundly ambivalent about female mysticism—with good reason. The unmediated divine contact claimed by these mystics was a potential threat for the hierarchy, and a source of power and independence for the women who experienced it.[69] On the other hand, the ecstasies and visions of the medieval women mystics were affirming the real presence of Christ in the Eucharist, a doctrine the clergy had been attempting to define and promulgate since the tenth century. Increasing the centrality of the Eucharist strengthened the priest's power and prestige: In his hands, "God was incarnated as in the Virgin's womb."[70] But the new doctrine was much resisted, and a concerted clerical effort had been initiated to educate and convert the masses to it.[71] The most successful teaching tool in this campaign was the circulation of elaborate miracle stories that focused on the Eucharist. Most of these stories concerned the mystical experiences of female virtuosi: being given communion directly by Christ, living miraculously on the Eucharist alone, seeing a vision of Jesus in the host, and so on.[72] Thus, even though accepting the legitimacy of women's mysticism set up an alternative source of power in the church, the clergy supported it because its Eucharistic emphasis coincided with their own.[73]

At the same time as they stood to benefit from female mysticism, however, the clerics were careful to insure that the women's activities did not get out of hand. The result was an especially nuanced dialectic of power and submission on the part of both parties. Both secular and religious priests believed that women mystics had a privileged relationship with God that they themselves lacked. As a result, the women served as "spiritual masters for their confessors and directors and thereby . . . teachers of the spiritual life even in their own age."[74] Yet the same friars who so admired women mystics had the "operant ecclesiastical authority" over them, and could give or withhold grace from them by their provision or refusal of the sacraments.[75] The women "both dominate[d] their confessors as spiritual mothers and [clung] to them as vulnerable advisees, needful of a guarantee of othodoxy."[76]

Medieval women's mysticism performed other services useful to the clergy. Their pronouncements and the clergy-written stories of their lives were useful to deter heresy.[77] The general upsurge of religious enthusiasm sparked by the mystics helped arouse popular fervor for the crusades. The support of women mystics was also valuable to clergy engaged in factional disputes among themselves. Priests and bishops beset by hostile rivals could immeasurably strengthen their positions by enlisting the support of

these women. For example, Hildegard of Bingen's prophecies were frequently cited by secular priests in denouncing their Franciscan rivals.[78]
The bishop of Liege, newly installed in a diocese riven by factions, enlisted popular support by validating the visions of Juliana of Cornillon and
establishing the feast of Corpus Christi as she and her Dominican advisors
had requested.

This dialectic of support and opposition, of benefits offered and liabilities feared, profoundly influenced the type of virtuoso spirituality the
women mystics developed. For example, their clerical biographers were
fascinated by the bizarre and the miraculous aspects of the women's experiences, and emphasized these aspects in their writings.[79] Subsequent
generations of female virtuosi were influenced by the men's stories, and
interpreted their own experiences in similar terms. The friars saw the
women as liminal figures, marking the boundaries of clerical power without threatening it.[80] The women, in their turn, adopted a rhetoric of
weakness that masked their great influence.

Still another example of an attempt to enlist clerical support for ideological innovations in religious virtuosity was the issue of how rigidly
separated religious life ought to be from the secular world. The hierarchy
had, in general, opposed any blurring of boundaries between the secular
and the monastic, and had emphasized the superior dignity of the
cloister.[81] This was especially true for women's groups. As a result of this
ecclesiastical attitude, uncloistered communities were seen as slightly heretical, or at the very least as inferior to "real"—cloistered—religious
life.[82] The women in active communities were often influenced by this
belief, and many gradually adopted a variety of "superior" monastic practices that vitiated their founder's original aims.[83] The founders waged an
intense ideological war against this notion. According to Vincent de Paul,
for example:

> When a mistress of the Charity School is tempted to leave her work to
> enter a religious house, let her take care what she is doing. She is aban-
> doning a state that is more evangelical, more arduous, more poor, more
> despised in the world, for another more comfortable, more honorable,
> but which is useful only for herself . . . In wishing to shut herself into a
> monastery, she is like a cowardly soldier who wants always to be in gar-
> rison, never out marching on campaign. She is leaving the spiritual war
> which she joined for God and for Jesus, in order to rest and to live at
> ease, in a safe place, unconcerned for the interests and the glory of her
> King.[84]

Other founders felt it necessary to stipulate that, if their community ever
opted for cloister, it would forfeit all of its property. Still other communities self-consciously developed an alternative symbol system that ranked

their active ministry *above* other forms of religious virtuosity; for one seventeenth-century community, teaching was a holy activity, explicitly compared to the role of the priest at mass.[85]

Despite the intense ecclesiastical opposition to their "mixed" secular/ monastic lifestyle, groups of both male and female virtuosi were able to bargain, first for the toleration and later for the active approval, of including precisely such a lifestyle in their new ideological frame. The Jesuits, for example, offered the papacy a force with which to re-establish its authority over lands endangered by Protestantism—but at the price of accepting the very mixture of "lay" and "religious" practices it was currently condemning at the Council of Trent.[86] The benefits of the Jesuits' activities were sufficiently attractive that Rome accepted their unorthodox spirituality in 1540. At first, such a concession was only for male communities. Later, however, the activities of the seventeenth- and nineteenth-century women's congregations were so useful that the Church authorities eventually approved their lifestyle as well.

A final example of the bargaining process between religious communities and the hierarchy, and of the clergy's influence on the shaping of virtuoso ideologies, is the amount of adaptation the Church permitted to the European communities that had migrated to non-European settings such as the nineteenth-century United States. The bishops and priests were of several minds about how much, if any, inculturation was desirable for these groups.[87] On the one hand, many Church officials believed that American freedom and independence were "dangerous tendencies" and that "religious life could never join forces with [them] to form a new, vital and valid expression of that ancient institution."[88] On the other hand, *some* adaptations of religious life to American culture seemed desirable to many bishops, in order to improve the orders' usefulness and their chances for survival in a new environment.[89]

The question of how closely American congregations should conform to the European model was a source of contention and negotiation between the sisters and the European-born priests. The Kentucky Dominican sisters ran afoul of a Spanish Dominican priest in the 1820s. The cleric insisted that the women must be cloistered like European nuns and must dissolve their school, their only source of income. When they refused, he ordered them to disband and refused them access to the sacraments.[90] In contrast, Bishop John Carroll petitioned Rome for authority to dispense the contemplative Carmelite sisters in his diocese from their strict cloister so that they could operate a school—a radical departure from the European model. The Carmelites resisted the Americanizing pressures imposed by Carroll, preferring to conform to their European rule.

The conflicting pressures from the clergy and hierarchy were complicated by the general Americanization process that was occurring in all of
the U.S. congregations, as a natural result of their ever-increasing numbers of American-born novices.[91] The tendency of bishops to detach the
sisters in their dioceses from European motherhouses hastened this transformation. The sisters' participation as nurses in the American Civil War
also heightened their sense of identity as U.S. citizens. By the late nineteenth century, the now-Americanized older congregations experienced
additional conflicts when they interacted with more newly arrived immigrant clergy. The customs of the Sisters of Mercy "differed markedly from
those of the German School Sisters of Notre Dame, who were required to
ask permission of their Redemptorist director every time they stepped outside their convent walls."[92] The Redemptorists, scandalized by the more
independent Mercy sisters, reduced their salaries and complained that
they "lacked proper respect for priests."

As additional groups of Catholic immigrants arrived in the United
States, the question of Americanizing religious orders took on new and
controversial implications. For late-nineteenth-century immigrant groups,
the availability of schools operated by sisters from their own homeland in
their native German, Italian, French, or Polish was essential for keeping
their faith unsullied in a materialistic, Protestant American environment.
Lay immigrants' pressure over retaining their native language was what
had led to the establishment or importation of many congregations in the
first place. "In English you must count your dollars, but in German you
speak with your children, your confessor and your God."[93] Many second
generation Irish-American bishops, however, were embarrassed by the
"superstitious" folk beliefs and outlandish customs of the newer arrivals,
and wanted them to conform to middle-class American culture as quickly
as possible.[94] The sisters were often put in an uncomfortable middle position between the ethnic groups to whom they ministered and an unsym-
pathetic and assimilated Irish-American hierarchy who were less sanguine
about Catholic practices and values different from their own.[95]

Conclusions

The above issues are only a few examples of the ways in which Church
officials might interest themselves in the ideological frames of religious
virtuosi, and of how the virtuosi might bargain for ecclesiastical support.
Even a cursory reading of the histories of religious orders can yield many
other examples of ideological contention.[96] Medieval bishops objected to
begging as a component of mendicant spirituality, and tried to persuade
the friars to abandon the practice. The idea that the nonordained mendicants could preach and evangelize was basic to their ideological frame,

but was also a source of contention with the bishops. In these as in so many other issues, communities of virtuosi secured the support of the ecclesiastical hierarchy, either by offering resources or services the hierarchy desired, or by modifying their ideological frame along lines that the hierarchy favored.

These examples also show the importance of ideological hegemony, and why religious communities fought so among themselves. Once a particular ideological frame was established, it both outlined which issues could be contended and furnished the very vocabulary with which the struggle would be conducted. "The monastic life was the first to organize and define itself. It thus became 'exemplary.' Each new form of life was confronted with the same question: did it conform to the [monastic] model?"[97] Thus, subsequent groups such as the mendicants, whose ideological frame was quite different from that of the monastics, gradually adopted "the office recited in common, silence inside their houses and convents, the reading of spiritual books at meals . . . a distinctive habit, tonsure, etc."[98] Since an existing ideology could lure a later version from its original vision, and since a new ideology could twist and infiltrate a prior one, the adherents of each would feel obliged to resist the other. The support of the clergy and bishops was vital in this struggle for hegemony, and often for the very existence of the order itself.

Enlisting the Support of Secular Elites

Types of Ideological Support

While the support of the Church hierarchy for its new ideology of religious virtuosity was undoubtedly the most important resource for a religious community to secure, a group could also enhance its chances for hegemony by enlisting the support of secular elites. Such individuals often had—or could be persuaded to have—definite opinions about what kinds of activities were holy and proper for a religious virtuoso, and about what the purpose of virtuoso spirituality was in the larger scheme of things. At times when the hierarchy was less convinced of the value of a new virtuoso ideology, the active support of lay elites could substitute, at least in part, for the lack of clerical assistance.

To be sure, the lay elites did not support an order's ideological frame by writing hagiographies of its founder. Nor did they produce learned theological treatises on the superiority of this or that element of virtuoso spirituality. But the laity could and did make their own personal evaluations of the relative merits of various virtuoso lifestyles, and could support their preferred model with political and material resources. By bestowing these resources on some groups and withholding them from others, lay elites could help determine which ideological frame would prevail. In both the late Roman and the early medieval periods, for example, eremitic and monastic lifestyles were viewed by wealthy benefactors as superior to those of the ordained clergy, and the hermits, monks, and nuns who followed them were looked upon as spiritual athletes. "Many Christians, who engaged in their own limited ascetic practices on certain days, and many more who may never have made the effort to control their diet and to strengthen themselves as 'athletes' did, nevertheless admire those who achieved such discipline."[99] Similarly, many patrons considered the active, self-supporting lives of the thirteenth-century Beguines to be superior to those of cloistered nuns and gave them extensive financial support.[100] By comparison, at times when the laity considered the followers of some particular model of religious virtuosity to be useless burdens on society, their support dropped off and the fortunes of that particular virtuoso ideology waned.[101]

Lay patrons who were also civil rulers could support a virtuoso group's ideology in additional ways. Kings might simply decree that all religious orders within their realms must adopt a particular Rule or practice. Thus the late fourth-century emperor Valens declared the desert hermits idle parasites and demanded that they be forced to return to the cities and perform some useful service.[102] Later Eastern emperors such as Justinian, wishing to bring about some degree of conformity in monastic law, drew up detailed legislation regulating almost every aspect of religious life. In Western Europe, Charlemagne ordered all monasteries to conform to the Benedictine Rule, a circumstance that cemented the ascendancy of that particular form of monastic spirituality. The emperor Napoleon supported the nineteenth-century teaching congregations with both property and government funds, thus insuring their model's hegemony over that of the French contemplative orders.

Bargaining for Ideological Support

As in their dealings with the hierarchy, religious orders were able to secure the ideological support of lay elites by offering them specific material and spiritual benefits in return. Schulenberg points out that founding a monastery composed of one's own relatives was one way the nobility of the early Middle Ages could retain their wealth within their own family.[103] For social-climbing *dévots* of seventeenth-century France, sponsoring a teaching congregation was a way of emulating the activities of the upper class. In addition to such material or status benefits, lay elites might also be interested in virtuoso spiritualities for other reasons. One of the duties of medieval monks and nuns, for example, was to pray for the well-being and stability of the kingdom. Rulers were thus strongly concerned that monasteries be well-regulated and not filled with lax members, whose prayers would presumedly be less efficacious.[104] Noble lay patrons, too, were concerned that the members of the monasteries they had founded were "earning their keep" by praying fervently and effectively for their benefactors' souls. Both rulers and the wealthy nobility, therefore, had a deep interest in the kind of virtuoso spirituality practiced by relgious orders, and frequently intervened to assure themselves that it was being performed correctly. A similar example of lay influence on virtuoso spirituality occurred in nineteenth-century America. Lay immigrants prized their particular ethnic variant of Catholicism, and exerted pressure on religious orders to retain and practice it.

At times, some specific element of the new framework's sprituality would be especially appealing to lay patrons, and would induce them to increase their support. Rubin mentions the attraction of the Cistercians' more affective prayer style, while Little cites the mendicants' development of a coherent moral theology to meet the needs of the new merchant class.[105] Still another attraction of many groups was the opportunity they offered for the laity to become auxiliary members through participation in Third Orders and spiritual fraternities.[106] Such elements rendered some versions of religious virtuosity far more attractive than others in the eyes of potential lay patrons, who then redirected their support toward the version they favored.

Religious virtuosi were also not above using political lobbying to secure the support of lay elites for their particular ideology. Several groups benefitted by being linked to entire networks of potential patrons, as Taylor has so painstakingly demonstrated for the seventeenth-century French congregations.[107] In general, therefore, the orders interacted with lay elites as they did with their ecclesiastical ones: by bargaining for their ideological support.

Internal Struggles for Ideological Hegemony

As chapter 8 has pointed out, the ideological frames of many religious orders contained internal inconsistencies and areas of confusion. Practically every Roman Catholic religious community that has existed for any length of time has experienced significant internal dissention over these discrepancies. The male Carmelites encountered much resistence among their members when they attempted to replace their eremitical frame with a mendicant one; the prior general of the order, Nicholas Gallicus, resigned in protest over the issue in 1271.[108] The Franciscans underwent several schisms over whether they should (or could) adhere to the pristine rule of

St. Francis. Some of the resulting factions, such as the Spirituals, were ultimately condemned as heretics because of their insistence on rigid poverty.[109] This, however, did not discourage later offshoots such as the Observants and the Capuchins from insisting the same thing. The Carthusians debated whether their members might undertake pastoral work and evangelization, or whether they should continue only to "preach with their hands" by copying manuscripts.[110] In the first one hundred years after their founding, the Jesuits developed two distinct strains of spirituality: one "cautious and soberly ascetical," suspicious of contemplation and given to methodical and moralistic styles of prayer, and the other "expansive and syncretistic," which valued affective mysticism.[111] The former ultimately won out over the latter. Even among nineteenth-century teaching congregations, which generally had not developed distinct charisms, ideological disagreements might arise over the precise mixture of ministerial activity and contemplation:

> As the young community [of Sisters of Mercy] developed, two visions of religious life grew side by side, one emphasizing contemplative spirituality and one the active life. Ascetical practices common to cloistered communities appealed to Mary Anne Doyle's sense of religious devotion; Catherine [McAuley] grasped and taught the asceticism of compassionate service, discouraging not only those practices which would render sisters "incapable of the duties of the institute," but any which would "diminish the quality of their service."[112]

The medieval canons and the seventeenth-century French sisters similarly vacillated between the monastic and the apostolic life, with fervent partisans on either side.[113]

Internal Resources in the Struggle for Ideological Hegemony

In the struggle to establish the supremacy of its version of virtuoso spirituality, each faction within an order attempted to avail itself of a number of valuable resources. One of these was a network through which like-minded recruits could be enlisted. For example, a key determinant in the ascendency of the "intellectual" faction in both the Franciscans and the Dominicans was undoubtedly these groups' access to students in the medieval universities. The mendicant scholars could enlist larger numbers of like-minded recruits than their wandering evangelist brethren could. The Jesuits benefitted from a similar source of recruitment for their new virtuoso ideology in the sixteenth century, as did the seventeenth-century teaching congregations.[114]

Another helpful resource was the literary and speaking skills of the new ideological faction's adherents. The writings of Origen, which emphasized the perfectability of the human soul through ascetical practices, are credited with playing a major role in the development of the eremitical model of religious life within the early Church.[115] Bernard of Clairveaux's published sermons had a similarly profound influence in turning Cistercian spirituality away from the study and ritual of Cluny and toward affective mysticism. St. Bonaventure's official biography of St. Francis profoundly influenced how his brother Franciscans viewed their founder, especially since Bonaventure had all other biographical versions destroyed.[116] Similarly, Hugh of St. Victor's commentary on the Rule of St. Augustine was accepted as official by other Augustinian canons. The translation into French of the mystical writings of St. Teresa of Avila and, twenty years later, of St. John of the Cross, sparked a wave of entrances into contemplative religious life among French women. To the extent that a new model of religious virtuosity possessed such apologists among its adherents, therefore, its hegemony over competing models would be facilitated.

It is important to note that, simply because a particular faction within a religious order possessed a talented spokesperson or a set of influential patrons, this did not necessarily insure that their vision would be adopted in toto. As Tarrow and others have pointed out, the leaders of a social movement group often cannot control how the rest of the members will adapt or change their ideological frame.[117] The particular amalgam of elements that ultimately emerged from the negotiation process may have been quite different from what any of the contending factions, or their leaders, had envisioned.

It is also important to note that not all splits in religious communites were the results of ideological differences. This is especially true of nineteenth-century women's congregations, for whom the virtuoso ideology was largely imitative and peripheral. While some nineteenth-century congregations did experience ideological tensions, they were more likely to subdivide because of ethnic antagonism, or because the bishops of their various dioceses had summarily detached them from each other, or because of disagreements over what kind of ministry the community was to engage in.[118] After such divisions, however, the congregations may have gone on to develop differences in their ideological frames.

Conclusions

The ascendency of a given ideological variant for religious virtuosity was never foreordained. As contending factions within and outside religious communities negotiated and bargained with each other, as they instigated or withstood persecution and ostracism, their definition of who religious virtuosi were and what purpose they served often underwent profound alterations. Ascetic practices and prayer forms rose in popularity, then waned and were discarded. In the process, a community might tear itself apart or be suppressed by a hostile king or bishop. New variants might lure away recruits or attract the financial support of a fickle laity. The fortunes of religious communities were thus intimately connected with the fortunes of their virtuoso ideologies.

But even those communities whose ideologies remained unchanged were not immune to the vicissitudes of the outside world, or to the danger of dissolution. The following chapters will explore the various causes, internal and external, that eventually resulted in the decline of even the most vigorous and widely accepted religious community.

Part Three

Perspectives on Movement
Decay: Decline Periods of
Religious Orders, 400–1800

Chapter 10

Previous Decline Periods in Religious Orders: Social Movement Perspectives

It is a common observation among students of collective action that social movements—including religious social movements—display cyclic rhythms of mobilization and demobilization.[1] "There are historical periods characterized by social movement, and there are periods of institutionalization and absorption, when movements more or less disappear as their ideas are incorporated to re-form established patterns or are discarded."[2] This implies that, insofar as religious orders are organizational manifestations of virtuoso movements, their periods of explosive growth would typically be followed by decline and stagnation—times when few new communities were founded and when existing groups shrank in size or even became extinct.

This is, in fact, the case. Medieval monastic life declined in the eighth and ninth centuries after its initial expansion period, and again in the late twelfth and thirteenth centuries after the revivals of Cluny and Citeaux.[3] The mendicant friars diminished in numbers and fervor during the fourteenth century, were revitalized, and declined again in the fifteenth.[4] So bad had the reputation and morale of these orders become by the early sixteenth century that "more than once it was proposed to the Holy See that all but four orders of men, and almost all orders of women, be suppressed."[5] The explosion of new orders in sixteenth- and seventeenth- century Europe was followed by a retrenchment in the eighteenth century. Existing institutions produced relatively few visionary leaders, vocations declined, and the entire Church suffered "a certain chilling of its life of faith."[6]

At times, a cycle might be specific to a given order or a given location; religious life might be decaying in one country even as it was being revitalized in another. "From the mid-thirteenth century onwards, there was a dearth of founders and saints in England. No new orders like the Servites, no new branches like the [fourteenth and fifteenth century] Minims or the Carmelite nuns . . . appeared; no saint arose such as the Catherines of Siena or Genoa, no mystics like Suso or Ruysbroeck, no preachers like Bernardine, Antoninus or John Capistran. . . . The later monastic reforms . . . did not penetrate to this country. The old machinery still ran on, though the rhythm was gradually slackening."[7] At other times, the decline cycle might spread beyond an individual order or locality to affect all religious communities. In any case, however, social movement cycles of growth and decline do appear to have occurred in Roman Catholic religious life.

While social movement theories agree on the *existence* of social movement cycles, they are less clear on the reasons *why* such cycles occur. As Tarrow puts it: "We know much more about what triggers a cycle of mobilization than we do about the factors that lead to its decline."[8] Extrapolating from the research and theories covering social movement growth, some have hypothesized that movement declines are related to an increasing scarcity of key resources, or to the reluctance of outside elites to provide their previous levels of support.[9] Others have cited the discrediting of the movement's ideological frame.[10] The present chapter will attempt to develop these hypotheses for social movement decay, and to explore where and how they might apply to religious orders.

Resource Deprivation and the Decline of Religious Communities

The most obvious explanation for the decline of religious communities would be that environmental changes had deprived them of ready access to key resources. Religious orders had thrived because they enjoyed a dependable source of fresh and enthusiastic recruits and because ecclesiastical and civil elites had found it expedient to provide them with material, political, or spiritual support. Anything, therefore, that made men and women less willing or able to join religious life, anything that alienated or disenchanted their former patrons, could threaten a community's very existence. On a more basic level, religious orders needed the wherewithal to secure food and shelter for their current members. They were thus also vulnerable to economic cycles and to any technological, social, or ideological developments that might reduce the demand for their services.

The Declining Number of Recruits: Sources and Results

A wide variety of outside forces might contribute to the diminishing number of entrants to religious communities during their periods of decay. Actual population decline due to the Black Death, the Hundred Years' War, or the Viking invasions meant that fewer young women and, especially, fewer young men were available for recruitment.[11] The economic or social conditions that had motivated families to dedicate a son or daughter to religious life during one period might later change, and parents would become correspondingly adverse to fostering vocations in their children. Similar social or economic changes might render widows reluctant to enter a monastery after the death of their husbands or might make their kin hostile to the idea. Such familial reluctance has been documented for the periods of monastic decline in the Middle Ages, as well as for eighteenth-century France.[12] Existing orders might also find that their potential recruits were being siphoned off by newer religious groups or even by secular movements. The rising mendicant orders, for example, drew the most fervent thirteenth-century youth into their own ranks, to the detriment of monastic vocations.[13] Still later, the popularity of secular fields of study and the decline of theology and philosophy in the university schools meant that the fifteenth-century mendicants, whose domination of intellectual life had attracted so many promising students to their ranks in previous centuries, now saw the brightest young men seek careers outside the Church.[14]

The declining recruitment of monks, nuns, and friars had several undesirable effects. Many religious orders had a large number of institutions—monastic houses, schools, priories, and the like—which their decreased membership was unable to fill, or even to maintain properly.[15] Financially precarious houses with only a few members were vulnerable to abuses, whether in the Middle Ages or in later periods. Some orders, such as the fourteenth-century Dominicans, attempted to replenish their membership by initiating "a lamentably undiscriminating recruiting policy."[16] The lax members thus admitted only exacerbated the community's difficulties.

Financial Difficulties

Orders might also decline due to their increasing inability to secure the necessities of life. Such economic difficulties could arise from a number of sources. Inflation might erode the value of monastic revenues, a circumstance that historians document for women's groups in both the Middle Ages and late-seventeenth-century France.[17] Several medieval orders, such as the eleventh-century Cluniac monasteries and the fourteenth-century Benedictines, succumbed to financial mismanagement, most notably the temptation "to maintain institutional grandeur and domestic living standards at a time of falling real income."[18] However, while financial difficulties were often a source of communal decline, they were not universally a factor. Knowles presents persuasive evidence that sixteenth-century English men's monasteries, at least, were not as insolvent as they have been portrayed by their Reformation critics.[19]

Women's orders, however, were notably poorer than men's, in part because they were required to observe a more rigid cloister than was imposed on the monks. Medieval women's monasteries, therefore, could rarely be self-sufficient.[20] In later time periods, the imposition of cloister forced the women to confine their recruitment to the aristocracy, a tactic that drastically limited the number of possible entrants. The women's financial situation was also affected by the rise of a more Eucharistic-centered and clerically dominated mentality after the twelfth century, which meant that lay donations tended to flow more to the priests who could provide these essential rituals. "The lay donor who endowed a monastery hoped to reap spiritual benefits from his gift, and the most highly valued of these was one that women could not provide: women could not celebrate mass."[21] All the nuns could do for their petitioners was to say private prayers. With the increasing popularity of the rosary and other lay devotions in the later Middle Ages, wealthy men and women may have felt that their own prayers were just as good as those of the nuns. In addition, the women's religious communities had to pay stipends to the clergy who heard their confessions and said masses for their dead sisters—spiritual services that, in former times, had not been thought necessary.[22] Other good causes, such as evangelization, education, or social work, competed with the monasteries for the faithful's donations. After the beginning of the thirteenth century, monastics found it increasingly difficult to compete with the "highly visible and fashionable friars" for lay support.[23] In seventeenth-century France, popular opinion increasingly esteemed the services performed by the *filles seculieres* over the prayers of cloistered nuns, and lay donations reflected this change.[24]

Changes in spirituality affected the monasteries' financial well-being in other ways. The increased amount of time that eleventh-century male religious were expected to spend in prayer reduced the time left for revenue-producing activities.[25] Later spirituality also de-emphasized giving money to shrines; whereas in the twelfth and thirteenth centuries shrine offerings had been an important part of monastic revenue, by the sixteenth century this source had become insignificant.

Financial difficulties obviously made it difficult for religious communities to provide food, clothing, and shelter for their current members.

But there were additional adverse effects as well. Many orders were forced to restrict the number of new entrants because they could not provide for them. "It was [their] chronic financial problems, rather than a shortage of postulants, that imposed limits upon the number of recruits entering the greater Benedictine establishments."[26] Once orders ceased being self-sufficient, they often began to be regarded as parasites on society.[27] Civil authorities might then become less willing to allow lay donors to will property to these communities. As a result, an order's financial difficulties helped sink it more and more deeply into a state of decline: The fewer resources it had, the less able it was both to recruit new members and to attract additional donations.

Loss of Other External Support

In addition to ceasing their provision of financial support, ecclesiastical and civil actors might refuse to provide the other resources needed by a community. Religious order and diocesan priests, always reluctant to dissipate their energies in providing spiritual services for nuns, became even more adverse to doing so in the thirteenth and fourteenth centuries.[28] The new male mendicant orders, especially, contended that the spiritual care of nuns was a distraction from their real work of lay evangelization. The deprivation of spiritual services was always a severe blow for the women's groups.

Another important survival resource—again, especially for women—was the extended network of friendship and mentoring that existed between convents. These could, in some eras, be quite empowering.[29] When, in other periods, increased cloister restrictions prevented religious women from creating and maintaining these networks, their resulting isolation often lessened their communities' chances for survival.

A community might not merely lose the support of influential outsiders, it might also become the target of their active ill will. Both civil and ecclesiastical authorities often initiated policies that were detrimental, or even fatal, to religious life. A decree of the Emperor Valens in 370 c.e. set in motion a mass deportation of the Egyptian hermits. This completely destroyed the early monastic and eremitical movement in some areas.[30] Medieval ecclesiastics at first limited and then ultimately proscribed membership in the Beguines. Reformation rulers summarily turned monks, friars, and nuns out of their houses and confiscated their property. Pope Clement XVI dissolved the Jesuits in 1772. During the French Revolution, thousands of male religious across Europe were imprisoned, executed, or exiled. While the nuns of the revolutionary period were, for the most part, spared the fate of the men, their property was often confiscated and they were forbidden to accept new members. Many of the large-scale extinctions of religious life can be traced to a civil or ecclesiastical decision either to extirpate or severely limit religious orders.

It is important to realize, however, that persecution did not always have this effect. As students of other communal movements have observed, religious groups often "gain strength when put to the test."[31] Historians of nineteenth-century congregations in the United States, Canada, and Ireland have noted scores of cases where communities flourished in spite of severe interference—and at times even attempted extermination—at the hands of both civil and religious authorities.[32] But persecution or severely restrictive civil laws could be a final blow for religious communities that had already been declining in fervor, undergoing financial difficulties, or having trouble attracting new recruits.[33]

Competition for Resources and Ecological Niches

As the growth and expansion phases of a social movement run their course, its field of action often becomes crowded with an increasing number of social movement organizations, each of which is searching for a unique institutional identity and mission to distinguish itself from its fellows. Competition for scarce resources—or for recruits—may become more and more fierce as the number of social movement organizations rises.[34] Societal changes and technological innovations may eliminate the particular ecological "niche" a social movement organization had filled, forcing it to stake its claim over some new task or mission.[35] In so doing, of course, the organizations may come into conflict with the previous occupant(s) of the new niche, a conflict that may end in the demise of one or the other of the competitors.

The decline phases of religious life were frequently marked by just such destructive competitions. Secular institutions might also compete with religious orders: One French medieval order, dedicated to constructing bridges to facilitate missionary evangelization, declined when secular governments assumed this task.[36] Knowles describes how the Inns of Court in fifteenth- and sixteenth-century England gradually usurped the intellectual leadership formerly provided by schools of theology at the universities.[37] Civil agencies or private voluntary associations in both the thirteenth and the nineteenth centuries took over works of charity formerly performed by religious orders.[38] The rise of a professional class of lay scribes and artists in the fourteenth century, and the invention of printing in the fifteenth, struck at the root of another monastic occupation: "In the late fifteenth century [copying manuscripts] was a fossilized and artificial occupation from which the sense of urgency and of achievement had disappeared. No substitute occurred to take its place. . . . One of the troubles in the monasteries of the late fifteenth century was undoubtedly the absence of satisfactory and satisfying occupation."[39] Other developments in knowledge often impacted negatively upon the works traditionally performed by religious orders. In the late nineteenth century, government regulations concerning professional requirements for teachers, nurses, or social workers threatened to bar all or most of the members of religious community from ministries they had performed for years, or at least to render the orders' schools and hospitals—staffed as they were by "less qualified" workers—less desirable in the eyes of their potential clientele.[40]

Conclusions

A primary factor in the decline and demise both of individual religious orders and of entire virtuoso movements within Catholicism, was the changes in their surrounding environments that made key resources—recruits, money, spiritual and political assistance, a clientele for their services—more and more difficult to obtain. This situation might be due to natural societal and economic developments over the centuries, or it might be the result of active, malign intervention by some civil or ecclesiastical authority. Table 10.1 attempts to summarize these external sources of communal decline. At times, several factors combined to insure an order's collapse; at other times, a single cause was sufficient.

A loss of resources was, however, neither necessary nor sufficient by itself to assure the collapse of a widespread movement of virtuoso spirituality. At other times and in other places, religious orders could weather circumstances even more adverse than these and emerge, not only unscathed, but actually strengthened. In order to understand fully the decline periods in Roman Catholic religious life, therefore, it is necessary also to study them from the perspective of frame alignment theory.

Frame Alignment and the Decline of Religious Communities

A unifying ideological frame is a fundamental necessity for any social movement, as well as for the particular organizations affiliated with it. "Social ideologies provide formalized codifications of expected behavior and socially acceptable ideals; they set forth visions of reality that define the nature and preferred behavior of, and the interrelationship between, men and society. *Ideologies arise in a particular socio-historical context; when that context changes, the system of norms and prescriptive behavior patterns associated with a given ideology ceases to be congruent with reality.*"[41] The frame

Table 10.1 External Sources of Communal Decline

	Declining or Limited Recruit Pool: War, Plague, Saturated Market	Economic Forces: Inflation, Financial Mismanagement	Interfering or Unsupportive Patrons	Competition for Clients/Works; Obsolescence of Occupation	Intervention, Persecution, Neglect by Ecclesiastical Authorities	Intervention, Persecution by Civil Authorities
Late 4th Century Egypt	Frazee 1982: 269, 277 Hostie: 82					Frazee: 264, 277
Men's Monasticism, 8th–10th centuries	Hostie: 82	Wynne: 99 Lawrence: 125, 129–30 Little: 68	Lawrence: 132–34			Lawrence: 80
Women's Monasticism, 8th–10th centuries	Schulenberg: 215, 222 Lawrence: 80, 105 Hostie: 82	Schulenberg: 225 Johnson: 219–25	Schulenberg: 233		Schulenberg: 227–29	Schulenberg: 230
Beguines, 14th century					Lawrence: 233–34 McDonnell: 524–38 Bynum, 1987b: 128 Neel: 243, 246	
Male and female Monasticism, 13th–14th centuries	Lawrence: 274–76, 281 Hollermann: 44–45 Knowles: 312 Hostie: 142 Ashley: 58	Lawrence: 275 Johnson: 111, 225, 259 Bynum, 1987b: 126 Hollermann: 44	Johnson: 45–46	Lawrence: 280 Little: 150–60 Johnson: 251, 258–59 Knowles: 308	Lawrence: 223 Johnson: 89–93, 101, 251 Bynum, 1987b: 128	Johnson: 46

Male and female religious orders, 15th and 16th centuries	Donovan: 15 Tugwell: 25 Lawrence: 276 Johnson: 256 Knowles: 4–7	Knowles: 140–42, 219–25	Knowles: 4–7	Taylor: 54 Clear: 45 Hollermann: 44–46	Hollermann: 48–49 Knowles: 66, 191–98
Religious Orders and Congregations, 18th century France and Quebec	Rapley: 187 Langlois: 145, 333	Rapley: 181, 185	Rapley: 182, 187	Rapley: 168–69	Rapley: 182 Langlois: 97 Hollermann: 54, 68–70 Hostie: 216, 219

alignment of a given ideology of religious virtuosity with its larger societal environment could never be taken for granted; it needed to be constantly reassessed and renegotiated. Established religious communities, however, were often reluctant to recreate their ideological frames in this way. As the discrepancy between their ideology and the needs of their surrounding society widened, religious orders faced the most serious threat to their growth and survival.

External Sources of Dealignment

Individuals within a society commonly have a mental image, or "maze-way," to describe the shape and functioning of that society, as well as of their own place within it.[42] The original success of a religious community's ideological frame had depended on the ability of its virtuoso adherents to articulate or embody the "resonance" between their lifestyle/ beliefs and the strains or deficiencies in the societal mazeway.[43] Brown and Rausch, for example, speak of the dualism of Hellenistic culture—"a haunting sense of the distance between God and humanity, between the heavenly and the earthly" in the larger society—that had spurred the fourth-century hermits to their solitary ascetic striving for spiritual perfection.[44] After a few centuries, however, the concerns of Hellenistic dualism paled before new developments. The hermit's solitary quest for spiritual perfection no longer spoke to a culture suffering from the collapse of the Roman Empire; the ordered life of the sixth-, seventh-, and eighth-century monasteries was much more appealing.[45] By the eleventh and twelfth centuries, however, the external chaos that had made monastic order attractive had once again diminished, as Europe gradually rebuilt its social and economic infrastructure. The increasing differentiation and complexity of society created in its turn new strains, to which the monasteries' spirituality of prayer and manual labor was largely irrelevant. As medieval Europe moved from mechanical to organic solidarity, "people felt an urgency, unlike anything we see in the early Middle Ages, about defining, classifying and evaluating what they termed 'orders' or 'lives' or 'callings'."[46] The increasing complexity of society was reflected in new spiritual practices both within and outside of the monasteries, from the preoccupation with order and precedence in medieval religious processions to the expressions of liminality and symbolic role reversals in monastic rituals and writings.[47] The ritual sophistication and affective spirituality of Cluny and Citeaux flourished in this new atmosphere, and previous variants of monastic spirituality declined.

By the thirteenth century, the rising mercantile economy had created an additional strain: the need to provide an ethical justification for the entire monetary system of an urban society, with its attendant complications of private property, fair prices, profit, and professional fees.[48] Religious virtuosi were also struck by the widespread urban poverty of the period, by the conspicuous consumption of the wealthy, and by the ignorance of the common people and their vulnerability to heresy.[49] The ideological framework of traditional monastic spirituality contained neither the vocabulary nor the concepts to deal with these concerns, but the new mendicant friars made them their primary focus. Still later, the ideology of the Reformation posed new dilemmas for religious orders. The collectivist spirituality of the Middle Ages, in which the concept of personal conversion had been a rather foreign concept, was yielding to the Reformers' insistence that each individual Christian, in order to be saved, must make an informed assent to his or her faith.[50] The "world-affirming" activism of the Reformers challenged the more quietistic, "world-rejecting" virtuoso spirituality of the Middle Ages, and required its reformulation into a disciplined, proactive version such as that adopted by the Jesuits.[51] At the same time, the societal differentiation of the thirteenth through sixteenth centuries meant that the Church in general, and religious life in particular, was gradually displaced from its central position in society and became more and more marginal to the culture as a whole.[52] In each of these eras, therefore, societal mazeway changes meant that the formerly congruent forms of religious virtuosity lost their relevance for the surrounding culture and had to be replaced with new formulations.

In addition to contending with large-scale cultural mazeway changes, Roman Catholic religious virtuosi also had to contend with opposing ideological frames held and advanced by groups outside the Church. Some of these frames attacked the very existence of religious life. The Protestant reformers, for example, rejected the whole idea of a "more perfect" virtuoso lifestyle.[53] Sixteenth-century Protestants found the erotic mysticism of the Beguines and the Cistercian nuns highly offensive, and denounced their Eucharistic spirituality as well. Nineteenth-century Protestants also objected to central elements of the Catholic orders' ideological frames: They viewed celibacy as "flouting the laws of God and Nature," and considered the vows of obedience and poverty as subverting the patriarchical authority of the family.[54]

In addition to external theologies that attacked the validity of *any* form of virtuoso spirituality, Catholic religious orders were sometimes threatened by religions that substituted competing virtuoso groups of their own. Gnostic study circles provided an alternate form of religious virtuosity to men and women in the third century.[55] The twelfth century abounded in groups of "ecstatic laymen who renounced marriage and formed self-contained conventicles" affiliated with the Cathars and the Albigensians.[56] The ideological frames for religious virtuosity advanced by these groups often appealed to the same pool of recruits from which the religious orders had traditionally drawn their members.

At times, various secular ideologies might also threaten the frames developed by the religious communities. The agnostic and deistic mood of the Enlightenment devalued most Christian institutions and beliefs.[57] Nineteenth-century secularism, with its emphasis on science and reason, seemed to deny the very legitimacy of both the priesthood and religious life. The meaning systems constructed in practically every nineteenth-century intellectual discipline "eliminated from experience all that [was] not susceptible to verification and measurement; everything, that is, which belonged traditionally to the dimension of the sacred."[58] Secular disciplines such as Freudian psychoanalysis interpreted all piety as pathological; Marxists labeled it the opiate of the people.[59] Sociologists considered religious movements to be "nostalgic attempts to rediscover the core of a lost civilization," engaged in primarily by misfits who were incapable of mature functioning in the present day.[60]

As a result of competition and/or devaluing by other ideologies, religious orders sometimes had difficulty both in attracting recruits and in socializing them once they had entered.[61] In response, many communities were tempted to confine their recruitment efforts to encapsulated populations isolated from the mainstream of an increasingly hostile society.[62] While such tactics assured a continuing supply of recruits, they also allowed the orders to avoid the kind of ideological work that would have been necessary to meet the challenges posed by competing ideological frames.

Internal Sources of Dealignment

External challenges were not the only causes of ideological dealignment in religious orders. Dynamics internal to the communities could also lead to "a certain moral decadence" or laxity, in which common life declined and enthusiasm for prayer and ascetical practices waned.[63] It was rare, in fact, for a community to exist for more than 150 years *without* experiencing some decay.[64] Lax observance and declining fervor have been observed for ninth-century monasteries in England and Gaul and for the twelfth-century Cluniac houses, for the fourteenth- and fifteenth-century Dominicans, Franciscans, Premonstratensians, and Carmelites, for the sixteenth-century Benedictines in Germany, for the English monks and mendicants of the same century, for the eighteenth-century French teaching congregations, and for their contemporaries in colonial America.[65]

These declines could not be due solely to external circumstances since they took place in widely varying environments. Rather, a number of internal dynamics have usually cooperated to make some decay of each

order's original fervor almost inevitable. First among these was the rou-
tinization of the founder's charismatic authority after his/her death and
the demise of the founding generation of members.[66] In many other communal groups, the transfer of the vision from the founding generation who
had chosen it as adults, to the "sabra" generation who had been raised in
it from childhood, resulted in a dilution of commitment.[67] It may at first
glance seem that members of celibate religious orders would be spared this
difficulty, since they recruited only adult members. But religious communities often accepted candidates at extremely young ages. Many parents in
fourth-century Egypt, for example, gave their young sons to local monasteries to be raised as monks.[68] Orphaned children might also be placed
there. The acceptance of child oblates continued into the Middle Ages
and had both positive and negative results. On the one hand, the system
provided monasteries with a simple and routinized means of recruitment
and made it possible to exercise total control over the socialization of
these potential members.[69] The ending of child oblation has even been
cited as a prime reason for the decrease in monastic membership in the
late Middle Ages.[70] Women who entered the convent as small children
experienced additional benefits. They often found there a "home away
from home," where they were welcomed by their sisters and aunts.[71] Such
women, raised in an all-female environment, were less likely to be influenced by the contemporary stereotype of the female sex as morally and
intellectually inferior to men, and more likely to develop confidence in
their own abilities.

On the other hand, the consecration of children to religious life often
made for lax members when these children became adults. Not all medieval child oblates wanted to be monks. A similar problem occurred in
seventeenth-century France and in nineteenth-century Ireland and the
United States, as the age of entrants to religous life declined. Whereas an
average age range of the mid- to late-twenties had been common for the
entrants to newly founded communities, congregations a generation later
were accepting postulants in their late- and even middle-teens.[72] Critics
feared that younger entrants might be overly influenced by the wishes of
their parents. "According to Vincent de Paul, this made for insipid, un-
motivated religious. 'They do not have a true vocation, since they were
put there by their parents, and stay there out of human respect.' "[73]

Another difficulty lay in the training given to new members. As the
order matured and institutionalized, the type of training necessary to so-
cialize its new recruits also changed. Whereas the first members had been
able simply to model themselves on the living example of the founder,
later generations were confronted with the task of systematizing the behavioral and belief elements of the order's ideological frame—and then
imparting the resulting package to individuals who had never personally

experienced the ethos and esprit of the community's early days. Often the arrangements for doing this were haphazard or even nonexistent. The early Franciscans had no novitiate training at all for their members.[74] Some seventeenth-century French convents also had no novitiate, but merely assigned each new entrant to an older nun as a mentor. At other times, formerly rigorous socialization procedures might fall into disuse. In twelfth-century Cluny, the year-long novitiate of the previous century had been reduced to one week—hardly a sufficient period in which to discern an applicant's aptitude or vocation.[75] Abandonment of former socialization procedures was especially likely in times of communal decay. In declining orders with few entrants, there was little incentive to train a novice director and establish a systematic form of novitiate.[76] Long-standing orders with many entrants, on the other hand, often relied on an excessively rigid and bureaucratic "mass production" system that stifled individual growth and creativity—the very qualities that would someday be necessary in adapting the order's ideological frame to any new environmental challenges.[77]

Still another source of ideological decay was the very prosperity that many orders experienced. In this, Roman Catholic religious communities have paralleled other communal groups in which fewer opportunities for sacrifice resulted in decreased commitment.[78] Lax observance appears to have increased in several monastic groups as they became wealthy: Cluny, Citeaux, and the fifteenth-century English Benedictines all experienced this problem.[79] McDonnell charts a similar process with the Beguines; Roche with the medieval canons.[80] As the fourteenth-century Dominicans became wealthy, a class system developed in which the friars and masters of theology, who controlled the better preaching territories, could keep the financial stipends they received and use them to live in luxury while others in the order lacked bare necessities.[81] The first superior of the seventeenth-century Filles de Notre Dame at la Fleche noted that "great temporal wealth ruins religious houses," and that "there is as much to fear from seeing them too rich as too poor."[82] The early years of many communities "were dogged by uncertainty and lack of funds . . . and yet it was often during these very years that the number of entries was the highest."[83] The wealth of the communities' later years also led to role specialization and correspondingly divided interests, to remoteness of the monastery's rulers from those they ruled, and to "endless feuds over money and possessions, minimal spiritual fervor among noble ladies of idleness, and the widespread adoption of a secular lifestyle."[84]

Another form of success that proved a decidedly mixed blessing was recruitment success. The assimilation of a large number of new members within a short time has traditionally posed problems for communal groups, since it makes it difficult to involve all members in the group's activities.[85] Growth may also lead to factionalization and to the establishment of imitators, which crowd the organization's field of action. The dynamics of large, impersonal commnities are often perceived by members in a negative light when compared with the more intimate group of earlier days. In addition, the quality of new recruits often varies in inverse proportion to quantity.[86] With so many novices to care for, it is difficult to give attention to the spiritual growth of each individual. As one Jesuit complained in the early twentieth century: "Solidly trained Jesuits simply cannot be produced on a mass production basis. The difficulty is enhanced by the fact that I have been appointed with no previous theoretical or practical training. With little or no time to read, it becomes difficult to do justice to the instruction of the novices. With constant pressure of crowds one's energy is constantly being drained."[87] Rapid growth often left the order's leaders scrambling to catch up: "From 1633, when the first few young women entered Mlle. le Gras's house until 1658, when the company, now numbering 800, received its letters of registration from parlement, the picture is the same: the founders were always led ahead by events, struggling to control and solidify their immensely successful institute."[88] In such situations, the ideological "edge" of the original small group may become blunted, as their frame stretches to accommodate an ever-wider variety of incompletely assimilated individuals.[89]

Ideological Decay

At the start of any enterprise, human beings can never anticipate all of the eventualities the future will hold. As they age, therefore, "all human communities . . . (utopian or not), require . . . 'ideological work' to accommodate its constitutional principles to its current contingencies."[90] Particpants in the newly founded social movements observed by Snow et al spent a large percentage of their time recounting and accounting for their activities, thus building up the ideological frames that informed and justified the movement itself.[91] Once this ideology had been concretized in the group's daily life, however, its members usually became less willing to continue deconstructing and reconstructing it as external and internal circumstances changed. Institutionalized practices, offices, and rewards had come to depend upon the established ideology, and various subgroups had developed strong vested interests in their continuance. Furthermore, since human beings are "cognitive misers," they are normally unwilling to expend the necessary energy to think through possible inconsistencies in their ideological frame and prefer instead to accept it as a given.[92] As newly fashionable spiritualities or secular ideologies supplanted and devalued the virtuoso emphasis of previous eras, as inflation or technological innovations rendered their traditional ministries economically unviable,

and as new recruits with different backgrounds and often inadequate training replaced the enthusiastic pioneer generation, religious orders needed
to initiate correspondingly profound changes in the ideological frames that
had given meaning and legitimacy to their members' efforts. For both psychological and institutional reasons, however, this was rarely done. For
the most part, the response of the orders was to attempt "to resuscitate the
older patterns" rather than to construct something new.[93] The result was
that an order's ideological frame became less and less relevant, both to its
surrounding environment and also to its newer members.

A progressive value and belief diminishment—the reverse of Snow et
al.'s frame amplification processes—often occurred.[94] Formerly central
values were diluted and discarded. For example, the primary element of
the monastic model of virtuoso spirituality was the monks' or nuns' life of
prayer and work in community. Yet, by the fourteenth century, "monastic
women and men often slept in their own rooms instead of in one large
dormitory. . . . Much more commonly, monastics ate alone, in small
groups, or in the infirmary where the meals intended for the ill were more
palatable than usual refectory fare."[95] The disintegration of their common
life, Johnson held, was both a symptom and the cause of a pervasive waning of the monastic ideal.

The element of poverty—a key ingredient in the mendicant and the
Beguine versions of virtuoso spirituality—was similarly devalued by the
very groups that had formerly professed them. By the late thirteenth century, the Beguines were purchasing vineyards so that their wines could attract more wealthy patrons and members.[96] The Carmelites experienced
declines both in their observance of communal life and in their practice
of personal and communal poverty. The Dominicans de-emphasized poverty in favor of ministerial effectiveness. The Jesuits in eighteenth-century
Maryland became preoccupied with the material value of their land holdings and displayed a "pastoral lethargy" in fulfilling their spiritual tasks.

As the founding values of a religious order lost their importance, the
incentive for following the rules and customs that had safeguarded these
values also declined.[97] The lifestyle prescribed by the order in earlier
times had been an exciting challenge for an elite group of virtuosi trained
and marshalled to attain the order's transcendent goal. Now, the goal was
devalued and the means to achieve it were widely disregarded. As an example of this process, one might compare the enthusiasm of Citeaux in
the twelfth century with Benedictine establishments two hundred years
later. While the later monastic life may have had "some attraction for the
sons of the gentry or of the burgher class who were in search of security
and status," it "offered no challenge to the fervent aspirant in search of
spiritual fulfillment."[98] Such aspirants usually went elsewhere, "either to
the eremitical orders or to newer kinds of religious organization. . . .

What the Benedictine abbeys offered their recruits was security, social status, and a career similar to that of the secular clergy without the distraction of pastoral responsibilities."[99] Life in some orders might actually be a *detriment* to spiritual progress: "While it was no doubt still possible for an individual [monk] to live a strict and holy life, he could only do so by refusing to take advantage of any relaxations or to solicit any favors. Whereas the monk . . . of the twelfth century would have needed to take deliberate action to escape the full regular life, the monk of the late fourteenth century would have needed equal determination to remain within its ambit."[100]

As the internal priorities diminished, outside values often took their place. English abbots and priors began to live lives that were quite similar to those of country squires.[101] The fifteenth-century Premonstratensians adopted a wide variety of secular customs. The distinction between the secular and the religious life thus became blurred. "This was the consequence of relaxation, of a centuries-long process of self compromise by religious orders."[102] As the orders became less differentiated from other types of associations, there was less incentive for virtuosi to join them.[103]

Not only might an order's values and practices decline, the very belief systems that underlay its ideological frame might also disintegrate under the pressures of external changes and internal inattention. As communal practices were abandoned and as members no longer gathered for periodic reconstruction of their interpretive frames, it became less and less likely that they would continue to retain those beliefs that were most at variance with their surrounding culture.[104] Stein documents this process for the nineteenth-century Shakers, who gradually lost their unified world view, becoming embarrassed about the "excessive" practices of their earlier days and reluctant to seek new converts.[105] Similarly, as their world changed around them and as their traditional doctrines appeared more and more irrelevant, the members of religious orders drifted from fervent mobilization in defense of their ideological frame.

Every religious order, therefore, was ultimately vulneraerable to the same sort of alienation Zablocki has documented for contemporary communes.[106] Collective self-investment waned, and eventually the community was transformed into an association where "members regain virtually full personal autonomy and the commune becomes a co-operative venture in support of its members' individual self-interests. Many of these latter types last for two or three decades, but rarely are they able to produce a second generation."[107] The rest of the world increasingly regarded the group's ideology as anachronistic, an opinion that was often shared by the group members themselves.[108]

The decline of the community's ideology was often hastened by internal divisions into possibly antagonistic factions. Competing interest groups frequently developed: the ordained versus the lay members, the intellectuals versus the activists, the traditionalists versus the innovators.[109] At times, these divisions split the community, with each faction continuing on its separate way. At other times, the entire group squandered its energies on destructive infighting and disintegrated under the pressure of external events.

Conclusion

Sociologists studying communal groups have traditionally defined a successful community as one that managed to survive for longer than twenty-five years. Using this criterion, Kanter found that only eleven of the ninety-one nineteenth-century communes she studied could be classified as successes.[110] Similarly, Miller examined 150 communes existing between 1860 and 1960 and found only 10 percent to be successful.[111] Catholic religious orders appear to exhibit similar mortality levels. While some Church historians cite a survival rate of 25 percent to 35 percent for religious communities,[112] this figure undoubtedly excludes hundreds of ephemeral attempts that never attained official status.[113] The combination of external changes that deprived communities of essential resources or rendered their ideological frames irrelevant, and of internal changes that attenuated each group's commitment to its ideology, inevitably posed severe challenges to religious orders. And yet some orders did manage to survive for centuries before collapsing—far longer than students of other intentional communities would have predicted. To understand the factors behind a successful religious community's survival, and why even these communities eventually deteriorated, it is necessary to apply hypotheses developed in the study of other intentional communities.

Chapter 11

Religious Orders as Intentional Communities: the Maintenance of Commitment

The sociologists who have studied religious communal groups hold that their ideological frames are absolutely central to their existence.[1] Religious virtuoso ideologies usually relate to some dominant theme of the larger culture, whether in support or opposition—or both. When a religious order's ideological frame resonated with the dominant concerns of the surrounding society, *and* when various other material, social, and political incentives existed, the community existed in a state of creative efflorescence, similar to the "white hot mobilization" analyzed by Lofland.[2] With little encouragement from movement leaders, large numbers of enthusiastic recruits entered and willingly devoted all of their energies to spreading the community's message.

However, once the concerns of the larger culture had drifted away from the issues addressed by the virtuoso ideology, and once the founding generation had died and the founder's charisma had been routinized, the recruitment and retention of members was a different matter. White hot mobilization, difficult as it is to achieve, is even more difficult to sustain.[3] Religious communities were inevitably faced with a dual problem: whether to attempt to revive their members' initial fervor or to devise alternate mechanisms for retaining them and mobilizing them in service of the common goal. Whichever path of action an order chose, the tactics for accomplishing it had serious drawbacks. Attempts to rekindle the members' initial enthusiasm were often divisive and liable to backfire in destructive ways. Relying on other commitment mechanisms instead of on the members' fervor, however, tended to perpetuate an increasingly hollow, institutionalized shell, which was vulnerable to abrupt and catastrophic collapse. The cycles of growth and decline experienced by individual religious orders were at least partly due to the inherent dynamics of the necessary communal practices they had perforce adopted in order to insure their survival.

Revitalization Techinques

When faced by declining member commitment to their founding ideology, some communal groups attempted to revive their initial fervor. This could be done in a number of ways. Most revitalization tactics, however, were extremely dangerous for the survival of the group, and leaders usually drew back from their full implementation. *Few communal groups have ever managed to rekindle their members' enthusiasm successfully.* Several historical examples, drawn from both Catholic and other religious traditions, will document this assertion.

In his history of the Shakers, Stephen Stein describes the events known as "Mother Ann's Work," a period between 1837 and 1845 in which scores of Shakers experienced visions and received prophetic messages.[4] On the one hand, the events of this period rekindled in the second generation of Shakers—who had never known Mother Ann personally—a feeling of belonging and dedication that they might otherwise have lacked. On the other hand, there was "much confusion" and tension between rival groups claiming different revelations. The whole episode dismayed the Shaker leaders "because it was impossible to establish objective standards for separating legitimate from inauthentic gifts," and they ultimately took steps to restrict and suppress the movement.[5] Some of the most disruptive visionaries left the society, and the community's leadership reasserted its authority by promulgating the millennial laws of 1845, "the strictest and most rigid in Shaker history."[6]

A few religious communities have attempted to revitalize their founding fervor by permitting new charismatic leaders to develop. But since a charismatic leader will, by definition, lead the rest of the community in the direction of his/her personal vision—a direction that may well be different from the one espoused by the original founder—the appearance of such an individual within an established community is usually divisive. The other members, who had known the new charismatic leader when he/she was a mere fellow disciple of the original founder, may legitimately question his/her qualifications for taking up the founder's role. Furthermore, group processes such as "Mother Ann's Work" often result in the appearance of *several* charismatic contenders at once—a situation that leads rapidly to organizational chaos.[7] Religious groups, therefore, usually avoid this revitalization tactic.

For similar reasons, Roman Catholic religious orders did not usually respond to their periods of declining commitment by attempting to rein-itiate their charismatic foundation phase. The major exception to this pattern is the Franciscans. Perhaps because the charismatic life of St. Francis and his famous *Testament* served as a more radical alternative to the official Franciscan *Rule*, or perhaps because the absolute mendicant poverty he embodied was an untenable lifestyle when lived over long pe-riods of time, the community's many revivals continued to have a strong charismatic component.[8] Although this spontaneity was "fertile source of tension and disorder" and resulted in frequent splits and schisms within the Franciscan order over the centuries, it was also a source of tremendous creative vitality.[9]

A second way to revive decaying enthusiasm and restore the white hot mobilization of the founding period is to seek out internal enemies and unite the members against them.[10] This technique, however, is even more divisive than attempting a charismatic reflowering, and few, if any, reli-gious orders have chosen to adopt it. Most commonly, religious commu-nities have reacted to the decline of their members' enthusiasm by initi-ating the commitment-maintaining mechanisms discussed in chapter 2.

Maintenance Techniques

Communal Commitment Mechanisms and Community Survival

Every community must insure that its members remain sufficiently com-mitted to its goals that they will be willing perform whatever tasks are nec-essary to achieve them. Close, fulfilling and nonexclusive relationships must also be fostered among the members while outside ties are de-emphasized, and it must be possible to exercise authority over the mem-bers' activities without alienating them.[11] Continuance, cohesion, and control are thus the three basic "problems of commitment" faced by all communities.[12] The ideal way to address these problems, if reviving the original level of "white hot mobilization" is not feasible, is to foster an "institutionalized awe" in the members with respect to the community's ideology, as that ideology is enfleshed in the community itself and in its leaders.[13] Leaders may cultivate—or be invested with—a charismatic aura by the progressive separation of their lives from the day-to-day rou-tines of their followers. Rituals may be established to re-enact the tran-scendent meaning of the group's ideology. Myths may be formulated to condense it to readily comprehensible form. These practices, however, may not be sufficient, especially in periods when the values and beliefs of the surrounding culture are seriously at variance with those of the communal group. At such times, successful communities must engage in almost constant ideological work to keep their common vision alive in their members.[14]

Ideological commitment, therefore, is necessary but not sufficient to insure communal success. "No one stays in an intentional community because of ideology; the ideology will only be adhered to if the community gives one a feeling of home. Conversely, the stresses of living in a community would be intolerable if there were no ideological backing to one's life in it."[15] According to Kanter, a successful community *must* reinforce its ideological commitment with cathetic ties between the members ("affective commitment") and with the promise of concrete material and spiritual benefits that outweigh the costs involved ("cognitive commitment").[16] As chapter 2 has outlined, commitment mechanisms such as common activity and boundary maintenance, shared sacrifice and mortification, drawing members from a similar background and eliminating divisive internal cliques, are "cultural universals," reinvented or borrowed time and again by successful communities to reinforce their members' ideological, affective, and cognitive commitment.

Commitment Mechanisms in Roman Catholic Religious Orders: Variations

In general, the monastic model of religious virtuosity utilized more of these communal commitment mechanisms than did either the mendicant or the eremitic versions. Communities of monks or nuns were expected by their Rule to live, work, and pray together, and relatively strict cloister restrictions were maintained to prevent contamination of the monastic ideal by outsiders. Deindividualizing mortification practices were also part of monastic life: monks and nuns had no personal property and very little privacy or free time. A form of public, communal confession known as the "Chapter of Faults" was often practiced, in which members were expected to accuse themselves before the assembled community of even their most secret violations of the Rule. As a result, religious orders with a large number of monastic practices were often able to survive for extended periods. The isolation of their members from the outside world, their regularly ritualized re-enactment of their ideological frame, the sacrifices and mortifications demanded of them, all served to bolster their ideological commitment with both cathetic and utilitarian motives. Perhaps for this reason, monastic practices were often adopted even by adherents to other models of religious virtuosity.

The mendicants, in contrast, were the "weakest and most vulnerable" of the forms, precisely because they enployed so few of the commitment mechanisms and relied instead on irregular and sometimes chaotic revitalizations of their founding spirit.[17] The Beguines, too, omitted many commitment-enhancing practices. "Some beguines lived at home with their families, others worked for their livelihood. . . . Others lived unattached lives, begging for sustenance."[18]

Without the safeguards of commitment mechanisms, it soon became difficult for the mendicant orders to address Kanter's three basic problems of commitment. Within a hundred years of their founding, both the Dominicans and the Franciscans were experiencing severe problems controlling the activities of their wide-ranging friars.[19] The mendicants' cohesion was also threatened as subgroups split off from the community, and then split again and again among themselves. Without a common reworking of their basic ideological frame, disputes arose over exactly what a Dominican spirituality entailed or exactly what was required by true Franciscan poverty. Eventually, the mendicant model was at least partially stabilized by the adoption of monastic versions of the commitment mechanisams:

> St. Dominic founded the Order for preaching, a role previously restricted only to bishops. Dominic wanted all aspects of Dominican life to support this preaching mission, and moved his friars out of monasteries and into "convents," where they would come together after having been out preaching. Observances such as those in monasteries . . . were not important to him if they did not support the life of preaching. Yet, in every reform of the Order since Dominic's death in 1221, monastic observances rather than the preaching of the friars has been stressed.[20]

The Jesuits, later, were able to remedy some of the difficulties inherent in combining member commitment with scattered evangelization ministries by initiating a prolonged training period and subsequent annual retreats. During these times, communal commitment mechanisms were extensively and thoroughly practiced, so that the Jesuit would be able to do without them later.[21] But even among the Jesuits, a variety of monastic practices were gradually introduced for all members, in order to enhance their commitment.[22]

Like other intentional communities, therefore, Roman Catholic religious orders varied in their ability to elicit sustained commitment in their members. The monastic model, because it provided an effective set of mechanisms to help in this process, was the longest-lived version, and other variants of religious virtuosity usually found it expedient to adopt some monastic practices to solve their problems of continuance, cohesion, and control. Table 11.1 attempts to outline the extent to which the various models of virtuoso spirituality initially possessed—or were later able to adopt—mechanisms to enhance and preserve their members' ideological commitment.

Table 11.1 Communal Commitment Mechanisms in Religious Orders

	Common Ideology/Self-definition	Shared Sacrifice	Common Activities	Boundary Maintenance
Eremitic Model	**High** Brown 1988: 170 Brown 1985: 431	**High** Wynne: 15 Lawrence: 6 Pagels: 89 Frazee: 263, 265 Brock & Harvey: 21 Brown 1988: 202, 221	**Low (initially)** Lawrence: 6 Rausch: 41, 43 Frazee 1988: 115 **Moving to** **High** Frazee 1982: 272–73 Lawrence: 9	**High** Wynne: 16–19 Frazee: 265 Lawrence: 1 Brown 1988: 271, 356 Brown 1985: 429
Monastic Model	**High (initially)** Johnson: 100, 230 Pennington: 206–7 Lawrence: 98 **Low** Lawrence: 108, 200	**Moderate (men) High (women)** Lawrence: 176 Bynum 1987a: 208 Francis: 441 Bynum 1987b: 131 **Moving to** **Low** Rausch: 51 Little: 68 Lawrence: 200, 277 Johnson: 133 Knowles: 310–314	**High (initially)** Wynne: 98–103 Francis: 441 Hostie: 147 **Moving to** **Low** Johnson: 193 Lawrence: 278	**High (initially)** Rausch: 55 Wynne: 141 Lawrence: 176 Johnson: 235–36 **Moving to** **Low** Knowles: 314 Rapley: 25
Canons	**Low** Bynum 1982: 36–37 Hostie: 121 Reinke: 160–61 Zinn: 219	**High** Zinn: 218 **Moving to** **Low** Francis: 443 Froese: 21–22 Knowles: 316	**High** Zinn: 218 **Moving to** **Low** Reinke: 159–60	**Low** Little: ch. 7 Froese: 21

Beguines	**Low** McDonnell: 136–37, 430 Neel: 242–44	**Moderate/High** Rausch: 30 Bynum 1987a: 208 Neel:247 Bynum 1987b: 131 **Moving to** **Low** McDonnell: 14–15, 486, 508	**Low** McDonnell: 180 Neel: 243–44	**Low** Bynum: 1987b: 124 **Moving to** **High** McDonnell:164
Mendicants	**Low** Rausch: 74 Francis: 445 Lawrence: 250 Hostie: 155 Reinke: 171 Tugwell: 18, 23 Egan: 52–53	**High** Tugwell: 19 **Moving to** **Low** Little: 203 Tugwell: 19, 25 Egan: 54	**Low** Tugwell: 22, 24 Hostie: 148 Rausch: 73–77 Francis: 446 Little: 160 Ashley: 58, 91 Knowles: 314 **Moving to** **High** Ewens 1989: 33 Ashley: 61	**Low** Knowles: 314 Hostie: 154
Apostolic Orders	**High** Wynne: 198 Rapley: 170–74 McDonnell: 136 Coser: 120–23	**Low** Coser: 124 Rapley: 144–45 Rausch: 30 D'Allaire: 225 Hostie: 182	**Low** Coser: 121 Hostie: 182 Francis: 439 **Moving to** **High** Rapley: 111 McDonough: 138–153 Becker: 26, 164	**Low (male orders)** Rausch: 91 Francis: 439, 447 Hostie: 182

The Institutionalization of Commitment

As was the case with revitalization tactics, the use of commitment-maintaining techniques by an intentional community also involves corresponding liabilities. Foremost among these is that *the mechanisms eventually supplant the very ideological commitment they were designed to protect.* The original vision of the group had manifested itself "in radical enthusiastic movements that express[ed] ideals of equality," whereas later institutionalized structures led to "established routines, rules, traditions and rationalizations that confirm[ed]" the principles of hierarchy and bureaucracy."[23] Orthodox adherence to a pre-established ideology replaced creative ideological ferment, and, as a result, the community was less able to stimulate its members' inner life. Cathetic bonds to one's fellow members, instead of being a means to the community's transcendent end, became an end to themselves. The group might even become so internally cohesive that it had extreme difficulty absorbing new entrants, with the result that the members were less and less interested in attracting any—a condition Miller terms "encapsulation."[24]

The first generation of community members had to be creative rebels in constructing and living a new ideology of communal life. The second generation had to be conformists.[25] The master frame constructed by the innovative founders of the community constrained the beliefs, values, and activities of its later members—and of the members of other communities founded later in the same movement cycle—to imitate the original pattern. Innovation became confined to increasingly minute regulations, which, once elaborated and embellished, assumed equal weight with the more basic practices of the group. As the surrounding environment changed, the boundary maintenance mechanisms of the group, originally developed to protect its ideological frame, now served to isolate its members from seeing the need for change. Incorporating even the most minor changes became risky, since the rituals and common practices of the community had endowed all with an equally sacred status. Instead of reconstructing its ideological frame to correspond with the concerns of a changed society, therefore, the community was more likely to increase its vigilance in adamant support of the old model.

This is precisely the sequence of events that occurred during the decline periods that were inevitably experienced by any religious order that adopted monastic practices to preserve and enhance its members' commitment— however useful these practices had initially been in insuring the group's survival. A "hardening of institutional forms" and a corresponding decline in creative enthusiasm has been observed for the medieval Beguines and Dominicans, for the late-seventeenth-century filles seculieres, and for the congregations of late nineteenth-century Ireland, France, and the United States.[26] Hierarchy was increasingly stressed; ever more minute regulations were substituted for the spirit of obedience or community.[27] As one Jesuit observed about this process in the early twentieth century:

> I agree that we were "locked in" [to following minute rules]. . . . "Being on time for dinner" became sacrosanct, so that if you were aiding the dying but arrived one minute after grace had been said, you could be told *not* to come in. It was not as though you were joining your *family* for a meal, it was more like military inspection.[28]

Institutionalization of existing practices was often facilitated by ecclesiastical or civil laws that mandated them.[29]

As the threat of a changing outside world impinged upon an increasingly beleaguered order, defense tactics multiplied; creative adaptation did not. Reformers among the thirteenth-century Benedictines, faced with the challenge of a new urban commercialized economy, found even their attempts to restore a more faithful adherence to traditional monastic practices stonewalled by recalcitrant abbots jealous of their own autonomy.[30] Creative adoption of the mendicants' scholarship or pastoral practices was of course out of the question for these Benedictines. Attempts to reform the fifteenth-century Premonstratensians likewise met with strong resistence.[31] By the sixteenth century, even the formerly flexible mendicant friars were reluctant to change.[32] In the early twentieth century,

> The written record—the rules posted by rectors, the correspondence of superiors, and similar materials—leave the impression that as times changed (for the worse, so it was perceived), vigilance increased. New rules were added, almost none abandoned. Prohibitions outweighed incentives. Refutational minutiae swamped exhortations to keep up with new developments. . . .
>
> The intellectual covering around the mystical core—scholastic philosophy and theology—had grown increasingly stale. Because this shell was thought to be practically immutable, most Jesuits spent less time attempting to adapt the ideas to contemporary realities than mastering their formal intricacies and tinkering with their paralogical properties.[33]

The commitment mechanisms were thus a two-edged sword. Without boundary maintenance, common activities, sacrifice and mortification, communities were short lived and ephemeral, subject to destructive schisms and heterodox excesses. But, *with* the commitment mechanisms, religious orders became hollow shells held together, as generation succeeded generation, not by the members' commitment to the founding ideology (which, in any case, had become increasingly maladapted to the

concerns of a changed socio-cultural environment), but instead by iner-
tia, by in-group affiliative bonds, and by the personal benefits that could
be gained from membership. Such communities abruptly collapsed when
confronted either with hostile persecutions or with new and enthusiastic
orders built on some innovative model the established orders could
not match.

Interestingly—especially since they often had a less distinct ideological frame to begin with—women's religious congregations appear to have
been less vulnerable to the previous catastrophic declines than were the
men's communities. Both at the time of the Reformation and during the
French Revolution, the women were less likely to accept the offer of monastic dissolution and reversion to lay life.[34] Perhaps this was simply because women had fewer alternatives and religious life thus remained more
attractive to them. Women's communities may also have been less threatening to secular governments and therefore less likely to be objects of official persecution than were the men's groups. Over the centuries,
however, religious communities of women have experienced the same institutionalization pressures and gradual erosion of commitment that occurred with the men's orders, even if they were usually less susceptible to
sudden collapse.[35]

Conclusion

"Social groups, like individuals, pass through stages: birth, infancy, ado-
lescence, adulthood, old age and death."[36] Several times in Catholicism's
history, waves of religious communities have burst upon the scene and
flourished, only to institutionalize, rigidify, and ultimately decline, as a
result of a repeated pattern of internal and external causes.

What about the present period? Can the current disintegration of religious congregations be traced to similar causal dynamics? Is a new wave
of religious foundations likely to arise? The following chapters will attempt
to address some of these questions. Chapter 12 will give a brief historical
overview of the events experienced by one set of Catholic religious communities—American women's congregations—from 1950 until 1992.
Chapters 13 and 14 will analyze these events as causal factors in the
"frame dealignment" of the orders' ideology, and will also examine the decay of the traditional commitment mechanisms that had once supported
it. Finally, Chapter 15 will discuss the withdrawal of the environmental
resources that had been essential to the sisters' lifestyle. Our basic hypoth-
esis will be that the decline of religious orders during the present period is
the result of an exceptionally malign conjunction of factors, which has led
to their being disadvantageously positioned in all three dimensions—
ideologically, communally, and environmentally. In former periods of

ideological decline, or in periods of communal laxity, lack of environmental alternatives might still encourage women to remain within religious orders. In periods when resources or environmental niches were lacking, the sisters' ideology might still be firm. *Today, all three elements are missing.* It is this, we will argue, that is behind the orders' current collapse.

PART FOUR

The Present Collapse:
Religious Orders in North
America and Europe,
1950–1992

Chapter 12

A History of U.S. Religious Orders, 1950–1990

In the introduction to his study of twentieth-century American Jesuits, Peter McDonough argues that, between 1900 and 1950, the order was a "motivational metaphor," which permeated the entire lives of its members.

> As the metaphor approximates not only a preference but a perception of organizational reality, an institution becomes virtually indistinguishable from an enveloping way of life, grounded in behavioral, cognitive, and affective reinforcements. Besides being a mechanism for action, it constitutes a context of understanding and a habit of feeling. The perceived integration of the three dimensions make changes along any one of them hard to disentangle from the rest. Around the time of Vatican II, all these supports came undone for the Jesuits.[1]

And not for the Jesuits alone. Most of the religious orders and congregations established during the great foundation period of the nineteenth century had, by the middle of the twentieth, established themselves quite firmly as institutional metaphors. Their motivating ideology of religious virtuosity had enjoyed hegemonic superiority for well over a hundred years and had achieved official recognition by Rome in the 1917 Code of Canon Law. Their recruiting channels and their sources of support had become routinized: Pastors often erected parish schools even before the church was finished; parents dutifully sent their children there; the schools regularly funneled a proportion of their graduates into seminaries and novitiates; newly ordained or professed religious returned to teach in the schools and inspire subsequent generations to devote their lives to God. Old motherhouses, hospitals, and academies were outgrown and new ones constructed. By the early 1960s, membership in

U.S. religious communities was reaching its peak of over 200,000 women and men.

Why did it all collapse so quickly? Subsequent chapters in this section will argue that religious orders have experienced the simultaneous breakdown both of their ideological frames and of the environmental resources on which they had formerly depended. The speed and extent of these breakdowns happened partly because the orders discarded many of the internal commitment mechanisms that had formerly shielded their distinctive ideology from outside contamination, and partly because external events, both in Catholicism and in the surrounding American culture, destroyed their recruitment sources. As a result of these mutually exacerbating factors, the orders have suffered an almost 50 percent drop in their membership over the past thirty years. Roman Catholic religious communities thus provide a particularly dramatic example of the effects of ideological and environmental change on social movement organizations. This is especially the case for the women's congregations, the largest but also the most rapidly disintegrating component of religious life.

Prior to analyzing the causal factors that brought about the orders' decline, however, it is necessary to describe the historical background in which these factors operated. The present chapter will briefly outline the key events that have affected religious communities during the second half of the twentieth century, using as a case study the active congregations of women operating in the United States.

The Seeds of Change: 1950–1962

It would surprise many Catholics to learn that, however unchanging the lifestyle of "the good sisters" may have seemed during the 1940s and 1950s, it was precisely this period of seeming stability that contained the seeds of the subsequent revolutionary changes. It would probably further surprise them to discover that the original impetus for change had come from the·pope himself.

In late 1950, the Sacred Congregation for Religious (the Vatican department responsible for religious orders and congregations around the world) convened its first General Assembly of Religious. Some 4,000 superiors and representatives of religious communities attended this meeting, and heard Pope Pius XII call them to adapt their "excessively strict" cloister restrictions and reduce whatever nonessential and archaic customs were hindering their apostolates.[2] The pope repeated his directive the following year, at a meeting of teaching sisters. In addition to adapting their religious customs, Pius XII urged the teaching orders to give their members professional training equal to or better than that of their secular counterparts. It was the strangeness of outdated costumes and customs and the strain of being sent into ministry without proper training, the pope felt, that was behind the alarming drop-off of religious vocations in Europe after World War II. In a 1952 address to the International Congress of Major Superiors, he urged:

> In the training of your sisters for the tasks that await them, be broad-minded and liberal and admit of no stinginess. Whether it be for teaching, the care of the sick, the study of art or anything else, the sister should be able to say to herself, "My superior is giving me a training that will put me on an equality with my secular colleagues." Give them also the opportunity and the means to keep their professional knowledge up-to-date. This is important for your sisters' peace and for their work.[3]

The pope suited his own actions to his words. In 1956, he established the Regina Mundi Institute in Rome "for the training, education and formation of religious women in the sciences and disciplines."[4]

Almost no year passed during the 1950s without some new directive being issued by the pope to religious orders.[5] These directives, however, did not call for *essential* changes in the underlying ideological frame of religious life, but merely for "a renewal of the primitive spirit of the congregations and an adaptation of that spirit to present-day needs."[6] That Pius XII still subscribed fully to the traditional ideological frame for Roman Catholicism's religious virtuosity is shown by his other pronouncements. In his 1954 encyclical *Sacra Virginitas*, for example, he extolled virginity and religious life as superior to the married state for achieving holiness—a position dating to the time of Origen.

At the request of the Sacred Congregation, the U.S. religious communities held their first national congress at Notre Dame in 1952. A prime concern of those attending was the professional and spiritual education of the young entrants into their communities. Protestant Americans had criticized Catholic schools as being educationally inferior and staffed by inadequately trained teachers. To meet these criticisms, several sisters had written books and papers urging that young sisters have the opportunity to complete their bachelor's degrees before they began teaching or, if that were not possible, at least by the time they made their final vows.[7] The congress also called for more psychological screening of new applicants.

Also in 1952, at the annual meeting of the National Catholic Education Association in Kansas City, a panel discussion took place on the implications of the pope's remarks to teaching sisters the year before. As a result of this panel, a committee was created to survey religious communities about the problems they were experiencing in educating their young sisters. The responses to the survey indicated that "three critical difficulties" prevented the superiors of religious communities from providing the kind of education called for by the pope: 1) the amount of *time* needed to complete these degrees, in the face of pastors' and bishops' demands for more sisters to staff the growing school system; 2) the *cost* of protracted schooling, especially at a time when "in almost 50% of communities, the average annual cost of living per capita exceeds the average annual salary of the teaching sisters," and 3) a *lack of understanding* on the part of both the clergy and the sisters themselves as to why all this education was needed.[8]

Following this survey, in 1954, the U.S. women's communities established the Sister Formation Conference, which recent writers have called "the single most critical ground for the radical transformative process" of religious life that would occur after Vatican II.[9] The SFC provided, first of all, the impetus and the informational resources that enabled American sisters to become the most highly educated group of nuns in the Catholic Church, and among the most highly educated women in the United States.[10] Pius XII's new Regina Mundi Institute in Rome had been a disappointment to the communities, since it enrolled only a handful of American sisters and provided mainly theological training. As one SFC member remarked, "it is no great compliment to be a counterpart or anything else of Regina Mundi. Father Heston [a member of the Sacred Congregation for Religious] admitted to me that its value was chiefly cultural—to get the feel of Rome for a year or so—not so much academic."[11] The SFC wanted more for its sisters. By 1962, its Education Resources Committee was collecting and disseminating information on the best programs of higher education for sisters and opportunities for financial aid.

The primary vehicle for the SFC's efforts was its *Sister Formation Bulletin,* "the first publication ever undertaken *by* sisters *for* sisters on a national basis."[12] Begun with an initial mailing of one hundred copies, the *Bulletin's* circulation reached 11,000 by 1964.[13] Its offerings included translations of top theological writings from Europe, as well as the sisters' own articles on education, vocations, and psychological testing. Announcements of meetings and workshops, suggested bibliographies for postulants and novices, and a wide variety of other topics were also included.[14] A 1956 issue reported on a survey of students in Catholic high schools, which indicated that young people saw sisters as "separated from and oblivious to the world, out of touch with reality, [and] uninformed about modern problems."[15] This was used to buttress the SFC's call for more modern and professional training. There are even indications in the *Bulletin* of an early feminist consciousness. The "Proceedings" for the SFC's 1956–1957 meetings note that "possibly too much insistence has been laid on the view that woman is to fulfill her social role by being passive, and that God has fashioned her more to endure than to act."[16]

In 1956, again because of the direct prodding of the Vatican, the heads of men's and women's religious communities in the United States established two umbrella groups: the Conference of Major Superiors of Men (CMSM) and the Conference of Major Superiors of Women (CMSW). There is some evidence that only one body had originally been envisioned, but that the women insisted on two separate organizations. The public reason given for the separation was that sisters far outnumbered male religious, and that, since they were more concentrated in education, their concerns differed from those of the men, who were mostly priests working in a variety of ministries. However, marginal notes in a 1956 draft of the statutes show that the sisters were also wary lest control of a unified body be concentrated in male hands.[17] In any event, CMSW was established as a separate entity, with a membership of 235 heads of women's religious communities in the United States.

By 1960, therefore, a wide-ranging organizational base had been established among the American religious orders and congregations, focusing primarily on the educational and spiritual reforms requested by the pope ten years earlier. According to at least one author, however, these developments affected primarily the leadership the the various communities. Except, perhaps, for some of the youngest sisters—the postulants, novices, and "junior professed" in the newly revamped formation programs—the life of the average nun was unaffected. "Even though superiors had been exhorted directly by the Pope to make significant changes in religious life, the possibility of this being accomplished was limited by the superior's own conviction or lack of it. Even when she was convinced of such a need, the question still remained, how? Lastly, there was the problem of convincing the rank and file sisters of the need for adaptation."[18]

The Impact of the Second Vatican Council: 1962–1970

On October 11, 1962, the recently elected Pope John XXIII opened the Second Vatican Council—the first "ecumenical council" of the Church's leaders to be called in almost a century. No member of a women's order or congregation was permitted to participate in, or even to attend, the first two sessions, although a limited number of sisters were admitted as auditors in 1964 and 1965. The council's decisions, however, would deeply affect religious communities. Of prime importance were the two documents on the Church, *Lumen Gentium* and *Gaudium et Spes*. The former emphasized that *all* members of the Church had received an equal call "to the fullness of the Christian life and the perfection of charity," simply by virtue of their baptism.[19]

The importance of this seemingly innocuous statement cannot be stressed enough. *In one stroke, it nullified the basic ideological foundation for eighteen centuries of Roman Catholic religious life.* The traditional ideology had postulated a kind of three-tiered hierarchical ranking of the clerical, religious, and lay states. This elitist view of the religious/lay distinction, which held that only vowed members of religious orders could achieve true spiritual perfection, had enjoyed unchallenged supremacy at least since the early Middle Ages.

Now, however, the Vatican Council was stating that all baptized Catholics were called to holiness, not just the members of religious orders. Religious life, the document maintained, was not "a kind of middle way between clerical and lay conditions of life. Rather it should be seen as a form of life to which some Christians, both clerical and lay, are called by God."[20] Since sisters were not ordained clerics, they must be lay, and equal in their call to holiness with all other lay Catholics. "Dislodged from a protected, clearly demarcated (and elite) 'state,' sisters suddenly found themselves laity."[21]

The council's document on "The Church in the Modern World" (usually referrred to by its Latin title, *Gaudium et Spes*) also contained ideological implications for religious life. Traditionally, one of the basic purposes for a separate state of religious virtuosity within Catholicism had been that such a lifestyle modeled the purity and perfection of the spiritual realm to a sinful and fallen world. (See chapter 6, p. 112, above.) The world-rejection motif was strongest in the eremitic and monastic variants of religious life, but followers of subsequent versions also considered "the world" to be a polluting influence that was best avoided. "Throughout Christian history, holiness has often been identified with separation from 'the world.' In response to the threat of contamination by 'the world,' ecclesiastical legislation over the centuries increasingly sought to protect women by insisting that they be cloistered."[22]

Gaudium et Spes, however, proclaimed that the Church was to be in *solidarity* with the very world its religious orders had so long shunned. While perhaps not as traumatic as the implications of *Lumen Gentium*, which had attacked the very definition of religious life, the world-affirming stance of *Gaudium et Spes* did contradict the world-rejecting assumptions that had inspired the pervasive cloister and ministerial restrictions of many communities.[23] And dropping the boundary maintenance fostered by these cloister restrictions had ominous implications for the ability of religious communities to keep their distinctive ideology—already eroded by *Lumen Gentium*—protected from competing secular ideologies.

It is likely that neither Pope Paul VI (John XXIII had died the preceding year) nor the bishops of the council realized the full implications of their statements.[24] As a result, Rome's official pronouncements gave very mixed signals on the question of whether or not religious orders were still a superior virtuoso state within the Church.[25] In a May 1964 address, for example, the pope referred to "the universal vocation of all the faithful to holiness of life" that would surface later that year in *Lumen Gentium*. In the same speech, however, he also emphasized the special importance of the religious state, "a state of life which keeps in view the constant growth of charity."[26] The council's 1965 Decree on the Adaptation and Renewal of Religious Life (officially entitled *Perfectae Caritatis*—the title itself indicates that religious were still being viewed according to the traditional ideological frame, as a state "more perfect" than that of the laity) compounded the confusion. In this decree, the bishops stated that renewal was to be based on the Gospels and the spirit of each order's founder, apparently leaving it to the discretion of the individual order exactly how to renew itself. This seemed to endorse independent initiative and pluralism among the communities. At the same time, however, Pope Paul VI was stressing that the bishops and the papacy were to have the final say on the direction and content of all renewal efforts. "It is clear from its later disputes with some communities that [Rome] expected that women religious would concentrate on minor external changes in their habits, their daily schedules of prayer and other activities, and their relationships to the larger Catholic community."[27] The differences between Rome's and the communities' interpretations of what their renewal would entail emerged shortly after the end of the council, when all religious communities were ordered to convene, within three years, a special legislative session (a "general chapter") to implement the council's inadequately defined reforms. With several different—and conflicting—versions of what the Vatican was calling for, the orders soon became embroiled in intense controversy, both internal and external.

The Conference of Major Superiors of Women had followed the procedings of the Second Vatican Council with great interest. (CMSW's president, Sister Mary Luke Tobin, S.L., was the sole American sister permitted to be an auditor during the 1964 and 1965 sessions.) Accordingly, the conference commissioned Sister Marie Augusta Neal, S.N.D., a sociologist teaching at Emmanuel College in Boston, to conduct a survey of the entire professed membership (157,000 sisters) in its component orders. Despite the length of the survey (twenty-three pages, 649 questions), 88 percent of the sisters who received it responded.[28] For many, simply completing the survey was a consciousness-raising experience: By asking whether a sister had read a particular modern theologian's writings, for example, or whether she had attended "meetings of people other than her fellow community members," the survey legitimated such activities for many respondents who would not otherwise have thought of doing so on their own.[29]

Meanwhile, in compliance with the Vatican's decree, religious communities began holding their special general chapters, to decide how they would go about implementing the mandated renewal. Almost immediately, the contradictions in the original documents began to surface. The IHM Sisters of Los Angeles, California, held their renewal chapter in 1967 and initiated a set of wide-ranging changes.[30] Cardinal James McIntyre of Los Angeles, who had regarded the order with suspicion for years because of its liberal leadership, immediately demanded that the sisters reverse their chapter's decisions or else withdraw from the thirty-one schools they staffed in his diocese.[31] The sisters unanimously refused to do so. A 1968 papal investigation into the issue ended by ordering the IHM sisters to retain a uniform dress (that is, a religious habit), to remain in their traditional apostolate of teaching, and to obey the bishops. Cardinal Antoniutti of the Vatican's Sacred Congregation for Religious wrote to the heads of all American communities denouncing the changes the IHM sisters had initiated as "completely contrary to religious life."[32] The cardinal "sternly warned that communities must secure Vatican approval" before putting their reforms into effect.[33]

The cardinal's comments caused a storm of protest among the U.S. communities, both male and female. Many issued public statements supporting the sisters.[34] The 1969 General Assembly of CMSW also introduced a resolution in their support. Reverend Edward Heston of the Sacred Congregation was present at this assembly. In his address to the members, he emphasized that "the needs of a religious community must be secondary to the directives of a bishop to that community." It was their duty, he said, to accept the guidance of the hierarchy in their renewal.[35] The majority of the sisters ignored Father Heston's objections and continued their discussion—an action that a scandalized minority of the members thought disrespectful. The IHM sisters themselves ultimately divided into two groups, a larger group of 455 younger members (average age, thirty-six) who were determined to continue experimenting with renewal, and a smaller group of some fifty older members (average age, sixty-two), who wished to remain loyal to the hierarchy. In 1969, the younger group was forced to dissolve as an official religious congregation. As a priest who witnessed the incident remarked: "The wording [of the document reducing the sisters to the lay state] was frigid and legal, with never a word of appreciation for these sisters' years of generous service. The older sisters felt trapped."[36] Two other religious communities suffered similar attempts by the hierarchy to annul their renewal decisions. One, the Glenmary sisters, was also forced to dissolve.[37]

Not only were the active congregations affected by the Vatican's retrenchment, the cloistered contemplative orders also found their renewal attempts thwarted. In July 1969, one month before a scheduled meeting of contemplative nuns, the SCR issued the decree *Venite Seorsum* forbidding the women to attempt any experimentation with cloister. The decree was issued without consulting the nuns themselves, and over their protests.[38] The nuns nevertheless met together and founded the Association of Contemplative Sisters—a necessary umbrella group, they felt, since the SCR had forbidden them to join the active congregations in CMSW. The ACS, however, never received Rome's official approval.

In addition to its effects on individual communities, the rethinking of religious life initiated by the Second Vatican Council was also having an impact on CMSW itself. The group's original statutes had asserted that the conference "depend[ed] immediately on the Sacred Congregation for Religious" in "perfect allegiance" to the U.S. hierarchy.[39] Many members now felt that the conference's name and charter did not reflect its shift of focus away from hierarchical models and toward developing creative and responsive leadership.[40] After hiring a management consulting firm, the conference changed its name to the Leadership Conference of Women Religious (LCWR) and adopted new bylaws that defined sisters as "ecclesial people" and the Church as "the people of God."[41] The Sacred Congregation for Religious was not consulted in the change, and refused to give formal approval to the new name for three years.

Reaction and Rebellion: 1970–1986

A number of the superiors in LCWR were troubled by its change of focus and its abrogation, as they saw it, of allegiance to Rome. The 1969 General Assembly's public support for the IHM sisters, in direct defiance of the demands of the SCR representative present, "shocked and alienated" them as a "direct affront to the legitimate authority of the Church over religious life."[42] Between 1970 and 1971, therefore, these sisters formed a more conservative group, the Consortium Perfectae Caritatis, and withdrew from LCWR. This departure of its most conservative members had the effect of moving LCWR further to the left in its own ideology. Throughout the 1970s and 1980s, the Consortium engaged in repeated attempts to persuade the Vatican to designate it as the official representative of U.S. religious communities and to withdraw recognition from LCWR. Since the number of superiors who were members of the consortium was only a fraction of the number in LCWR, however, their efforts were ineffective.[43]

Several events occurred during the 1970s that heightened the tension between LCWR and the Roman authorities.[44] In 1975, the first Women's

Ordination Conference was held. The SCR ordered LCWR, as the official representative of American sisters, to dissociate itself completely from the conference's proceedings and goals. The LCWR board unanimously refused to do so. In 1979, on the occasion of the new pope's visit to the United States, Sister Theresa Kane, RSM—the president of LCWR for that year—greeted John Paul II before a national television audience by telling him that the Church "must respond" to its own call for affirming the dignity of all persons by allowing women to become ordained. The pope visibly registered his disapproval of such audacity.

John Paul II was more inclined than his predecessor to take an activist role in reasserting the Vatican's authority over religious life. In several addresses and letters, he revealed his concern that religious orders were becoming too secularized, too preoccupied with social concerns, and not sufficiently involved in the service of the Church.[45] In 1983, he directed American bishops to conduct a study of women's religious congregations in their country, with special attention given to the reasons for the precipitous drop in vocations.[46] Despite official denials, the directive was widely seen by sisters as an attempt by Rome to reverse the renewal of their orders. This impression was strengthened by the fact that the Sacred Congregation for Religious released a document entitled "Essential Elements in Church Teaching on Religious Life" simultaneously with the pope's letter.[47] According to the SCR, all religious orders and congregations were required to have a corporate apostolate and recognized houses in which the members would live together, and to give public witness through the wearing of a standard habit or religious garb. Since, by this time, many sisters were living and working apart from other members of their congregations, and since over a third of them no longer wore a habit, they viewed the "Essential Elements" as a repudiation of their lifestyle.[48] In spite of the sisters' apprehensions, however, the bishops' final report basically affirmed their efforts and attributed the decline of religious vocations, not to the pernicious effects of their renewal, but to the negative impact American cultural changes and the Second Vatican Council's elevation of the laity had had on their communities.[49]

Tensions between LCWR and Rome reached a height late in 1984. During the American presidential campaign of that year, several U.S. bishops had condemned Geraldine Ferraro, the Democratic Party's vice-presidential candidate, for her position on abortion. Some of the bishops' statements had appeared to imply that Catholics were bound in conscience not to support the Democratic ticket. In response, a group of Catholics took out a full-page ad in the *New York Times* on October 7, 1984, in which they stated that U.S. Catholics held a diversity of opinions on abortion, and that debate on the issue should not be stifled. Among the signers were twenty-six nuns and three religious priests and brothers.

In December, the heads of the sisters' communities (all of whom were members of LCWR) received letters from the SCR demanding that they force the signers to retract their statement, on penalty of expulsion if they refused. Several of the superiors immediately contacted LCWR, which held three meetings of the communities involved during December and January. These meetings enabled the sisters to identify and explore their options, to develop a shared perspective on the legal issues, and to give each other mutual support.[50] One of the ad's signers, Sister Margaret Farley, R.S.M., had already been scheduled as a main speaker at LCWR's 1985 General Assembly. Both the U. S. bishops and the Vatican officials now exerted strong pressure on LCWR to cancel her invitation. When LCWR refused, both Archbishop Quinn (who was heading the Pontifical Commission to study religious life) and Pio Laghi, the apostolic delegate, "rescinded their acceptance of invitations to celebrate liturgy and speak at the assembly."[51] Ultimately, a face-saving compromise was devised through the sisters' efforts, and most of the twenty-six signers were able to issue clarifications, not retractions, of their statements. A few, however, left their orders.

Throughout the 1970s and 1980s, the basic ambiguity of the Vatican's stance on the renewal of religious orders continued to resurface. On the one hand, the 1983 revised Code of Canon Law contained only 173 canons on religious orders—as compared to over 2000 in the 1917 compilation—and left many issues and policies to the discretion of the individual congregations. On the other hand, the hierarchy's repeated attempts to dictate policy to individual communities appeared to contradict the decentralization and pluralism implied in both the Vatican documents and the 1983 code:

> The SCR's handling of renewal exemplified the strongest contradictions of Vatican II: renewal was discussed in terms that emphasized decentralization and an openness to the modern world, but in fact SCR sent ambiguous messages about the limits of the reform process, occasionally seemed to intentionally act secretively, and then eventually decided that, most important, the authority structure of the Church must remain unchallenged.[52]

The confused signals and lack of due process in disputes were deeply alienating to American religious orders.

Confronting Decline; 1986–1992

Throughout the 1970s and early 1980s, the members of religious orders, while cognizant of—and somewhat worried about—the large number of departures from their commuinities and the paucity of new applicants, strongly resisted the idea that their communities would disappear as a result. Especially among women's communities, there is almost no documentary evidence that the possibility of organizational demise was a seriously considered reality that affected either the policies of the congregations or the daily lives of the sisters.[53]

Beginning in 1986, however, several events forced the communities to consider these issues. In May of that year, the *Wall Street Journal* published a front-page article entitled "Sisters in Need: U.S. Nuns Face Crisis as More Grow Older With Meager Benefits."[54] The article cited an estimated two billion dollar gap between the money available for the sisters' retirement and the amount needed, and recounted numerous stories of nuns going on public welfare, selling their motherhouses, and having meatless meals in order to make ends meet. The bishops and religious orders established the Tri-Conference Retirement Office[55] to address this need and, in 1987, authorized the first of a series of annual collections to create a retirement fund. The Tri- Conference's publications and activities had the effect of raising the consciousness of the men and women in religious orders regarding the financial implications of their communities' decline. A second sobering event occurred in the latter years of the decade, when several smaller communities were forced to merge with other orders. The news of such mergers was an additional impetus that led the leadership and members of religious orders to consider the possibility of such a fate happening to them. But even more disturbing revelations were about to come.

Between 1989 and 1992, a major study was being done of the men and women in U. S. religious orders. Funded by the Lilly Endowment, the study included a national survey of a randomly sampled 9,999 religious priests, brothers, and sisters, as well as more detailed interviews with the leaders of religious communites and with individuals identified as particularly knowledgeable about religious life.[56] In addition to funding the original research, the endowment allocated $500,000 for the dissemination of its findings. Accordingly, in September 1992, the study's preliminary conclusions were published in the *New York Times*, the *Chicago Sun-Times*, the *Washington Post*, the *Boston Globe*, and in scores of other secular and church-related newspapers. The report was sobering in its assessment: "Without significant change, religious life in the United States will continue to decline, and, more important, those who most need the help of these orders will not be cared for."[57] The leadership of LCWR reacted somewhat defensively to the study's conclusions, which seemed to imply that the renewal of religious orders over which LCWR had presided during the past thirty years had had less than positive results.[58] Still, as their membership dropped below the 100,000 mark—an almost 50 percent decline from the 1960s high—and as their median ages approached seventy, religious communities were forced to acknowledge that their very existence might be in danger.

In the midst of these disturbing developments, several actions by the pope and the SCR gave renewed evidence that a serious discrepancy continued to exist between Rome's expectations for religious orders and the willingness of the orders to conform to them. On June 22, 1992, the SCR announced the formation of a new "Council of Major Superiors of Women Religious," parallel to LCWR, to represent approximately 10,000 U.S. sisters in more conservative communities.[59] LCWR, by way of comparison, still represented over 90,000 sisters in 1992. LCWR and the Conference of Major Superiors of Men immediately protested the Vatican's action and noted that, whereas LCWR membership was open to all, membership in the new council depended on adherence to a set of preordained criteria and was subject to approval by the council's board. Christian Brother Paul Hennessy, the president of CMSM, stated that "these women declared themselves more authentically religious [than the women in LCWR] and more loyal to the Holy See. . . . We feel that special recognition given to a small group is offensive and is not unifying."[60] The new Council also had an episcopal liaison directly with Rome, something neither LCWR nor CMSM had. Many observers felt that this would enable the council to bypass the U.S. bishops. Several U.S. bishops expressed only reluctant consent to the Vatican's decision and emphasized their continuing support for LCWR.[61]

The new council aligned itself unambiguously with the traditionalist views on religious life. Both its statutes and the keynote speaker at its first national assembly appeared to subscribe to the pre-*Lumen Gentium* ideology that there were three forms of Christian discipleship (not two as the Second Vatican Council had stated) and that the religious life was a more uncompromising and better response to the gospel call than that of the laity.[62] Their statutes' preamble, for example, while briefly mentioning that every person was indeed called to holiness in imitation of Christ, also asserted that sisters were bound by a specific call "to live for God alone." This implied that the rest of the laity were not so bound.[63] The group also emphasized its subordination to the Church's hierarchy. The official episcopal liaison was "to be invited to council assemblies, be informed of all important council business, and be consulted beforehand on all committee appointments and all plans of the board regarding the council's annual national assembly. The liaison must be notified of any proposed changes in the council's statutes before they are sent to Rome for approval."[64] In contrast, the LCWR and CMSM met several times a year with the National Conference of Catholic Bishops, a process indicating a relationship more of equals than of superior and subject.

While U.S. religious orders were digesting the implications of the new Council of Major Superiors, another announcement from Rome was causing consternation among religious orders in other countries as well. In January 1992, the pope announced that a special worldwide Synod of Bishops would be convened in 1994 to discuss religious life. The uneasiness of religious orders over how much input they would be allowed to have in a conference of clerics (most of whom were *not* members of religious orders themselves) was exacerbated when the preliminary outline of the synod topic, its "Lineamenta," was released in November 1992. Critics immediately noted that this document's discussion of the nature of religious life was very similar to that of the much maligned 1983 "Essential Elements"; that it was narrowly monastic in focus and gave little consideration to any forms of religious life after 549 A.D., that it assumed religious life to be superior to lay life, that it failed to consider the experiences of women's communities and "totally ignored the challenge of Christian feminism," and that it "did not refer in any significant way" to the "paradigm change" that had been initiated by the Second Vatican Council or to the prophetic dimension that had so carefully been developed since then as a new theological basis for religious life.[65] The role of the vows was treated in a "confusing" manner, reinstating the "flight from the world" model that many had thought repudiated by *Gaudium et Spes*.[66] Modern society was discussed "in a tone which denotes derision or at best cynicism . . . for example, 'the cult of freedom' or . . . 'a mistaken idea of feminism.' It gives the impression that human dignity and rights are to be lesser values" in religious life than they are elsewhere."[67]

Most alarmingly for many observers, the "Lineamenta" laid a heavy stress on obedience to the hierarchy and devotion to the pope.[68] This appeared to indicate that the real objective of the synod was not, as its declared purpose had stated, "to introduce the topic and to foster a preliminary study of it,"[69] but rather "to bring religious fully into line with the requirements of the present pontificate and with the 'Directives' (to use his own word) of John Paul II in person. The Roman authorities have been concerned for a long time about 'dissident' religious . . . and, more recently, about some 'dissident' religious bishops (e.g. Archbishop Weakland of Milwaukee, who has openly queried the official position on the status of women in the church)."[70] Past synods, one critic noted, had produced final documents that were essentially similar to the lineamenta that had preceded them. The conclusions of the 1994 synod were likewise felt to be foreordained. "Briefly, the "Lineamenta" contain what John Paul II wants to say to religious today through the synod as intermediary."[71] Whether or not the orders would listen remained to be seen.

The above section is a very brief summary of a historical process that has been treated more extensively elsewhere.[72] An outline of the main events is given in table 12.1.

The following chapters will examine the causal factors underlying the decline of American religious orders during the latter half of the twentieth century, using the theoretical model developed in chapters 2 through 11. Why did the events outlined above have such dramatically negative results, especially when they had originally been envisioned as beneficial? Why was there such negative reaction among religious orders when the Vatican attempted to "rein in" the renewal? In chapters 13 and 14, we will explore one possible explanation for the communities' decline: that the new Church teachings caused the collapse of the ideological frame that had legitimated religious life in previous centuries. We will also explore the organizational dilemmas occasioned by the adoption of a new ideological frame for religious communities, and the implications of these dilemmas for the orders' willingness—and ability—to respond to Rome's demands.

Table 12.1 Key Dates in the Renewal and Decline of U.S. Religious Orders

1950:	(Nov. 26–Dec. 8) First General Assembly of Religious held in Rome. Pope Pius XII calls for adaptation and renewal.
1951:	(September) Meeting of women's teaching congregations in Rome.
1952:	First U.S. Congress of Religious Communities held at Notre Dame. National Catholic Education Association meeting in Kansas City.
1954:	Establishment of the Sister Formation Conference (SFC).
1956:	Establishment of the U.S. Conference of Major Superiors of Women (CMSW) and the Conference of Major Superiors of Men (CMSM).
1959:	Death of Pius XII; election of John XXIII. John XXIII announces the convening of an "Ecumenical Council."
1962:	(Oct. 11) Vatican Council II opens.
1963:	Death of John XXIII; election of Paul VI.
1964:	Vatican Council document *Lumen Gentium* published.
1965:	(Oct. 25) Vatican Council issues *Perfectae Caritatis*, the Decree on the Adaptation and Renewal of Religious Life.
1966:	High point of membership in U.S. religious orders and congregations: 181,421 women and 45,300 men.
1966–1968:	"Sisters' Survey" developed and disseminated by CMSW.
1967–1968:	Controversy between Cardinal James McIntyre of Los Angeles and the Sisters of the Immaculate Heart of Mary.
1969:	(July–August) Contemplative nuns meet at Woodstock, Md., despite the opposition of bishops and the Vatican, to consider how to apply the second Vatican Council's call for renewal to their lives. Publication of the Vatican decree *Venite Seorsum* mandating cloister for contemplative nuns.
1970:	High point in the number of departures from U.S. religious orders: 4,337 women left religious life in this year.
1971:	CMSW changes its name to the Leadership Conference of Women Religious and adopts a new set of by-laws.
1970–1971:	Formation of the Consortium Perfectae Caritatis, in reaction to CMSW/LCWR policies of 1967–1971.
1975:	First Women's Ordination Conference.
1979:	Sister Theresa Kane, R.S.M. addresses Pope John Paul II during his visit to the U.S.
1980:	First follow-up to the 1967 "Sisters' Survey."

Table 12.1 Continued

1983:	(Jan.) Revised Code of Canon Law published.
1983:	(May 31) John Paul II directs American bishops to conduct a study of American religious communities, and appoints a special commission, directed by Archbishop John Quinn, for the purpose.
1983:	(May 31) "Essential Elements of Religious Life" published by the Vatican's Sacred Congregation for Religious.
1984–1985:	Controversy over the signing of the abortion statement in the *New York Times*.
1986:	*Wall Street Journal* article on retirement needs of religious communities; U.S. bishops and religious orders establish the Tri-Conference Retirement Office.
1992:	(January) Pope John Paul II informs the superiors of religious orders that he has decided to convene, in 1994, a Synod of Bishops to discuss the topic "Consecrated Life in the Mission of the Church and in the World."
1992:	(June) Council of Major Superiors of Women Religious established by the SCR. LCWR fears that this is an attempt by Rome to decertify LCWR as the official representative for U.S. religious communities and to replace it with a more conservative organization.
1992:	(September) Results released of nationwide study on the Future of Religious Orders in the United States.
1992:	(November) The "Lineamenta" (that is, the outline and discussion questions) for the 1994 Synod of Bishops is published.

Chapter 13

The Collapse of an Ideology, I: The Purpose of Religious Life

The years immediately following the Second Vatican Council saw a profound shift in the way members of religious communities defined both their activities and the very reason for their existence. Such an ideological transformation would be disruptive in the best of circumstances, and the 1960s and 1970s were *not* the best of circumstances. Inherent contradictions rendered the adoption of a new self-definition impossible. The resulting "ideological limbo," it will be argued, was a major causal factor in the decline of religious communities.

Methods of Research

In order to trace the changes in how members of religious communities felt about themselves and about their lifestyle, it is necessary to study the written definitions and justifications advanced for religious life and its component activities during the years both before and after the Vatican Council. Of the many possible sources for these articulations, the one most readily available to the U.S. researcher is the Jesuit "trade" periodical, *Review For Religious*. The bimonthly *Review* has been continuously published since 1942 and bound copies are available in most Catholic college and university libraries. It contains articles written by priests and nuns on various topics, amd has also printed many of the directives from the pope and the SCR pertaining to religious life. The selection of articles reflects the decisions of a small and extremely stable editorial board, composed largely (and, until 1978, completely) of Jesuits.[1] It also reflects, of course, the pool of articles submitted to the editors for consideration in any given year.[2]

Because of the duration and breadth of its coverage, the *Review* has been called "the most pertinent" periodical for any study of the renewal of religious life during the past four decades.[3] This section will expand previous analyses of articles appearing in the *Review*, in an attempt to discover the impact of ecclesial and societal events upon those who subscribed to it. What effect did Pius XII's call for religious to update their customs and modernize their education have on the average members of the communities? How rapidly and to what degree did the sisters and the religious priests and brothers become aware of the implications of *Lumen Gentium*'s "universal call to holiness"? How much internal division resulted from the strains of renewal and the controversies with the Vatican? Answers to these questions might be gleaned both by observing the relative proportion of articles devoted to a given topic over the years, and also by analyzing the content of the articles themselves.

Preliminary Findings

Table 13.1 lists the types of articles that have appeared in the *Review* since 1950. An examination of the table reveals some interesting patterns. Prior to 1962, the most frequently represented category was that of general spirituality, which included articles on the virtues, sin, exemplary lives of the saints, and prayer. An average of 26 percent of the articles were devoted to these topics each year. A small but steady stream of psychological articles during the 1950s treated such topics as the use of psychological testing for new applicants and mental illness among religious. Another category (averaging somewhat more than 18 percent of each volume) included articles on the spirituality of particular orders, as well as articles on daily life in a religious community (the keeping of hours of silence, cloister, and so on). Had there been any articles on the adaptations called for by Pius XII, they would have been placed in this category. In fact, however, there were few such articles. Between 1950 and 1955, the *Review* simply published Pius XII's pronouncements without commentary. Such texts have been listed in the "Roman Documents" section of table 13.1. In 1955 and 1956, the *Review*'s regular canon law columnist compiled several collections of these pronouncements, again without commentary, and also authored two technical articles on the specific legal changes the pronouncements called for.[4] Not until 1957, and then only in response to a reader's request, did the *Review*'s "Questions and Answers" column print a one-page list of bibliographic references concerning the renovation and adaptation of religious orders Pius had called for seven years before. Of the

Table 13.1 Average Proportion of Articles, by Topic, in *Review for Religious*,
1950–1992

Years	General Theo. & Scripture	General Spirituality	Theology of Religious Life	Vows, General	Poverty	Chastity
1950–62	5.1%	26.2%	3.1%	0	•••	••
1963–69	4.5%	12.3%	6.4%	•••	2.6%	3.9%
1970–86	4.9%	30.6%	1.7%	1.1%	1.6%	2.0%
1987–92	4.7%	34.0%	•••	•	0	••

• One article on this topic during entire period.
•• Two articles on this topic during entire period.
••• Three articles on this topic during entire period.
Note: A full table, listing the figures for each year from 1950 until 1992, is given in appendix A.

six paragraphs in this bibliography, the first three simply listed the relevant Vatican documents, while the fourth cited the decrees of the National Conference. During the entire decade, only two *Review* articles addressed the possible ways in which individual communities might begin to carry out Pius XII's call.[5]

Notably sparse during this period were articles dealing with the vows, or any theological attempts to explain what, in essence, religious life actually *was*. There were also relatively few articles on the ministries the various orders performed, and many of the ministerial articles that did occur were simply anecdotal recountings of the life of a nursing sister or a teaching brother.

The years of the Second Vatican Council and immediately afterward reveal a sudden change. Articles dealing with general spirituality dropped precipitously, comprising less than half the proportion of each volume that they had occupied in the 1950s. Conversely, articles devoted to renewal and adaptation dramatically increased. Topics such as "preparing for and planning change, reorganizing government structures, studying the charism of the founders, experimentation with community forms and with the adaptation of the habit"[6] began to occur far more frequently—an upsurge reflected in the "Spirituality and Practice of Religious Life" column of table 13.1. This pattern in the *Review's* articles mirrored a trend Kolmer found in books published for religious communities at the same time: "One finds a strong emphasis on structural renewal and an attempt simply to understand what is going on."[7] The *Review's* articles on the spirituality and practice of religious life peaked in 1969 at 45.2 percent of that volume and have remained at a somewhat elevated level ever since.

In addition to the plethora of articles on various renewal topics, there were also more attempts to articulate an overall theology of religious life

Obedience	Spirit & Pract. of Religious Life	Canon Law, Roman Documents, Papal Writing	Psych.	Ministry & Social Justice	Misc.	Average Number of Articles per year
2.3%	18.6%	20.7%	8.1%	3.3%	11.5%	(31)
5.9%	27.9%	16.1%	7.7%	5.4%	6.5%	(64)
1.2%	26.5%	7.7%	5.8%	8.2%	8.8%	(84)
...	30.4%	6.8%	5.4%	12.5%	4.0%	(91)

than there had been in the 1950s (6.4 percent of each year's articles after 1962 compared to 3 percent before that time). There were also many more articles on the vows (11–12 percent of each volume), but fewer reprints of Vatican documents.

The number of articles devoted to topics of ministry or social justice remained surprisingly low throughout the 1960s, averaging only about 5 percent of each year's total. As Kolmer has stated, "There was little mention of the social climate in the country at large in this literature of renewal. One might believe that the social protests for civil rights did not exist if one had to learn about them from publications about religious life at this time."[8] The organizational upheavals attendant upon renewal simply eclipsed other concerns, at least insofar as can be estimated from published articles in the *Review* and elsewhere. This contrasts with a recently growing mythology that religious orders developed a widespread social consciousness in the early 1960s.[9]

Beginning in about 1973, articles on general spirituality, prayer, and the like began to increase again in the *Review,* and they have, on average, comprised between 30 percent and 35 percent of each volume ever since. Articles on the spirituality and practice of religious life declined slightly in the 1970s (from 29 percent to about 27 percent of each volume), but rose again in the 1980s and 1990s. Treatments of the vows and the theology of religious life also declined, but did not rebound. By the 1990s, there were few articles on either topic. The number of ministry/social justice articles did begin to increase after 1976, and comprised the third most frequently represented category by 1990.

Within the "Spirituality and Practice of Religious Life" category, specific topics show interesting patterns. Articles on vocational recruitment appeared briefly in 1980 (five articles) and then disappeared until 1985. There have been about one or two articles per year on this topic since that time. The number of articles on the training of new candidates once they had been recruited also increased when compared to the 1960s and early 1970s—precisely as the number of actual candidates to be trained decreased. In the years since 1982, there have been, on average, three or four of these articles per year. Articles about retirement and about aging religious began to make a consistent appearance during the 1970s; articles about individuals transferring from one order to another occurred sporadically from 1975 on. Only in 1989, however, did the first articles on the possibility of an order's disintegration and death begin to appear, along with a few accounts of the merging of groups too small to continue existing on their own. Surprisingly, there were only a few articles either on women's ordination, or, explicitly at least, on women's spirituality, and there were no articles on the struggles between the sisters and the Vatican.

A simple listing of the types of articles appearing in the *Review* does, therefore, confirm some of the observations made earlier in chapter 12. The lack of any articles during the 1950s defining the overall purpose of religious life and, especially, the almost total absence of articles on the vows of chastity and poverty, indicate that these concepts were relatively unproblematic at the time. (Conversely, the *presence* of articles on obedience during the 1950s may indicate that this *was* a contested concept, even then.) The extremely small number of articles exploring the implications of Pius XII's call to renovation and adaptation confirms Kolmer's observation that the leadership-level developments sparked by the pontiff's call had little effect during their first decade.[10] The orders' concern with renewal following Vatican Council II is reflected in the sudden upsurge of articles on the spirituality and practice of religious life at that time. Some of these patterns may be preliminary indications that cherished myths among religious about their renewal processes were not, in fact, the case: The relative lack of articles on ministry and social justice during the 1960s appears to contradict liberals' perceptions of religious activism at that time, while the increase in articles on spirituality during the 1970s and 1980s (in a proportion *higher* than was usual during the 1950s) would seem to refute the conservative assumption that members of religious orders got "more worldly" when they discarded the habit and cloister.[11]

Before these changes in the basic ideological frame for religious life can be confirmed, however, one would have to analyze the actual content of the articles. The following section will attempt this task. Articles in the *Review* which relate to the distinction—if any—between the religious and the secular lay states will be summarized and critiqued. To supplement this analysis, sixteen of the most recently published "trade" books aimed at members of religious orders will also be surveyed.[12] Finally, summaries of the "mission statements"—short paragraphs defining the fundamental purpose or philosophy—for over 650 religious orders will be reviewed and analyzed.

Ideological Component I: The Meaning and Purpose of Religious Life

Formulations prior to 1962

In the decade immediately prior to 1962, there were few, if any, attempts to articulate a theology of religious life—to explain either what distinguished such a lifestyle from the lay state or why one would want to follow it. The books and articles written for religious communities "were superficial discussions of the spiritual life with heavy emphasis on the practice of such virtues as humility, trust, obedience and modesty," and were largely lacking in theological or scriptural underpinnings.[13] The sisters, brothers, and priests who wrote them appear never to have questioned that religious life was superior to being married,[14] that it was the best way of attaining spiritual perfection,[15] or that it was essentially and eternally unchanging.[16] There was no need to explain or justify the lifestyle any further. "Religious life is the same in its essentials all over the Catholic world. It consists of life in a community with the three vows of poverty, chastity and obedience under a lawful superior."[17] Only rarely, and only in the very last years before the Vatican Council, did writers on religious life even begin to hint that it was "not completely exact" to say that the lifestyle was a higher state than that of the average lay Christian.[18]

Whatever distinctiveness was postulated for a particular model of religious life applied mostly to the male orders. As was mentioned in chapter 7 (pp. 140–141, above), many of the women's congregations had never really had a distinct ideology to build on. "What founders and foundresses [of nineteenth-century women's congregations] [had] responded to was not a call to reinvent religious life but a call to meet a felt need in society: a need for education, or health care, or social work. They responded to that need by founding a congregation to meet it. . . . Consequently, they did not create . . . a new form of life or a new spirituality."[19] With a derivative and largely unexamined self-definition that was essentially the same as that of dozens of other religious congregations, new recruits learned what religious life was by memorizing a uniform "catechism" of received, unchanging knowledge. Rote answers to questions such as "What is a vow?" or "What is perfection?" gave the novice a set of definitions, a body of rules, and distinctions among degrees of virtue and culpability—all presented as unchanging fact.[20] With equal rigor, young sisters were introduced to the order's most minute customs, "including such details as the proper way to eat a banana or crush the shell after having consumed an egg."[21] Often, it was these minute customs, not the larger ideological frame, that distinguished one community from another.

Post Vatican II Formulations: 1962–1992

As was mentioned in chapter 12, the Vatican Council's documents redefined the levels of membership in the Church in such a way as to undercut—seriously—the traditional ideological frame for religious life. The
Review's authors recognized almost immediately that, in the post-Vatican
Catholicism described by *Lumen Gentium*, there was "no proper place" for
them, and they eagerly awaited the council's further pronouncements on
this issue.[22] When the long-awaited decree on religious life (*Perfectae caritatis*) was finally promulgated in 1965, however, members of religious communities were disappointed. In their eyes, the document did not advance
the same kind of groundbreaking theology in redefining the place of sisters
and male religious in the Church that *Lumen Gentium* had exhibited in
defining the role of the laity.[23] The role of ordained male religious was
especially unclear—were they priests first or monks/friars first? There was
a complete lack of any theology of religious priesthood that could satis-
factorily distinguish it from secular, diocesan priesthood.[24]
       Disappointment with the new decree translated almost immedi-
ately into opposition, as is reflected in the *Review* articles. A 1967 author
characterized it as "somewhat routine and uninspired," and pointed out
that the original draft had completely ignored the most fundamental legitimating belief in the orders' ideological frames—that the Holy Spirit
had been active in their foundations.[25] The author—a priest—also complained that "religious women have not had a word to say about all the
legislation that concerns them."[26] Criticism of the decree continued in
subsequent decades. A 1991 author called it merely "a revamp of the theology of the vowed life outlined by St. Thomas Acquinas in the thirteenth
century."[27]
       Despite such criticism, the Vatican hierarchy made no attempts to de-
velop a more satisfactory articulation. The 1983 "Essential Elements," for
example, merely reiterated the traditional definition of what constituted
religious life. Without a dynamic and positive statement from the council
specifying a new meaning and purpose for religious communities, the writers in the *Review* and elsewhere were forced to depend on *Lumen Gentium*,
the very document that had denied them any distinct place in the church.
With their sacred underpinnings thoroughly undermined by this document, religious orders were vulnerable to critics who wondered why they
should exist at all. In fact, articles bitterly attacking the very idea of religious life were beginning to appear in the Catholic press: One 1968
writer in the *National Catholic Reporter* labeled the lifestyle "gnostic and
jansenistic in its opposition to the world so that it is poisoned in its roots.
As an 'esoteric subculture,' with its 'stoic discipline' and 'unhealthy spirituality,' it is a countersign and parody of Christian baptism."[28] Religious

communities were thus put on the defensive even as they were attempting to begin their renewal process.

The first task, therefore, was to delineate a new purpose for religious life and to describe how (if at all) it differed from the life all baptized Christians were called to lead. Table 13.2 summarizes the definitions proposed, in the *Review* and elsewhere, between 1963 and 1991. While a few of these writers continued to maintain that the religious state *was* different— that it was more contemplative, more intense, more communal— than that of the laity, an even larger number of authors specifically denied that it was superior in any way. This left them with the task of devising a new definition of, and legitimation for, the very lifestyle their readers had taken for granted for so many years. And, by the mid- to late 1980s, a coherent alternative definition had, in fact, been proposed: the *Review's* authors now held that all Christians were indeed called to the same holiness, but that religious were called to *an increased level of visibility* in living out this call. Thus, they were to serve as prophets or public witnesses to the rest of the Church.

It is immediately evident, however, this formulation did not achieve unambiguous hegemony as the new ideological frame for religious life. First of all, the *Review's* various authors differed in exactly what message the newly prophetic religious were supposed to be witnessing to the rest of the Church. The new definition also failed to receive the Vatican's approval: The word "prophetic" never once appeared in the 1992 "Lineamenta."[29] In addition to these problems, other authors ignored the "prophetic witness" definitions and claimed that religious life was simply one way among many equally valid ways of responding to Christ's friendship or living one's baptismal consecration. Such a lack of definition could become tautological: "So, how might we go about defining religious life? . . . I remember once asking a mathematician friend: 'What is mathematics?' She answered: 'Mathematics is new every day. I guess you could say mathematics is what mathematicians do.' This definition is a good model for us in our efforts to define religious life. Religious life is what religious do."[30]

Results of Frame Delegitimation

The Vatican Council's "universal call to holiness" drastically weakened the definitional boundaries that had made religious life a separate and privileged state within the Church. The impact of this delegitimation was swift and profound. By 1969, the LCWR-sponsored "Sisters' Survey" found that its respondents were almost evenly divided on the issue of whether their life was distinct: 48.1 percent agreed that "religious have a greater call to holiness and apostolic responsibility than do Christian lay-

Table 13.2   Suggested Definitions for Religious Life:
Ways to Distinguish the Religious from the Lay State

Religious life is distinct from the lay state:

in achieving perfection through living the vows
(Tillard, 1963; Brezik, 1989)

as a more intimate encounter with Christ; a more integral response to the Christian vocation
(Hogan, 1983)

religious are more contemplative; laity more active
(Johnston, 1969)

religious live the evangelical counsels all the time; laity live them sporadically or partially
(Schleck, 1965; Kiesling, 1986; Moreno, 1992)

religious life is lived in community
(Garvey, 1972; Doyle, 1973; Brinkman, 1971; O'Connor, 1987)

Religious life is a public/prophetic witness:

not a greater or a different holiness from that of the laity, but a different level of visibility:
Schleck, 1969; O'Connor, 1990: 5

a witness to the baptismal calling to holiness which all have received
(Haring, 1963; O'Reilly, 1968; Tambasco, 1973; Sheets, 1985; Reck, 1986)

a witness to the Church as Bride of Christ
(Hinnebusch, 1963)

a witness to the "absolute priority of God's interests," or that fulfillment is possible only in Christ
(Tillard, 1964a; Garcia, 1980; Quinn, 1983b; O'Connor, 1987; Arbuckle, 1988: 67; Merkle, 1992: 106, 143)

a witness to Christ's presence in the world
(Woodward, 1987:246; Munley, 1988:188)

a witness to gospel values and/or the spirit of the beatitudes
(Munley, 1988:188; Schneiders, 1986:94)

a witness to the eschatological Kingdom of God/the life to come
(Tillard, 1964b; John, 1965, Danielou, 1965; Martelet, 1965; Fichtner, 1966; Tillard, 1967; Larkin, 1968; Schleck, 1969; McKenna, 1992; Donovan, 1989c; Neal, 1990: 69)

a witness of universal "archetypical values" to all humankind
(O'Murchu, 1991: 48, 54; Munley, 1992: 1)

Table 13.2 Continued

Religious life is merely one way among many equally valid ways

of responding to Christ's friendship
(Fink, 1968)

of achieving holiness or likeness to Christ
(Schleck, 1969; Futrell, 1969; Ewen, 1984; Fitzpatrick, 1980)

of living one's baptismal consecration
(Schneiders, 1987)

Authors specifically denying that religious life is superior to lay life:

Holstein, 1961; Haring, 1963; Tillard, 1964; Dodd, 1964; John, 1965; Schleck, 1965; Tillard, 1967; S. Elaine Marie, 1967; Fink, 1968; O'Reilly, 1968; Schleck, 1969; Johnston, 1969; Futrell, 1969; Knight, 1973; Tambasco, 1973; Lozano, 1983; Casey, 1988; Schneiders, 1988; O'Murchu, 1991; Merkle, 1992.

men [sic]," while 44.8 percent disagreed.[31] Popular books read by religious began to proclaim their essential identification with the laity: "Everyone is called to be a monk today. . . . The call is general."[32] The roles advanced for members of religious orders became less and less distinguishable from those assigned to all baptized believers: One author stated that the purpose of religious priests, brothers, and sisters was to be "engaged in the ministry of action. They are actively involved in making economic, political and moral decisions by which they define the message of Christ in the human consequences of what they do."[33] It was hard to see how this purpose differed from the calling of any lay Christian.

A symbol—and a consequence—of this weakening of the "wall of separation" which had formerly divided the religious from the secular life, was the modification or discarding of a distinctive religious habit. By 1982, for example, 55.6 percent of U.S. sisters had made major changes such as shortening the habit's skirt to street-length, abolishing scapulars and wimples, and simplifying the veil. Another 34 percent had ceased wearing any form of habit at all.[34] Other aspects of the boundaries between religious and secular life were also blurred. Communities adopted psychological screening processes for new applicants that were borrowed from the secular world; entrants retained their given names instead of adopting new, "religious" ones. Some religious orders began to resemble self-help groups: "One community declared one of its five goals for integrating new members to be that each 'deepens her understanding of self; spiritually, psychologically, socially, emotionally, sexually.'"[35] A critic termed this the "therapeutic" or "me-istic" model of religious life, in which the primary function of the religious community was "to serve the individualistic and narcissistic or self-fulfillment needs of members."[36]

As a result of this boundary reduction, many members of religious communities rapidly lost their sense of "role clarity." A 1981 survey of some 2,100 Catholic women nationwide (including some 800 high school and college students and one hundred sisters) concluded that, not only were the lay respondents uncertain about the role of women religious in the Church, but the sisters themselves also exhibited "a sense of ambiguity" about their mission.[37] The 1990 national survey of 10,000 men and women in religious communities found that only 55 percent of the sisters reported high role clarity, while a full 30 percent were in the "low role clarity" category.[38] The authors of this survey considered this decline in role clarity "the most compelling result" of their study.[39]

Lack of role clarity can also be seen in the "mission statements" of the congregations. Most religious communities have written statements to define their corporate purpose. Key excerpts from these statements are published in a yearly *Formation Directory*, along with other pertinent information about each order or congregation, to assist the persons who might consider entering religious life.[40] Of the 651 active U.S. communities listed in the 1992 *Directory*, 84.9 percent of the women's groups and 61.5 percent of the men's orders had submitted mission statements as requested. Table 13.3 analyzes the specificity of these statements, both for orders confined to one particular ministry and for orders serving a variety of needs. Specific mission statements were any that mentioned a ministerial focus ("We continue the work of education of youth.") or geographical limitation ("We serve the missions in East Africa." "We dedicate ourselves to ministries of service, primarily in the Dioceses of Peoria and Springfield."), as well as any that referred to a specific founder's spirituality, example, or rule. Vague mission statements, on the other hand, failed to distinguish an order's role either from that of other communities or from the general call given to all baptized Christians. *Only 25 percent of the women's communities had mission statements that could be considered specific under the above definition.* Even congregations confined to a specific ministerial work often did not mention it in their mission statements.

What few differences did exist in the vague mission statements of most of the women's congregations were subtle and did not fully distinguish them from other groups. For example, an unusually high proportion (75.6 percent) of the Benedictine women's communities mentioned community living in their mission statements (as compared to only 21 percent that mentioned St. Benedict or the Benedictine *Rule*). But many other congregations also mentioned community, if not quite so consistently. Six of the Dominican congregations mentioned study in their statements; few non-Dominican groups did so. But thirty-two other Dominican congregations did *not* mention study as part of their mission. Most St. Joseph

Table 13.3 Definitional Specificity in Mission Statements: U.S. Religious Orders, and Congregations, 1992

	Women's Communities		Men's Communities	
	%	(N)	%	(N)
Communities with vague mission statements[a] in diversified ministries:	63.4	(263)	46.1	(48)
Communities with vague mission statements[a] in specified ministries:	10.8	(45)	3.8	(4)
Communities with specific mission statements[b] in diversified ministries:	13.0	(54)	15.3	(16)
Communities with specific mission statements[b] in specified ministries:	12.8	(53)	34.6	(36)
No mission statement submitted:	—	(67)	—	(65)
	100	(482)	100	(169)

[a] Examples of vague mission statements:
  "Rooted in the Eucharist and personal prayer, we continue the mission of Jesus by striving to be and to experience Christ's redeeming presence as we affirm and empower one another and those we serve, especially the poor." (#2210)
  "We work for justice and act for peace because the Gospel urges us. We commit ourselves to improving the condition of those who suffer from any injustice, oppression and deprivation of dignity." (#4530)
  "The [—] Sisters are ecclesial women sharing a vision and responding to the call of God. Sustained by a deep prayer life and empowered by our communal and vowed life, we dare to seek new ways to serve the Church. Open to risk, we trust in God and walk in courage." (#2796)
[b] Examples of specific mission statements:
  "To reach retreatants by opening our doors to them and to all who come for care and meetings." (#2140)
  "[We] make the merciful love of God visible to women and girls who have been wounded emotionally and spiritually, and rejected by society . . . [Our] mission is evolving into various ministries that touch . . . also families." (3998)
  "[We] staff a junior college, have several priests and two brothers on parishes." (9074)
  "[We] . . . live in community and share the spirit of the cross by consecration of self . . . and by . . . apostolic activities in everything which pertains to the priesthood and to the religious life: teaching and formation of future priests, . . . confessions for priests, seminarians and sisters, retreats and conferences to priests, seminarians and sisters. . ." (#8760)
Source: Eleace King and Thomas P. Ferguson, eds. CARA *Formation Directory for Men and Women Religious, 1992*. (Center for Applied Research in the Apostolate, Georgetown University, P.O. Box 1601, Washington, D.C.)

congregations mentioned a commitment to unity; they did not claim this emphasis to be unique, however, nor were they clear on how unity would be realized. Many orders had some reference to their title in their mission statements: the Sisters of Providence usually mentioned God's providence; the Daughters of Wisdom, the Sisters of the Holy Faith, and the Sisters of the Holy Family referred to these concepts. But rarely was it specified what role providence, or wisdom, or faith was to play. It is in analyzing the congregations' mission statements that the inheritance of their suppressed distinctiveness—the centuries when women's communities were forced to conform to monastic cloister, the foundation of nineteenth-century women's congregations by clerics who were more concerned with their labor than their distinctive spirituality—is appallingly evident.

As might be expected, the mission statements of the men's orders—when they submitted them, which they were less likely to do than the women,—were more specific. The male groups were more likely to equate their mission with staffing a particular institution or with following their written Rule, statements the women's groups rarely made. Male orders were also more likely specifically to cite the example or charism of their founder than were the women's groups: 12 percent of the women's Franciscan congregations as compared to 37 percent of the male Franciscans submitted statements that made specific reference to the spirit of St. Francis. Nevertheless, a plurality even of the male orders submitted mission statements that were too vague to give nonmembers a clear idea of who they were or what goals they espoused.

Anecdotal accounts and case studies supplement the findings of the national surveys and the analysis of the mission statements. One *Review* author told of conducting a workshop for the men and women in religious communities who were in charge of training new entrants. After a thirty-minute discussion, "none in that group, composed primarily of individuals appointed by their congregations to aid in the formation of young religious, was able to express in a manner which could be understood and accepted by the others there what is most characteristic and distinctive of religious life."[41] Several studies have found a high degree of role confusion among religious priests, who were torn between their priestly identity and their (much less well- defined) identity as members of a religious order.[42] A case study of one Texas women's congregation found "a sense of anomie in terms of the purpose or mission of religious orders in the contemporary world."[43] Their old identity had been abrogated by the Second Vatican Council, and the new formulations—religious life as prophetic witness, religious life as merely one lifestyle choice among many—had not proved sufficient replacements. The promulgation—and repromulgation—of often vague mission statements in no way alleviated members' loss of role clarity.[44]

Contradictions in the New Ideological Frame

In part, this role ambiguity has persisted because there are several fundamental contradictions between contemporary religious life and the communities' ability to enact the one clear articulation of purpose that has been advanced for them in the post-Conciliar era—that of being prophetic witnesses. The first of these contradictions is the *dilemma of visibility*. It is difficult for a group to witness to a value or belief if its members cannot be identified as belonging to it. Many religious orders have discarded an identifiable habit or uniform dress as unnecessary for their new mission: "Jesus did not wear a habit and he certainly gave public witness."[45] Increased freedom of job choice has also made it difficult for communities to staff their institutions, which could have served as an additional vehicle for corporate visibility.[46] In addition, their new freedom to live and work where they chose also made religious free *not* to be prophetic.[47] As they moved increasingly into secular positions, critics charged, religious risked "identifying with their milieu to the point of becoming invisible."[48] One study found that, as a result of their invisibility, sisters were not strongly perceived by the Catholic laity as women of faith and prayer, nor as living witnesses to an identification with the poor.[49] The more its members became unidentifiable, therefore, the more difficult it became for any order, as a corporate entity, to fulfill its newly defined prophetic role. Of course, some of the individuals in the order may be giving strong witness—*as individuals*—to various Christian virtues. But, as one commentator noted, religious communities "have done a great deal to foster the prophetic individuals in their midst. At the same time, they have done very little to function as prophetic groups."[50]

A second contradiction is the *dilemma of diversity and individualism*. As congregations began to rearticulate their new identities, they attempted to consider the opinions of each and every member in the process. While this new emphasis on increasing individuality was welcomed by some as a liberation from the previous "herd mentality,"[51] it in fact made it extremely difficult to agree on any goals at all for the community, other than to advance some very general aims that could encompass the works and interests of all the members.[52] "Lost in this increasing pluralism is a sense of the purpose of it all. In some congregations, there has been such a diffusion of energies that it is difficult to see what remains in common."[53] No clear criteria could be given to measure whether and to what extent the community had moved toward its new role of prophetic witness, for fear of alienating those of the membership who did not agree.[54] In articulating how they would achieve their new identity, therefore, religious communities had to confine themselves to "pious and safe abstractions" rather than moving "to a more dangerously concrete level."[55] The orders' mission statements are a striking indication of this tendency.

A third contradiction is the *dilemma of professional versus religious identity*. By 1980, 94 percent of the sisters responding to the "Sisters' Survey" had bachelor's degrees and 43 percent had at least one master's.[56] In the absence of a distinct role for themselves as religious, many of these sisters felt the pressure to fit their behavior and their self-definition to the powerful professional paradigms current among their lay colleagues. "The result can be seen clearly in generations of religious who are often professional educators, social workers, or nurses first, and religious second."[57] The 1990 Nygren/Ukeritis survey found that, the more professional education reported by a respondent, the less role clarity he/she had.[58] As at least one recent author has noted, absorbing the dominant cultural values of professionalism and efficiency can interfere with a group's ability (and willingness) to be prophetic.[59]

The flurry of articles and books on the theology of religious life, which appeared in the *Review* and elsewhere, did indeed formulate a new ideological frame to define a meaning and purpose for this form of religious virtuosity within the Church. But the rising individualism of the communities' members and their competing identities as professionals prevented the specific and concrete *enactment* of the new ideology within a given community.[60] Lack of corporate visibility (whether through common dress or community-run institutions) made it all the more difficult for the order as a whole to be seen fulfilling its prophetic role. Instead, many religious communities evolved into voluntary associations of individuals held together largely by affiliative ties.[61] By the mid-1980s, the editor of the *Review* was complaining that religious themselves "are a very major part of the reason for the fall-off in vocations. And this, at the base, is because, as a group, we have lost credibility. We no longer really know who we are. I find so much of our public image to be self-serving pretentiousness and grandiosity that is utterly lacking in credibility—and even worse, that is utterly boring."[62]

Conclusions

By the mid-1980s, belief in the superiority of a religious vocation over that of the average lay Catholic had been largely destroyed. Deprived of their former place and role in the Church, religious communities were left to devise a new ideological frame that would legitimate their existence. The most commonly suggested replacement, however, was unable to be realized on a communal basis. This led to a lack of role clarity and, ultimately, to the communities' inability to project a corporate image that would attract new entrants.

The legitimation or purpose of religious life was not, however, the only aspect of the communities' ideological frame that had to be rebuilt after the Vatican Council. In chapter 14, we will explore another aspect that underwent profound changes: the living of the vows.

The Collapse of an Ideology, II: the Vows and Community Life

The basic definition of religious life was not the only aspect of the orders' ideological frames that underwent drastic modifications in the years after the Vatican Council. The traditional articulations of the vows were also attacked by many writers, who saw them as irrelevant at best or as psychologically destructive at worst. As one *Review* author complained, "If sexuality, property and the exercise of personal judgment and decision are the raw material for growth into personhood, as is recognized today, will not the vows frustrate the maturity which is essential for a life of prayer and action?"[1] To meet such criticisms, the vow of obedience was totally redefined and diluted in its application; the vow of poverty's external obligations were completely reworked (even if its internal spirit remained theoretically the same); and the vow of chastity, while relatively unchanged, shed many of the peripheral practices Victorian society had attached to it.

Obedience

Traditional Formulations

During the 1950s, obedience was ranked first among the vows—surpassing even chastity in importance.[2] The number and content of the articles on obedience in the *Review* reflected this emphasis. Typical formulations emphasized the duty of the subject to fulfill all of the commands of the superior, even if they were unwise or imprudent: The subject was to trust that God's providence would draw good even out of a superior's mistakes.[3]

The highest form of obedience was *intellectual* obedience—to want what the superior wanted and to obey, not perforce, but with joy. Obedience was "giving up, out of love for the obedient Christ, the most precious thing that we have, our own will."[4] Writers frequently acknowledged, however, that this vow was the hardest for modern youth and was perhaps the reason why more young people did not enter religious life.[5]

There were other problems with obedience besides its unattractiveness to the young. During the early twentieth century, there had been a proliferation of new rules and minutiae and an increased autocratism, especially in the women's communities.[6] Both of these factors led to pent-up dissatisfaction and alienation among the rank and file members. In addition, by the end of the 1950s, psychologically trained religious were beginning to question the healthiness of the vow as it had traditionally been presented.[7] At the Sister Formation Conference's annual meeting at Notre Dame University in 1962, for example, one paper outlined examples of "the debilitating effects of some concepts of obedience on sisters' mental health."[8] Still another difficulty concerned the disjunction between religious obedience and professional autonomy:

> Observers have noted that it was in ministry settings, actually, that sisters had the opportunity to exert the autonomy of adults, in contrast to the dependence and docility expected in the convent. Instances abound. The administrator of a large teaching hospital not only ran the institution effectively but dealt with her peers in the field and with civic officials. The college president oversaw governance, finances and curricula. The scholarly anthropologist conducted field research with grant funding. The high school drama coach staged the annual musical to which an entire town flocked. All these women then returned to the convent, where they had to ask permission to stay up past 9 P.M. and where their lives were governed by the regulations of canon law and community custom.[9]

Finally, the submission required by the vow of obedience began to be criticized by some, not merely as psychologically dangerous, but as actually immoral: "After the disclaimers of guilt by obedient Nazis at the Nuremberg trials, religious men and women can no longer honestly idealize total submission to the will of another human being as a good."[10]

The Impact of Vatican II

Perfectae caritatis, the Vatican Council's 1965 decree on the adaptation and renewal of religious life, sent confusing signals about how the vow of obedience was to be "renewed." On the one hand, the document emphasized that obedience was to be defined in such a way as to respect the dignity of the individual. On the other hand, however, "not to be weakened . . . is the superior's authority to decide on what must be done and to require the doing of it."[11] The confusion was reflected in the 1969 "Sisters' Survey." While the majority (54.9 percent) of the survey's respondents disagreed with the statement, "The essence of religious life is the continual renunciation of one's own will," a strong minority (33.9 percent) continued to agree with it.[12] By the late 1960s, obedience thus had several definitions: "blind compliance with a superior's command; exercise and initiative for the sake of the common good, even in spite of the superior's command; community consensus; questioning and arguing a command with a superior in the style of 'the new executives,' and so forth."[13]

During these years, a new and more internalized definition of obedience was formulated, one that explicitly repudiated the old model of subjugation to a superior as "false and naive."[14] The new interpretation stemmed from the Latin root of the word—*obaudire*—and stressed that obedience was "an attitude of openness to the providential plan of God," a "life lived with alertness to the Spirit," a "search for God's will and its realization in ever newer forms," a "means to develop as an adult," or even "the actualization of one's own destiny."[15]

> Obedience, within this context, is primarily understood as fidelity. To be obedient demands that one uses all of one's capacities, that one creates. Further, being obedient calls for contemplation and continued conversion. Being obedient together means calling forth each person's gifts, reverencing each one's mystery, acknowledging and transforming each one's blurred sight.[16]

The "signs of the times" were thus given equal or even greater weight than the dictates of the community's superiors in revealing the will of God in one's personal life.[17] The former belief in the divine origin of communal authority was de-emphasized: "Communities democratized their systems of governance, legitimizing obedience to a superior in the style of a public servant rather than an infallible representative of God."[18]

Within the *Review*, treatments of obedience reflected three main tendencies. From 1963 to 1966, there were several traditional articles that continued to emphasize the divine authority of the superior. A second category current at this time stressed that superiors should be more consultative or more loving and that subjects should be more free, but did not doubt that a superior was necessary. (This position seems to be the official one taken in the Vatican Council documents.) Later articles in this category held that obedience was functional in religious communities because of sinful human nature or because, organizationally speaking, all groups must have a leader.[19] After the mid-1970s, however, both of these categories declined, and almost all articles in the *Review* treated obedience solely from the third perspective, that of listening to the will of God. Table 14.1 summarizes these changes.

However, several dilemmas arose from a conception of obedience that appeared to be primarily a matter of internal, personal attitude. The first was to explain how this new vow of obedience differed from the simple openness to the will of God required of all Christians.[20] Several authors also worried that, in a reaction to the excesses of the past, religious were now denying the very existence of *any* legitimate communal authority.[21] The lack of clearly defined authority, they felt, could lead to the tyranny of the group and the crippling limitation of elected officials' power "by the excessive and unreasonable use of communal discernment,"[22] or to "mediocre management, representing the least common denominator within an organization."[23] Others wondered whether the openness called for by the new definition was even possible: "Discernment is an exciting concept today," stated one *Review* author, "but few people, lay or religious, have the detachment to do a dependable job of it."[24]

Most of these criticisms ceased after the mid-1980s, however, as did most of the articles on obedience—from any perspective. In part, this was because the authors had a tendency to shy away from divisive topics.[25] However, it may also have resulted partly because, under the hegemony of the internalized, personalized definition, the vow had been shorn of any specific *communal* meaning. By 1982, for example, 75 percent of women's religious congregations in the United States reported having no local superior in some or all of their houses.[26] By 1989, only 11 percent of the sisters believed that "a truly obedient religious need seek no source other than her Rule and the will of her superiors to know what she should do."[27]

The reinterpretation of authority and obedience contributed to several of the conflicts and difficulties that arose in religious life during the 1970s and 1980s. The new emphasis on consultation and democracy within their own communities' governance structures led the sisters to expect the same treatment from the Vatican, and to become angry and alienated when it was not forthcoming.[28] The "radical de-sacralization of the Mother General and her authority" and the redefinition of obedience as one's own individual openness to the will of God had the net effect in many communities of reducing almost to nonexistence *any* instances when the vow of obedience impinged upon the life of the average sister.[29] "Technically, there was no question that the sisters remained bound by the vow of obedience; in fact, however, the range of obligations to which the vow bound them was reduced practically to nothing."[30] One recent author lamented that new constitutions and authority structures have re-

Table 14.1   Variations in the Definition of Obedience in *Review For Religious Articles*, 1963–1990

Year	Traditional Version: Emphasizes Superior's Authority	*Perfectae Caritatis* Definition: Superior Should Consult	Obedience as Listening to God
1963	Dubay ("Personal") Kruse ("Authority") Kruse ("Obedience")	Meyer Kelleher Hogan Dubay ("Under-standing") S. Theresa Mary	—
1964	—	—	—
1965	Gallen	Boisvert Tillard Dubay	S. Elaine Marie
1966	Schleck	M. Mary Viola Ward O'Rourke	—
1967	Greif	Gallen Laporte	S. Elaine Marie
1968	—	Cowburn	—
1969	—	—	Fichtner Auw Coursey
1970	—	M. Mary Francis	Sisters of Mercy
1971	—	—	Coulon & Nogosek Fink Ayo
1972	—	—	—
1973	—	Gau Dubay Knight* Goggin & Knight*	Tambasco Doyle
1974	—	Clancey* Dubay*	—
1975	—	—	DeMaria
1976	—	Regan	Hendricks
1977	—	—	Doohan
1978	—	—	Ratigan Jones
1979	—	—	Schineller Genovesi
1980	—	—	Fitzpatrick Agnew
1981	—	—	Winstanley
1982	—	Albrecht	Fitz
1983	—	Aschenbrenner*	Fitzgerald
1984	—	—	Ramsey
1985	—	—	O'Leary

Table 14.1   Continued

Year	Traditional Version: Emphasizes Superior's Authority	Perfectae Caritatis Definition: Superior Should Consult	Obedience as Listening to God
1986	—	—	—
1987	O'Connor	—	Korczyk
1988	—	—	—
1989	—	Aresto	—
1990	—	—	Whitehead McCarthy

*Denotes an article specifically critiquing the "Listening to God" definition of obedience.

sulted in superiors being "legislated into impotence."[31] There was often little indication that the central administration could command the sisters to do anything.[32]

The locus of power in religious communities changed. As sisters began to find their own jobs rather than relying on the motherhouse to place them, the motherhouse came to be dependent on the good will of the working sisters, who supplied it with funds. The author of one case study mentions the need for orders not to antagonize their wage-earning members by excessively intrusive demands.[33] Another notes that the only sanctions the California IHM sisters were able to apply to a recalcitrant member after the mid-1960s were either to drop her from the membership rolls (and thereby forfeit her financial contribution) or to deny her access to educational and spiritual functions.[34] Obedience, therefore, had become almost totally vitiated in its *corporate* meaning by 1990, although *individual* religious might, personally, still live lives of great openness to the Holy Spirit.

Poverty

Traditional Formulations

Unlike obedience, the vow of poverty was given very little attention either in the *Review* or in other publications on religious life before Vatican II.[35] The few articles that did occur seemed to presume both an internal and an external component. Externally, the canonical obligation assumed by the vow primarily limited the individual's right to dispose of anything without first asking the permission of his/her superior to do so.[36] More important than such external observances, however, was one's *internal* spirit of poverty. This was manifested in an indifference to expensive comforts and possessions.[37] Religious were urged not to be anxious about material things, but rather to be dependent upon God. The authors of the 1950s explicitly denied that the vow of poverty was incompatible with material possessions (provided, of course, that these possessions were communally held), but several did feel that there was *some* connection between material goods and poverty of spirit. For example, both Pius XII (1955) and John XXIII (1962) held that the vow of poverty required religious communities to forego surplus goods and ostentation. One *Review* author warned his women readers against collecting knickknacks.[38] In general, as with obedience, the sisters took the vow of poverty much more literally than did the men. Unlike their male counterparts before the mid-1960s, "individual sisters, except those in very specific roles, handled no personal budget at all."[39]

Post-Vatican Formulations

After 1963, a number of articles began to critique the way the vow of poverty had traditionally been interpreted in daily life. Just because a religious did not own but merely used some item did not, some noted, prevent him/her from developing a proprietary attitude toward it that negated the spirit of poverty.[40] The communal use of material goods did not witness what the world saw as poverty, others insisted, since the community as a whole might be quite well off.[41] The old interpretation of the vow had led to personal irresponsibility, security, and a middle-class lifestyle.[42] Worse still, the old practices of poverty were meaningless to the young recruits, who wanted to do more.[43] Between the 1960s and the 1980s, there was a pronounced erosion in the willingness of men and women in religious orders to subscribe to what had traditionally been considered the external dimension of the vow. In 1967, 40 percent of the respondents to the "Sisters' Survey" had believed that "vowed poverty means dependence on superiors, such that the use of all things falls under the authority and control of those who are set over the common life." By 1989, only 11 percent agreed with this statement.[44]

In general, however, the post-Vatican II authors continued to accept the *internal* dimension of the spirit of poverty as detachment from worldly things and dependence on God.[45] A few new connotations, however, were also added. Poverty now meant to place all one's possessions—including one's time and talents—in the service of Christ, renouncing possessiveness over them.[46] It meant accepting one's limitations,[47] and treating people as more important than things.[48] All of these internal attitudes were part of following the example of the poor Christ.[49]

For the external practice of communal ownership and asking permission to use material goods, some of the post-Vatican II authors substituted

various levels of actual material poverty. Inspired by an increased awareness of the actual conditions experienced by so many of the world's poor,
they argued that, without *some* material poverty, poverty of spirit meant
nothing.[50] Few of these authors advocated absolute destitution, however.
Most advised a lifestyle roughly equal to that of the average working-class
household; of choosing, in a spirit of simplicity, to resist the consumerism
of modern society and to have less rather than more.[51] The congregation
as a whole, they argued, should also prune itself regularly of its power,
wealth and prestige.[52]

As the 1970s progressed, other external criteria were also advanced
for living the vow of poverty. The *Review's* first mention of a vowed obligation to stand with and work for the betterment of the poor occurred in
1969, and then quite regularly after that.[53] Service to the poor was mentioned in 26.5 percent of the mission statements submitted to the 1992
CARA Formation Directory by the women's communities and in 24 percent of the men's statements, an indication that the communities were
taking this new obligation to heart.[54] Some authors interpreted the vow as
requiring them to critique their culture's treatment of the poor or to work
for redistributive justice—topics that also occurred in the orders' mission
statements.[55] In the late 1980s, still another external criterion for poverty
was advanced: that the vow bound its adherents to ecological stewardship
of the earth and of all creation.[56]

As with the vow of obedience, these new formulations of poverty
posed some definitional problems. Authors disagreed over the relative
weight to be given to the vow's internal and external components, and
over exactly what behaviors the external components should entail. Unlike virginity, the practice of which was fairly unambiguous, poverty could
never be absolute; therefore, its practice admitted of different degrees—
and types—of observance.[57] Poverty, stated one 1969 *Review* writer, "is
seen in many ways: a community possession of goods; care of the poor and
downtrodden; the spirit of *anawim*, of emptiness before God without reference necessarily to the question of material possession; the lack of concern for providing material goods (an unnecessary bother that is relieved
by the vow); actual physical poverty, and so forth."[58]

The distinction between the vowed poverty of religious and the poverty all baptized Christians were called to practice also became progressively less clear: Should not *all* Christians accept their limitations? feel
dependent on God? try to better the lot of the poor? steward the earth and
creation? "Poverty," stated one *Review* author as early as 1966, "needs to
be seen as an integral part of the Christian vocation, common to both lay
and religious."[59] The fact that the difference between Christian poverty
and vowed poverty was unclear further hampered the ability of religious
communities to fulfill their new role as prophetic witnesses to it.

Markham's 1981 survey of Catholic laywomen found that they did not perceive sisters as living a life of poverty and simplicity, nor did they believe that religious women were adequately serving the poor.[60] Furthermore, the dilution of obedience and the rise of individualistic interpretations of poverty meant that it was difficult to mobilize members to make greater communal sacrifices on its behalf, whatever their mission statements might say. One Canadian author noted the rise of a "class system" in some religious communities after 1968: Members working in relatively well-paying secular occupations were beginning to experience a higher standard of living than those in less remunerative fields.[61] As a rule, another author noted, the more general the call "for human caring and sharing, the higher the assent; the more specific the call for commitment to action in applying the justice agenda . . . the more individuals resist."[62] The 1990 survey of male and female religious, for example, found only a "moderate" level of commitment actually to work with the poor.[63] Like obedience, poverty ultimately came to be seen as an *individual preference* rather than a group commitment.[64]

Chastity

Traditional Formulations

Since the third century, celibate chastity has been universally considered *the* essential component of religious virtuosity within the Catholic Church; indeed, one theologian calls it "the ultimate, irreducible charism of religious life."[65] And yet, except for a few articles on modesty, there were no articles on this vow in the *Review* before 1961.[66] Any mention of chastity in other articles usually focused on aspects that might be considered rather peripheral today: reading "dangerous literature," for example, or avoiding undue attachments and "particular friendships."[67] The primary *reason* given for virginity during the 1950s, however, was the same as it was to be later: to free the religious to focus single-heartedly on Christ in a mystical union that many authors, both before and after Vatican II, compared to being "wedded to God."[68]

Unlike poverty and obedience, therefore, the basic content of and reason for the vow of chastity was not changed by Vatican II. And while peripheral observances such as definitions of appropriate reading material or modest deportment may have changed, the core of the vow—both its internal meaning and its basic external observance—did not. *Alone among the three vows, chastity still involved an identifiable behavior that set the members of religious communities apart from non-members.*[69] Furthermore, for women religious at least, the observance of the vow was a source of great spiritual meaning: The sisters responding to the 1990 survey ranked chastity as "the most meaningful and the least difficult" of the three vows.[70] And yet, even this aspect of religious life did not escape unscathed in the reworking of the ideological framework that followed the Vatican Council.

Post-Vatican Formulations

The early *Review* authors had had no doubt that consecrated virginity was better than being married. As late as the 1960s, one can still find a few articles in the magazine that asserted that "the objective excellence of virginity over marriage cannot be called into question," that it was "far more precious to God" and therefore "superior to matrimony."[71] Other authors in the 1960s and later, however, vigorously denied the superiority of chastity.[72] Furthermore, an increasing number of articles in the *Review* and elsewhere began to reflect the awareness that a celibate lifestyle might be considered psychologically unhealthy, or even impossible.[73] As the director of a psychological treatment center for members of religious orders put it: "We find that many of the neuroses we treat are aggravated by styles of spirituality and community life that encourage religious . . . to try to be happy without giving and receiving genuine affection and warm love."[74] By 1967, 65 percent of the respondents to the "Sisters' Survey" agreed that "the traditional way of presenting chastity in religious life has allowed for the development of isolation and false mysticism among sisters."[75]

Under these attacks, religious found themselves needing to defend the one aspect of their lives that was still readily identifiable. As one author in the *Review* ruefully remarked: "A celibate vocation remains very much on the defensive today. If formerly marriage was considered a second- rate vocation, it is clear that the atmosphere of sexual fulfillment as a necessary ingredient for maturity and personality growth has left the celibate vocation almost in need of a "singles lib" movement."[76] Or another: "Whereas formerly, religious assured the laity that, even though they were married, they could still attain true sanctity, now the laity have to assure religious that, even though they are celibate, they can still achieve true personhood and first-class citizenship as human beings."[77]

So why should anyone choose celibacy, if married life is just as holy and if chastity might be dangerous to one's psychic and spiritual health? Some authors in the *Review* held that, like poverty, obedience, and religious life in general, consecrated virginity was a prophetic sign of God's love for the Church, or of the end of time when all would attain perfect union with the divine.[78] But it was not always clear just *how* chastity witnessed to these concepts, and some authors vigorously denied that such were sufficient reasons to choose the lifestyle: "Frankly, I am not impressed by being told that I am an eschatological sign because I am a celibate. I really do not think that men and women who come into contact with me are going to experience a love that is redeeming simply by being aware that I can point to a way they will love one another in heaven."[79] For these writers, the reason for vowing chastity was simply unexplainable: It was based on one's individual, personal experience of the love of God. For still others, celibacy was merely a useful by-product, a side effect of one's dedication to ministry or service, and the idea of "mystical marriage" was an embarrassing and outdated metaphor.[80] Others retorted by reasserting the superiority of celibacy, with its single-hearted focus on God, over marriage, and using this superiority as the reason for the vow.[81]

Conclusions

Thus, by the 1980s, the original ideological frame that had legitimated and described Roman Catholic religious for eighteen centuries had been largely destroyed. Religious life was no longer a superior route to holiness; obedience and, to a lesser extent, poverty no longer meant what they once had; chastity was not holier than marriage and might even be unhealthy. While an internally consistent alternative definition—religious life as prophetic witness—had been constructed by the theologians and religious writers in journals such as the *Review*, structural changes in the daily lifestyle of sisters and (to a lesser extent) religious priests and brothers had prevented the new frame from being enacted on a corporate basis. Nor was the new ideology upheld with the same unanimity as the old had been, for religious communities had deprived themselves of some of the very communal commitment mechanisms that might have reinforced their new beliefs.

Ideological Maintenance: The Role of the Community

Throughout most of the history of Catholicism, the major growth periods in its religious orders occurred—at least in part—because some new or revised ideological frame for religious virtuosity had been formulated which successfully addressed key dilemmas or concerns in the surrounding secular culture. As a result, there was less initial need for communal commitment mechanisms to safeguard members' adherence to the ideology. Men and women from the cultural centers of their society—from the families of the governing or merchant elites, from capital cities and other large metropolitan centers—found in religious life compelling answers to the strains, deficiencies, and rising problems of their age.

For communities founded during the nineteenth century, however, this was not the case. As several writers have pointed out, the Church had reacted to the aftermath of the French Revolution and the rise of nineteenth-century liberalism by withdrawing into a fortress mentality, which canonized the theologies and societal arrangements from the Middle Ages and condemned any attempts to update Church teachings as "Modernism."[82] The new nineteenth-century religious congregations reflected this retrenchment. In contrast to the ideological creativity of previous growth periods, the nineteenth-century orders were based on a resuscitation of seventeenth-century models, often mixed—especially for the women's groups—with cloistral restrictions and spiritual ideologies dating from even more remote periods. The model's assumption of the religious virtuoso's superiority took little or no account of the egalitarianism of the post-revolutionary era; its concept of obedience ignored the fundamental tenets of Western liberal democracy; its formulations of chastity and poverty were untouched by the insights of Freud or Marx. And the discrepancies only grew worse as the years progressed. As one author noted, "the typical American cultural values of personalism and personal fulfillment, freedom and self- determination, pluralism, democratic self-criticism, egalitarianism and an emphasis on productivity and success have sometimes clashed with an older form of rigid religious life."[83]

Since the ideological frame that defined and described nineteenth- and early twentieth-century religious life failed to resonate with the predominant beliefs and values of mainstream Western culture, the congregations drew their recruits primarily from the marginalized subcultures that had been less influenced by such discordant ideas.[84] Once these new members were recruited, it was necessary to *keep* them isolated from the pernicious influence of mainstream beliefs and values. The communal commitment mechanisms so often employed by other intentional communities were used by religious orders for this purpose: living and working together, often under the same roof; boundary maintenance against outsiders through distinctive dress and severely limited contact; shared sacrifice and mortification practices.[85] As the ideological frame for religious life became less and less congruent with mainstream Western culture, and as the formerly marginalized subcultures of the nineteenth century became increasingly assimilated in the twentieth, such commitment mechanisms became more and more necessary—and more and more rigidly applied.

> In pre-Vatican II days, we were almost completely culturally different from our contemporaries. We wore dress that could in no way be confused with secular clothes. We followed the horarium of an agrarian monastery so that we were up when other people were in bed, and in bed when most other people were up. . . . The whole system hung together as a separate sociological reality.[86]

In former times within their own communities and institutions, religious could define reality as they wished and the definitions were unquestioned. Religious could say, for example, that poverty means dependence by permission and is perfectly compatible with corporate wealth and personal comfort, or that true freedom is found in abdication of one's personal will to that of a superior who, even when wrong, speaks with the voice of God, and no one questioned the truth of these positions.[87]

However, if the boundary maintenance, common living, and other commitment mechanisms that held the model together were ever allowed to weaken, then the values and beliefs of mainstream secular culture, *which the basic ideological frame of nineteenth- and twentieth-century religious orders had never addressed,* would no longer be able to be excluded. In the years following the Second Vatican Council, it was precisely these communal commitment structures that were discarded.

Criticisms of Community

Under both the 1917 and the 1983 versions of canon law, members of religious orders and congregations have been required "to live in a house of their own institute under the authority of a religious superior."[88] In the late 1960s and 1970s, however, many sisters, brothers, and priests in religious orders began to question this requirement. Authors began to note the similarity between life in a religious "community" and life in the "total institutions" described by Erving Goffman.[89] The analogy was not a favorable one. Critics charged that the traditional practice of residing in large numbers under one roof was extremely alienating. "The old saying about being lonely in a crowd is really true, and it can be just as true for a priest in a religious order as for anyone else. It was certainly so in my case, and I do not hesitate to name loneliness as the prime reason for my leaving the religious life."[90] A consistent theme in the new articles was that the quality of time together was more important than the mere quantity.[91] Many writers began to question whether mere physical presence to one another was necessary or valuable in religious life at all. According to one survey done in 1980, 23 percent of the sisters responding either were undecided or disagreed with the statement that their community lifestyle gave an important witness to the larger Christian community.[92] In place of common *living* to unite a congregation, the writers of the 1970s and 1980s stressed the centrality of a common *vision,* or of mutual support and a common *identity,* either of which could occur, they maintained, even among members who lived apart from each other.[93] The writers were less clear on exactly how this vision, support, and identity would be achieved. As a result of their questioning, however, the ideological basis for common living was severely undermined.

New Living Patterns

By the early 1980s, it was evident that the women, at least, in religious congregations had profoundly altered the size and type of the local groupings in which they lived. The 1982 "Sisters' Survey" found that 10 percent of the respondents lived, either alone or with one or two other sisters, in rented apartments or houses. This was a pronounced contrast to 1968, when almost all had resided in convents.[94] The trend away from large group living in parish convents continued throughout the decade. By the time of the 1989 "Sisters' Survey," 40 percent of the respondents were living either alone or in groups of fewer than six.[95] The "Sisters' Survey" figures probably understate the extent of the change, since the remaining 60 percent included retired sisters residing in the orders' infirmaries. A more accurate estimate may be reflected in a 1990 study of eight congregations, which examined only those active sisters living away from their motherhouses. This latter study found that 40 percent of the addresses were for sisters living alone in apartments, and that only 33 percent of the addresses, on the average, were for convents.[96] In some orders, fewer than 20 percent of the addresses could be identified as convents. In addition to being less likely to live with their fellow community members, the members of religious orders were also less likely to work together.[97] In both their living and work situations, therefore, members of religious orders during the 1980s and 1990s were far less likely to come into daily contact with the other members of their communities. Even those members who still resided under a single roof were less likely to pray, eat, or recreate together.[98] Members of many orders, one critic remarked, no longer *lived in* community but merely *related to it* functionally: They attended its bi-annual meetings or sent in their monthly salary checks, but otherwise lived their own lives.[99]

Results

By 1990, therefore, the boundary maintenance and common lifestyle that were necessary to safeguard their order's ideological frame had largely eroded among many sisters, and, to a lesser extent, among religious priests and brothers.

> Most religious can recall the days when they did not know anybody outside their own congregation. Today, many would probably say that some of their best friends are people not in their own congregations, even people who are not in religious life. These broader contacts have effectively

undermined the closed sociology of knowledge which made religious ready and able to accept as true whatever was promulgated in their own group. Today, religious mix with "outsiders," and in general, have a larger frame of reference for judging the validity of what is promulgated by Church or congregation.[100]

What this means, of course, is that the members also find it easier to *reject* the validity of any ideological frame—old or new—proposed for religious life.

Instead of drawing their ideas and values from fellow community members, with whom they may rarely have interacted, the nuns, priests, and brothers in religious orders often substituted other reference groups. Some now identified more with their professional colleagues: "Most religious became, foremost, practitioners of their profession and, incidentally, persons who lived in community as traditionally defined. . . . Community truly became secondary: a place to live and, in ever-limited ways, a place to take part in spiritual experiences."[101]

Others exhibited greater attachment to the one or two or three fellow members with whom they lived than they did to the rest of the order: The 1990 study of eight women's congregations found that the residents at each local address were far more likely to have lived for extended periods with the same group of sisters than they had been in the mid-1960s.[102] Whereas, in 1964, the largest congregations tended to move their sisters from convent to convent more frequently than the smaller congregations did (a tactic that kept their members more connected with the entire order and less split into cliques or friendship groups), this was not the case in 1990. As a result, the sisters' attachment to their congregation was more likely to attenuate in favor of loyalty to one or two "housemates."[103] In any event, their more dispersed living and working arrangements caused many religious to migrate "to the periphery of their congregations, often living lives that reflect significant ministerial contributions but which have little to do with their congregations or religious life."[104]

Even the common spiritual focus of the orders may have declined. It is true that the 1980 "Sisters' Survey" found that 80 percent of the respondents stressed the importance of prayer, and that some 53 percent either spent an hour or more each day in meditation or else regularly studied and reflected on the Bible.[105] And, as chapter 13 has reported, the proportion of *Review* articles on prayer and the spiritual life was higher after 1975 than at any other point in the journal's history. However, some observers have wondered whether the spiritual interest thus exhibited was not "a cosmopolitan, personalized spirituality," a "shopping around" for the latest trends in spiritual experience, rather than a devotion to a coherent spiritual focus, specific and unique to the order, which could unite its members and help support its ideological frame.[106] Another critic complained that the increased attention given to creation theology, centering prayer, eastern forms of mystical meditation, and charismatic renewal had made sisters "gentle" and inward-looking, and thus less likely to be prophetically active in society.[107] This was a further abrogation of their newly defined corporate role.

Conclusions

By the 1990s, the old ideological frame that had defined Roman Catholic religious life had collapsed, and the new definitiitions formulated to replace it had failed to achieve a full and lived hegemony. Religious orders were to be prophets to the Church and the larger society—but their interpretation of ministry, community, and obedience prevented them from fulfilling this role. Individual religious were defined as those who live their baptismal call in the vowed life—but these vows were either inadequately defined or else defined in such a way as to apply indiscriminately to *all* Christians.[108] "The dominant language of religious life . . . shifted from theological constructs to social and psychological paradigms," that were inadequate to explain what was distinct or desirable about the lifestyle.[109]

As a result of the collapse of their ideological frame, members of religious congregations have suffered am "alarming" loss of identity.[110] Instead of alarm, however, the members of many religious orders have developed defense mechanisms which prevent them from addressing the problem.[111] One consultant listed the common and self-defeating patterns of operation that result:

1. Statements of mission or charism that are vague and general enough to include all the various interests in a congregation.
2. Difficulty in making choices, particularly in the area of long-term planning, because there is no deeply shared vision on which to base these choices.
3. An emphasis on the personal growth and development of the members, as well as a tendency to interpret community in terms of the needs of the members, work as an individual project, and spirituality as a private concern.
4. The near impossibility of sustaining corporate commitments.[112]

The decay of U.S. religious orders, therefore, presents a compelling example of the necessity of a coherent, relevant, and lived ideological frame for the survival of a social movement. As religious orders lost role clarity, as their interpretation of the vows waned and fragmented, their ability to plan and work for their future survival also disintegrated.

There are, however, still other reasons for the decline of religious orders. Chapter 15 will explore another contributing factor: the loss of key environmental resources.

The Withdrawal of Resources

The collapse of its ideology, while a key element in the dramatic decline of religious orders, is not the only factor that contributed to it. Like any organization, religious congregations have always depended on support from their surrounding environment.[1] During the past twenty-five years, the orders have experienced a significant loss of necessary environmental resources: the support of the Church hierarchy, the demand of the laity for their services and, most importantly, the formerly reliable sources of their new recruits. This "Resource Demobilization" has interacted with the "Frame Dealignment" and the abandonment of their common commitment mechanisms, discussed in the two preceding chapters, to produce the orders' collapse. This chapter will briefly examine the most significant resources religious congregations have lost since 1960.

Resource I: Recruits

Chapter 1 described the drastic reduction in the numbers of young men and (especially) of young women entering religious orders both in North America and in Western Europe. In part, this decline has been due to changing environmental conditions, which have made traditional Catholic religious life much less attractive to prospective entrants. In contrast to table 4.1 (pp. 66–67, above), lay Catholics today do *not* experience the shortage of marriage partners, the lack of other opportunities to develop and use their talents, or the fear of dying in childbirth that had formerly motivated entrants to religious orders. Moreover, life as a sister or a religious brother is not seen as a source of social status, Church power, or financial security—if anything, the opposite is true.

A second reason for the decline of recruits is that several compelling disincentives prevent the current members from encouraging them. As a result, the members make no attempts to counteract the pervasive environmental influences that deter young Catholics. In fact, some religious may actively *discourage* potential entrants.

Environmental Factors in the Decline of Religious Vocations

Perhaps the most obvious environmental change impacting the willingness of young men and women to consider entering a religious order is the perceived rise in alternate opportunities for them.[2] This is especially true for women, of course, but young Catholic men also have a more open occupational ladder today than their immigrant great-grandfathers had in a former era when perhaps the only educated professional in a parish was its priest. The rise of alternative career opportunities also affected those who had already entered. Their professional education often provided them with attractive career options outside the community, thus preparing for their "economically viable exodus" from the order.[3] In response to these widening horizons, some orders began to emphasize the opportunity for self-abnegation and sacrifice offered by religious life—hardly as attractive a recruitment incentive as stressing the order's unique social and educational benefits once had been.[4]

A second environmental factor was the changing image of nuns—and of religious priests and brothers—in the public mind. As immigrant cultures faded and were assimilated, the subcultural status once given to priests and nuns was replaced by images from the mainstream culture.[5] In both its news and its entertainment media, however, the mainstream culture has depicted sisters either as childish and silly or else as victims of constant clerical oppression, and has paid scant attention to their more inspiring or heroic activities.[6] News stories depicting priests and brothers as sexual predators have a similarly deterrent effect. Such images have added to the popular perception that members of religious orders are immature at best or psychologically damaged at worst, an impression that naturally repels healthier candidates.[7] Recent surveys of Catholic laywomen have shown that they have negative opinions of sisters, viewing them as weak, ineffectual, and irrelevant.[8] In addition to these negative stereotypes, the widespread media attention given to the orders' seemingly intractable financial problems may also deter younger people from entering.[9]

A third environmental factor was the loss of the orders' traditional recruitment channels. The closing of boarding schools and academies, and the withdrawal of sisters from teaching in diocesan grade and high schools, removed them from contact with the young Catholics who might have been persuaded to join them.[10] In addition, parents and other family members are much less willing to encourage a son or daughter to join a religious community than were the parents of previous generations; they are more likely, in fact, actively to discourage such a notion.

> At the time of Vatican II, the family which had a member in a religious order was considered "respectable' and had status in local society. Convent life was considered a good, safe and even enhanced form of life. . . . Today, 25 years later, the picture is very different. A sister's life is looked on as somewhat stunted and one that even good Catholic parents would not encourage their daughters to pursue . . . sisters no longer enjoy status. They experience rejection and devaluation on a wide scale.[11]

Finally, parish priests are less likely to channel young men and women into religious orders than they formerly were.

By the late 1980s, therefore, a combination of environmental changes had made religious orders much less attractive to the young men and women who, in former days, had served as their chief recruitment pool. The opportunities for a fulfilling ministry and an education which the orders had once offered could now be obtained elsewhere; the social status gained by entering had dissipated and been replaced by social opprobrium; parents no longer urged the lifestyle on their offspring; the absence of religious personnel in the schools made it unlikely that most Catholic teens had ever even met a religious sister or brother. And the main characteristic of religious congregations that did appear attractive to potential entrants—their communal lifestyle—was precisely the one being most rapidly discarded.[12] It was hardly likely, in these circumstances, that many young Catholics would be attracted to religious orders.

Internal Factors: Recruitment Disincentives

An additional factor in the drop in entrants has been the growing reluctance of the current members of religious orders to invite others to join them. Previous research has shown that encouragement by a religious priest, brother, or sister was once the single most important element in a young person's decision to enter a seminary or novitiate.[13] These same studies now show an almost total absence of such recruiting on the part of the members of present-day religious orders.[14]

There are several reasons for this. The first and most obvious is the lack of role clarity described in the preceding chapter. Some members of religious communities did not think it was moral or ethical to invite people to join a group that was so uncertain about its purpose and future.[15] Lack of role clarity has thus had a significant effect on many orders' recruitment success, both by deterring their members from inviting other people to enter and by deterring the potential entrants directly. In contrast, communities that continue to project a clear role have been somewhat more successful in attracting recruits. A 1975 survey, for example, found that wearing a distinctive habit and having a specific community apostolate were both highly correlated (at .778 and .900 respectively) with the number and percentage of young members in a religious congregation. A 1991 study resulted in similar findings.[16]

For the women's congregations, an added disinclination to recruit new members was provided by the rise of feminism among nuns and the consequent increase in their anger at the Church's hierarchy. Prior to the early 1970s, the isolation of most sisters from any direct experience of working for a male employer, and their concentration in institutions run and staffed entirely by females (where they had opportunities for mentoring and career advancement most other women could only dream of), had combined to keep them unaware of the disadvantages of their position.[17] After the mid-1970s, however, many nuns left their own schools and hospitals to accept positions in parishes and diocesan offices, where they were exposed—often for the first time—to the blocked mobility and structural inequality that other women experienced. With their previous background as professionals within all-female institutions, the sisters were even less predisposed to accept these limitations than their lay co-workers were. As the various structural models for the rise of gender consciousness would predict,[18] alienation and anger quickly surfaced among nuns working in comparatively powerless positions. One result was "patriarchical flight"— the withdrawal of many sisters from *any* Church employment, to seek jobs elsewhere.[19] Other sisters formed consciousness-raising support groups with their fellow sisters working in parish ministry:

> The sisters [in the support group] got together and interpreted their experiences in the light of feminist ideology. Short articles with titles such as "How to Survive in a 'Church' That Doesn't Want You" were circulated, and the group's prayers were always deliberately inclusive. On one occasion, a litany of praise for Jewish and Christian foremothers was used to open a meeting; on another, an autumn day of prayer was structured completely around reflection on the lives of famous women working for peace and justice.[20]

More quantitative studies support these anecdotal accounts. A content analysis of the chapter documents and mission statements of eighty-eight women's congregations found that concern for the oppression of women in church and society occurred in 34 percent of them.[21] A 1990 survey of administrators working for dioceses, parishes, and religious orders found that the sisters in these positions were far more dissatisfied with Church employment policies than were either the priests or the lay administrators.[22]

Particular events also contributed to the nuns' rising sense of anger and alienation. Some of these—the struggles of the California IHM sisters and the New York Times abortion ad controversy—have already been mentioned. Other, less well-known, occurrences also became important as symbols of the inferior status of women religious in the Church. Quinonez and Turner report one such incident at the 1982 Joint Assembly of LCWR and CMSM. The planners of the assembly's liturgy had asked ten of the participants—five men and five women—to assist in the distribution of communion. As these persons approached the altar, the presiding Vatican officials publicly rebuffed the five women and refused to allow them to assist their male counterparts. "Many LCWR members, until then supportive but not especially devoted to the women's issue, date their awakening to that event."[23]

In addition to the impact of specific events, the leaders of LCWR were radicalized by their continuing interaction with the SCR officials. Since LCWR's leadership was frequently rotated, this meant that a large pool of women were returned to their own communities with their consciousness dramatically raised:

> In 1980 a group of former LCWR presidents and executive directors gathered for three days to reflect on conference history. Each was asked to make an audio tape of her recollections of important events and issues during her time of leadership in the Conference. Independently, and prior to group discussion, every woman who participated in meetings between [the SCR] and the LCWR described experiences [of conflict with the SCR]. One recalled an [SCR] official reading, one after another, a list of objectionable passages he had culled from papers given . . . at the 1977 [LCWR] Assembly. Another said . . . "They expect [LCWR] . . . to have no thoughts of our own but simply to report everything that comes from Rome." Another added, "My faith was shaken many times in those years of struggling with the raw power of those men."[24]

The SCR routinely refused to answer LCWR's repeated requests to be represented on the Vatican commissions that dealt with their lives. The pope, too, refused to meet with them. The SCR also repeatedly attempted to insert statements about obedience to the pope in the sisters' new constitutions, whether or not such explicit obedience had been part of the orders' tradition.[25]

According to one theorist, "perhaps one of the most sociologically inflammatory methods of democratizing is to claim to decentralize power, and even create new, internally strong institutional organs . . . but in fact to grant these organs little or no authority."[26] This "negative autonomy" often leads to the radicalization of those excluded. By 1990, both national surveys and anecdotal accounts were uncovering a deep reservoir of alienation from the institutional Church among women in religious orders. The Nygren and Ukeritis study found that "religious, in particular, are clear in their lowered respect for the magisterial authority of the church and the U.S. hierarchy in general."[27] Several authors have reported that some sisters no longer attend even Sunday Mass because of the offensiveness of a male-celebrated liturgy.[28] Many communities are considering the desirability of renouncing their official ("canonical") status altogether, despite the intense reservations of canon lawyers as to the wisdom of such a tactic.[29] In such an atmosphere of tension and disillusionment, it is hardly surprising that these sisters hesitate to invite young women to join them in their subjection to what they perceive as an oppressive Church structure.

A final reason why members of religious orders—both men and women—are apathetic about recruitment is that, for many of them, *the order is no longer their primary source of reference.* One case study discovered many sisters for whom membership was simply "a matter of convenience" and who could articulate quite precisely the limits to their commitment.[30] For these women, the prospect of the order's demise through lack of new members is not a threatening one. Moreover, even those sisters, priests, and brothers who do identify with their religious orders may do so in a way that discourages recruitment. The 1990 national survey found that the primary bond holding many men and women in religious orders was their "sense of affiliation"—their friendships with other members—rather than any larger sense of the order's purpose or mission.[31] Closed groups of friends generally have little incentive to recruit others to join them and may, in fact, be perceived by outsiders as an exclusive clique. For all of these reasons, therefore, religious orders have lost both their traditional sources of recruits and their own personal incentives to find new sources.

Resource II: External Supports

In addition to a dependable supply of new recruits, religious orders also need other resources from their environment. Whatever services or occupations they perform must be sufficiently valued by the surrounding society so that they may exchange them for the money and the material goods they need to survive. Potentially powerful actors in church and state must be favorably disposed—or at least neutral—toward them. In the years after Vatican II, many of these external supports were also lost by religious orders.

Ministerial Changes: The Loss of an Environmental Niche

By the mid-twentieth century, both internal and environmental changes had profoundly altered the way religious orders were able to operate their traditional ministerial institutions. The socioeconomic and geographic mobility of third- and fourth-generation American Catholics often left orders either staffing wealthy suburban schools that could well have afforded to hire lay teachers, or else struggling to keep sparsely attended inner city schools afloat in neighborhoods that now held few Catholics. Some schools closed and others were forced to merge, a move that reduced or eliminated the influence of any particular order.[32] The orders' hospitals were transformed by Medicare and Medicaid into "private enterprise systems, rendering human service competitive and, hence, less commitment-oriented, again a disenchanted, pragmatic turn from an altruistic calling."[33] Bureaucratic procedures and values were adopted, often indistinguishable from the procedures of secular institutions: "Size, sophistication and government funding have made [our schools and hospitals] new entities. We compete for jobs, we are promoted, we are fired. It is a very new religious vocation."[34]

As a result of these changes, religious orders have lost their environmental niche. With their hospitals having, on average, fewer than 1.5 sisters engaged in bedside nursing; with parish grade schools having few or no sisters on staff, it became less and less evident why sisters were needed for ministry at all.[35] The indistinguishability of bureaucratized religious institutions from similarly bureaucratized secular schools and hospitals also made the institutions' reason for existence less obvious. The loss of their environmental niche has occurred among religious orders in other countries besides the United States: In Canada during the 1960s, for example, the Quebec government took control of social and health care services formerly run by religious orders. The state thus replaced the orders as "the most visible presence in provincial life."[36]

The loss of their environmental niche had substantial negative effects upon religious communities—effects so profound that Ebaugh calls the re-establishment of such a niche "perhaps the greatest challenge to religious orders today."[37] Since, for many congregations, their ministerial work had been their chief defining characteristic, its loss left them unable to explain how they differed from other orders, or from lay Catholics in general. It also became progressively less clear what good, if any, the religious orders as corporate entities served in the Church:

> Given the diversity of occupations among members today, it is virtually impossible for religious orders to construct their mission and environmental niche in terms of specific works. Instead, many orders are struggling to redefine their purpose in more abstract, ideological terms such as

"the witnessing of Christian values," "standing with the poor of society," and "dedication to furthering the mission of Jesus in the world." But these redefinitions of purpose are difficult to justify in terms of their necessity to society.[38]

Ecclesiastical Hostility

The obverse of the alienation which many religious feel toward the Church hierarchy is the hostility and distrust many of the hierarchy feel toward them. As early as 1969, Cardinal Antoniutti, then head of the SCR, denounced "the erroneous ideas about the promotion of women" held by some sisters, ideas that "smothered their natural instinct toward humble and retiring self-giving."[39] This negative opinion of U.S. women's communities has become widespread among the Vatican hierarchy. When Quinonez and Turner asked U.S. Archbishop Thomas C. Kelly, O.P., what he believed was the SCR's major objection to women in U.S. religious orders, he immediately answered "their feminism."[40] Many of the sisters' new constitutions contained expressions of their identity as "vowed women" or "women in the Church"—expressions the SCR officials found objectionable. The sisters, the Vatican officals said, were putting too much emphasis on being *women* when they should be identifying themselves as being *religious*.[41] According to the Vatican's Cardinal Ratzinger:

> A feminist mentality . . . [has entered] into women's religious orders. This is particularly evident, even in its extreme forms, on the North American continent. . . . Active orders and congregations are in grave crisis: the discovery of professionalism, the concept of "social welfare" which has replaced that of "love of neighbor," the often uncritical and yet enthusiastic adaptation to the new and hitherto unknown values of modern secular society, the entrance into the convents, at times wholly unexamined, of psychologies and psychoanalyses of different tendencies: all this has led to burning problems of identity—with many women, to the collapse of motivations sufficient to justify religious life.[42]

With such a negative opinion of U.S. sisters, it would hardly be surprising if the SCR were to prefer that they all leave religious life. Such a departure would remove from the Church the group that has most openly challenged the SCR's authority.[43]

It is in this context that we can understand the recent establishment of the new Council of Major Superiors of Women Religious as an alternate representative body for American nuns. Ever since their separation from LCWR in 1970, the members of the conservative Consortium Perfectae Caritatis had hoped to replace it as the official representative of U.S. religious communities. However, as Burns has pointed out, LCWR had too much power at that time to be so lightly discarded. It had by far the larger membership, and its leaders had spent years developing a sophisticated network of contacts and organizational expertise.

> The Vatican could have [replaced LCWR], but only by creating enormous controversy and ill will within the Church, possibly alienating not only women religious, but also a good number of American Catholic laywomen. Even if directed only at superiors, such a purge would have inflicted crippling damage on the morale and administrative abilities of sisters' communities, which, incidentally, provided an enormous supply of labor in Catholic schools, parishes and hospitals.[44]

Thus, even though the SCR was ideologically much closer to the consortium's positions than it was to those of LCWR, and even though the SCR's officials were more and more disturbed by the "feminist bug" that seemed to have infected the LCWR's membership, the power of the latter organization staved off any recognition of a competitor for twenty years.

The establishment of the new council (and its immediate absorption of the consortium's members and functions) indicates a change in the balance of power between the SCR and LCWR. The leaders of LCWR had long dreaded such a move, rightly fearing the eventual loss of the benefits of their public status.[45] By 1992, however, they were helpless to prevent the initial moves that have been taken toward their ultimate disenfranchisement. The sisters' labor was no longer essential for the running of the Church's educational and health institutions. They were becoming a less and less visible presence to the American laity, who might otherwise have championed their cause. And their public expressions of alienation may have led the SCR to decide that recognizing a competing group could hardly alienate them further. Finally, the implications of offending a constituency whose median age is almost seventy are obvious to Vatican officials. However upset the LCWR communities may be to be disenfranchised, their outcry will not last long.

The sisters also have few overt supporters in the episcopacy. In contrast to the bishops in the nineteenth century, today's prelates no longer believe that non-Catholics are condemned to hell and that religious orders are necessary to save them. And whereas a strong and devoted cadre of nuns as a valued presence diocesan schools and hospitals may once have been necessary for an episcopal career, in the presence of obsteperous religious in one's diocese today is an episcopal liability. John Paul II has made it a prime goal of his papacy to reclaim control of the selection of U.S. bishops and to replace the liberal candidates appointed under Paul VI with more conservative ones.[46] Fidelity to the Church's official teachings and loyalty to Rome are the key issues in episcopal selection and promotion.[47] Such pressures have a chilling effect; as one bishop said, "It isn't simply a raw lust for bigger dioceses. It is much more subtle. It is the wish to be clean and credible in the eyes of those who are perceived to be at the center of power. You see, then you will be able to do so much more good. That is why you want to be careful what you say and what you do. It isn't for yourself. It is for a good cause. . . . That is one of the biggest problems today."[48] In such a climate, too vocal a championing of the liberal LCWR in any conflict with the Vatican could torpedo an episcopal career. Bereft of supporters and lacking much of their former power, sisters in the majority of U.S. communities will soon be unable to make any effective response to attempts by Rome to exert greater control over them. If the SCR decertifies LCWR, or if the 1994 Bishops' Synod attempts to enforce the rules and definitions in its "Lineamenta," many individual sisters may opt either to leave or else to remove their communities from official ("canonical") status. Either tactic would be a further blow to an already dying institution.

Conclusions

The evidence presented in the past four chapters strongly indicates that the future of most current religious orders is limited indeed. Their ideological frame has been destroyed far more thoroughly than during any of the previous decline periods and, more importantly, no commonly accepted alternative has been developed to take its place. Whereas, in previous eras, incipient religious communities were able to counter clerical hostility by mobilizing lay support, or to neutralize episcopal opposition by enlisting papal support, present groups stand alone and bereft of allies. Benefits that had formerly seemed so attractive to potential entrants can now be obtained more easily elsewhere. Increasingly, even the members themselves wonder whether a legitimate place should exist for them in the Church.

The disappearance of an organizational feature that has been an important part of a denomination for as long as religious orders have been a part of Catholicism is a momentous occurrence indeed. If it does, in fact, happen that religious orders cease to exist within the Catholic Church in North America and Western Europe—however thriving such groups may be in other parts of the world—the ramifications will be profound. Both Catholicism and Protestantism, both the secular and the sacred aspects of Western culture, will change in fundamental ways. The concluding chapter will explore some of these ways by analyzing the changed and changing roles of religious virtuosity.

Chapter 16

Conclusions

Recently, several major studies have focused on religious fundamentalism in the United States and elsewhere around the world. As one author has pointed out, such research is useful in illuminating broad theoretical issues in a variety of disciplines.[1] For sociologists of religion, case studies of fundamentalism illustrate the social construction of a religious phenomenon—in this case, the dialectical interdependence of heresy and orthodoxy. Organizational theorists find interest in descriptions of how the fundamentalists were excluded from denominational bureaucracies in the past and how, through the development of alternative structures, they have recently been able to reassert control.[2] Still another organizational topic is the effect of bureaucratization on developing fundamentalist sects. Finally, studies of fundamentalism confront theologians with an important question: "How is it that when religious belief and practice are brought in harmony with reasonable requirements of the secular world, so often they lose their power to attract and satisfy?"[3]

It is a contention of this chapter and, indirectly, of the entire book, that studies of religious virtuosity could be similarly useful. The social construction of virtuoso spiritualities—which sometimes overlap with and sometimes vigorously oppose fundamentalism—has been the topic of chapters 6, 7, and 8. Another topic is the fate of religious virtuosity in a cultural context that denies it legitimacy—a primary focus of chapter 10. Organizational issues such as how to contain and channel virtuosi within a church, or how organizational resources help determine the shape and context of virtuoso spiritualities, were touched upon in chapters 5 and 9. And chapters 13 and 14 outlined a key issue currently confronting Catholic theologians: How, if at all, does the call of lay religious virtuosi differ from that of all baptized Christians?

The Social Construction of Contemporary
Religious Virtuosity

At least since the early nineteenth century, the concept of religious virtuosity has been devalued within the institutional center of Western culture. Virtuoso spirituality has therefore been confined primarily to
peripheral subcultures: to rural or immigrant Catholics, for example, or to
Protestant sectarians on America's nineteenth-century frontier or in small
Southern towns. Upwardly mobile individuals from these populations usually discarded their distinctive virtuoso beliefs and behaviors upon assimilating to the mainstream. The marginalized origins of religious virtuosi,
and the tendency of their wealthier or more educated co-religionists to
abandon them for more compromised denominations, reinforced their traditional suspicion of the American cultural center—of the media moguls,
the educational bureaucracies, the business and governmental establishments—which seemed indifferent or hostile to their most basic values.
Both Catholic religious orders and Protestant sects were built upon a basic
opposition to "the world," whose blandishments committed saints should
resist at all costs.

Despite its denial of virtuoso spirituality, however, contemporary culture has not been immune to the social disarticulations that produce utopian movements. Nor is the American and Western European "center,"
for all its avowed secular emphasis, completely lacking in individuals predisposed to envision utopian solutions in religious terms. Persons inclined
toward spiritual virtuosity continue to surface in all sectors of the pluralistic American religious economy and form markets ripe for targeting by
some sect or denominational subgroup.[4] The opportunity thus exists for
present-day virtuoso communities, which had previously confined themselves to peripheral populations, to rework their ideological frames and address the "sharpest anguish" of postmodern Western culture.[5] Whichever
sect or denomination can construct such a frame within its boundaries
will attract a new population of virtuosi and experience rapid growth. The
hegemony of their new virtuoso ideology will then constrain the development of subsequent groups.

In recent decades, a virtuoso form of evangelical Protestantism has
begun to attract not only the uneducated rural poor but also middle-class
suburban professionals.[6] While this virtuoso spirituality may not yet appeal to the intellectual and cultural leaders of American society, it *does*
attract growing segments of the middle class. *And, with the demise of its
religious orders, Catholicism can offer little competition.*

For this reason, the decline of Catholic religious communities is at
least as important for the Church's future as is its priest shortage, even if
the latter has received far more attention. For centuries, Catholicism has
combined an institutionalized virtuoso status—the ordained priest-

hood—with a succession of "nascent" lay communities.[7] This internal outlet for its lay virtuosi has at least partially shielded the Catholic Church from the fissive and emigrant tendencies endemic in institutional Protestantism. With the decline of religious orders, however, such shielding no longer occurs. Researchers have estimated that as many as 100,000 U.S. Catholics convert every year to Protestant evangelism.[8] Catholics of Spanish background defect to Protestant denominations at a rate of about 60,000 per year, usually joining precisely those types of sectarian groups that provide the virtuoso opportunities Catholicism no longer offers them.[9] Unless and until a new Catholic ideology can be formulated that allots a clear and valued place to lay religious virtuosi, the drain of its most committed members will continue.

What might be the elements of a new Catholic virtuoso spirituality? The ideological package currently developing in American Protestantism combines religious virtuosity with fundamentalism, in restrictive and sectarian church organizations that exclude the less-committed from their ranks.[10] A second, less denominationalized, variant advances a quasi-"Gnostic" and privatized virtuosity, a quest for personal transcendance through various esoteric "New Age" practices.[11] Of course, neither of these variants are the only forms religious virtuosity can take. But they will exert great pressure upon any new version of Catholic religious virtuosity to conform to their models. At the same time, powerful political forces within the Catholic hierarchy remain committed to the pre-1965 version of religious life and have mobilized to defend it.

In such an environment, the attempted articulation of new ideological frames for religious virtuosity within the Catholic Church offers an unparalleled opportunity for sociologists of knowledge to study the factors that influence their formulation and development. This chapter can only outline some of the areas that merit such study. For example, a surprising number of new religious "orders" have been established within Catholicism during the last two decades, and some are showing significant growth. The Monastic Fraternity of Jerusalem, for example, was founded in Paris in the mid-1970s and has since grown to some fifty professed members and at least one hundred lay associates.[12] Several other new monastic groups—notably the Monastic Fraternity of Peace—have been recently established in Spain. In the United States, the Fellowship of New Religious Communities had sixty-three aspiring Catholic congregations on its 1993 mailing list, and there are at least two dozen other new communities that are not members of this association. In addition to new communities of vowed, celibate men and women, a number of lay groups that include married couples are also thriving. Ireland has eight charismatic covenant communities with a total of some 500 members.[13] The Emmanuel charismatic covenant community, begun in 1972, now provides about one-fourth of the seminarians for the Paris archdiocese.[14] The San Egidio community, begun in Italy in 1968, counts some 15,000 members world-wide.[15] The Focolare Movement is 1.5 million strong and growing.[16]

The new groups exhibit several common characteristics. Responding to the "sharpest anguish" of current Western culture, most focus on spirituality and community, rather than on ministerial service.[17] Many groups have adopted a monastic lifestyle, devoting over half of their days to common prayer or meditation and working outside the community only part-time, if at all.[18] An additional, subsidiary focus of many new groups is a strong spirit of poverty, which is interpreted both as personal material renunciation (several of the new communities have written into their constitutions that they will never own land or buildings), as well as working exclusively with the poor. Even among these communities, however, prayer remains their primary focus. The Capuchin Friars of the Renewal in the South Bronx, for example, have a notice posted on their front door firmly reminding beggars not to ring the doorbell during the friars' hours of prayer. As the founder of a new group of sisters in the same area expressed it: "Our original reason for coming [to the South Bronx] was *never* the work, but rather to be *religious* within this setting."[19]

Many of these new communities are strongly conservative in their theology of religious life, and appear to be replicating the traditional model. Rome, of course, encourages this.[20] But the young men and women who enter these communities do not personally remember pre-Vatican II religious life, and do not necessarily believe that what they are doing is the same thing.[21] Thus, a certain amount of creative innovation is present in many groups. Several of the founders of new women's communities also show at least an incipient feminist sensitivity to the power implications of their relationship with male co-orders or the ordained hierarchy. Future studies in the sociology of knowledge could profitably explore the ways traditional Catholic ideological frameworks for religious virtuosity are being reworked, whether consciously or unconsciously, by these new communities, in order to address the assumptions and values of late-twentieth-century and early twenty-first-century American culture.

In addition to the influence of traditional models, however, Catholic virtuoso groups often show the influence of the other ideological frames for religious virtuosity. Many of the charismatic covenant communities and some of the new religious congregations exhibit strongly traditional sex-role divisions and a tendency toward doctrinal literalism, which is reminiscent of Protestant fundamentalists. Some of the longer-established orders have begun to borrow Native American or Eastern prayer styles. To study the cross-fertilizations of traditional Catholic mysticism with Jungian archetypes, or of Protestant Pentecostalism with Catholic integralism and secular feminism, as these hybrids proliferate, flourish or collapse, would be a fascinating contribution to the sociology of knowledge. Researching the virtuoso movements in Catholicism, however, can also provide valuable insights in other disciplines.

The Organizational Implications of Religious Virtuosity

The Rise—and Decline—of Alternate Ecclesiastical Power Centers

The present transformation of religious virtuosity within Catholicism could provide an absorbing research agenda for organizational sociologists. Coleman's brief description of how the Church hierarchy "tamed" the Catholic Charismatic Movement and contained it within Catholicism's institutional boundaries is one example of the type of studies that could be done.[22] Another extremely fertile theoretical question in this area would be to examine the implications of having large and flourishing virtuoso groups coexisting in the same dioceses or parishes as the secular clergy. As chapter 15 of this book has argued, priests and bishops today have few organizational incentives to support the founding of new religious orders, since such groups, if successful, would serve as alternate centers of power. The Vatican, however, has actively supported the establishment of conservative orders and quasi orders such as Opus Dei or Communion and Liberation, and these groups have enjoyed substantial growth as a result.[23] This presents local bishops with the dilemma of whether or not to support the establishment of these groups within their dioceses. Supporting Opus Dei would demonstrate a bishop's loyalty to Rome, but, as a personal prelature with direct Vatican connections, its presence in the diocese could also seriously undermine his own episcopal authority.

Still another issue, and one that might engage feminist organizational theorists, is the relative merit of having separately institutionalized religious communities of (nonordained) women virtuosi, as compared to admitting women into the ranks of the clergy where they often find themselves occupying the least powerful and least upwardly mobile positions. Studies of several Protestant denominations have shown that ordained women are less likely to attain positions as pastors of large churches, and are more likely than their male counterparts to leave the active ministry.[24] If, as the conservative faction of the Southern Baptist Convention has shown, a disenfranchised group can capture control of a church organization by establishing and mobilizing alternative organizational networks,[25] might not forming a similarly insurgent community of female virtuosi be a more feasible route to church power than ordaining women into the present structure?

Related to the problem of what structures would best enfranchise and empower women (or other minorities) within the Catholic Church is the fact that the traditional model for religious virtuosity currently espoused by the Vatican is one in which such minorities occupy an extremely peripheral and subordinate place.[26] Official church hierarchies typically resist supporting any organized form of religious virtuosity which they are not able to control. *But self-determination of one's virtuoso spirituality is precisely the characteristic that is most attractive to lay virtuosi.* Until this kind of self-determination is again available in the Catholic Church, many virtuosi will seek it elsewhere. The loss of almost one out of ten members of American Catholicism's largest ethnic group to virtuoso Protestant sects, and the defection of a disproportionate number of what was traditionally its most devout gender—the gender which formerly supplied three-fourths of its religious virtuosi—are "ecclesiastical failure[s] of unprecedented proportions."[27] And yet prevailing organizational constraints, both within religious orders and in the hierarchy, are likely to prevent them from offering a viable alternative.

Established Religious Orders and the Dynamics of Organizational Change

In addition to the implications which organized religious virtuosity—or the lack of it—has for power and opportunity within the larger Catholic Church, the *internal* dynamics of religious orders as they adopt or fail to adopt new ideological frames would also be an interesting object of study. Organizational cultures constrain both members and leaders to view problems in structured ways. Ingrained patterns from previous solutions inhibit the formation of new insights.[28] And powerful intraorganizational factions may oppose the implementation even of necessary change. For example, one recent study has noted that the New England Congregationalists of the nineteenth century were unable to revise their seminary programs and evangelization procedures to incorporate Charles Finney's "immensely successful" frontier revival campaigns, even though failure to do so resulted in the loss of thousands of potential adherents.[29] More recently, the National Council of Churches has continued to follow policies that alienate a majority of their constituents. Religious organizations have often chosen death or stagnation rather than change.

There is some evidence that similar constraints are operating within the established religious orders, resulting in the inability of both leaders and members to initiate any specific organizational remedies for the problems that face them. Previous research has indicated that sisters, priests and brothers typically choose administrators, not leaders, for their communities. A recent study of such administrators found "little evidence of [their] ability to think structurally or to provide creative solutions," especially when attempting to enunciate specific strategies for institutional transformation.[30] The leaders lacked a clear image of their communities' identity and mission, and confined themselves instead to expressing overall values that gave little practical direction for the future. A similar inability surfaces quite regularly in the popular books and articles written by and for the members of religious orders. Even authors who were quite articulate in describing the problems facing their communities faltered when prescribing remedies for them.[31] This failure to articulate overall strategy leads to "an incrementalism that emphasized maintenance concerns" over organizational revitalization.[32]

Even if a solution could be envisioned, other intraorganizational dynamics might inhibit its implementation. The practice of seeking consensus on major decisions is often paralyzing, and prevents truly visionary leaders from initiating major changes either in the order itself or in its ministerial institutions. "Many leaders noted that, in attempting to focus the group on a collective action, responsibility to do so is thwarted because of the leader's lack of authority to act. Thus, opportunities for impact are lost because the group lacks a process for decision making in such realms."[33] Religious orders thus provide an example of organizational resistence to ideological and operational change, even to the point of courting extinction. Since, as many researchers have pointed out,[34] organizational decline and death are rarely studied, the internal dynamics of religious orders provide an opportunity to observe the political and ideological factors that operate in such situations.

For centuries, religious orders defined what it meant to be truly Catholic. No other model of holiness was available for the non-ordained; the "Third Orders" and sodalities of popular Catholic piety were modeled on the spiritualities developed and practiced, in their most rigorous form, by the orders themselves. Catholic culture was mediated through the sisters and brothers who taught in Catholic schools and the religious order priests who gave the parish "mission" revivals and educated the diocesan seminarians.[35] Most of the authors of devotional books, magazines and tracts were members of religious orders; as were many of the most popular Catholic fictional writers. One might argue that it should not have been so, or that, even if such a situation was acceptable in the past, today's laity have matured and are capable of performing these tasks for themselves. But a Catholicism without religious orders, such as is imminent in Western Europe and North America today, will be a fundamentally different Catholicism than has ever existed before. This book has attempted to provide a theorietical and methodological background for studying this change, and perhaps—for those like myself who are interested in doing so—for avoiding it.

Glossary

abbot, abbess: The head of an autonomous monastery of a religious order. In the early Middle Ages, an abbot or abbess had roughly the same juridical powers as the bishop of a diocese. Usually elected for life.

Association of Contemplative Sisters (ACS):   Unbrella association for contemplative orders of nuns; parallel to LCWR, which contemplative orders are not permitted to join. Has never received official recognition from the Vatican.

breviary: A book containing the complete order of the Divine Office for every day.

brother: A nonordained male member of a religious congregation or noncloistered order.

canon law: Official church law. Revised in 1917 and 1983.

canonical status: Official standing given to a religious order or congregation within the Catholic Church.

canons: Members of communal groups of secular priests in the Middle Ages. Usually staffed the cathedral. Unlike monks, canons were permitted to retain some control over their personal property.

cenobitic: Referring to communal religious life as lived in a monastery, as compared to the eremitical life lived by hermits.

chapter: The governing legislative body of a religious order or congregation.

congregation: A religious community whose members are bound by simple rather than solemn vows and which is not chartered directly by Rome. Religious congregations are therefore subject to varying amounts of episcopal oversight, unlike religious orders. Since 1752, no new religious orders have been permitted by Rome. Male religious communities founded since that time have avoided episcopal interference by organizing as "pious societies" not bound by vows. Women, however, were not permitted to form pious societies. All religious communities of women founded since 1752, therefore, are congregations.

Conference of Major Superiors of Men (CMSM):   Umbrella association of the heads of all major U.S. communities of men.

Conference of Major Superiors of Women (CMSW):   Umbrella association of the heads of all major U.S. communities of women. (See also Leadership Conference of Women Religious.)

constitutions: The rules or guidelines, originally drawn up by the founder and later modified by various chapters, which stipulate the basic purpose and the daily life of religious orders or congregations. Today, constitutions must be approved by the Sacred Congregation for Religious in Rome.

convent: The local dwelling of some members of a religious order or congregation. Although current usage limits "convent" to dwellings of women religious, in the Middle Ages, convents could be the local houses of male religious as well.

Council of Major Superiors of Women Religious (CMSWR):   New umbrella organization established in 1992 for the conservative American communities.

Decree on the Appropriate Renewal of Religious Life: 1965 Vatican document mandating that religious orders and congregations adapt and update their lifestyles according to the spirit of their original founder. (See also *Perfectae Caritatis.*)

Divine Office: The official collection of psalms, scriptural, and devotional readings and other prayers, which are chanted or said daily by monks, nuns, and some of the other religious communities at specified hours throughout the day and night. The two most important of the "hours" of the Divine Office are Lauds and Vespers.

eremitic: Pertaining to the life and spirituality of hermits. (See cenobitic.)

Essential Elements in the Church's Teaching on Religious Life: 1983 document issued by the Sacred Congregation for Religious.

evangelical counsels: The vows and practice of poverty, chastity, and obedience.

exemption: A privileged status obtained by some monasteries that freed them from the jurisdiction of their local bishop.

formation: Usually, the initial probationary instruction period prior to the individual's full commitment to the community in final vows. May last between three and ten years, and is usually comprised of an indeterminate period of affiliation or postulancy prior to entrance, a year of canonical noviatiate, and one or more additional years of novitiate or temporary vows.

friar: The nonordained (male) member of a mendicant order such as the Franciscans or Dominicans.

Gaudium et Spes: Vatican Council document on the role of the Church in the modern world.

indulgence: The commutation of a certain period of canonical penance, enabling the penitent who had confessed his/her sin to substitute for his period of penance some specified act (a pilgrimage, for example) or work of charity (contributing to the building of a church, for example) or prayers.

Leadership Conference of Women Religious (LCWR): Name, after 1971, of the Conference of Major Superiors of Women, the umbrella association of the heads of U.S. women's communities.

Lumen Gentium: The Vatican Council's definitive document on the theological nature of the Church.

monk: The male member of a contemplative religious order.

novice: Member of a religious community during the first year or years after official entrance and prior to the first profession of vows. Canon law stipulates that all new members of religious orders must have at least one full year of "canonical novitiate," during which time the novice does not engage in an active ministry or secular studies, but instead devotes his/her time to studying scripture, theology, and the history of the religious community he/she has chosen to enter. Many congregations also require an additional year of novitiate, during which time other studies or ministries may be undertaken.

nun: Officially, a female member of a contemplative religious order. Colloquially, "nun" and "sister" are often used interchangeably.

Opus Dei: "The Work of God" 1) expression used by St. Benedict to refer to the Divine Office. 2) a new religious group founded by Jose Maria Escriva de Balaguer in the early 1930's.

order: A religious group officially chartered by the pope and exempt from episcopal jurisdiction over its internal affairs. No new orders have been permitted since 1752.

Perfectae Caritatis: The Vatican Council's 1965 decree mandating the renewal of religious communities.

postulant: Traditional term for a person seeking admittance to a religious community. Usually lives with the community during this probationary period. Some women's congregations have recently substituted terms such as "affiliate" or "associate" for candidates at this stage.

prior, prioress: The head of a nonautonomous house of a religious order, or of some autonomous religious congregations (especially of women) in the Benedictine or other monastic tradition. Has less discretionary power than an abbot or abbess and is elected or appointed only for a specific term of office.

regular clergy: Clergy who are members of a religious order, as opposed to secular clergy who live in the world and do not belong to a religious order.

religious: When used as a noun, a person who is a member of a religious congregation. Thus, one speaks of a "male religious" or of "women religious."

religious life: Life in a religious community, usually under some form of vows.

rule: The constitution and other directives that outline the way of life of a religious community.

Sacred Congregation for Religious: The Vatican department with authority over Roman Catholic religious communities worldwide. This department has had several names since 1950: the Congregation for Religious and Secular Institutes, the Congregation for Institutes of Consecrated Life and Societies of Apostolic Life, and so on. For the sake of simplicity, I have used the original title here.

secular clergy: The parish priests and bishops of a diocese. Secular clergy do not take vows: they retain ownership of their own property, for example. The secular priest's celibacy and obedience to the local bishop are administrative regulations, not vows.

sister: Officially, the female member of a religious congregation. Colloquially, "sister" and "nun" are often used interchangeably.

Sister Formation Conference (SFC):   Established in 1954 by U.S. women's congregations to promote the education and religious training of sisters.

vow: A formal promise by which an individual binds himself/herself to assume certain extra obligations not normally incumbent upon the average Christian. Members of religious communities usually pronounce three vows: poverty, chastity, and obedience.

"Universal Call to Holiness":   Doctrine advanced by *Lumen Gentium* that all baptized Christians are called to a life of holiness, that the life of vowed religious is not superior to the life of the laity.

Appendix

Proportion of Articles, by Topic, in *Review for Religious*, 1950–1992

Year	General Theo. & Scripture	General Spirituality	Theology of Rel. Life	Vows, General	Poverty	Chastity
1950	8.3%	33.3%	4.2%	—	4.2%	—
1951	—	38.2%	5.9%	—	—	—
1952	3.2%	29.0%	3.2%	—	—	—
1953	9.1%	27.3%	—	—	—	—
1954	11.8%	20.6%	8.8%	—	—	—
1955	3.3%	23.3%	—	—	—	—
1956	—	32.0%	—	—	—	—
1957	3.8%	23.1%	3.8%	—	3.8%	—
1958	10.3%	24.1%	—	—	—	—
1959	3.3%	23.3%	—	—	—	—
1960	3.7%	25.9%	7.4%	—	—	—
1961	5.3%	28.9%	5.3%	—	—	2.6%
1962	4.5%	11.4%	2.3%	—	2.3%	2.3%
1963	9.1%	18.2%	3.6%	—	1.8%	1.8%
1964	3.4%	11.9%	13.6%	1.7%	1.7%	5.1%
1965	3.5%	17.5%	8.8%	—	1.8%	3.5%
1966	6.0%	7.5%	4.5%	—	3.0%	—
1967	5.8%	15.9%	1.4%	1.4%	2.9%	5.8%
1968	4.3%	7.2%	5.8%	—	2.9%	7.2%
1969	—	8.2%	6.8%	1.4%	4.1%	4.1%
1970	4.6%	18.5%	—	4.6%	—	1.5%
1971	3.1%	14.0%	3.1%	1.6%	3.1%	4.7%
1972	7.4%	18.5%	4.9%	1.2%	1.2%	4.9%
1973	6.4%	23.9%	3.7%	—	—	—
1974	2.5%	36.2%	1.2%	—	1.2%	—
1975	4.3%	24.6%	—	1.4%	4.3%	5.8%
1976	4.9%	26.8%	—	—	1.2%	—
1977	6.4%	33.0%	5.3%	1.1%	3.2%	4.3%
1978	2.2%	40.0%	—	2.2%	4.4%	—
1979	6.1%	35.4%	—	2.4%	1.2%	2.4%
1980	9.9%	32.1%	—	1.2%	—	1.2%
1981	5.9%	36.5%	—	—	2.3%	2.3%
1982	3.2%	35.1%	1.1%	—	2.1%	4.2%
1983	9.7%	29.0%	2.2%	—	2.2%	—
1984	3.4%	32.1%	2.3%	—	—	1.1%
1985	3.4%	38.6%	1.1%	1.1%	—	1.1%
1986	—	45.1%	3.2%	1.1%	1.1%	—
1987	2.3%	39.1%	1.1%	—	—	—
1988	5.5%	36.3%	1.1%	—	—	4.4%
1989	7.1%	34.7%	—	—	—	—
1990	5.4%	27.2%	—	1.1%	—	—
1991	5.5%	37.4%	—	—	—	—
1992	2.3%	29.5%	1.1%	—	—	1.1%

Obedience	Spirit & Pract. of Rel. Life	Canon Law, Roman Docs., Papal Writing	Psych.	Ministry & Social Justice	Misc.	No. of Articles
—	12.5%	8.3%	12.5%	4.2%	12.5%	24
—	23.5%	11.8%	11.8%	—	8.8%	34
—	22.6%	19.4%	—	6.4%	16.1%	31
—	12.1%	18.2%	6.1%	9.1%	18.2%	33
2.9%	17.6%	8.8%	5.9%	8.8%	14.7%	34
3.3%	36.7%	6.7%	—	3.3%	23.3%	30
4.0%	16.0%	20.0%	4.0%	4.0%	20.0%	25
—	15.4%	38.5%	7.7%	—	3.8%	26
—	17.2%	34.5%	6.9%	—	6.9%	29
3.3%	13.3%	36.7%	10.0%	—	10.0%	30
11.1%	11.1%	29.6%	11.1%	—	—	27
2.6%	15.9%	18.4%	13.2%	—	7.9%	38
2.3%	27.3%	18.2%	15.9%	6.8%	6.8%	44
18.2%	14.5%	10.9%	14.5%	1.8%	5.4%	55
—	15.2%	22.0%	11.9%	5.1%	8.5%	59
7.0%	19.3%	19.3%	8.8%	1.8%	8.8%	57
6.0%	37.3%	14.9%	7.5%	9.0%	4.5%	67
2.9%	24.6%	17.4%	1.4%	13.0%	7.2%	69
5.8%	39.1%	17.4%	5.8%	1.4%	2.9%	69
1.4%	45.2%	11.0%	4.1%	5.5%	8.2%	73
1.5%	33.8%	9.2%	6.2%	4.6%	15.3%	65
1.6%	31.2%	4.7%	3.1%	7.8%	21.9%	64
—	30.9%	3.7%	2.5%	4.9%	19.7%	81
2.8%	22.9%	15.6%	5.5%	4.6%	14.7%	109
2.5%	23.8%	12.5%	—	2.5%	17.5%	80
—	31.9%	4.3%	5.8%	5.8%	11.5%	69
3.7%	22.0%	8.5%	7.3%	14.6%	11.0%	82
1.1%	23.4%	6.4%	7.4%	5.3%	3.2%	94
1.1%	18.9%	3.3%	10.0%	10.0%	7.8%	90
—	17.1%	9.8%	8.5%	13.4%	3.7%	82
1.2%	25.9%	7.4%	4.9%	11.1%	4.9%	81
1.2%	28.2%	5.9%	9.4%	5.9%	2.3%	85
—	23.4%	6.4%	5.3%	12.8%	6.3%	94
2.2%	28.0%	5.4%	7.5%	10.8%	3.2%	93
1.1%	33.3%	6.9%	4.6%	10.3%	4.6%	87
1.1%	31.8%	8.0%	4.5%	8.0%	1.1%	88
—	22.0%	13.2%	6.6%	6.6%	1.1%	91
1.1%	27.6%	10.3%	5.7%	8.4%	4.6%	87
—	26.4%	6.6%	4.4%	13.2%	2.2%	91
1.0%	26.5%	6.1%	9.2%	11.2%	4.1%	98
1.1%	37.0%	4.3%	7.6%	12.0%	4.3%	92
—	30.8%	5.5%	2.2%	14.3%	4.4%	91
—	34.1%	8.0%	3.4%	15.9%	4.5%	88

1. The Extent of the Problem

1. *Official U.S. Catholic Directory*, 1993. The number of diocesan ("secular") priests and bishops is 33,900.

2. See Schoenherr and Young (*The Catholic Priest in the U.S.*, 3; *Full Pews and Empty Altars*, 29) and the *Official U.S. Catholic Directories* for 1966 and 1993. As chapter 3 will explain, there is an official difference in canon law between religious "orders" and religious "congregations." The former are composed of cloistered *nuns*; the latter of active *sisters* who teach, nurse, and so on. The figures for both groups are combined here, however, and unless otherwise indicated, this book will use the terms interchangeably.

3. Finke and Stark, *The Churching of America*, 135, 261.

4. See Neal (*Catholic Sisters*, 18) for the 1960s' figures; Briody and Sullivan ("Sisters at Work," 319) for the 1981 figures; and King (1992 *CARA Formation Directory*, 2) for the 1990 figures. The pattern for male orders is similar to that of the women: McDonough (*Men Astutely Trained*, 562, n. 5) notes that the average number of young men entering the U.S. Jesuits each year between 1959 and 1964 was 312, whereas, by 1970–1973, the average number entering had dropped to eighty-eight.

5. Duncan, "Where Do Nuns Come From?" 122.

6. King and Ferguson, *1992 CARA Formation Directory*, 4,

7. See Woodward et al. ("The Graying of the Convent," 50) for the median age of nuns; see Schoenherr and Young (*The Catholic Priest*, 11; *Full Pews and Empty Altars*, 32) for the median age of diocesan clergy.

8. Popko, "Leadership in the 1990s," 3.

9. Ebaugh (*Women in the Vanishing Cloister*) makes this argument.

10. Dumont-Johnson, "Les communautes religieuses," 98. Turcotte ("Les congregations masculines," 318) reports similar figures (a drop of 26 percent) for the Quebec communities.

11. Flannery, 1991 Editorial, 81.

12. Gogan, "Lay Community and Church Survival," 179.

13. See Langlois (*Le Catholicisme*, 47, 521) for statistics on the French religious orders; see *Inside the Vatican* ("Imported Nuns") for the Italian figures. Some Eastern European countries show similar declines. Modras ("Materialism," 3) notes that, in Poland, the number of entrants into religious orders fell 25 percent between 1989 and 1990, and another 25 percent between 1990 and 1991. See also Kerkhofs ("Confidence in the Spirit," 295) for a confirmation of the Polish figures.

14. See, for example, Hoge (*The Future of Catholic Leadership*), Hoge et al. (*Patterns of Parish Leadership*), and Schoenherr and Young (*The Catholic Priest; Full Pews and Empty Altars*), among the many researchers who have studied the priest shortage.

15. Flannery, 1992 Editorial, 343. The countries included in these figures were Ethiopia, Kenya, Malawi, Sudan, Tanzania, Uganda, Zambia, and the Seychelles. Overall, according to O'Connor (*Witness and Service*, 161), the number of local sisterhoods in Africa increased 280 percent between 1978 and 1985, while the number of brothers increased 340 percent.

16. Jones, "Christian Brothers," 15.

17. Jones, "A Close Look at the Jesuit Orders," 21.

18. *Religion Watch*, "Counting Jesuit Losses," 4. See also Jones ("A Close Look," 21).

19. Regan, "Religious Life in Brazil," 120.

20. See Neal ("Who They Are," 162) and Grady ("Catholic Church Personnel," 5) for the Catholic figures. See Stein (*The Shaker Experience*) and Kephart (*Extraordinary Groups*, 40, 192) for Shaker and Amish figures.

21. Chmielewski et al. (*Women in Spiritual and Communitarian Societies*, 5) point out that studies of Roman Catholic sisterhoods are rarely included in communitarian literature.

22. Hatch, *The Democratization*, 4, 200.

23. Among the historians, see Hatch (*The Democratization*), Westerkamp ("Enthusiastic Piety"), Moran ("Sinners Are Turned Into Saints"), Cross (*The Burned-Over District*), and Bilhartz (*Urban Religion*; "Sex and the Second Great Awakening"). Among political scientists, see Barkun (*Disaster*; *Crucible*). Among sociologists, see Finke and Stark (*The Churching of America*; "How the Upstart Sects") and Gordon-McCutchan ("The Irony").

24. Weber (*From Max Weber*, 287–88) defines the term "religious virtuoso." See chapter 2, below.

25. Hostie, *La vie et mort*, 82.

26. Wynne, *Traditional Catholic*, 209.

27. See, for example, the studies by Kanter (*Commitment and Community*; *Communes*) and Zablocki (*Alienation*; *The Joyful Community*).

28. Thompson, "Discovering Foremothers," 284.

29. Kolmer, "Catholic Women Religious," 1–2.

30. Oates, "Organized Voluntarism," 141–42.

31. Dolan, ed., *The American Catholic Parish*. For example, there is an extensive anecdote (329) about a priest missionary in North Dakota whose sled caught fire. In contrast, Sister Blandina Segale, S.C., who protected an entire Colorado town from Billy the Kid and built several adobe convents with her bare hands, is given half a paragraph (184). The Sisters of Loretto, the foremost pioneer missionaries in an extensive area of the West, are relegated to a single paragraph (183).

32. Schneider, "American Sisters and the Roots of Change," 55.

33. Thompson, "Women, Feminism and the New Religious History," 140–41.

34. See Brown ("The Notion of Virginity"; *The Body and Society*), Donovan ("The Spectrum of Church Teaching"; *Sisterhood as Power*), Kraemer ("The Conversion of Women"), Fontaine ("The Practice"), McNamara (*A New Song*), and Frazee ("Late Roman and Byzantine Legislation"; "The Origins of Clerical Celibacy").

35. See, for example, Bynum (*Jesus as Mother*; *Holy Feast*; "Religious Women"), Elkins (*Holy Women*), Lawrence (*Medieval Monasticism*), Little (*Religious Poverty*), P. Johnson (*Equal in Monastic Profession*), and Schulenberg ("Women's Monastic Communities").

36. See Rapley (*The Devotes*), Kavanaugh ("Spanish Sixteenth Century Carmel"), Luria ("The Counter-Reformation"), and O'Malley ("Early Jesuit Spirituality").

37. See Clear (*Nuns*) for Ireland; Denault ("Sociographie generale") and Jean (*Evolution des communautes*) for Quebec; Langlois (*Catholicisme*) for nineteenth-century France.

38. See Ewens ("The Leadership of Nuns," "Women in the Convent," "The Vocation Decline"), Kennelly ("Historical Perspective"), Misner ("*Highly Respectable,*" "Women in the Convent,") and Oates ("Organized Voluntarism," "The Good Sisters").

39. Tarrow, *Struggle, Politics and Reform*, 43.

40. Tarrow, *Struggle*, 44. While Tarrow was talking about political movements, his observations apply equally to religious orders.

41. Ibid., 45.

42. Ibid., 42.

43. Hannigan, "Social Movement Theory," 317.

44. Ibid., 318.

45. Tarrow, *Struggle*, 50–51.

46. Diamond, "From Organization to Society," 475.

47. Tarrow, *Struggle*, 50.

48. Biernatzki, *Roots of Acceptance*, 48.

49. See, in addition to Biernatzki (*Roots of Acceptance*), Berry (*America's Utopian Experiments*) and Diamond ("From Organization to Society"). See Turcotte ("Sociologie et histoire") for a theoretical discussion of the intersection of these disciplines.

50. Kanter (*Commitment*) examined nineteenth-century communes; Zablocki (*Alienation, The Joyful Community*), B. Berger (*The Survival of a Counterculture;* "Utopia and its Environment"), and Veysey (*The Communal Experience;* "Ideological Aspects") examine contemporary ones.

2. Theories of Ideology and Social Movements

1. Weber, *From Max Weber*, 287.

2. Ibid.

3. See Geertz, *The Interpretation of Cultures*, 196.

4. Denault, "Sociographie generale," 26.

5. Ibid., 30.

6. See Hill (*The Religious Order*, 201) and Casteras ("Virgin Vows," 131–33).

7. Rausch, *Radical Christian Communities*, 85.

8. See Little (*Religious Poverty*, 201) and Hill (*The Religous Order*, 28).

9. Tappert, *The Book of Concord*, 80. See also Knowles (*Bare Ruined Choirs*, 63).

10. Weber, *From Max Weber*, 291.

11. Coser, *Greedy Institutions*, 103.

12. Warner, *New Wine*, 28.

13. See Hill (*The Religious Order*, 12), McGuire (*Religion*, 128) and Rausch (*Radical Christian Communities*, 94).

14. Gannon, "Catholic Religious Orders," 161. See also Lawrence (*Medieval Monasticism*, 11).

15. Turner, *Religion and Social Theory*, 96.

16. Coser, *Greedy Institutions*, 120.

17. See Hostie (*La vie et mort*, 288) and Langlois (*Catholicisme*, 599).

18. Conover and Feldman, "How People Organize," 96. See also Converse ("The Nature of Belief Systems," 207).

19. Brown, *The Body and Society*, 202–08.

20. Hill (*The Religious Order*, 40) makes this argument. But see Kieckhefer ("Imitators of Christ," 1) and Cohn ("Sainthood on the Periphery," 45) for the view that even Catholic Christianity had a more individualistic emphasis than Judaism, and thus was more likely to produce individual virtuosi.

21. Kurtz, *The Politics of Heresy*, 29–30. Coleman (*The Evolution*, 36) makes a similar point.

22. Hollerman, *The Reshaping*, 409.

23. McGuire (*Religion*, 109), Kraemer ("The Conversion," 306), Sered ("Conflict," 26), Dews ("Ann Carr," 84), and Foster (*Women, Family and Utopia*, 226) give examples of this.

24. Swidler, "Culture in Action," 273.

25. See Rapley (*The Devotes*, 171) for legends of Mary; see Brown (*The Body*, 328) for legends of St. Thecla.

26. Weber, *From Max Weber*, 288.

27. Weber, *The Sociology of Religion*, 187. See Zimdars-Swartz (*Encountering Mary*, 140) for an example.

28. Zimdars-Swartz, *Encountering Mary*, 184.

29. K. Woodward, *Making Saints*, 174, 186.

30. Weber, *The Sociology of Religion*, 193.

31. See Rapley (*The Devotes*, 33) for the Visitation Sisters, and Wynne (*Traditional Catholic Religious Orders*, 173) for reactions to St. Francis of Assisi.

32. Wynne, *Traditional*, 243–44.

33. Kieckhefer, *Unquiet Souls*, 192.

34. Ibid., 13, 190.

35. Turner, *Religion*, 89.

36. Ibid., 101.

37. Ibid., 92.

38. See Jean (*Evolution*, 117) for an example.

39. Coser, *Greedy Institutions*, 109.

40. See Little (*Religious Poverty*, 135–60), Rapley (*The Devotes*, 11–20), and Bartholomeuz (*Women Under the Bo Tree*, 148, 233) for examples.

41. See Hill (*The Religious Order*, 201) and Casteras ("Virgin Vows," 131–33) for examples.

42. See Berger (*The Sacred Canopy*, 24) and Luckmann (*The Invisible Religion*, 53).

43. Yinger, *The Scientific Study*, 7.

44. Finke and Stark, *The Churching of America*, 251.

45. Durkheim, *Elementary Forms*, 62.

46. Turner, *Religion*, xxi.

47. Bukowczyk, "Mary the Messiah," 26–30; Strassberg, "Polish Catholics in Transition," 192.

48. Woodward and Nagorski, "The Troubled Altar," 43. See also Modras ("Materialism," 3) and Kerkhofs ("The Spirit of Jesus," 295).

49. Berger and Luckmann, *The Social Construction*, 116.

50. See Burns ("The Politics of Ideology," 1125) and Swidler ("Culture," 280).

51. A. Wallace, "Revitalization Movements," 265. See also Levitas (*The Concept of Utopia*, 181).

52. See Brown (*The Body*, 221), and Bynum (*Jesus as Mother*, 70–75) for examples.

53. See Manuel (*Utopias and Utopian Thought*, 70), Levitas (*The Concept*, 14), and B. Berry (*America's Utopian Experiments*, 229, 238) for these arguments.

54. Tarrow, *Struggle*, 12.

55. See Burns ("The Politics," 1125), Ferree and Miller ("Mobilization and Meaning," 38–61) and Klandermans ("The Social Construction of Protest," 83).

56. Wallace, "Revitalization Movements," 270.

57. Klandermans, "The Formation and Mobilization of Consensus," 179.

58. See Snow and Benford ("Ideology," 199), Tarrow (*Struggle*, 13) and Klandermans ("The Formation and Mobilization," 175).

59. Snow et al., "Frame Alignment Processes," 467. See Hatch (*The Democratization*, 65) for an example.

60. Gamson ("Commitment and Agency," 40, 45; "The Social Psychology," 57) makes this point.

61. Snow et al., "Frame Alignment," provide these categories.

62. Ibid., 469. See Hill (*The Religious Order*, 85–88) for examples.

63. Snow et al., "Frame Alignment," 473–76.

64. Quoted in Snow et al., "Frame Alignment," 476. Italics in original.

65. Snow and Benford, "Ideology," 208–10.

66. Snow and Benford, "Master Frames," 149.

67. Langlois, *Catholicisme*, 216.

68. Friedman and McAdam ("Collective Identity," 168) discuss the perils of becoming so inclusive that there is no incentive to join; Snow et al. ("Frame Alignment," 477) discuss the development of intragroup conflict.

69. Snow et al., "Frame Alignment," 477.

70. See Tarrow (*Struggle*, 4), Snow and Benford ("Ideology," 211; "Master Frames," 134), and Zald ("Looking Backward," 341).

71. See Tarrow (*Struggle*, 50) and Snow et al. ("Frame Alignment," 477).

72. See Lawson ("Religious Movements," 5) and Jenkins ("Resource Mobilization Theory," 529) for this argument.

73. See, for example, Bromley and Shupe ("Financing New Religions").

74. Jenkins, "Resource Mobilization," 533.

75. McAdam, *The Political Process*.

76. Little, *Religious Poverty*, 185.

77. Lawson ("Religious Movements," 9), Gerlach and Hine (*People, Power and Change*, 80–83) and Tarrow (*Struggle*, 51–52) mention this advantage.

78. See Gamson ("Political Discourse," 219) and Klandermans ("The Social Construction," 91).

79. Snow and Benford, ("Master Frames," 144–45) state that movement organizations that arise early in a movement cycle create the hegemonic master frames that will constrain later groups.

80. See Etzioni (*A Comparative Analysis*, 41–42) for the dynamics of normative organizations. See Wittberg ("Outward Orientation," 101–02) for a discussion of why normative organizations may choose to dissolve.

81. Lawson, "Religious Movements," 3.

82. Klandermans, "Mobilization and Participation," 586.

83. See Gamson ("The Social Psychology," 56) and Friedman and McAdam ("Collective Identity," 157).

84. Klandermans, "Mobilization and Participation," p.586.

85. See Kanter (*Commitment and Community*, 64–65), Shenker (*Intentional Communities*, 71), and Hall ("Social Organization," 679).

86. Kanter, *Commitment*, 67–72.

87. See Kanter (*Commitment*, 94–102) and Zablocki (*The Joyful Community*, 64–65).

88. Robbins, *Cults*, 83.

89. Aidala ("Social Change," 292), Coser (*Greedy Institutions*, 106), and Foster (*Women, Family and Utopia*, 189) all make this point. According to Brian Berry (*America's Utopian Experiments*, 204), Dorothy Day once stated that "single persons can live in a communal society but not families." Thus she discouraged married persons from living in Catholic Worker houses.

90. Kern (*An Ordered Love*, 97), Zablocki (*The Joyful Community*, 172), Kanter (*Commitment*, 86), and Robbins (*Cults*, 82) all note this requirement. Friedman and McAdam ("Collective Identity," 165) note that *all* boundary maintenance techniques serve to differentiate in-group from out-group members, thus reinforcing the community's collective identity.

91. Kanter, *Commitment*, 79–86. See also Festinger (*When Prophecy Fails*).

92. Kanter, *Commitment*, 79. See Zablocki (*The Joyful Community*, 185) for examples of this.

93. Kanter, *Commitment*, 103.

94. See Foster (*Women, Family and Utopia*, 85), DeMaria (*Communal Love*, 9), and Zablocki (*The Joyful Community*, 178, 251) for examples.

95. Kanter, *Commitment*, 112.

96. Hall, "Social Organization," 686.

97. Finke and Stark (*The Churching of America*, 19–21) argue that, in a monopolistic religious environment, there is actually *more* apathy and unbelief than in a pluralistic one. Thus a religious order in, for example, eleventh-century Italy would have had to shield its members even more rigorously than a century or so later, when competitors such as the Waldensians and Albigensians had stirred up the general level of religious fervor.

98. See Hostie (*La vie et mort*), Knowles (*Bare Ruined Choirs*, 304), and Cada (*Shaping the Coming Age*).

99. Cada, *Shaping*, 66.

100. Both Cada (*Shaping*, 19) and Rausch (*Radical Christian Communities*, 38–39) use this term.

101. Lawrence (*Medieval Monasticism*, 3) and Gannon ("Catholic Religious Orders," 161) note this development.

102. Brown (*The Body and Society*, 170) and Kraemer ("The Conversion of Women," 306) discuss this doctrine.

103. Brown, *The Body*, 215.

104. Rausch, *Radical*, 41. See Frazee ("Late Roman," 265).

105. Brown, *The Body*, 263.

106. See Morris (*The Lady Was a Bishop*, 12) and Hostie (*La vie et mort*, 9) for the Egyptian figures; Brown (*The Body*, 306) provides the data for the Antioch church.

107. See Gannon ("Catholic," 162) and Lawrence (*Medieval Monasticism*, 7–10).

108. Examples of the variations are provided by Thacker ("Monks, Preaching," 139) and Charles-Edwards ("The Pastoral Role," 67), who note that "monasticism" in early medieval England and Ireland referred to several different kinds of communities, and that it was also often difficult to distinguish between monastic and nonmonastic churches.

109. See MacQuarrie ("Early Christian Religious Houses," 131).

110. Hostie (*La vie et mort*, 85) and Lawrence (*Medieval Monasticism*, 176) both make this point.

111. See Schulenberg ("Women's Monastic communities," 212–14) for the figures in this and the following sentence.

112. Bynum, *Holy Feast*, 14.

113. See Rausch (*Radical*, 54), and Lawrence (*Medieval Monasticism*, 217–18).

114. See Lawrence (*Medieval Monasticism*, 228) and Bynum ("Religious Women," 122–23).

115. These figures are from Hollerman (*The Reshaping*, 40) and Elkins (*Holy Women*, 45).

116. Little, *Religious Poverty*, 4.

117. Ibid., 30.

118. Bynum, *Jesus as Mother*, 10. See Johnson (*Equal*, 251).

119. See Rausch (*Radical*, 66), Little (*Religious Poverty*, 119), and McDonnell (*The Beguines*, 35) for the Humiliati and the Waldensians.

120. See Rausch (*Radical*, 73) and Cada (*Shaping*, 30) for these figures.

121. See Rausch (*Radical*, 79), Hinnebusch ("How the Dominican Order," 1309), and Ashley (*The Dominicans*, 27) for the Dominican figures.

122. Bynum, *Jesus as Mother*, 175. See also Coakley ("Gender and the Authority of the Friars").

123. See McDonnell (*The Beguines*), Little (*Religious Poverty*, 132) and Rausch (*Radical*, 70–71).

124. Rubin, *Corpus Christi*, 167.

125. See Bynum (*Holy Feast*, 18) and Lawrence (*Medieval Monasticism*, 222) for these figures.

126. See Ewens ("Women in the Convent," 33), for example.

127. Taylor, *From Proselytizing*, 17, 22.

128. Rausch, *Radical*, 86.

129. Hollerman, *The Reshaping*, 43, 49.

130. From the 1561 Dominican General Chapter, quoted in Hinnebusch ("How the Dominican Order," 1314).

131. Rausch, *Radical*, 86, 90.

132. Knowles, *Bare*, 302.

133. Cada, *Shaping*, 38.

134. O'Malley, "Early Jesuit Spirituality," 7.

135. Coser, *Greedy Institutions*, 122–23.

136. Wynne, *Traditional*, 220.

137. Rausch, *Radical*, 89.

138. See Buckley ("Seventeenth Century French Spirituality," 44) and Foley ("Uncloistered Apostolic Life," 38) for these figures. According to Dolan (*The American Catholic Experience*, 19), Spanish mysticism became "almost a literary mass movement" in the sixteenth and seventeenth centuries.

139. See Foley (*Uncloistered Apostolic Life*, 28) for the Troyes figures; see Rapley (*The Devotes*, 20, 182) for the data on Rheims and Paris.

140. Rapley, *The Devotes*, 84.

141. Taylor, *From Proselytizing*, 467–69. According to Vacher (*Des regulieres*, 130), the French Sisters of St. Joseph established thirty-three separate houses between 1649 and 1669.

142. Gannon, *Catholic Religious Orders*, 167.

143. See Padburg ("The Context," 22), Roche ("The Male Religious," 766), O'Connor (*Witness and Service*, 150), and Wynne (*Traditional*, 244) for the statistics in this and the following sentences.

144. Hinnebusch, "How the Dominican Order," 1318.

145. Ashley, *The Dominicans*, 192–93.

146. See Cada (*Shaping*, 38) and Hostie (*La vie et mort*, 218–20).

147. Padburg, "The Context," 22.

148. Langlois, *Catholicisme*, 97.

149. See Cada (*Shaping*, 39) and Cain ("Cloister," 918) for this assertion.

150. See Misner (*Highly Respectable*, 31), Murphy and Liu ("Organizational Stance," 39), and Kennelly ("Historical Perspectives," 83) for the figures in this and the following sentences.

151. See Ewens ("Women in the Convent," 18; "The Leadership of Nuns," 101), Dolan (*The American Catholic Experience*, 220, 356), and Finke and Stark (*The Churching of America*, 135). Finke and Stark report that the number of women in religious orders in the United States went from twelve or thirteen per 10,000 Catholics in 1850 to 36.5 per 10,000 Catholics in 1890, even as the Catholic population was increasing tenfold.

152. Ewens ("The Leadership of Nuns," 103) and Finke and Stark (*The Churching*, 134) report these figures.

153. See Clear (*Nuns*, xvi, 35) and Luddy ("Catholic Women") for the Irish figures; Denault ("Sociographie," 42–43) for Quebec; Langlois (*Catholicisme*, 152, 308, 520, 545) for France; Bukowczyk ("Mary the Messiah," 24–25) for Poland; and Flannery, (1992 editorial, 193–94) for Russia.

154. Cada, *Shaping*, 43. See Kennelly ("Historical Perspectives," 90), Oates ("The Good Sisters," 107), Clear (*Nuns*, 107), Denault ("Sociographie," 61–63), and Langlois (*Catholicisme*, 324) for the proportion of sisters in the United States, Quebec, Ireland, and France who were engaged in teaching.

155. Ewens, "Women in the Convent," 33.

3. Contemporary Roman Catholic Religious Life

1. Ebaugh and Ritterband, "Education and the Exodus From Convents," 257.

2. See Weber (*From Max Weber*, 287–88) and Gannon ("Catholic Religious Orders," 173).

3. Cunneen, *Sex Female, Religion Catholic*, 81.

4. Fichter, *The Pastoral Provisions: Married Catholic Priests*.

5. Osborne, *Priesthood*, 188, 286.

6. See Sullivan ("Beneficial Relations") for a description of seminary life in the first half of the twentieth century. See Goffman (*Asylums*) for a description of a total institution.

7. Stuhlmueller, "Biblical Observations," 153.

8. The procedures of most orders, citing the vow of poverty, still require that sisters work within a budget approved by their congregation's leadership and that periodic financial reports be sent to the congregation, along with any surplus funds. There is some evidence, however, that this formal rule is less strictly observed in practice, at least by a few sisters.

9. See Gannon ("Catholic Religious Orders," 159), McGuire (*Religion: the Social Context*, 128) and Turcotte ("L'eglise, la secte," 99; "A l'intersection," 65, 72).

10. See Wach (*Sociology of Religion*, 173–86) for a discussion of *ecclesiolae*.

11. See Taves (*The Household of Faith*, 89–101) for this example.

12. Bellant, "Ohio Bishop," 5.

13. Farrell, "New Generation of Seers," 1. See also Taves (*The Household of Faith*, 101).

14. Kieckhefer, "Major Currents," 101.

15. Bynum, "Religious Women," 129.

16. Hillery, "Monastic Occupations." See also Hillery (*The Monastery*, 110).

17. King amd Ferguson, *1992 CARA Formation Directory*, 203, 215–19.

18. Denault, "Sociographie generale," 61; King, *1991 CARA Formation Directory,* 6.

19. For the active communities, the CARA *Formation Directory* is a better resource than the *Official Catholic Directory.* The former lists only those communities sufficiently established in the United States to have separate "formation," or training, programs for their members, while the latter also includes entries for small, two to five member convents that are merely outposts of orders located primarily abroad.

20. See Neal (*Catholic Sisters in Transition,* 24), the *Official Catholic Directory* for 1966, and Gannon ("Catholic Religious Orders," 178) for the U.S. figures.

21. Denault, "Sociographie," 61–63.

22. Neal, "Who They Are," 162. Turcotte (*Les chemins,* 22) notes a similar decline in a men's teaching order in Quebec.

23. Figures are calculated from the 1993 *Official Catholic Directory* and the *Retirement Needs Survey of U.S. Religious-III* (Arthur Anderson & Co. 5–6). This may slightly underestimate the percentage of active members engaged in teaching, since the Anderson retirement percentages are from 1989. If, as is probable, a larger number of the orders' membership are now retired, then the 15,866 women religious and the 4,581 men still teaching in 1993 would form a higher percentage of the remainder. See also Neal ("A Report on the National Profile," 36), however, for supporting evidence.

24. Fichter, *A Sociologist,* 80.

25. See, for example, Wallace ("Women Administrators," 289; *They Call Her Pastor*).

26. Neal, *Catholic Sisters,* 24.

27. Thompson, "Women, Feminism and the New Religious History," 159, n.32.

28. Gannon, "Catholic Religious Orders," 171–72.

29. Ewens ("Women in the Convent," 33), Donovan (*Sisterhood As Power,* 49; "Spirit To Structure," 10–11), Thompson ("Discovering Foremothers," 274), and Jean (*Evolution,* 251) all make this point.

30. McDonough, "Beyond the Liberal Model, " 103.

31. See Hostie (*La vie et mort,* 122) for the historical verification of this statement; see King (*1991 CARA Formation Directory* 8) and Nygren

and Ukeritis ("The Future of Religious Orders," 260–61) for current figures.

32. Ebaugh, *Out of the Cloister,* 25–26.

33. This does not, of course, mean that members of religious communities never desire to marry. Many obviously do, and this desire has been a prime motivator behind the exodus from religious life over the past few decades. But there has been very little agitation, among either current members or ex-members, for the vow of celibacy to be abolished as a part of religious life, nor for married ex-members to be permitted to rejoin their former orders. Only recently have members of a very few orders begun to explore granting full membership to married persorsons. To the best of my knowledge, few if any communities have actually done so.

34. de Bhaldraithe, "The Eucharist in Religious Communities," 303, n.8.

35. Oates, "The Good Sisters," 177.

36. See Thompson ("Discovering Foremothers," 288) and Deacon (*Handmaids,* 235) for the nineteenth century congregations' attempts to win pontifical status.

37. Kantowicz, *Corporation Sole.*

38. Oates, "Organizing for Service," 156.

39. Oates, "Organized Voluntarism," 158.

40. See Oates ("The Good Sisters," 184), Curry ("Financial Sponsorship"), and Dolan (*The American Catholic Experience,* 289).

41. Deacon, *Handmaids,* 373.

42. See Byrne ("Sisters of St. Joseph," 26) and Oates ("The Good Sisters," 192, 199).

43. See the National Association of Treasurers of Religious Institutes (*Compensation Survey, 1992–1993*) for the data in this paragraph.

44. See, for example, Fialka ("Sisters in Need").

45. See Arthur Anderson & Co. (*Retirement Needs Survey IV,* 3–4) for the information in this and the following sentence.

46. Tri-Conference Retirement Office, private communication, August 24, 1993.

47. Tri-Conference Retirement Office, private communication, September 2, 1993.

4. Personal Incentives for Membership

1. Ferree and Miller ("Mobilization and Meaning," 54) make this point.

2. See Klandermans ("Mobilization and Participation"), McAdam (*The Political Process*), and Ferree and Miller ("Mobilization and Meaning").

3. Klandermans ("The Formation and Mobilization of Consensus," 175) and Eyerman and Jamison (*Social Movements*, 55) make this argument. Burns, ("The Politics of Ideology," 1125) provides an example.

4. Gamson, "Political Discourse", 227.

5. See Ferree and Miller ("Mobilization and Meaning," 43), Eyerman and Jamison (*Social Movements*, 146), and Burns ("The Politics of Ideology," 1124).

6. See McCarthy and Zald (*The Trend of Social Movements*; "Resource Mobilization and Social Movements"), Lawson ("Religious Movements and Social Movement Theory"), Eyerman and Jamison (*Social Movements*), and McAdam et al. ("Social Movements").

7. See McAdam et al. ("Social Movements"), Lawson ("Religious Movements and Social Movement Theory"), and Eyerman and Jamison (*Social Movements*).

8. See Brown (*The Body and Society*, 144) for demographic pressures in the late Roman Empire, McDonnell (*The Beguines*, 83) for medieval Germany, Johnson (*Equal in Monastic Profession*, 23) for medieval France, and Hill (*The Religious Order*, 300), Casteras ("Virgin Vows", 131), and Prelinger ("The Female Diaconate", 166) for nineteenth-century England.

9. McDonnell (*The Beguines*, 83) and Lawrence (*Medieval Monasticism*, 72) make this observation for medieval Europe.

10. Bynum (*Holy Feast and Holy Fast*, 19; "Religious Women in the Late Middle Ages," 126) traces religious entrances to medieval dowry and inheritance customs. Clear (*Nuns in Nineteenth Century Ireland*, 136) and Nolan, (*Ourselves Alone*, 29–36) make the same point for nineteenth-century Ireland.

11. Brown (*The Body and Society*, chap. 1) cites the fear and danger of childbirth as a factor in third- and fourth-century religious vocations; Bynum ("Religious Women," 126) finds the same motivation in medieval women; Taylor (*From Proselytizing*, 423) in seventeenth-century France;

and Clear (*Nuns*, 135, 140), Dumont-Johnson ("Les communautes religieuses," 93), and Thompson ("Discovering Foremothers," 287) in nineteenth-century Ireland, Quebec, and the United States, respectively. Bartholomeuz (*Women Under the Bo Tree*, 261) notes a similar motivation among Buddhist nuns in comtemporary Sri Lanka.

12. Elkins (*Holy Women*, xx) makes this point.

13. Rapley, *The Devotes*, 5, 11. See also Taylor (*From Proselytizing*, 312) for seventeenth-century France, McNamara (*A New Song*, 37, 45) for third-century Rome, and McDonnell (*The Beguines*, 85) for medieval Europe.

14. See Clear (*Nuns*, 5, 19) and Nolan (*Ourselves Alone*, 29, 36) for the assertions in this paragraph.

15. Clear, *Nuns*, 143.

16. Luddy, "Catholic Women."

17. Casteras, "Virgin Vows", 136. See also Clear (*Nuns*, 138–39).

18. Langlois, *Le Catholicisme au feminin*, 643. Translation mine. See Bukowczyk ("Mary the Messiah," 24) and Prelinger ("The Female Diaconate," 163) for information on Poland and Germany.

19. See Brown (*The Body and Society*, 276), Donovan (*Sisterhood as Power*, 11), Knowles (*Bare Ruined Choirs*, 306), Courtenay ("Spirituality," 111), Little (*Religious Poverty*, 173–76), and Lawrence (*Medieval Monasticism*, 260) for documentation of opportunities in European religious orders. For Spanish Colonial America, see Lavrin ("Women and Religion," 46). For French Canada, see Allen ("Women in Colonial French America," 80) and Dumont-Johnson ("Les communautes religieuses," 88). For nineteenth-century England and Poland, see Hill (*The Religious Order*, 254, 272) and Bukowczyk ("Mary the Messiah," 24).

20. Kenneally, *The History of American Catholic Women*, 43. See also Ewens ("The Leadership of Nuns," 107), Mannard ("Maternity of Spirit," 305–06), Thompson ("Discovering Foremothers," 288), and O'Brien (*Journeys*, 426).

21. Kenneally, *The History*, 63.

22. Little, *Religious Poverty*, 161.

23. Johnson, *Equal in Monastic Profession*, 100.

24. See Clear (*Nuns*, 140, 151) for Ireland, Dumont-Johnson ("Les communautes" 86–91) for Quebec, and Oates ("Organized Voluntarism," 149) and Ewens ("Women in the convent," 17) for the United States.

25. See Clear (*Nuns*, 14–20), Lavrin ("Women and Religion," 43), and Denault, ("Sociographie," 101).

26. Rapley, *The Devotes*, 187.

27. See Rausch (*Radical Christian Communities*, 39) and Donovan (*Sisterhood as Power*, 7) for fourth-century Egypt, Clear (*Nuns*, 135) for nineteenth-century Ireland, and Jean (*Evolution*, 154) for Quebec.

28. See Brown (*The Body and Society*, 143), Donovan (*Sisterhood as Power*, 26), Fontaine ("The Practice of Christian Life," 454, 464) and Osborne (*Priesthood*, 146, 150, 190) for the rise of clerical status in the fourth and fifth centuries.

29. This point is made by Osborne (*Priesthood*, 189, 193, 207), Bynum (*Jesus as Mother*, 9, *Holy Feast*, 57; *Fragmentation and Redemption*, 63), Rubin (*Corpus Christi*, 13, 35, 50), Lerner (*The Creation*, 73), Turner (*Religion and Social Theory*, 152), and Johnson (*Equal*, 257).

30. See Rapley (*The Devotes*, 25) for seventeenth-century France, Nolan (*Ourselves Alone*, 36) for nineteenth-century Ireland, and Dolan (*Catholic Revivalism*, 196) and Thompson ("Women, Feminism and the New Religious History," 143) for nineteenth-century America.

31. See Donovan ("The Spectrum of Church Teaching," 213) and Brown (*The Body and Society*, 119, 382) for the influence of Origen. See Little (*Religious Poverty*, 120) for the teaching of Peter Waldes, and Rapley (*The Devotes*, 5) and Buckley ("Seventeenth Century French Spirituality," 28) for the writings of Teresa of Avila.

32. See Wynne (*Traditional Catholic Religious Orders*, 62), Rausch (*Radical Christian Communities*, 42), Bynum (*Jesus as Mother*, 18) and Kraemer ("The Conversion of Women," 201).

33. See Brown (*The Body and Society*, 151, 175, 244), Hill (*The Religious Order*, 23, 276), Bynum (*Jesus as Mother*, 9, "Religious Women," 120, *Holy Feast*, 128, *Fragmentation and Redemption*, 135), Kieckhefer ("Major Currents," 99), Coakley ("Gender and the Authority," 454) and Rubin (*Corpus Christi*, 120, 323) for these assertions. See Zimdars-Swartz (*Encountering Mary*, 40) for a nineteenth-century example.

34. Levesque, "Les communautes religieuses," 179.

35. See Brown (*The Body and Society*, 266, 276) for the fourth-century virgins, and Morris (*The Lady Was a Bishop*) and Bynum (*Holy Feast*, 128) for medieval abbesses.

36. Haas, "Schools of Late Medieval Mysticism," 141.

37. Foley, "Women as Evangelizers."

38. Ewens, "The Leadership of Nuns," 107. See also Deacon (*Handmaids*, 350–380) and Thompson ("Women, Feminism and the New Religious History," 148) for specific examples.

39. Scott, *Ideology and the New Social Movements*, 114. See also Oberschall (*Social Conflict and Social Movements*).

40. Turner, *Religion and Social Theory*, 90. This pattern of middle-class recruitment is similar to the millennial movements discussed by Barkun (*Crucible of the Millennium*, 43).

41. See Brown (*The Body and Society*, 262–63), Lawrence (*Medieval Monasticism*, 36, 49, 60, 178, 217), Bynum ("Religious Women," 126), Little (*Religious Poverty*, 68), Kieckhefer (*Unquiet Souls*, 193), Neel ("The Origins of the Beguines," 248), Johnson (*Equal in Monastic Profession*, 14), and Rausch (*Radical Christian Communities*, 57) for the assertions in this paragraph.

42. Lawrence, *Medieval Monasticism*, 126.

43. D'Allaire, "L'hopital general de Quebec," 65, 96. According to Foley (*Uncloistered Apostolic Life* 53), the Congregation de Notre Dame did attract some women of lower socioeconomic backgrounds.

44. See Taylor (*From Proselytizing*, 167) and Clear (*Nuns*, 88–90).

45. See Tugwell ("The Spirituality of the Dominicans," 20), Lawrence (*Medieval Monasticism*, 231, 248), Little (*Religious Poverty*, 117–133), Ashley (*The Dominicans*, 27), Bynum (*Holy Feast*, 18), and Neel ("The Origins of the Beguines," 250).

46. Rapley, *The Devotes*, 187. See also Taylor (*From Proselytizing*, 311). Vacher (*Des regulieres*, 57–58) notes that the first Sisters of St. Joseph were also from the middle or working classes.

47. Langlois, *Le Catholicisme*, 614.

48. Ibid.

49. Casteras, "Virgin Vows," 131. See Prelinger ("The Female Diaconate," 176).

50. See Langlois (*Le Catholicisme*, 266, 273, 614) and Clear (*Nuns*, 49–51).

51. Misner, *"Highly Respectable and Accomplished Ladies"*, 107. Dolan (*The American Catholic Experience*, 87) notes that earlier, in the colonial period, there were no convents in the United States at all. Only the very

wealthy, who could afford a journey to Europe and a high dowry, could send their sons and daughters to religious orders.

52. See Oates ("The Good Sisters," 175) and Deacon (Handmaids, 62–63) for these figures. O'Brien (Journeys, 219, 510) notes that many Sister of Mercy communities expressly recruited their members from Irish convents to make up for a dearth of local applicants. Most of the vocations to the North Dakota Mercy community, for example, came from Ireland.

53. Byrne, "Sisters of St. Joseph," 270.

54. Deacon, Handmaids, 62–63. See also Peterson and Vaughn-Roberson (Women With Vision, 38).

55. Thompson, "Sisterhood and Power," 152–53.

56. O'Brien, Journeys, 52.

57. Lawrence (Medieval Monasticism, 180) documents one instance of this with the Cistercian conversi.

5. The Mobilization of Resources by Religious Orders

1. See Kanter (Commitment and Community, 46–49) and Zablocki (Alienation and Charisma, 39), as well as chapter 2, above, for lists of these commitment mechanisms.

2. See McAdam et al. ("Social Movements"), Lawson ("Religious Movements and Social Movement Theory"), and Eyerman and Jamison (Social Movements, 25).

3. See McDonnell (The Beguines, 240), Rapley (The Devotes, 173–74) and McDonnell (The Beguines, 235) for information on the indulgences and other spiritual benefits offered to recognized religious orders and their patrons.

4. O'Connor (That Incomparable Woman, 53) documents the reluctance of families to send their daughters to Mary Ward's new—and un-approved—community; Rapley (The Devotes) makes a similar point with regard to seventeenth-century French congregations. O'Brien (Journeys, 52, 173, 577) describes how hostile bishops and pastors funneled vocations away from several nineteenth- and early twentieth-century Mercy communities in the United States. On the other hand, the Idaho Mercy community had recruits directed to them from all over the country by friendly clerics, and Clifford (The Story of Victory Noll, 107) notes the role

the bishop of Fort Wayne, Indiana, played in publicizing the Missionary Catechists of Our Lady of Victory. This was an invaluable source of new vocations for the group.

5. Rausch (*Radical Christian Communities*, 78) and Little (*Religious Poverty*, 117) make this point.

6. See Rapley (*The Devotes*, 172) and Foley (*The Uncloistered Apostolic Life*, 154).

7. Vidulich, *Peace Pays a Price*, 56–58.

8. See Schulenberg ("Women's Monastic Communities," 229–32) for belief about medieval women's capacity for religious virtuosity, Little (*Religious Poverty*, 35) for medieval merchants, and Rapley (*The Devotes*, 5) for seventeenth-century French women.

9. See Bynum ("Religious Women," 122–23; *Holy Feast*, 15), Ashley (*The Dominicans*, 44), Johnson (*Equal in Monastic Profession*, 181–82), and McDonnell (*The Beguines*, 171, 187–90) for spiritual services required by women's communities and the reluctance of men's communities to provide such services.

10. Johnson, *Equal*, 219. See Schulenberg ("Women's Monastic Communites," 225), Johnson (*Equal in Monastic Profession*, 251), Coakley ("Gender" 446), and Lawrence (*Medieval Monasticism*, 228) for the financial dependence of women's monasteries.

11. McDonnell, *The Beguines*, 119.

12. Johnson, *Equal in Monastic Profession*, 89.

13. See Kiefer (*In the Greenwood*, 39) for an example.

14. McDonnell (*The Beguines*) notes this danger for the Middle Ages, Rapley (*The Devotes*) for seventeenth-century France, and Regan and Keiss, (*Tender Courage*) for nineteenth-century Ireland.

15. Rapley, *The Devotes*, 182. See also Taylor ("From Proselytizing," 531).

16. Regan and Keiss, *Tender Courage*, 61.

17. See Rubin (*Corpus Christi*, 168) and Clear (*Nuns*, 50–51).

18. See Wynne (*Traditional*, 63) and Rausch (*Radical Christian*, 43) for the sixth-century monks; Bynum (*Holy Feast*; "Religious Women"), Rubin (*Corpus Christi*), Rapley (*The Devotes*), and Taves (*The Household of Faith*, 89) for medieval and Reformation women. See Thompson ("Women," 152–53) for the nineteenth century.

19. See Zinn ("The Regular Canons," 219), Little (*Religious Poverty*, chap. 7), and Bynum (*Jesus as Mother*, 36) for the conflict between the medieval canons and the monastics; see Little (*Religious Poverty*, 127–28) for the Cistericans and the Waldensians. See McDonnell (*The Beguines*, 185, 343) for the male religious orders and the Beguines, Rapley (*The Devotes*, 53) for seventeenth-century France, Regan and Keiss (*Tender Courage*, 32) for nineteenth-century Ireland, and Jean (*Evolution des communautes*, 133–34) for nineteenth-century Quebec.

20. McDonnell, *The Beguines*, 442.

21. Rapley, *The Devotes*, 32. See also O'Connor (*That Incomparable Woman*, 72).

22. See Vidulich (*Peace Pays a Price*, 40, 50) and McQuade ("My Dear Lord").

23. See Little (*Religious Poverty*, 169) and Clear (*Nuns*, 30).

24. Johnson, *Equal*, 95.

25. Clear, *Nuns*, 149.

26. See Healy (*Sisters of Mercy*, 54) and Sullivan ("Mother Cabrini") for these examples.

27. Jean, *Evolution*, 116, 188.

28. See Kenneally (*The History of American Catholic Women*, 46) and Thompson ("Discovering Foremothers," 288).

29. Jean, *Evolution*, 121–23.

30. Fitzgerald, "The Perils," 49–50.

31. Hill, *The Religious Order*, 217, 194.

32. Ibid., 214.

33. Prelinger, "The Female Diaconate," 185.

34. On papal exemption of religious orders, see Lawrence (*Medieval Monasticism*, 87). See also Donovan (*Sisterhood as Power*, 11) and Johnson (*Equal*, 136).

35. Frazee, "Late Roman," 263. See Thacker ("Monks, Preaching and Pastoral Care," 149–150) for seventh- and eighth-century England, McDonnell (*The Beguines*, 457) and Hinnebusch ("How the Dominican Order Faced Its Crises," 1309) for the French bishops and the mendicants.

36. Coakley, "Gender," 499. See also McDonnell (*The Beguines*, 194).

37. See Coleman (*The Evolution*, 29) for the seventeenth-century Netherlands, and Engh (*Frontier Faiths*, chap. 8) for Bishop Amat in nineteenth-century California.

38. O'Connell, "John Ireland," 112. According to O'Brien (*Journeys*, 396, 528) Bishop Ireland was also hostile to the Sisters of Mercy and to any religious order "he did not feel he could control."

39. Rapley, *The Devotes*, 177.

40. Rapley (*The Devotes*, 177) reports these inspections for seventeenth century France; Johnson (*Equal in Monastic Profession*, 70) documents similar incidents in the Middle Ages.

41. Oates ("The Good Sisters," 179–83), Clear (*Nuns*, 55–58), and Rapley (*The Devotes*, 49–71) each document dozens of cases of episcopal interference in these matters.

42. See Byrne ("Sisters of St. Joseph," 244) for seventeenth-century France, and Denault ("Sociographie," 107) for nineteenth-century Quebec.

43. Johnson, *Equal*, 67.

44. Ibid., 71.

45. See McNamara (*A New Song*, 68) and Pagels ("What Became," 299) for the appeal of the Gnostics, Neel ("The Origins of the Beguines," 245) for the Cathars, Bynum ("Religious Women," 123) for the Waldensians, and Rapley (*The Devotes*, 11–20) for the Protestant reformers.

46. Quoted in Donovan (*Sisterhood as Power*, 120).

47. Schulenberg, "Women's Monastic Communities," 224. See O'Brien (*Journeys*, 167, 459) for scandals in various nineteenth-century Mercy communities which required episcopal intervention.

48. Brown (*The Body and Society*, 224) mentions this for the fourth century hermits, Lawrence (*Medieval Monasticism*, 38) for the Middle Ages, and Rapley (*The Devotes*, 186) for seventeenth-century French communities. But see Bynum (*Jesus as Mother*, 185) for an opposite view.

49. Quoted in Rapley, *The Devotes*, 186.

50. See Lawrence (*Medieval Monasticism*, 38) and Donovan (*Sisterhood as Power*, p.19).

51. Rapley, *The Devotes*, 33.

52. McDonnell, *The Beguines*, 136, 442.

53. Lawrence, *Medieval Monasticism*, 17. See also Gannon ("Catholic Religious Orders," 163).

54. McDonnell, *The Beguines*, 151.

55. Rausch, *Radical Christian Communities*, 65. See also Wynne (*Traditional Catholic*, 62) and Donovan (*Sisterhood*, 34).

56. See Hill (*The Religious Order*, 23), Brown (*The Body and Society*, 119, 144), McNamara (*A New Song*, 67, 75), Bynum (*Holy Feast*, 220), Coakley ("Gender," 454), Rubin (*Corpus Christi*, 323), Rausch (*Radical Christian Communities*, 67–68), Little (*Religious Poverty*, 127–28), and Rapley (*The Devotes*) for examples in this paragraph. See Zimdars-Swartz (*Encountering Mary*, 184) for a recent example.

57. Quoted in Jean (*Evolution*, 21). Translation mine.

58. Brown, *The Body and Society*, 350–56.

59. Schulenberg, "Women's Monastic Communities," 217. See also Elkins (*Holy Women*, 15–16) for an account of similar episcopal support in twelfth-century England.

60. Taylor, *From Proselytizing*, 679–93, 706–26. See O'Connor (*That Incomparable Woman*, 49) for Bishop Blaine's support of Mary Ward.

61. Coleman, *The Evolution*, 33.

62. Langlois, *Le catholicisme*, 264.

63. See Engh (*Frontier Faiths*) for the story of Bishop Amat. See Thompson ("Cultural Conundrums," 215–16) for a list of bishops and priests who invited other religious communities to this country. See *Not With Silver* (125) for a description of how a priest of the Precious Blood Order recruited the Precious Blood sisters for work in Ohio.

64. These data were compiled from a short questionnaire sent to the archivists of all the active religious congregations of women listed in the 1992 *CARA Formation Directory* (King, 1992) that had been founded prior to 1950. Of the 361 questionnaires mailed, 295 were returned, a response rate of 81.7 percent. The questionnaire asked the archivists to supply the year and the country in which their communities had been founded, and (if not founded in the United States) when and by whom they had been invited to this country. Each archivist was then asked to name the person(s) *whom their order considered to be their primary founder.* As Langlois

(*Catholicisme*, 164–67) points out, there are problems with this method, since the foundation periods of individual orders could not always be clearly attributed to a specific individual. In many groups, the person who was *claimed* as founder—the cleric or the woman he worked with—changed over time. Given the present tendency of women's communities to emphasize the role of their woman founder, the role of the male clerics may be actually underestimated by this method.

65. See Osborne (*Priesthood*, 179) and Coleman (*The Evolution*, 141, 182). See also Provost ("The Papacy," 196–97), Lawrence (*Medieval Monasticism*, 87), Osborne (*Priesthood*, 211), and Donovan ("The Spectrum of Church Teaching," 218) for examples of how religious orders were able to profit from the competition between the papacy and the bishops.

66. Little, *Religious Poverty*, 169. See also Donovan (*Sisterhood*, 14) and Lawrence (*Medieval Monasticism*, 261).

67. Brown, *The Body and Society*, 260.

68. Brown (*The Body and Society*, 266) documents this for the early Church; Coakley ("Gender") for the medieval friars.

69. See Bynum (*Jesus as Mother*, 175–85; *Fragmentation and Redemption*, 46).

70. Brown, *The Body and Society*, 356.

71. Heft, "From the Pope to the Bishops," 65.

72. O'Brien, "A Historical Perspective," 114.

73. O'Connell, "John Ireland," 110. See Light ("Catholic Evangelism"), however, for an opposing view.

74. Gleason and Salvaterra, "Ethnicity," 31–33.

75. Dolan, *The American Catholic Experience*, 171.

76. See Langlois (*Le Catholicisme*, 225) and Byrne ("Sisters of St. Joseph," 244) for the foundations by French priests. See Jean (*Evolution*, 120) for a similar occurrence in Quebec.

77. Burns, "The Politics of Ideology," 1131–1132. See also O'Connell ("Ultramontanism," 201–202) and Langlois (*Le Catholicisme*, 262).

78. Portier, "Church Unity," 35. See also Heft ("From the Pope to the Bishops," 66).

79. O'Brien, "A Historical Perspective," 114. See also Leonard ("Ethnic Tensions," 197).

80. Heft, "From the Pope to the Bishops," 69. See also Leonard ("Ethnic Tensions," 197).

81. See Dolan (*The American Catholic Experience*, 355) and Thompson ("Women, Feminism," 143) for this argument.

82. Jean, *Evolution*, 170. See also Langlois (*Le Catholicisme*, 214, 266).

83. Thompson, "Women, Feminism," 143.

84. Levesque, "Les communautes," 180.

85. See Schulenberg ("Women's Monastic Communities," 237), Hollermann ("The Reshaping of a Tradition," 33–38), Tugwell ("The Spirituality of the Dominicans," 15), and Little (*Religious Poverty*, 160) for the missionary role of the monastics and mendicants; see Rapley (*The Devotes*, 40–49) for seventeenth-century France.

86. Coser, *Greedy Institutions*, 118.

87. O'Connell, "Ultramontanism," 206. See also Coleman (*The Evolution*, 141).

88. Neel, "The Origins," 245. See also McDonnell (*The Beguines*, 4) and Bynum (*Fragmentation and Redemption*, 198).

89. See Schulenberg ("Women's Monastic Communities," 226), Finke and Stark (*The Churching of America*, 134), Dolan (*The American Catholic Experience*, 289), and Oates ("Organized Voluntarism"; "The Good Sisters") for examples of the functional benefits of religious orders in solving problems for the hierarchy.

90. Hellman, "The Spirituality of the Franciscans," 44.

91. See Schulenberg ("Women's Monastic Communities" 225) for the early Middle Ages, Neel ("The Origins," 253) for the Premonstratensians, Hellman ("The Spirituality," 37) for the Franciscans, Rapley (*The Devotes*, 33, 49) for seventeenth-century France, Jean (*Evolution*) and Foley (*Uncloistered Apostolic Life*, 89, 119) for eighteenth century Quebec, and Ewens ("Women in the Convent," 33), Hollermann ("The Reshaping," 67), and Clear (*Nuns*, 48) for the nineteenth-century. On the other hand, Elkins (*Holy Women*, 47) reports that religious women of twelfth-century England readily accepted episcopal oversight as a trade-off for the bishops' protection and financial support.

92. Rapley, *The Devotes*, 33.

93. Dolan, *The American Catholic Experience*, 121.

94. Thompson, "Women, Feminism," 149.

95. Kenneally, *The History*, 44.

96. Taylor, *From Proselytizing*, 396. For the examples of bishops thwarting unification efforts in seventeenth-century France, see Rapley (*The Devotes*, 71). For nineteenth-century Canada, see Jean (*Evolution*, 70, 131). For nineteenth-century France, see Langlois (*Le Catholicisme*, 258). For the Sisters of Notre Dame, see their *Outline History*, 22. For the Sisters of St. Joseph in the United States, see Byrne ("The Sisters of St. Joseph," 257–58).

97. Clear, *Nuns*, 58.

98. See Clear (*Nuns*, 59), Lozano (*Foundresses, Founders*, 67), Langlois (*Le Catholicisme*, 244–45, 251), Jean (*Evolution*, 131), Hollermann (*The Reshaping*, 171–75) and Thompson ("Women, Feminism," 151–52) for the incidents mentioned in this paragraph.

99. Quoted in Byrne ("The Sisters of St. Joseph," 259).

100. See Oates ("The Good Sisters," 178), Hollermann ("The Reshaping," 350–52), Kenneally (*The History*, 47–48), O'Brien (*Journeys*, 170, 309), Byrne ("The Sisters of St. Joseph," 260), D'Allaire (*L'hopital general*, 195), and Clear (*Nuns*, 61–62) for the incidents recounted in this paragraph.

101. Thompson, "Women, Feminism," 151.

102. O'Toole, *Militant and Triumphant*, 224–25.

103. See Vidulich (*Peace Pays a Price*, 57), Clear (*Nuns*, 56, 60), Oates ("Organized for Service," 152–53) and Jean (*Evolution*, 89) for the incidents listed in this sentence.

104. Oates ("The Good Sisters," 191; "Organized for Service," 155), Clear (*Nuns*, 59–60), Thompson ("Women, Feminism," 149), Kenneally (*The History*, 47–48), and Hollermann (*The Reshaping*, 119, 194, 235) all contain examples of the episcopal diversion of funds. Kiefer (*Log Cabin Days*, 32), Thompson ("Women, Feminism," 146–47), and O'Brien (*Journeys*, 157) recount attempts to make orders sell their motherhouses. Clifford (*The Story of Victory Noll*, 75) notes that the founder of the twentieth-century Missionary Catechists required that the sisters in New Mexico send their *weekly* itemized expense accounts back to him in Indiana for his approval; O'Brien (*Journeys*, 309) reports that Bishop Power of Worchester, Massachusetts would not allow the Sisters of Mercy in his diocese to own the land on which their institutions were built and kept them dependent on him even for shoes and clothes.

105. Kenneally's chapter on congregations of sisters in the nineteenth-century United States contains descriptions of thirty-seven separate instances of episcopal interference—seven involving the Sisters of Mercy alone. Other authors (Byrne, Kiefer, Ewens) list additional incidents which Kenneally does not mention. The anonymous author of *Not with Silver* (143–45), records that the founder of the Sisters of the Precious Blood (a priest) appointed the subprioress of the order, even though the sisters' official constitutions had required her election. He also defined the limits of the subprioress's role under his authority. Clear's account of sisters in nineteenth-century Ireland lists eighteen instances of clergy interference in just seven pages (61–68); these, she says, are only "the tip of the iceberg." Langlois (257) gives sixteen cases of French bishops detaching the sisters working in their dioceses from their motherhouses elsewhere.

106. See Kenneally (*The History*, 10, 46) and Oates ("The Good Sisters," 183) for these examples.

107. Oates, "The Good Sisters," 179.

108. See Oates ("The Good Sisters," 178), Jean (*Evolution*, 89, 136–37), Deacon (*Handmaids*, 107), Healy (*Sisters of Mercy*, 180), Kenneally (*The History*, 49), Clear (*Nuns*, 60), Sisters of Divine Providence ("Mother Maria," 18–19), Sisters of Notre Dame (*Outline History*, 22), Surles (*St. Therese Couderc*, 14), Lubich and Lazzarin (*Joan Antida Thouret*, 123–37), Hollermann ("The Reshaping," 148, 201), Kiefer (*Log Cabin Days*, 29), Thompson ("Women, Feminism," 146), and Deacon (*Handmaids*, 303) for the incidents recounted in this paragraph.

109. Langlois, *Le Catholicisme*, 166.

110. Flannery, 1992 Editorial, 42–43. This same editorial is also the source for the information on Mary McKillop.

111. Langlois, *Le Catholicisme*, 264.

112. See McLaughlin ("Creating and Recreating," 300) and Johnson (*Equal*, 71) for delaying tactics by medieval communities of women. See Donovan (*Sisterhood*, 11) and Engh (*Frontier Faiths*, chap. 8) for men's communities.

113. See Deacon (*Handmaids*, 140) and Oates ("Organizing for Service," 154). Becoming a pontifical congregation also protected the communities from having bishops in other dioceses detach convents of their sisters to set up new communities.

114. Thompson, "Discovering Foremothers," 288.

115. See Deacon (*Handmaids*, 136–37) for the incidents in this and the following sentence.

116. Johnson (*Equal*, 80) documents this practice for the Middle Ages; Deacon, (*Handmaids*, 142) for the nineteenth century United States. See also Rapley (*The Devotes*, 179) for the Ursulines of Nantes, Clear (*Nuns*, 58) for the Dominicans of Galway, Ewens ("Women in the Convent," 20) for the Carmelites of Maryland, and O'Toole (*Militant and Triumphant*, 113) for the Daughters of Charity.

117. Oates, "The Good Sisters," 181.

118. Thompson, "Women, Feminism," 143.

119. Quoted in Kenneally (*The History*, 45). See Clear (*Nuns*, 61) for a similar example in nineteenth-century Ireland.

120. See Misner (*"Highly Respectable"*, 74), Engh (*Frontier Faiths*, 152–53), and Deacon (*Handmaids*, 243) for the efforts of U.S. communities to obtain civil incorporation. See Langlois (*Le Catholicisme*, 415) for the state charters of nineteenth-century French congregations.

121. See Brown (*The Body and Society*, 263–65) and Frazee ("Late Roman," 263) for examples of this in the fourth century. See Schulenberg ("Women's Monastic Communites," 237) for the early Middle Ages, and Bynum (*Jesus as Mother*, 9) for the later Middle Ages.

122. Johnson, *Equal*, 53–61. See Rapley (*The Devotes*, 149) for seventeenth-century French teaching orders; see Regan and Keiss (*Tender Courage*, 21) and Clear (*Nuns*, 46) for nineteenth-century Ireland.

123. Byrne, "The Sisters of St. Joseph," 259. See also Nolan (*Ourselves Alone*, 88).

124. Deacon ("Handmaids," 140–45, 380), Thompson ("Women, Feminism," 148), O'Brien (*Journeys*, 346), and Ewens ("The Leadership of Nuns," 107) recount instances of sisters withdrawing from a school, or even from a diocese, if they were displeased. See also Rapley (*The Devotes*, 86), Byrne ("The Sisters of St. Joseph," 265), Langlois (*Le Catholicisme*, 415), and the Sisters of Notre Dame (*Outline History*, 22).

125. Deacon, *Handmaids*, 351.

126. Deacon (*Handmaids*, 111, 250, 333, 389) provides these figures.

127. Wynne (*Traditional Religious Orders*, 244), Langlois (*Le Catholicisme*, 120), D'Allaire (*L'hopital general*, 133), and Cain ("Cloister and the Apostolate," 918) provide examples of this.

128. See Taylor (*From Proselytizing*, 399–400) for Anne D'Autriche's efforts on behalf of the Daughters of Charity. See Langlois (*Le Catholicisme*, 120, 323–26) for nineteenth-century France.

129. See Lawrence (*Medieval Monasticism*, 73), MacQuarrie ("Early Christian Religious Houses," 14), Little (*Religious Poverty*, 203), and Langlois (*Le Catholicisme*, 120) for the political benefits gained by rulers in supporting religious orders.

130. See Lawrence (*Medieval Monasticism*, 127), Foot ("Anglo Saxon Minsters," 212), Rapley (*The Devotes*, 84), D'Allaire (*L'hopital general*, 2), Hufton (*The Poor*, 142–44), Dolan (*The American Catholic Experience*, 289), Clear (*Nuns*, 100), and Ewens ("Women in the Convent," 26) for the examples of social services provided by religious orders in various centuries.

131. Lawrence, *Medieval Monasticism*, 73.

132. See Frazee ("Late Roman," 260) for fourth-century Rome and Little (*Religious Poverty*, 203) for Frederick II.

133. Knowles, *Bare Ruined Choirs*, 76.

134. Wynne, *Traditional Catholic*, 244. See Denault ("Sociographie," 45), Jean (*Evolution*, 216) and O'Connell ("John Ireland," 112).

135. Oates, "The Good Sisters," 172. See also Ewens ("Women in the Convent," 25).

136. Hollermann, "The Reshaping," 84–85, 144.

137. See Brown (*The Body and Society*, 350–56) for the economic objections of secular authorities in fourth-century Rome, McDonnell (*The Beguines*, 270–76) for the medieval low countries, Knowles (*Bare Ruined Choirs*, 138–39) for sixteenth-century England, and Taylor (*From Proselytizing*, 169), Langlois (*Le Catholicisme*, 346), Vacher (*Des regulieres*, 104), and Rapley (*The Devotes*, 185) for seventeenth- and nineteenth-century France.

138. Rapley (*The Devotes*, 182) reports such economic fears for seventeenth-century France; McDonnell (*The Beguines*, 270–76) for medieval Europe, and Knowles (*Bare Ruined Choirs*, 130–35) for sixteenth-century England.

139. McDonnell (*The Beguines*, 276) and Taylor (*From Proselytizing*, 382) report these legal and licensing concerns.

140. Mannard, "Maternity of the Spirit," 306–07. See Brown ("The Notion of Virginity," 429), Kraemer ("The Conversion of Women,"

301–02), and McNamara (*A New Song,* 44–45) for similar concerns in fourth-century Rome. See Hill (*The Religious Order,* 278), Casteras ("Virgin Vows," 137), and Prelinger ("The Female Diaconate," 179) for nineteenth-century England.

141. Among them Schulenberg ("Women's Monastic Communities"), Rausch (*Radical Christian Communities,* 51), Johnson (*Equal* 18, 20), and Little (*Religious Poverty,* 203–05) for the Middle Ages; Jean (*Evolution,* 19) for eighteenth-century Quebec; Clear (*Nuns,* 42), and D'Allaire ("Jeanne Mance," 40) for seventeenth-century France; and Hollermann, (*The Reshaping,* 89) for the nineteenth-century United States.

142. See Rubin (*Corpus Christi,* 168) and D'Allaire ("Jeanne Mance," 40).

143. Rapley, *The Devotes,* 180. See also McLaughlin ("Creating and Recreating," 304) and Rapley (*The Devotes,* 86).

144. See Rapley (*The Devotes,* 53), Taylor ("From Proselytizing," 137), and Foley (*Uncloistered Apostolic Life,* 23).

145. Rosser, "The Cure of Souls," 276.

146. O'Brien (*Journeys,* 75, 195, 349, 418) recounts this belief and the subsequent incident.

147. Taylor, *From Proselytizing,* 112.

148. Ibid., 452–53.

149. See Schulenberg ("Women's Monastic Communities," 233) and Lawrence (*Medieval Monasticism,* 219) for the early medieval period, and McLaughlin ("Creating and Recreating," 302–09) and Taylor (*From Proselytizing,* 136, 243) for the later Middle Ages.

150. See Taylor (*From Proselytizing,* 388) for seventeenth century France and Langlois (*Le Catholicisme,* 631) for nineteenth-century France.

151. See Brown (*The Body and Society,* 244), Wynne (*Traditional Catholic,* 105), and Lawrence (*Medieval Monasticism,* 72).

152. See Pennington ("The Cistercians," 210) and Rausch (*Radical Christian Communities,* 56) for this incident.

153. See Johnson (*Equal,* 248–49) for medieval Europe, D'Allaire (*L'hopital general,* 144) and Foley (*Uncloistered Apostolic Life,* 52) for seventeenth-century Quebec, O'Connor (*That Incomparable Woman,* 39) for Mary Ward, and Clear (*Nuns,* 144) for nineteenth-century Ireland.

See Byrne ("The Sisters of St. Joseph," 249), Kiefer (*Log Cabin Days,* 11), and Deacon (*Handmaids,* 21) for the Sisters of St. Joseph, the Kentucky Dominicans, and the Wisconscin Franciscans, respectively.

154. Langlois, *Le Catholicisme,* 297.

155. Ibid.

156. Gerlach and Hine, *People, Power and Change,* 80–83.

157. See Rapley (*The Devotes,* 186) for seventeenth-century France; Denault, ("Sociographie," 66) for eighteenth-century Quebec; Clear (*Nuns,* 83–85) for nineteenth-century Ireland, and Oates ("The Good Sisters," 176) for the nineteenth-century United States.

158. See Denault ("Sociographie," 66), Deacon (*Handmaids,* 369–70), and Clifford (*The Story of Victory Noll,* 107).

159. See Byrne ("The Sisters of St. Joseph," 242–48), Healy (*Sisters of Mercy,* 141), Deacon (*Handmaids,* 103), and Levesque ("Les communautes religieuses," 185) for the activities of this society. Foley (*Uncloistered Apostolic Life,* 35) provides a similar example of lay support for the Society of Notre Dame de Montreal in eighteenth century France.

160. According to Deacon (*Handmaids,* 102), while the School Sisters of Notre Dame received 25 percent of their motherhouse income from the Ludwig Missionsverein in 1855, this had declined to 3 percent by 1866 (the year of the Verein's last payment). In all, the School Sisters of Notre Dame received $41,000 from the Verein, and another $9,400 as a personal gift from King Louis I. See also Hollerman (*The Reshaping,* 89).

161. Sewell, "Ideologies and Social Revolution," 58.

6. Frame Alignment and Religious Virtuosity

1. Snow et al. ("Frame Alignment Processes"), Klandermans ("Mobilization and Participation", "The Formation and Mobilization"), Melucci (*Nomads*), and Eyerman and Jamison (*Social Movements*) all make this argument.

2. Swidler, "Culture in Action," 273. See also Griswold ("A Methodological Approach," 4).

3. See Burns (*The Frontiers of Catholicism,* 9) for the distinction between the content and the structure of an ideology.

4. See Gamson ("Political Discourse," 242) for the role of myths, metaphors, and images in an ideological frame; see Converse ("The Nature of Belief Systems") for packages of beliefs.

5. Snow and Benford ("Master Frames and Cycles of Protest," 143) make this argument for political protest movements: that the construction of a new master frame is essential for the initiation of a new movement cycle.

6. Snow et al., "Frame Alignment Processes," 474–75. See Snow and Machalek ("The Sociology of Conversion," 170–75) for a discussion of global frame transformations among religious virtuosi.

7. See Snow et al. ("Frame Alignment Processes," 470) and Snow and Benford ("Ideology," 205–06) for belief and value amplification.

8. Gamson, "Political Discourse," 227.

9. See Snow and Benford ("Ideology," 208) and Gamson ("The Social Psychology," 70) for ideological conformation to individual beliefs. See Gamson ("Political Discourse," 220–21) for ideologies that either affirm or negate larger cultural beliefs.

10. See Turner (*Religion and Social Theory*, 96, 101) for an example of the elevation of material success; see Little (*Religious Poverty*, 201) for the elevation of poverty.

11. Gamson, "Political Discourse," 221. See also Erikson (*Everything In Its Path*, 81–93).

12. Little, *Religious Poverty*, 176–80.

13. Thompson, "Women, Feminism and the New Religious History," 159, n.32.

14. See Friedman and McAdam ("Collective Identity," 165) on the attraction of a collective identity in social movement recruitment.

15. See Lawrence (*Medieval Monasticism*, 180) for the Cistercians, and Little (*Religious Poverty*, 161) for the mendicants.

16. This point is made by Sewell ("Ideologies," 76), Swidler ("Culture in Action," 283), and Moaddel ("Ideology," 360). See Bates ("Lobbying," 8) for an example.

17. Skocpol, "Cultural Idioms," 91.

18. Eyerman and Jamison, *Social Movements*, 55. See also Klandermans ("The Formation and Mobilization," 175) and Melucci (*Nomads*, 25–34).

19. See Sewell ("Ideologies," 60) and Moaddel ("Ideology," 356) for examples of similar processes in secular movements.

20. Scott (*Ideology*, 104) gives an example of this in a secular social movement.

21. See Knoke (*Political Networks*, 67), Feree and Miller ("Mobilization and Meaning," 46), Macy ("Chains of Co-operation," 735), and Jenkins ("Resource Mobilization Theory," 538).

22. Knoke, *Political Networks*, 70–71.

23. Little, *Religious Poverty*, 160.

24. Lawrence, *Medieval Monasticism*, 24.

25. See Bates ("Lobbying," 12) for an example.

26. Snow et al. ("Frame Alignemnt Processes," 467) make this point for other social movements.

27. Eyerman and Jamison, *Social Movements*, 68.

28. Brown, *The Body and society*, 170, 235. See Coser (*Greedy Institutions*, 120) for the subordination of spiritual perfection to other goals.

29. Deacon, *Handmaids*, 21.

30. Dumont-Johnson, "Les communautes," 91. Translation mine.

31. Woodward, *Making Saints*, 71.

32. Lawrence, *Medieval Monasticism*, 3–10.

33. See Pennington ("The Cistercians," 208) for the male Cistercians, and Neel ("The Origins of the Beguines," 248) for the Beguines and female Cistercians. See also Bynum ("Religious Women," 131–32) and Tugwell ("The Spirituality of the Dominicans," 29).

34. Bynum (*Jesus as Mother*) makes this point.

35. Rausch (*Radican Christian Communities*, 56), Lerner (*The Creation*, 69), Bynum (*Jesus as Mother*, 85), and Pennington ("The Cistercians," 216) all make this point.

36. Brown, *The Body and Society*, 382. See also Brown ("The Notion of Virginity," 429–30).

37. See Brown (*The Body and Society*, 94, 400) for religious orders as models of Eden, Hill (*The Religious Order*, 107) for religious orders as models of the early Apostolic Church, and Hill (*The Religious Order*, 150) and Levesque ("Les communautes religieuses," 182) for religious orders as models of pre-Reformation or pre-Revolutionary Catholicism.

38. See Francis ("Towards a Typology," 441) and Lawrence (*Medieval Monasticism,* 26) for examples.

39. Bynum, *Jesus as Mother,* 36.

40. Woodward, *Making Saints,* 70.

41. Bynum (*Jesus as Mother,* 218; *Holy Feast,* 115), Brown ("The Notion of Virginity," 432–35; *The Body and Society,* 255) and Kieckhefer ("Major Currents," 31) emphasize the intercessory power of religious virtuosi. See Brown (*The Body and Society,* 263) for a discussion of the fourth-century religious virgins. See Johnson (*Equal in Monastic Profession,* 26, 61) and Lawrence (*Medieval Monasticism,* 69) for medieval families valuing a religious member's prayers.

42. Schulenberg, "Women's Monastic Communities," 219. See also Wynne (*Traditional Catholic,* 125).

43. Hill, *The Religious Order,* 28.

44. Bynum, "Religious Women," 127. See also Kieckhefer ("Major Currents," 71).

45. Bynum, *Jesus as Mother,* 10; "Religious Women," 128.

46. Wynne, *Traditional Catholic Religious Orders,* 123.

47. Coakley, "Gender and the Authority of the Friars," 451, 456.

48. Hollerman, *The Reshaping,* 409.

49. Quintal, *Herald of Love,* 139.

50. Rausch, *Radical Christian Communities,* 40, 42, 63–64.

51. Buckley, "Seventeenth Century French Spirituality," 44.

52. See Lawrence (*Medieval Monasticism,* 73) and Schulenberg ("Women's Monastic Communities," 217).

53. McDonnell, *The Beguines,* 187.

54. Coser, *Greedy Institutions,* 119–20. See Haas ("Schools of Late Medieval Mysticism," 143) for the de-emphasis of self-perfection and mystical union among the mendicant Dominicans. See Bynum (*Jesus as Mother,* 103) and Lawrence (*Medieval Monasticism,* 149), in contrast, for the medieval definition of the "*vita apostolica*" as life in a monastery.

55. Hostie, *La vie et mort,* 154. See also Foley ("Women as Evangelizers").

56. Quoted in Clear (*Nuns,* 103).

57. See Little (*Religous Poverty*, 190, 195) for repentence as a topic of mendicant preaching. See Clear (*Nuns*, 101–02) and Rapley (*The Devotes*, 21) for nineteenth-century Ireland and seventeenth-century France.

58. Clear (*Nuns*, 149).

59. McDonnell (*The Beguines*, 187) and Tugwell ("The Spirituality of the Dominicans," 16–17) both make this point.

60. Hostie, *La vie et mort*, 183–84.

61. Tugwell ("The Spirituality of the Dominicans," 26–27), Woodward (*Making Saints*, 354), and Dolan (*Catholic Revivalism*, 196) all make this point. Dobbeleare and Voye ("Western European Catholicism," 220) charge that official Catholic models of sanctity today actually exalt "the superiority of the simple" and downplay professional and intellectual success. This is in contrast to Greek Orthodoxy and Judaism, which, as Kieckhefer ("Imitators of Christ," 26) and Heschel ("The European Era," 7) argue, have traditionally emphasized the intellectual qualities of religious virtuosi as a key sign of their sanctity.

62. Hostie, *La vie et mort*, 184.

63. Byrne, "Sisters of St. Joseph," 243. See Healy (*Sisters of Mercy*) for the nineteenth-century Mercy sisters' ideological frame.

64. Byrne, "Sisters of St. Joseph," 249.

65. Hill, *The Religious Order*, 177–78.

66. Bynum, *Fragmentation and Redemption*, 17.

67. See Little (*Religious Poverty*), McDonnell (*The Beguines*), and Bynum (*Jesus as Mother*, "Religious Women") for the twelfth and thirteenth centuries, Rapley (*The Devotes*) and Dumont-Johnson ("Les communautes religieuses") for seventeenth-century France, and Nolan (*Ourselves Alone*), Langlois (*Le Catholicisme*), and Denault ("Sociographie") for nineteenth-century Ireland, France, and Quebec.

7. Elements of Virtuoso Ideologies in Catholic Religious Orders

1. See Snow and Benford ("Ideology," 205).

2. Brown, "The Notion of Virginity," 428–29.

3. McNamara, *A New Song*, 2, 38.

4. Brown, "The Notion of Virginity," 429.

5. See, for example, Paul's first letter to the Corinthians, 7:25–35.

6. Brown, *The Body and Society*, 67–68.

7. Brown, *The Body and Society*, 170. See also Woodward (*Making Saints*, 228).

8. Brown ("The Notion of Virginity," 429–30) and Pagels (*Adam, Eve and the Serpent*, 15, 80) both make this point. See Kitch (*Chaste Liberation*, 187) for a similar interpretation in a completely different environmental context.

9. Brown, "The Notion of Virginity," 430. According to Thacker ("Monks," 155–56), one early English abbot taught that marriage was actually sinful, while St. Bede ranked the married state as the "lowest category" of the Christian life.

10. Clear, *Nuns*, 152. See also Schneiders ("Reflections," 23–24) for virginity as a form of asceticism.

11. See Bynum (*Fragmentation and Redemption*, 201; *Jesus as Mother*, 14; "Religious Women," 127) for these arguments.

12. McNamara (*A New Song*, 55, 117, 123) and Pagels (*Adam*, 89) make this point for the early Church. Charles-Edwards ("The Pastoral Role," 68) notes that the bishops of early Ireland lost status if they were not celibate. See Kieckhefer ("Imitators of Christ," 143) and Fontaine ("The Practice of Christian Life," 450) for later examples.

13. See Bynum ("Religious Women," 131) for the Middle Ages, Rapley (*The Devotes*, 20) for seventeenth-century France, Clear (*Nuns*, 151) for nineteenth-century Ireland, and Mannard ("Maternity of the Spirit," 316) for the nineteenth-century United States.

14. Kenneally, *The History of American Catholic Women*, 17. See Woodward (*Making Saints*, 343) for Pius XII's encyclical.

15. See Elkins (*Holy Women*, 28–29). Schneiders (*New Wineskins*, 49–50) adds an additional two understandings of virginity in the early Church: as marriage to Christ and as a part of a larger commitment to service.

16. Brown, *The Body and Society*, 67.

17. Ibid., 119, 244.

18. Brown (*The Body and Society*, 263–73) and Schulenberg ("Women's Monastic Communities," 224) note variations in the bahavior of celibate women in the early and the medieval Church, respectively. See also

Rapley (*The Devotes,* 59–71) for a similar problem in seventeenth-century France.

19. Johnson (*Equal in Monastic Profession,* 235) makes this argument.

20. Clear, *Nuns,* 153.

21. Ibid., 74.

22. Ibid., 75. See McDonough (*Men Astutely Trained,* 159–60) for minute rules on dress and behavior among the Jesuits.

23. McNamara, *A New Song,* 1.

24. See McNamara (*A New Song,* 2, 55), Pagels (*Adam,* 20, 86), Brown (*The Body and Society,* 144, 175), and Kraemer ("The Conversion of Women," 301) for the attraction of virginity to women in the early Church. See Bynum ("Religious Women," 127) and Mannard ("Maternity of the Spirit," 310–11) for similar views in the Middle Ages and the nineteenth century.

25. Brown (*The Body and Society,* 88), McNamara (*A New Song,* 71), Bynum ("Religious Women," 126), Dumont-Johnson ("Les communautes," 93), and Kenneally (*A History,* 78) all make this point.

26. See Brown (*The Body and Society*) for male celibacy as a sign of virility in the fourth century. See McDonough (*Men Austutely Trained,* 7, 110) for a similar idea among Irish and German immigrants to the United States.

27. Rausch, *Radical Christian Communities,* 40–41.

28. Wynne, *Traditional Catholic Religious Orders,* 171–72.

29. Quoted in Hollermann (*The Reshaping,* 324).

30. Little, *Religious Poverty,* 68.

31. Clear, *Nuns,* 71.

32. Ebaugh, *Out of the Cloister,* 25.

33. Francis ("Toward a Typology," 446) and Tugwell ("The Spirituality of the Dominicans," 18–19) both make these points.

34. Francis, "Toward a Typology," 446.

35. Wynne, *Traditional Catholic Religious Orders,* 11.

36. Lawrence, *Medieval Monasticism,* 247. See also Francis ("Toward a Typology," 446). Schneiders (*New Wineskins,* 53) notes that, for St.

Francis, poverty played somewhat the same role that virginity played in earlier ideological frames.

37. See Rapley (*The Devotes*, 145) for the seventeenth-century teaching sisters. See Francis ("Toward a Typology," 443) for the medieval canons.

38. See Little (*Religious Poverty*, 23–25) and Bynum ("Religious Women," 115) for the appeal of poverty in the twelfth and thirteenth centuries.

39. See Lawrence (*Medieval Monasticism*, 248–50) and Little (*Religious Poverty*, 90, 101) for the arguments in this and the following sentence.

40. See Francis ("Toward a Typology," 441), Lawrence (*Medieval Monasticism*, 96), and Reinke ("Austin's Labor," 161) for these observations on obedience in early medieval monasteries.

41. Lawrence, *Medieval Monasticism*, 96.

42. Gannon, "Catholic Religious Orders," 165. See also Tillard ("Authority and Religious Life," 97.

43. See Lawrence (*Medieval Monasticism*, 191) for the Cistercians, Dominicans and Franciscans. See Donovan (*Sisterhood*, 16) for the Jesuits and Bynum (*Fragmentation*, 64) for the Beguines.

44. Francis, "Toward a Typology," 446.

45. Lawrence, *Medieval Monasticism*, 122.

46. Tugwell, "The Spirituality of the Dominicans," 23.

47. Rausch, *Radical Christian Communities*, 79.

48. Francis, "Toward a Typology," 446.

49. Lawrence, *Medieval Monasticism*, 254.

50. Lawrence, *Medieval Monasticism*, 49–57) notes the independence of abbesses in medieval England, Ireland, and Gaul. Vacher (*Des "regulieres,"* 20), on the other hand, notes the confusion of authority in seventeenth-century France.

51. Deacon (*Handmaids*, 219–20), Clear (*Nuns*, 53–65, 76), and Hollermann (*The Reshaping*, 347) note many instances of this.

52. Deacon, *Handmaids*, 220. See also 227–28 in the same volume for the difficulties recounted in the rest of this paragraph.

53. Coser, *Greedy Institutions*, 123. See also Lawrence (*Medieval Monasticism*, 29).

54. Tugwell, "The Spirituality of the Dominicans," 23, 26. See also Ashley (*The Dominicans*, 10).

55. McDonough, *Men Astutely Trained*, 160. See also Hostie (*La vie et mort*, 260).

56. Clear, *Nuns*, 76.

57. Mannard, "Maternity of the Spirit," 318.

58. Coser, *Greedy Institutions*, 122–24. See Hostie (*La vie et mort*, 185).

59. Coser (*Greedy Institutions*, 122), Donovan (*Sisterhood*, 8), and Lozano (*Foundresses*, 74) all make this point.

60. Lawrence, *Medieval Monasticism*, 6.

61. See Kanter (*Commitment and Community*), and Zablocki (*The Joyful Community, Alienation and Charisma*) for the necessity of obedience in communal groups.

62. For example, Clear (*Nuns*, 136) makes this point.

63. Gannon, "Catholic Religious Orders," 167.

64. Francis, "Toward a Typology," 443; Hollermann, *The Reshaping*, 408.

65. Osborne, *Priesthood*, 189; Bynum, *Jesus as Mother*, 10.

66. Rubin, *Corpus Christi*, 346.

67. Little (*Religious Poverty*, 188) and Bynum (*Jesus as Mother*, 60–70) both make this point.

68 See Kieckhefer (*Unquiet Souls*, 172), Newman ("Hildegard of Bingen," 170), Coakley ("Gender," 450, 452), Lerner (*The Creation*, 57), and Bynum ("Women Religious," 131) for mysticism in medieval women.

69. Bynum (*Holy Feast*, 77), Rubin (*Corpus Christi*, 169–70), and Kieckhefer (*Unquiet Souls*, 172) all note the women's Eucharistic devotion.

70. See Rausch (*Radical Christian Communities*, 55) and Rubin (*Corpus Christi*, 316) for examples.

71. Hostie, *La vie et mort*, 182.

72. Keating, *Open Mind, Open Heart*, 22.

73. See Rausch (*Radical Christian Communities*, 91) and O'Malley ("Early Jesuit Spirituality," 22).

74. Rapley, *The Devotes*, 144; Keating, *Open Mind, Open Heart*, 23.

75. Keating, *Open Mind, Open Heart*, 25.

76. See Hollermann (*The Reshaping*, 411–14), Clear (*Nuns*, 138), and Rapley (*The Devotes*, 144) for the discarding of the Divine Office by women's congregations—even Benedictine ones—in the seventeenth and nineteenth centuries.

77. Lawrence, *Medieval Monasticism*, 100.

78. See Coser (*Greedy Institutions*, 121) for the Jesuits; see Tugwell ("The Spirituality of the Dominicans," 22–23) and McDonnell (*The Beguines*, 189) for the Dominicans.

79. Quoted in Rausch (*Radical Christian Communities*, 79). See also McDonnell (*The Beguines*, 189).

80. Tugwell, "The Spirituality of the Dominicans," 18. See also Haas ("Schools," 153).

81. Tugwell, "The Spirituality of the Dominicans," 24.

82. Quoted in Hill (*The Religious Order*, 19).

83. See Wynne (*Traditional Catholic*, 11), Pagels (*Adam*, 82–85), Rausch (*Radical Christian Communities*, 40), Lawrence (*Medieval Monasticism*, 31), D'Allaire ("Jeanne Mance," 39), and Clear (*Nuns*, 137–38) for the role of asceticism among religious virtuosi in these periods.

84. Brock and Harvey, *Holy Women*, 21.

85. Bynum, *Fragmentation*, 54.

86. See Bynum (*Fragmentation*, 63; *Holy Feast*, 193, 220) for fasting as co-suffering and as a source of power.

87. Bynum, *Holy Feast*, 244.

88. Haas, "Schools," 141. See Bynum (*Fragmentation*, 187) for documentation of the following sentence.

89. Quoted in Coser (*Greedy Institutions*, 124). See also O'Malley ("Early Jesuit Spirituality," 7) for Jesuits and asceticism. See Rausch (*Radical Christian Communities*, 79) for Dominicans and asceticism.

90. See Hostie (*La vie et mort*, 182) for male societies and Rapley (*The Devotes*, 144–45) for the women's societies.

91. See Wynne (*Traditional Catholic*, 15) and Francis ("Toward a Typology," 441).

92. Rausch (*Radical Christian Communities*, 56) and Bynum (*Jesus as Mother*, 70–75) both make this point.

93. Hostie, *La vie et mort*, 143.

94. Rapley, *The Devotes*, 167–70.

95. See Donovan (*Sisterhood*, 13), Little (*Religious Poverty*, 160–61), and Hostie (*La vie et mort*, 144) for variations on monastic stability.

96. See Nolan (*Ourselves Alone*, 36) and Rapley (*The Devotes*, 5) for this argument in both nineteenth-century Ireland and seventeenth-century France.

97. For examples in various time periods, see Clear (*Nuns*, 150), Johnson (*Equal*, 249–50), and Rapley (*The Devotes*, 189).

98. See Bynum (*Jesus as Mother*, 70–84) and McDonough (*Men Astutely Trained*, 149, 306) for examples of communal values in the medieval and early twentieth-century men's orders.

99. Rausch (*Radical Christian Communities*, 41) and Turner (*Religion and Social Theory*, 101) both make this point.

100. Lawrence, *Medieval Monasticism*, 31–36.

101. Wynne, *Traditional Catholic*, 108.

102. Rausch (*Radical Christian Communities*, 47–48, 51), Lawrence (*Medieval Monasticism*, 127), and Schulenberg ("Women's Monastic Communities," 217) all make this point. See also Cubitt ("Pastoral Care," 204, 207) and Thacker ("Monks," 140, 147).

103. Taylor, *From Proselytizing*, 38.

104. Lawrence, *Medieval Monasticism*, 142.

105. Rausch (*Radical Christian Communities*, 70–71) and McDonnell (*The Beguines*, 137) both make this point.

106. Bynum, *Jesus as Mother*, 30–36.

107. Taylor, *From Proselytizing*, 34.

108. Wynne, *Traditional Catholic*, 147.

109. Hostie, *La vie et mort*, 123–25. See also Wynne (*Traditional Catholic*, 147)

110. Rapley, *The Devotes*, 24.

111. O'Malley, "Early Jesuit Spirituality," 9.

112. Taylor, *From Proselytizing*, 166.

113. See Rausch (*Radical Christian Communities*, 71, 91), Rapley (*The Devotes*, 189), and Hostie (*La vie et mort*, 182).

114. Little, *Religious Poverty*, 198–99.

115. Wynne, *Traditional Catholic*, 43, 87.

116. Taylor, *From Proselytizing*, 411–12.

117. Hollermann, *The Reshaping*, 50. See page 356 of the same volume for the example in the following sentence.

118. See Neel ("The Origins," 252) and McDonnell (*The Beguines*, 314, 321) for the Beguines' borrowings. See Hellman ("The Spirituality of the Franciscans," 32) and Little (*Religious Poverty*, 168) for the ideological indebtedness of the Franciscans. According to Schneiders (*New Wineskins*, 19), "pure forms" of religious life are far less common than "cross-fertilized" ones.

119. Bynum, *Holy Feast*, 26.

120. Bynum, *Fragmentation*, 75. See Rubin (*Corpus Christi*, 317).

121. See Rausch (*Radical Christian Communities*, 80) for St. Clare, Hostie (*La vie et mort*, 40) for St. Angela Merici, and Rapley (*The Devotes*, 33), Foley ("Uncloistered Apostolic Life," 43), and Taylor (*From Proselytizing*, 137) for the seventeenth century.

122. Donovan, "Spiritual Structure," 10–11. See also Ewens ("Women in the Convent," 33), Lozano (*Foundresses*, 3), and O'Connor (*Witness and Service*, 148) for these examples.

123. Langlois, *Le Catholicisme*, 197.

124. See Hollermann (*The Reshaping*, 313), Kiefer (*In the Greenwood*, 33), Oates ("The Good Sisters," 180, 183), and Ewens ("Women in the Convent," 20) for examples.

125. Misner, *Highly Respectable*, 20.

126. Jean, *Evolution*, 78.

127. Ibid., 107

128. Langlois, *Le Catholicisme*, 185–99.

129. Hostie, *La vie et mort*, 264–68.

130. Oates ("The Good Sisters," 176), Deacon (*Handmaids*, 55–60), and Thompson ("Sisterhood and Power," 161; "Cultural Conundrum," 219–23) make this point for the United States; Jean (*Evolution*, 143–47) and Gahan ("The Demographic Evolution") do so for Canada.

131. Jean, *Evolution*, 222.

8. Ideological Supports for Religious Virtuosity

1. See Bynum (*Jesus as Mother*, 57), Hostie (*La vie et mort*, 86), and Hill (*The Religious Order*, 93) for examples.

2. Rapley, *The Devotes*, 169.

3. Shipps (*Mormonism*, 46) makes a similar point: that the creation of new myths and symbols was a necessary task of the first Mormon generation.

4. Rubin, *Corpus Christi*, 8.

5. Bynum, *Holy Feast*, 278.

6. McNamara, *A New Song*, 14, 79–80.

7. See Brown ("The Notion of Virginity," 436) for the third and fourth centuries, for example, and Mannard ("Maternity," 307–08) and Kenneally (*A History*, 17) for nineteenth-century America.

8. McNamara, *A New Song*, 79. See Rapley (*The Devotes*, 145, 171), Foley (*The Uncloistered Apostolic Life*, 181), and Allen ("Women in Colonial French America," 81) for use of this myth—and that of St. Anne—in the seventeenth century.

9. Rapley (*The Devotes*, 172), O'Connor (*That Incomparable Woman*, 55–56), and Foley ("Uncloistered Apostolic Life," 41; *Uncloistered Apostolic Life*, 194) all cite this use of the Visitation story.

10. Rapley, *The Devotes*, 172–73. See also Foley ("Women as Evangelizers").

11. See McNamara (*A New Song*, 80), Rapley (*The Devotes*, 173), and Foley (*Uncloistered Apostolic Life*, 174).

12. Kieckhefer, "Major Currents," 87.

13. Bynum, *Fragmentation*, 158. See also Bynum (*Holy Feast*, 269; *Jesus as Mother*, 14–18).

14. Lawrence, *Medieval Monasticism*, 180.

15. Zimdars-Swartz, *Encountering Mary*, 7.

16. Bynum (*Jesus as Mother*, 18; *Holy Feast*, 26; *Fragmentation*, 131), Rubin (*Corpus Christi*, 168), and Hellman ("The Spirituality," 44) all make this point.

17. Buckley, "Seventeenth Century French Spirituality," 44.

18. Brown, "The Notion of Virginity," 438.

19. See Hellman ("The Spirituality," 33), Lawrence (*Medieval Monasticism*, 247), and Tugwell ("The Spirituality," 23).

20. See Brown (*The Body and Society*, 328), Kraemer ("The Conversion of Women," 302), McNamara (*A New Song*, 82), and Pagels (*Adam*, 20) for these uses of the myth of Thecla.

21. Pagels, "What Became," 300–01.

22. Rapley, *The Devotes*, 191.

23. McNamara, *A New Song*, 112; Brock and Harvey, *Holy Women*, 135.

24. See Rausch (*Radical Christian Communities*, 45) for Anthony; see McDonnell (*The Beguines*, 120) and Lawrence (*Medieval Monasticism*, 11) for Mary of Oignes.

25. See Zinn ("The Regular Canons," 218) and Reinke ("Austin's Labor," 158).

26. Woodward, *Making Saints*, 72–73.

27. See Lawrence (*Medieval Monasticism*, 149) and Foot ("Anglo-Saxon Minsters," 219) for the medieval monks, Zinn ("The Regular Canons," 218) for the canons, and McDonnell (*The Beguines*, 141) for the Beguines.

28. Tugwell, "The Spirituality," 15.

29. McDonough, *Men Astutely Trained*, 159, 460.

30. Hostie (*La vie et mort*, 261). Translation mine. See DeCock ("Turning Points," 59) and Foley (*The Uncloistered Apostolic Life*, 163) for examples.

31. See Shipps (*Mormonism*, 54, 63) for a similar process among the Mormons.

32. Lozano, *Foundresses*, 38, 54–58.

33. Egan, "The Spirituality of the Carmelites," 50–51, 58–59.

34. Tugwell ("The Spirituality," 23) and Ashley (*The Dominicans*, 2, 17) both make this point.

35. Woodward, *Making Saints*, 102.

36. Brown ("The Notion of Virginity," 432), Schneiders (*New Wineskins*, 49–50), and Pagels (*Adam*, 90) mention the metaphor for the third and fourth centuries; McDonnell (*The Beguines*, 105) and Coakley ("Authority," 451–452) for the Middle Ages; and Raymond ("Nuns," 206) for later periods.

37. See Kraemer ("The Conversion of Women," 303) and Raymond ("Nuns," 206).

38. Johnson, *Equal*, 63.

39. Bynum (*Jesus as Mother*, 18, 162; "Religious Women," 131), Rubin (*Corpus Christi*, 169) and McDonnell (*The Beguines*, 105) make this point for medieval religious; Buckley ("Seventeenth Century French Spirituality," 28) for the seventeenth century.

40. Clear (*Nuns*, 147) and Jean (*Evolution*, 136) give examples.

41. See McNamara (*A New Song*, 121) for clerical attitudes in the third century, and Mannard ("Maternity," 319, 323) for similar attitudes in the nineteenth-century United States.

42. See Bynum (*Jesus as Mother*, 18, 185) and Taves (*The Household of Faith*, 34) for devotion to the Sacred Heart in the Middle Ages and in the nineteenth century, respectively.

43. See Lawrence (*Medieval Monasticism*, 6, 31, 48) and Little (*Religious Poverty*, 198) for this metaphor in the Middle Ages. See McDonough (*Men Astutely Trained*, 146, 148) for a similar metaphor among the nineteenth-century Jesuits.

44. Dries, "The Americanization," 20.

45. Tugwell, "The Spirituality," 23. Ashley (*The Dominicans*, 13) makes a similar point. See Hinnebusch ("How the Dominican Order," 1309), however, for an opposing view.

46. See Reinke ("Austin's Labor," 171) for one of the first examples of this conflict.

47. Egan, "The Spirituality of the Carmelites," 51.

48. Ibid., 52.

49. Rosser, "The Cure of Souls," 273. See also Vacher (*Des "regulieres"* 36).

50. McDonnell (*The Beguines*, 189) and Coser (*Greedy Institutions*, 121) both make this point.

51. See Ashley (*The Dominicans*, 18).

52. See Ewens ("Women in the Convent," 33), Taylor (*From Proselytizing*, 22), McDonough (*Men Astutely Trained*, 136–53, 358), and Becker (*The Re-Formed Jesuits*, 26).

53. Ewens ("Women in the Convent," 24), Kenneally (*A History*, 44), and Hollermann (*The Reshaping*, 395–96, 412) all note this difficulty.

54. Wynne, *Traditional Catholic*, 110. See also Rausch (*Radical Christian Communities*, 51, 58), Pennington ("The Cistercians," 205), and Lawrence (*Medieval Monasticism*, 198), for discussions of this problem.

55. See Tugwell ("The Spirituality," 18), Haas ("Schools," 169), and O'Malley ("Early Jesuit Spirituality," 17).

56. Lawrence, *Medieval Monasticism*, 249. See also Wynne (*Traditional Catholic*, 172, 175), McDonnell (*The Beguines*, 189), and Tugwell ("The Spirituality," 19).

57. See Hellman ("The Spirituality," 44) for the Franciscans, Wynne (*Traditional Catholic*, 209) for the Carmelites, and Ashley (*The Dominicans*, 90) for the Dominicans.

58. See Clear (*Nuns*, 71–72) and Rapley (*The Devotes*, 145).

9. Determinants of Ideological Change

1. See, for example, Gamson ("The Social Psychology of Collective Action"), Klandermans ("The Formation and Mobilization of Consensus"; "The Social Construction of Protest"), Ferree ("The Political Context," 35) and Ferree and Miller ("Mobilization and Meaning").

2. See Swidler ("Culture in Action," 283).

3. See Swidler ("Culture in Action," 283") and Scott (*Ideology*, 104).

4. Tarrow, *Struggle*, 34–35, 83–87.

5. See Bynum (*Jesus as Mother*, 18) and Osborne (*Priesthood*, 189).

6. Rausch, *Radical Christian Communities*, 43.

7. deBhaldraithe, "The Eucharist," 298.

8. See Kieckhefer ("Major Currents," 97), Lerner (*The Creation*, 73), and Rubin (*Corpus Christi*).

9. McDonough (*Men Astutely Trained*, 138) provides an example of this with the Jesuits.

10. Lawrence, *Medieval Monasticism*, 71.

11. See Bynum (*Jesus as Mother*, 150–62; "Religious Women," 127).

12. See, for example, Coakley ("Gender," 456), Hellman ("The Spirituality," 40), and Bynum ("Religious Women," 129) for this observation.

13. Kenneally, *The History*, 43. See also Clear (*Nuns*, 152, 192).

14. Dumont-Johnson ("Les communautes," 81), Mannard ("Maternity," 306–09), and Rapley (*The Devotes*, 5) all make this point.

15. See Bynum (*Jesus as Mother*, 20–36) for the influence of loving one's neighbor on new forms of relgous life; Courtenay ("Spirituality," 113) for the revival of biblical study, and Byrne ("Sisters of St. Joseph," 254–55) for the influence of Jansenism on eighteenth- and nineteenth-century religious communities.

16. See Clear (*Nuns*, 149) and Jean (*Evolution*, 112).

17. Kenneally, *The History*, 9.

18. Ebaugh, *Women*, 80.

19. See McNamara (*A New Song*, 69–71) for the third-century Gnostics, McDonnell (*The Beguines*, 35) for the Albigensians, and Rapley (*The Devotes*, 11–20) for the Protestants.

20. See Little (*Religious Poverty*, 146, 160) for the medieval Franciscans and Dominicans. See O'Malley ("Early Jesuit Spirituality," 9–15), Hinnebusch ("How the Dominican Order," 1316), and Rapley (*The Devotes*, 11, 25) for the seventeenth-century orders.

21. Rapley (*The Devotes*, 168) gives examples of this.

22. Swidler ("Culture in Action," 273), Griswold ("A Methodological Approach," 4), and Tarrow ("Mentalities," 189) make this point for other, secular social movements. See also Hart ("Culture and Religion," 7, n. 1).

23. Clear, *Nuns*, 95.

24. McDonough, *Men Astutely Trained*, 138, 362.

25. Clear, *Nuns*, 95. See also Byrne ("The Sisters of St. Joseph," 267).

26. Clear (*Nuns*, 97, 99) and Hill (*The Religious Order*, 283) make this point.

27. Quoted in Donovan (*Sisterhood*, 45). See also Thompson ("Cultural Conundrums").

28. Deacon (*Handmaids*, 85) and Thompson ("Sisterhood," 151–55) make this argument.

29. Quoted in Byrne ("The Sisters of St. Joseph," 267–68).

30. See Hollermann (*The Reshaping*, 393) for the Benedictines and Deacon (*Handmaids*, 85–86) for the Wisconsin Dominicans. See also Thompson ("Sisterhood," 156).

31. Ewens ("Women in the Convent," 31) and Byrne ("The Sisters of St. Joseph," 265) give examples.

32. See Mannard ("Maternity," 315, 319) for the quotation in this and the following sentence. See also Oates ("Organized Voluntarism," 147).

33. Kenneally, *The History*, 15.

34. See Lawrence (*Medieval Monasticism*, 4), Hinnebusch ("How the Dominican Order," 1315, 1317), Taylor (*From Proselytizing*, 355, 408) and McDonough (*Men Astutely Trained*, 6) for the incidents in this paragraph.

35. See Coleman ("Catholic Integralism," 86) for a discussion of the nineteenth century "crisis of legitimacy" in the Catholic Church.

36. See Kurtz (*The Politics of Heresy*, 27) and Burns ("The Politics of Ideology," 1126–1129).

37. See Levesque ("Les communautes," 182–87), Dolan (*Catholic Revivalism*, 2), and Byrne ("The Sisters of St. Joseph," 248–49, 264) for the assertions in this paragraph.

38. See Burns ("The Politics of Ideology," 1129) and Ewens ("Women in the Convent," 19).

39. See Donovan (*Sisterhood*, 48), Dolan (*The American Catholic*, 111), Ewens ("Women in the Convent," 19), and Leonard ("Ethnic Tensions," 12–13).

40. See Vidulich (*Peace*, 40, 50) for an example.

41. See McDonough (*Men Astutely Trained*, 154–55) and O'Connell ("Ultramontanism," 205).

42. O'Connell, "Ultramontanism," 207. Burns ("The Politics of Ideology," 1133) and Becker (*The Re-Formed Jesuits*, 140) make a similar point.

43. Coleman, "Catholic Integralism," 77. See also McDonough (*Men Astutely Trained*, 374).

44. See McDonough (*Men Astutely Trained*, 156–57, 374–76) and Becker (*The Re-Formed Jesuits*, 140).

45. See Little (*Religious Poverty*, 173–83) and Flannery (1992 editorial, 42) for the mendicants and the Jesuits respectively. Ashley (*The Dominicans*, 212) also notes that Lacordaire, the founder of the nineteenth-century Dominicans, was sympathetic to the liberalism the Vatican so despised. Therefore, when nineteenth-century Dominicans confined themselves to rote memorization of the Vatican's "party line," they were also going against their most recent founder's philosophy.

46. See Converse ("The Nature of Belief Systems," 210) for a theoretical discussion of how opposing belief systems are linked to each other.

47. See Dolan (*The American Catholic Experience*, 315), Kurtz (*The Politics*, 47) and O'Connell ("Ultramontanism," 115) for a discussion of the Americanist controversies.

48. See Storch ("John Ireland") and McDonough (*Men Astutely Trained*, 73–74, 180) for the American orders' reaction to the Americanist charges.

49. Rubin (*Corpus Christi*, 8–9) and Bynum (*Fragmentation*, 17) give examples of the use of ecclesiastical networks to spread a virtuoso ideology.

50. See Lawrence (*Medieval Monasticism*, 11), Rausch (*Radical Christian Communities*, 36–38), and Frazee ("Late Roman," 264; "The Origins," 115) for the influence of Athanasius' biography of Anthony.

51. See Lawrence (*Medieval Monasticism*, 20–25) and Reinke ("Austin's Labor," 159) for the influence of Gregory's *Life* of St. Benedict.

52. See Rausch (*Radical Christian Communities*, 70), McDonnell (*The Beguines*, 120), and Neel ("The Origins," 244–45) for de Vitry's *Life* of Mary of Oignies.

53. See Elkins (*Holy Women*, 7) for Gocelin's biographies of Anglo-Saxon abbesses and Coakley ("Gender") for the medieval friars' biographies of women mystics.

54. Pagels (*Adam*, 85) and McNamara (*A New Song*, 122) recount this incident.

55. Kieckhefer, "Imitators of Christ," 6.

56. Bynum (*Holy Feast*, 20; "Religious Women," 127) makes this argument.

57. See Neel ("The Origins," 242–45), Lawrence (*Medieval Monasticism*, 233), and Taylor (*From Proselytizing*, 391) for these examples.

58. Lawrence, *Medieval Monasticism*, 88.

59. Tugwell ("The Spirituality," 16) and Lawrence (*Medieval Monasticism*, 25–27) both make this point.

60. Taylor, *From Proselytizing*, 122–29.

61. This process parallels the negotiation Zimdars-Swartz (*Encountering Mary*, 240) has noted for the Marian visionaries. The seer had less authority/influence in defining the apparition's meaning than one might suppose—interested clerics and even the general public often decided for the seer what it was that his/her vision meant.

62. See, for example, Pagels (*Adam*, 21–27), McNamara (*A New Song*, 1–2), Brown (*The Body and Society*, 137, 206) and Frazee ("The Origins," 109).

63. McNamara, *A New Song*, 55.

64. See Pagels (*Adam*, 21) and Brown (*The Body and Society*, 137) for Clement's opposition.

65. McNamara, *A New Song*, 58.

66. Francis ("Toward a Typology," 442–43), Brown (*The Body and Society*, 358), Osborne (*Priesthood*, 188), Frazee ("The Origins," 115), and Roche ("The Male Religious," 760) all make this observation.

67. See, for example, Brown (*The Body and Society*, 119), McNamara (*A New Song*, 65–68), Kraemer ("The Conversion," 30), and Pagels ("What Became," 300).

68. McNamara, *A New Song*, 124.

69. Rubin (*Corpus Christi*, 316–17), Lerner (*The Creation*, 57), Bynum ("Religious Women," 129), and Newman ("Hildegard of Bingen") all make this point.

70. Bynum, *Holy Feast*, 57. See also Rubin (*Corpus Christi*, 29–35), Bynum (*Fragmentation*, 46), and Osborne (*Priesthood*, 190).

71. Rubin (*Corpus Christi*, 319–34) and Osborne (*Priesthood*, 190–210) chronicle the attempts to win acceptance of the doctrine of the Eucharist.

72. See Bynum (*Holy Feast*, 77) and Rubin (*Corpus Christi*, 120).

73. See Bynum (*Jesus as Mother*, 185; *Fragmentation*, 13–16) for this argument.

74. Hellman, "The Spirituality of the Franciscans," 40. See also Coakley ("Gender," 456).

75. Coakley, "Gender," 449.

76. Bynum, "Religious Women," 129.

77. See Coakley ("Gender," 451, 455–456), Tugwell ("The Spirituality," 24), McDonnell (*The Beguines*, 160, 200–01), Bynum (*Fragmentation*, 198), and Neel ("The Origins," 244) for the examples recounted in this paragraph.

78. See McDonnell (*The Beguines*, 294) and Rubin (*Corpus Christi*, 172–74) for the examples in this and the following sentence.

79. See Bynum ("Religious Women," 136–37; *Holy Feast*, 208).

80. Coakley, "Gender," 459.

81. Rapley, *The Devotes*, 25

82. See McDonnell (*The Beguines*, 508), Rapley (*The Devotes*, 173), Taylor (*From Proselytizing*, 414), and Foley (*The Uncloistered Apostolic Life*, 208) for incidents indicating that women in apostolic orders were viewed as inferior to cloistered nuns.

83. Vacher (*Des "regulieres*," 209) notes this tendency for the seventeenth-century Sisters of St. Joseph. See also Rapley (*The Devotes*, 177), and Foley (*The Uncloistered Apostolic Life*, 24, 127).

84. Quoted in Rapley (*The Devotes*, 174).

85. Foley, *Uncloistered Apostolic Life*, 146.

86. Rapley, *The Devotes*, 25–30, 86.

87. Leonard, "Ethnic Tensions," 213.

88. Ewens, "Women in the Convent," 19.

89. Ibid., 19–24.

90. See Ewens ("Women in the Convent," 23) and Thompson ("Women, Feminism," 145–46) for these incidents.

91. See Byrne ("Sisters of St. Joseph," 251–55, 262), Deacon (*Handmaids*, 54–60), Oates ("The Good Sisters," 176), Hollermann (*The Reshaping*, 137), Thompson ("Cultural Conundrums"), and Kennelly ("Historical Perspectives," 86) for the arguments in this paragraph.

92. See Ewens ("Women in the Convent," 31) for this and the subsequent quotation.

93. Dolan, *The American Catholic Experience*, 169. See also Hollermann (*The Reshaping*, 88) and Thompson ("Sisterhood," 165; "Cultural Conundrums").

94. Dolan, *The American Catholic Experience*, 303.

95. See Engh (*Frontier Faiths*, 157–61) for an example of this conflict.

96. McDonnell (*The Beguines*, 464, 509) and Little (*Religious Poverty*, 127) recount these controversies.

97. Hostie, *La vie*, 122. Translation mine.

98. Ibid., 157. Translation mine.

99. Pagels (*Adam*, 83) See also McNamara (*A New Song*, 118) and Brown (*The Body and Society*, 268–320).

100. See McDonnell (*The Beguines*, 121), Rubin (*Corpus Christi*, 171), and Neel ("The Origins," 245) for the influence of lay patrons on the Beguines.

101. See Pagels (*Adam*, 84), Schulenberg ("Women's Monastic Communities," 225), Rapley (*The Devotes*, 182–83), and Taylor (*From Proselytizing*, 408) for examples of falling lay support in different historical epochs.

102. See Frazee ("Late Roman," 264, 271–79), Pennington ("The Cistercians," 205), Reinke ("Austin's Labor," 159), Lawrence (*Medieval Monasticism*, 74), Little (*Religious Poverty*, 203–05), Byrne ("The Sisters of St. Joseph," 246), and Langlois (*Le Catholicisme*, 126) for the examples in this paragraph.

103. Schulenberg, "Women's Monastic communities," 218–19. See Taylor (*From Proselytizing*, 112, 452) for seventeenth-century France.

104. Lawrence, *Medieval Monasticism*, 73–74.

105. Rubin (*Corpus Christi*, 166) and Little (*Religious Poverty*, 176–83).

106. Little, *Religious Poverty*, 206–10.

107. Taylor, *From Proselytizing*, 256, 318. See Pagels (*Adam*, 129–33) for an example from the third-century Church.

108. Egan, "The Spirituality," 53.

109. See Hill (*The Religious Order*, 98), Hellman ("The Spirituality," 44–49), Wynne (*Traditional Catholic*, 170, 175–77), and Rausch (*Radical Christian Communities*, 73–74) for ideological splits among the Franciscans.

110. Martin, "Popular and Pastoral Issues," 326.

111. O'Malley, "Early Jesuit Spirituality," 17. See also Keating (*Open Mind, Open Heart*, 22–23).

112. Regan and Keiss, *Tender Courage*, 107. According to O'Brien (*Journeys*, 38, 43), the Sisters of Mercy had other ideologically based conflicts. The Omaha community, for example, debated whether their charism allowed them to do any work for money at all.

113. Rausch (*Radical Christian Communities*, 65) and Rapley (*The Devotes*, 170–75.).

114. See Little (*Religious Poverty*, 175–76) and Tugwell ("The Spirituality," 17) for the mendicants. See Rapley (*The Devotes*, 49–59) and Rausch (*Radical Christian Communities*, 92) for the Jesuits and the teaching congregations.

115. See Donovan (*Sisterhood*, 7) and Brown (*The Body and Society*, 170) for the writings of Origen. See Pennington ("The Cistercians," 210) and Bynum (*Jesus as Mother*) for Bernard of Clairveaux.

116. See Hellman ("The Spirituality," 43) for the role of St. Bonaventure in Franciscan spirituality. See Reinke ("Austin's Labor," 165) for Hugh of St. Victor. See Rapley (*The Devotes*, 5) and Buckley ("Seventeenth Century," 28) for Teresa of Avila and John of the Cross.

117. Tarrow, *Struggle*, 191.

118. See Jean (*Evolution*, 143–47), Thompson ("Sisterhood," 160–65; "Discovering Foremothers," 281), Hollermann (*The Reshaping*, 164, 179), Byrne ("The Sisters of St. Joseph," 258–59), and Langlois (*Le Catholicisme*, 637) for examples of these types of divisions in the nineteenth-

century Canadan, American and French communities. See Deacon (*Handmaids*, 357–58) for disputes over ministry.

10. Previous Decline Periods in Religious Orders

1. See Knoke (*Political Networks*, 58), Tarrow (*Struggle*, 4), Klandermans ("Mobilization," 584) and Barkun (*Crucible*, 82).

2. Eyerman and Jamison, *Social Movements*, 63. See also Jenkins ("Resource Mobilization Theory," 534) and Tarrow (*Struggle*, 49).

3. See Johnson (*Equal*, 248–64), Schulenberg ("Women's Monastic Communities," 215, 221–34), Lawrence (*Medieval Monasticism*, 120), and Hillery (*The Monastery*, 8–9).

4. See Tugwell ("The Spirituality, 22–26), Egan ("The Spirituality," 57), Hellman ("The Spirituality," 46–47), and Wynne (*Traditional Catholic*, 177–207).

5. Padburg, "The Contexts," 21.

6. Jean, *Evolution*, 49. See also Rapley (*The Devotes*, 182–83), Taylor (*From Proselytizing*, 607–12), Coser (*Greedy Institutions*, 135), Langlois (*Le Catholicisme*, 142–43), Hollermann (*The Reshaping*, 53), and Hennessey ("A Look," 38).

7. Knowles, *Bare Ruined Choirs*, 314–15.

8. Tarrow, *Struggle*, 53.

9. Miller, "The End of the SDS," 280. Related to this is Warner's analysis (*New Wine*, 178–190) of contextual factors in church decline.

10. See Ferree and Miller ("Mobilization," 43) and Snow et al. ("Frame Alignment," 477).

11. Donovan (*Sisterhood*, 15), Lawrence (*Medieval Monasticism*, 105, 276), Tugwell ("The Spirituality," 25), and Schulenberg ("Women's Monastic Communities," 222) note these factors. Ashley (*The Dominicans*, 58) notes that the Black Death caused the sharpest decline in the order's history: between 30 percent and 50 percent of all friars died.

12. See Schulenberg ("Women's Monastic Communities," 187) and Johnson (*Equal*, 255–56) for the periods of monastic decline. See Rapley (*The Devotes*, 187) for eighteenth-century France.

13. See Knowles (*Bare Ruined Choirs*, 308) and Bynum (*Jesus as Mother*, 10).

14. See Knowles (*Bare Ruined Choirs*, 4–7) and Courtenay ("Spirituality," 110–11).

15. See Lawrence (*Medieval Monasticism*, 281), Schulenberg ("Women's Monastic Communities," 225), and Rapley (*The Devotes*, 182) for the documentation of this paragraph.

16. Tugwell, "The Spirituality," 25.

17. See Johnson (*Equal*, 225–59) for the medieval women's communities and Rapley (*The Devotes*, 181–82) for late seventeenth-century France.

18. Lawrence, *Medieval Monasticism*, 274–75. See also Lawrence (*Medieval Monasticism*, 129–30), Little (*Religious Poverty*, 68) and Knowles (*Bare Ruined Choirs*, 140–42).

19. Knowles, (*Bare Ruined Choirs*, 219–25).

20. See Wynne (*Traditional Catholic*, 99), Schulenberg ("Women's Monastic Communities," 225) and Johnson (*Equal*, 219–25) for the medieval monasteries. See Rapley (*The Devotes*, 53–71) for a similar problem in seventeenth-century France.

21. Lawrence, *Medieval Monasticism*, 219.

22. See Johnson (*Equal*, 111, 259–60) for these arguments.

23. Johnson, *Equal*, 259.

24. Rapley, *The Devotes*, 183.

25. See Johnson (*Equal*, 111) for the eleventh-century men's communities; see Knowles (*Bare Ruined Choirs*, 130) for the sixteenth century.

26. Lawrence, *Medieval Monasticism*, 130. See Rapley (*The Devotes*, 185) for a similar situation in seventeenth-century France.

27. See McDonnell (*The Beguines*, 270), Rapley (*The Devotes*, 182–85) and Langlois (*Le Catholicisme*, 346, 630, 639) for this problem.

28. See McDonnell (*The Beguines*, 187–90) and Johnson (*Equal*, 251–52) for male reluctance to provide spiritual services in the Middle Ages. See Thompson ("Women, Feminism," 150) for the denial of the sacraments in the nineteenth century.

29. See Thompson ("Discovering Foremothers," 288) for an example of the empowering effects of networks. See Bynum ("Religious Women," 128) and Johnson (*Equal*, 264) for the effects of the withdrawal of these networks.

30. See Frazee ("Late Roman," 264–65) for the effects of the Emperor Valens' persecution. See Lawrence (*Medieval Monasticism*, 234–35) and McDonnell (*The Beguines*, 505–15, 535–38) for the Beguines, and Knowles (*Bare Ruined Choirs*, 66–69, 191–98) and Rausch (*Radical Christian Communities*, 86) for Reformation rulers. See Langlois (*Le Catholicisme*, 97) and Hollermann (*The Reshaping*, 54–55) for the Revolutionary period.

31. Miller, "They Found a Formula," 89. See also Miller, "The End of the SDS," 281.

32. See Kenneally (*The History*, 43–52), Ewens ("Women in the Convent," 20–27), Hollermann (*The Reshaping*, 131, 146–50), Clear (*Nuns*, 48–53) and D'Allaire (*L'hopital general*, 132–33) for examples.

33. See Knowles (*Bare Ruined Choirs*, 44, 304–19) for examples in religious communities. See Miller ("The End of the SDS," 286) and McAdam ("The Decline," 304) for the effect of persecution on declining secular movements.

34. See Tarrow (*Struggle*, 55), Snow et al. ("Frame Alignment," 477) and McAdam ("The Decline," 304) for this argument.

35. See Gerber ("From Bottles to Bombs") and Sills (*The Volunteers*) for examples of this tactic.

36. Arbuckel (*Out of Chaos*, 2) recounts this incident.

37. Knowles, *Bare Ruined Choirs*, 4. See also Courtenay ("Spirituality," 111).

38. Johnson (*Equal*, 251) notes this for the thirteenth, and Langlois (*Le Catholicisme*, 632) for the nineteenth, centuries.

39. Knowles, *Bare Ruined Choirs*, 313.

40. See Langlois (*Le Catholicisme*, 631) and Clear (*Nuns*, 115, 128–29).

41. Kern, *An Ordered Love*, 7. Italics in original. See also Snow et al. ("Frame Alignment," 476).

42. Wallace, "Revitalization Movements," 266.

43. See Snow et al. ("Frame Alignment," 477) and Gamson ("The Social Psychology," 65) for a theoretical discussion of this argument. See Hostie (*La vie et mort*, 79) and Denault ("Sociographie," 27) for examples in religious orders.

44. See Brown ("The Notion of Virginity," 433–34) and Rausch (*Radical Christian Communities*, 43).

45. Lawrence (*Medieval Monasticism*) makes this point.

46. Bynum, *Jesus as Mother*, 89. See also Little (*Religious Poverty*, 35) and Ashley (*The Dominicans*, 52).

47. See Rubin (*Corpus Christi*, 263, 266) and Bynum (*Holy Feast*, 281) for these examples.

48. Little, *Religious Poverty*, 173–79, 195.

49. See Little (*Religious Poverty*, 25), Bynum (*Holy Feast*, 115) and Hostie (*La vie et mort*, 153).

50. See Deck ("The Challenge," 20) and Rapley (*The Devotes*, 11).

51. See O'Malley ("Early Jesuit," 9), Rapley (*The Devotes*, 11), and Coser (*Greedy Institutions*, 118).

52. Knowles, *Bare Ruined Choirs*, 304–06.

53. See Rausch (*Radical Christian Communities*, 84–85), Bynum (*Fragmentation*, 78), and Rubin (*Corpus Christi*, 354) for the hostility of the sixteenth-century reformers to Catholiic religious virtuosity.

54. Mannard, "Maternity of Spirit," 309–10. See also Casteras ("Virgin Vows," 137), Prelinger ("The Female Diaconate," 179), and Hill (*The Religious Order*, 298).

55. See Brown (*The Body and Society*, 119) and McNamara (*A New Song*, 68).

56. Bynum, "Religious Women," 122–23. See also McDonnell (*The Beguines*, 442).

57. See McRedmund ("The Jesuits in Ireland," 61), Taylor (*From Proselytizing*, 598–600), and Jean (*Evolution*, 49) for the Enlightenment; see Kurtz (*The Politics of Heresy*, 13–14, 23–25) for the nineteenth century.

58. Melucci, *Nomads*, 62.

59. See Finke and Stark (*The Churching*, 251–52).

60. Hannigan, "Social Movement Theory," 317.

61. Hill (*The Religious Order*, 38), Hollerman (*The Reshaping*, 53), and Froese ("On Reforming," 25) all note this problem.

62. See Langlois (*Le Catholicisme*, 146–51, 223–31, 402–03).

63. D'Allaire, *L'hopital general*, 225.

64. Hostie (*La vie et mort*, 82) and Lawrence (*Medieval Monasticism*, 120) both make this argument.

65. See Lawrence (*Medieval Monasticism*, 80) and Schulenberg ("Women's Monastic Communities," 224) for ninth-century monasteries; Lawrence (*Medieval Monasticism*, 108) for twelfth-century Cluny; Tugwell ("The Spirituality," 19–23), Hinnebusch ("How the Dominican Order," 1311), and Ashley (*The Dominicans*, 58, 90–91) for the fourteenth- and fifteenth-century Dominicans; Wynne (*Traditional Catholic*, 174–76) for the Franciscans; Froese ("On Reforming," 21) for the Premonstratensians; Egan ("The Spirituality," 57), Wynne (*Traditional Catholic*, 207–08), and Kavanaugh ("Spanish Sixteenth Century," 69–92) for the Carmelites; Hollermann (*The Reshaping*, 44) for the sixteenthteeth-century Benedictines; Knowles (*Bare Ruined Choirs*, 308–10) for sixteenth-century England; Rapley (*The Devotes*, 140), Lubich and Lazzarin (*Johan Antida*, 50), and Jean (*Evolution*, 49) for eighteenth-century French congregations; and Jean (*Evolution*, 50–53), Ashley (*The Dominicans*, 182), D'Allaire (*L'hopital general*, 225), Foley (*Uncloistered Apostolic Life*, 81), Hollerman (*The Reshaping*, 53–54), and Dolan (*The American Catholic Experience*, 123) for the eighteenth and early nineteenth centuries.

66. See Weber (*The Sociology of Relgion*, 60–61) for a theoretical discussion of this process. See Berger ("Hasidism," 377–78), Gannon ("Catholic Religious Orders," 170), and Denault ("Sociographie," 29) for examples, both in Catholic and in other religious groups.

67. Foster (*Women*, 115), DeMaria (*Communal Love*, 214–16), and Zablocki (*The Joyful Community*, 267–73) describe this problem.

68. See Brown (*The Body and Society*, 244) and Wynne (*Traditional Catholic*, 104).

69. Wynne, *Traditional Catholic*, 105.

70. Lawrence, *Medieval Monasticism*, 38.

71. Johnson, *Equal*, 20. See Bynum (*Jesus as Mother*, 185) for the argument in the following sentence.

72. Rapley (*The Devotes*, 186), Clear (*Nuns*, 80–81), and Oates ("The Good Sisters," 175) all note this problem

73. Rapley *The Devotes*, 187.

74. See Rausch (*Radical Christian Communites*, 73) for the Franciscans. See Wynne (*Traditional Catholic*, 192) for the seventeenth-century French convents.

75. Lawrence, *Medieval Monasticism*, 108.

76. Wynne, *Traditional Catholic*, 192.

77. See Knowles (*Bare Ruined Choirs*, 308) and McDonough (*Men Astutely Trained*, 374–75) for examples.

78. See Kanter (*Commitment*, 79–86; *Communes*, 494), Veysey ("Ideological Aspects," 29), and Zablocki (*The Joyful Community*, 35). Finke and Stark (*The Churching*, 43) quote Cotton Mather's epigram: "Religion brought forth prosperity, and the daughter destroyed the mother."

79. See Rausch (*Radical Christian Communities*, 51, 58), Wynne (*Traditional Catholic*, 131), Pennington ("The Cistercians," 205), Lawrence (*Medieval Monasticism*, 198), and Knowles (*Bare Ruined Choirs*, 310–12).

80. See McDonnell (*The Beguines*, 486) and Roche ("The Male Religious," 761).

81. Ashley, *The Dominicans*, 58, 91–92, 182.

82. Quoted in Rapley (*The Devotes*, 185). See Foley (*Uncloistered Apostolic Life*, 82) for a similar observation.

83. Rapley, *The Devotes*, 21.

84. Hollermann, *The Reshaping*, 44. See also Wynne (*Traditional Catholic*, 127), Knowles (*Bare Ruined Choirs*, 139–40, 312).

85. Miller ("The End," 282), Zablocki (*The Joyful Community*, 96), Fishman ("Religion and Communal Life," 773), Kanter (*Commitment*, 228), Foster (*Women*, 109), and Stein (*The Shaker Experience*, 64–65) all note this difficulty and those in the following sentences.

86. Knowles (*Bare Ruined Choirs*, 312), McDonough (*Men Astutely Trained*, 138–40), and Tugwell ("The Spirituality," 25) all note this difficulty in Catholic communities. See Bartholomeuz (*Women*, 292) for an example of this in another culture.

87. McDonough, *Men Astutely Trained*, 361.

88. Rapley, *The Devotes*, 84.

89. See Knowles (*Bare Ruined Choirs*, 108) and Coser (*Greedy Institutions*, 106) for this reason. As Foley notes (*Uncloistered Apostolic Life*, 30), the seventeenth-century French Carmelites strictly limited the number of new recruits they would accept, for fear that their spirit would become diluted by large numbers.

90. Berger, "Utopia," 419.

91. Snow et al., "Frame Alignment," 467.

92. The term is from Conover and Feldman ("How People Organize," 96). See also Shenker (*Intentional Communities*, 104).

93. Martin, "Popular and Pastoral Issues," 327.

94. Snow et al., "Frame Alignment," 469.

95. Johnson, *Equal*, 193–94. See also Ashley (*The Dominicans*, 58, 91–92, 182).

96. See McDonnell (*The Beguines*, 17), Egan ("The Spirituality," 57), Kieckhefer ("Imitators," 47–48), and Tugwell ("The Spirituality," 25) for these incidents.

97. See Knowles (*Bare Ruined Choirs*, 314), Froese ("On Reforming," 21), and Lawrence (*Medieval Monasticism*, 31) for examples.

98. Lawrence, *Medieval Monasticism*, 276.

99. Ibid., 280.

100. Knowles, *Bare Ruined Choirs*, 310.

101. See Knowles (*Bare Ruined Choirs*, 23, 33) for the English abbots. See Froese ("On Reforming," 21) for the Premonstratensians.

102. Rapley, *The Devotes*, 25.

103. Finke and Stark (*The Churching*, 145) make a similar point: that, when a church's tension with society wanes, it ceases to grow and ultimately declines itself.

104. Snow et al., "Frame Alignment," 467.

105. Stein, *The Shaker Experience*, 198, 246, 352. See also Whitworth (*God's Blueprints*, 79).

106. Zablocki, *Alienation*, 10.

107. Ibid., 289.

108. See Whitworth (*God's Blueprints*, 79).

109. See Rausch (*Radical Christian Communities*, 73–75), Wynne (*Traditional Catholic*, 172–77), O'Malley ("Early Jesuit," 17), Ashley (*The Dominicans*, 58, 90–91, 182), and Lawrence (*Medieval Monasticism*, 250) for examples.

110. Kanter, *Commitment*, 244–48.

111. Miller, *When Prophets Die*, 215.

112. See Cada et al. (*Shaping the Coming Age*, 60–66).

113. This argument is made by Thompson ("Women, Feminism," 138).

11. Religious Orders as Intentional Communities

1. See, for example, Shenker (*Intentional Communities*, 71).

2. Lofland, "White Hot Mobilization," 157–62.

3. Ibid., 162. Chmielewski et al. (*Women*, 5) question whether *any* intentional community can realistically keep the outside world at bay for very long.

4. See Stein (*The Shaker Experience*, 170–72) and Foster (*Women*, 45–46) for the information in this paragraph.

5. Stein, *The Shaker Experience*, 190.

6. Foster, *Women*, 38.

7. Ibid.

8. Hill (*The Religious Order*, 98) makes this argument.

9. Wynne, *Traditional Catholic*, 178.

10. See Coser (*Greedy Institutions*, 110) for examples.

11. Kanter, *Commitment*, 64.

12. See Hall ("Social Organization," 679) and Kanter (*Commitment*, 20–24).

13. Kanter, *Commitment*, 113–16.

14. See Berger (*The Survival*, 181) and Kitch (*Chaste Liberation*, 180).

15. Shenker, *Intentional Communities*, 142.

16. Kanter, *Commitment*, 67–72. Turcotte (*Les chemins*, 13) makes this argument for religious communities.

17. Knowles, *Bare Ruined Choirs*, 308.

18. McDonnell, *The Beguines*, 136.

19. See Tugwell ("The Spirituality," 22–24) and Ashley (*The Dominicans*, 58, 91–92, 182) for the Dominicans' lapses, and Kieckhefer (*Unquiet Souls*, 47–48) for the Franciscans.

20. Ewens, "Women in the Convent," 33. See also Ashley (*The Dominicans*, 61).

21. See Becker (*The Re-Formed Jesuits*, 164) for an example.

22. See McDonough (*Men Astutely Trained*, 138–53) and Becker (*The Re-Formed Jesuits*, 26).

23. Stein, *The Shaker Experience*, 66. See also Fishman ("Religious and Communal Life," 776) and Hill (*The Religious Order*, 45) for examples.

24. Miller, "The End of the SDS," 283.

25. See Heiling and Heiling ("Coping"), Snow and Benford ("Ideology," 212), Zablocki (*Alienation*, 264), and Kanter (*Commitment*, 150–56) for the arguments in this paragraph.

26. See McDonnell (*The Beguines*, 14) for this process among the Beguines, Tugwell ("The Spirituality," 25) and Hinnebusch ("How the Dominican Order," 1311) for the Dominicans, Taylor (*From Proselytizing*, 559) and Rapley (*The Devotes*, 149) for the filles seculieres, and Clear (*Nuns*, 158), Langlois (*Le Catholicisme*, 631–35) and Dries ("The Americanization," 17) for the late nineteenth and twentieth centuries.

27. See Rapley (*The Devotes*, 178), Dries ("The Americanization," 17), and McDonnell (*The Beguines*, 139).

28. Quoted in McDonough (*Men Astutely Trained*, 528).

29. See Jean (*Evolution*, 251) and Clear (*Nuns*, 158) for examples.

30. Lawrence, *Medieval Monasticism*, 279.

31. Froese, "On Reforming," 21.

32. Knowles, *Bare Ruined Choirs*, 57–58.

33. McDonough, *Men Astutely Trained*, 157.

34. See Knowles (*Bare Ruined Choirs*, 196–97) for the Reformation, and Langlois (*Le Catholicisme*, 80–82) and Cain ("Cloister," 917) for the French Revolution.

35. See McDonnell (*The Beguines*, 14), Taylor (*From Proselytizing*, 559), Rapley (*The Devotes*, 149), Clear (*Nuns*, 158), Langlois (*Le Cathol-*

icisme, 531–35), and Dries ("The Americanization," 17) for the institutionalization of women's communities in various periods.

36. Stein, *The Shaker Experience*, 121.

12. A Brief History of U.S. Religious Orders, 1950–1990

1. McDonough, *Men Astutely Trained*, 9.

2. Kolmer, *Religious Women in the U.S.*, 19–20.

3. Quoted in Ewens ("The Vocation Decline of Women Religious," 172).

4. Quoted in Kolmer, *Religious Women*, 22.

5. Kolmer, *Religious Women*, 21.

6. Schneider, "The Transformation of American Women Religious," 5.

7. Among the most famous of these works were Sister Bertrande Meyers, D.C.'s *The Education of Sisters*, published in 1941, and Sister Madeleva Wolff, C.S.C.'s 1949 paper, "The Education of Sister Lucy." According to Weaver (*New Catholic Women*, 81), the studies found that attempts to educate sisters were having "dismal" results. Because of the "appalling" constraints of trying to earn undergraduate and graduate degrees while still teaching full time, "sisters had not lost their [religious] fervor, but neither could they identify any positive results of their experience of higher education. 'As a matter of fact, in the majority of cases, the experience seems to have destroyed rather than nurtured any love of learning.' There appeared to be no discernible growth in leadership qualities, spiritual outlook or intellectual awareness."

8. Quoted in Schneider ("The Transformation", 6–7).

9. Quinonez and Turner, *The Transformation of American Catholic Sisters*, 6.

10. Ibid., 6.

11. Quoted in Schneider ("The Transformation," 24).

12. Schneider, "The Transformation," 19.

13. Ibid.

14. A list of the SFC's publications and other activities can be found in Kolmer (*Religious Women*, 23–26) and Schneider ("The Transformation," 19–20, 25).

15. Quinonez and Turner, *The Transformation*, 10.

16. Quoted in Schneider, "The Transformation," 33.

17. Quinonez and Turner, *The Transformation*, 94–95.

18. Kolmer, *Religious Women*, 27.

19. Ibid., 38.

20. Quoted in Quinonez and Turner, 37.

21. Quinonez and Turner, *The Transformation*, 37. Similar assessments of the impact of *Lumen Gentium* can be found in Arbuckle ("Religious Life in the U.S." 201; *Out of Chaos*, 81), O'Connor (*Witness and Service*, 154), Schneiders (*New Wineskins*, 24, 89), and Nygren and Ukeritis ("The Future of Religious Orders", 270), to name only a few sources.

22. Foley, *The Uncloistered Apostolic Life for Women*, 185.

23. This point is made by Schneiders (*New Wineskins*, 25), Leddy (*Reweaving Religious Life*, 14), and Clifford ("Women Missioned" 42), among others.

24. Weaver (*New Catholic Women*, 72), however, notes that a few theologians believe that *Lumen Gentium* was deliberate: that it was the end point in a "long effort by the hierarchy to demote nuns from their original status as members of the clergy."

25. Burns (*The Frontiers of Catholicism*, 143) makes this point. Even conservative writers such as O'Connor (*Witness and Service*, 130) admit that the Council's documents exhibit a basic ambiguity—while stating that religious are canonically lay, the documents do not treat them as such, but rather as a separate, third category.

26. Quoted in Kolmer (*Religious Women*, 38).

27. Burns, *The Frontiers*, 137. According to Becker (*The Re-Formed Jesuits*, 98), Paul VI was also dubious about the changes the male orders were instituting.

28. See Neal (*From Nuns to Sisters*, 5) and Quinonez and Turner (*The Transformation*, 46).

29. Quinonez and Turner, *The Transformation*, 46.

30. The initials stand for Sisters of the Immaculate Heart of Mary.

31. In 1963, the sisters had chosen Sister Anita Caspary as their Mother General. Sister Caspary, as president of the IHM's college, had incurred Cardinal McIntyre's wrath in the 1950s by inviting controversial speakers such as theologian Hans Kung to their campus.

32. Quoted in Quinonez and Turner (*The Transformation*, 83).

33. Quinonez and Turner, *The Transformation*, 153.

34. Among them, thirty-four Jesuits in that order's California formation house. See Becker (*The Re-Formed Jesuits*, 187).

35. Burns, *The Frontiers*, 144.

36. Stuhlmueller, "Biblical Observations," 163.

37. Burns, *The Frontiers*, 146. See also Weaver (*New Catholic Women*, 93).

38. Weaver, *New Catholic Women*, 104.

39. Quinonez and Turner, *The Transformation*, 27.

40. Ibid., 21.

41. Ibid., 27; Burns, *The Frontiers*, 151.

42. Quinonez and Turner, *The Transformation*, 153

43. According to Burns (*The Frontiers*, 258, n. 109), LCWR had 600 members in 1977—all of whom were heads of religious congregations. The Consortium had only eighty superiors in its membership, plus an undetermined number of other sisters, not in leadership, who were dissatisfied with the changes in religious life.

44. See Quinonez and Turner (*The Transformation*, 100) for the incidents in this paragraph.

45. See Kolmer (*Religious Women*, 59–61) for a summary of these statements.

46. John Paul II, "Letter to U.S. Bishops on Religious Orders," *Origins* 13(8): 129–33 (July 7, 1983). See Quinn ("Archbishop Quinn Discusses the Commission on Religious Life." *Origins* 13(8): 143–58) for an example of an official denial that the pope's directive was punitive.

47. Sacred Congregation for Religious, "Essential Elements," *Origins* 13(8): 133–42.

48. See Neal (*Catholic Sisters in Transition*, 42–43) and Burns (*The Frontiers*, 139) for this information.

49. Pontifical Commission. "U.S. Religious Life and the Decline of Vocations." *Origins* 16(25): 467–70.

50. Quinonez and Turner, *The Transformation*, 135.

51. Ibid., 138.

52. Burns, *The Frontiers*, 143–44.

53. See Wittberg ("Outward Orientation," 90–91) for a detailed analysis of this failure of women's congregations to consider the possibility of their demise. Several examples cam be briefly cited here: an edited compilation of the background papers for the papal commission investigating the decline of vocations to religious orders (Felknor, *The Crisis in Religious Vocations*) contained only *one* paper that even admitted that the continuation of present-day religious communities was highly doubtful. The other papers either ignored the possibility of institutional disintegration—the original impetus for the entire project—or else treated the membership decline as an opportunity with *positive* aspects. (See Gray, "The Vocation Crisis," 46–47) Similar concentration on the positive aspects of the decline—often to the complete exclusion of the negative aspects—can be found in Woodward (*Poets, Prophets and Pragmatists*, 15), Munley ("An Exploratory Content Analysis," 185), and in the LCWR's 1985 paper, "Reflection Upon the Religious Life of U.S. Women Religious." (In Foley, ed., *Claiming Our Truth*, 175).

54. Fialka, "Sisters in Need."

55. The name refers to the Conference of Major Superiors of Men, the Leadership Conference of Women Religious and the National Conference of Catholic Bishops.

56. Nygren and Ukeritis, "The Future of Religious Orders in the U.S.," 262–263.

57. Ibid., 257.

58. See the remarks of Donna Markham, O.P., the president of LCWR, as reported in Stepp, ("Religious Orders in Decline," G11–12). LCWR officials also objected to the study's findings on a lack of role clarity among religious, questioning how such a concept had been developed.

59. See *Origins* 22(9) for the relevant texts cited in this paragraph: the LCWR "Statement," Archbishop Quinn's response, and the new council's statutes.

60. Quoted in *Origins* 22(9): 159–60.

61. Flannery (1992 Editorial, 275–76) noted that Archbishop Quinn's acceptance of the Vatican's decision "in faith and obedience" is "an ecclesiastic code for 'with little enthusiasm' or words to that effect." "One cannot help wondering," Flannery stated," whether the establishment of the new council in the U.S. is a warning shot across the bows of religious orders and congregations, in preparation for the forthcoming (1994) Synod of bishops on religious life. Is the Congregation for Religious saying, in effect, that the views of religious life espoused by the council are the views which all religious should share?"

62. See the new council's statutes in *Origins* 22(9): 160, and Sheets, "Address to the New Council of Major Superiors," *Origins* 22(24): 413.

63. *Origins* 22(9): 160.

64. *Origins* 22(9): 160–61.

65. See Markham ("The Lineamenta," 103–04), Conference of Dutch Women Religious ("Comments," 349), Byrne ("The Real Mary Ward," 141), and Arbuckle ("The Survival of Religious Life?" 132) for these citations. One critic noted that the *only* mention of the status of women in the "Lineamenta" bemoaned "a mistaken idea of feminism" that "has laid claim to the right to participate in the life of the Church in ways which are not in keeping with the hierarchical structure willed by Christ."

66. Arbuckle, "The Survival of Religious Life?" 133.

67. O'Donoghue, "What Hopes for the Synod?" 215. See also Kerkhofs ("The Synod Lineamenta," 286).

68. Kerkhofs, "The Synod Lineamenta," 289.

69. Archbishop Jan Schotte of the Vatican Synod Secretariat, cited in *Origins* 22(26): 433.

70. O'Riordan, "Religious Life in a Time of Turbulence," 159.

71. Ibid., 160.

72. See, most notably, Quinonez and Turner (*The Transformation*) and Burns (*The Frontiers*, chap. 6). Earlier histories include Schneider ("The Transformation") and Kolmer (*Religious Women*).

13. The Collapse of an Ideology, I

1. Prior to 1959, the *Review* listed between three and five Jesuits as an editorial board. There was very little turnover on this board: only six

names appear during the entire 1942–1959 period. Two Jesuits served the entire seventeen years; another served thirteen years. A single editor, R.F. Smith, S.J., took over in 1959 and served until 1975, when he was replaced by Daniel F.X. Meenan, S.J. Under Meenan's editorial direction, a board of assistant editors was added, including a Sister of Mercy in 1978 and a School Sister of Notre Dame in 1984. Father Meenan retired in 1988 after a thirteen-year stint, and was replaced by the current editor, David L. Fleming, S.J. The *Review's* editorial board currently consists of Father Fleming, several other Jesuits, a Dominican sister and two lay persons. As a glance at appendix A would make clear, significant changes in the proportion of the *Review's* articles devoted to particular topics do *not* seem to have occurred at a time of editorial change.

2. According to the current editor, manuscripts are not solicited. The board meets several times a year to consider the approximately 250–300 unsolicited submissions, and selects between ninety and one hundred for publication. An effort is made to include articles representing as wide a variety of opinions as possible. (Editorial, *Review for Religious*, September/October, 1992, and David L. Fleming, personal communication.)

3. Kolmer, *Religious Women*, 31.

4. See Joseph F. Gallen's various articles in *Review for Religious* during 1955–56. The two that are more than edited compilations of Vatican documents are "Religious Clerical Formation and Sister Formation" (205–15 in issue 4) and "Renovation and Adaptation: What Can and Cannot be Changed" (293–318 in issue 6).

5. Sister Maria ("Preliminary to Adaptation") urged religious communities to undertake "painstaking research" into the spirit of their founders. Joseph Gallen compiled an "Examen on Renovation and Adaptation"—a series of questions for religious superiors to ask themselves about how well they were fostering renewal. Both of these articles were written in 1958–59.

6. Kolmer, *Religious Women*, 52.

7. Ibid., 45.

8. Ibid., 50.

9. See Quinonez and Turner (*The Transformation*, 69–70), Neal (*From Nuns to Sisters*, 4, 34), Weaver (*New Catholic Women*, 83–84), and Manion ("One Perspective on Change", 62) for examples of this mythology.

10. Kolmer, *Religious Women*, 27.

11. Nygren and Ukeritis (*The Future of Religious Orders*, 180) make this point. See Sheets ("Address to the New Council", 415) for an expression of the conservative myth that liberal religious have gotten less spiritual.

12. These books include Schneiders (*New Wineskins*), Arbuckle (*Out of Chaos*), Leddy (*Reweaving Religious Life*), O'Murchu (*Religious Life: A Prophetic Vision*), Quigley, ed. (*Turning Points in Religious Life*), Foley (*Claiming Our Truth*), DeThomasis (*Imagination: A Future for Religious Life*), Woodward (*Poets, Prophets and Pragmatists*), Neal (*From Nuns to Sisters*), Felknor, ed. (*The Crisis in Religious Vocations*), Schweikert ("Toward the New Millennium"), Quinonez and Turner (*The Transformation of American Catholic Sisters*), Merkle (*Committed by Choice*), Steinberg and O'Hara, eds. (*The Future of Religious Life*), and, on the conservative side, O'Connor (*Witness and Service*), and Becker (*The Re-Formed Jesuits*). This constitutes, I believe, the universe of all the books, except my own, published in the United States on religious life since 1985. A limited number of other works, most notably Turcotte's *Les chemins de la différence*, will also be cited whenever possible, to compare the U.S. experience with that of other countries.

13. Kolmer, *Religious Women*, 27.

14. See, for example, articles in the *Review* by DeLetter ("The Grace of Our Vocation," "Contemporary Depreciation of Religious Life"), Faherty ("The Destiny of Religious Women"), Balsam ("God's Living Sermon and Mystery"), Futrell ("Pius XII and the States of Perfection"), and Mullahy ("Community Life").

15. DeLetter ("The Grace of Our Vocation") and Callahan ("The Perfect Pattern for Religious Life").

16. The impression of the uniformity of religious life was strengthened by the fact that constitutions had become largely standardized after 1917. Quinonez and Turner (*The Transformation*, 35) tell of quoting a sentence from one order's constitutions to a mixed audience from several different religious congregations, and having all of the listeners chant it verbatim—from *their* constitutions. Manion ("One Perspective", 60) states that, prior to the 1960s, "every apostolic community, at least on paper, was a near carbon copy of a blueprint designed by outer authority. The size of the book and the style of the print may have been different, but the wording, with a few changes here and there, was the same. And for all the ways communities of religious women viewed themselves as distinct, thousands of them all over the country rose at the same hour and kept the same great silence at night."

17. Garesche, "The Spirit of Poverty," 19.

18. Holstein, "The Mystery of Religious Life," 319.

19. Schneiders, "Reflections on the History," 67. E. McDonough ("Beyond the Liberal Model," 183; "Charisms and Religious Life," 649) makes the same point.

20. Quinonez and Turner, *The Transformation*, 33.

21. Ewens, "The Vocation Decline," 173.

22. Tillard, "Religious Life: Sacrament of God's Presence," 200. See also Haring ("The Vocation of The Christian to Perfection"), Dodd ("Attitudes of Religious Toward Laity"), Galot ("Why Religious Life?"), and Danielou ("The Place of Relious in the Structure of the Church"). See also Dilanni ("Vocations and the Laicization of Religious Life," 208), who complains that, "in the admirable desire to affirm the intrinsic value of the secular world, to maximize individualism, and most of all to foster an egalitarianism in the church, we have been led in practice to affirm that there is little or no difference between lay and religious life."

23. Kolmer, *Religious Women*, 51.

24. O'Riordan, "Religious Life in a Time of Turbulence," 157.

25. Tillard ("A Point of Departure," 424) makes this criticism. See Hostie (*La vie et mort*, 261), DeCock ("Turning Points", 59), and Lozano (*Foundresses, Founders*, 38, 54–58) for examples of the attribution of founding events to the action of the Holy Spirit.

26. Tillard, "A Point of Departure," 437.

27. O'Murchu, *Religious Life*, 59. See also Merkle (*Committed by Choice*, 87).

28. Quoted in Larkin ("Scriptural-Theological Aspects," 1013).

29. Markham ("The 1994 Synod," 365) makes this observation.

30. Schneiders, "Reflections on the History," 75.

31. Burns, *The Frontiers*, 139.

32. Quoted in O'Murchu (*Religious Life*, 200).

33. DeThomasis, *Imagination: A Future for Religious Life*, 63.

34. Figures from Quinonez and Turner (*The Transformation*, 48).

35. Quoted in Burns (*The Frontiers*, 140).

36. Arbuckle, "The Survival of Religious Life?" 134.

37. See Markham ("Psychological Factors," 7; "The Decline of Vocations," in Felknor, 184).

38. Nygren and Ukeritis, "The Future of Religious Orders," 263.

39. Ibid., 271.

40. King and Ferguson, *1992 CARA Formation Directory*. The CARA staff edits the excerpts from the congregations' full statements, but these excerpts are submitted to the superior of each community for approval before being included. "Since I made a specific effort to determine and use the identifying characteristics, such as cenobitic life for the Benedictines, study for the Dominicans and gentleness for the St. Francis de Sales groups, I think it is fair to say that if these qualities are not published [in the CARA *Directory*], they weren't in the full statement." (Eleace King, personal communication, November 11, 1993.)

41. Reck, "Who Are We as Religious?" 50.

42. Arbuckle (*Out of Chaos*, 114) reported that, in a survey of one male religious order, 30 percent of the ordained members had "diocesan priest values, rather than those of religious life." Fagan ("The Identity of Religious," 78), Coleman (*The Evolution*, 183), and Turcotte (*Les chemins*, 149; "La recomposition," 524, 527) make similar assertions. The "Lineamenta," recent critics assert, has exacerbated this role conflict for religious priests. (See Markham, "The Lineamenta," 106).

43. Ebaugh, *Women in the Vanishing Cloister*, 26. Nygren and Ukeritis ("The Future of Religious Orders," 263) found that loss of role clarity could lead to "anxiety, reduced ability to meet role requirements, decreased ministerial satisfaction, lower trust and self-confidence, increased sense of futility and a greater propensity to leave a religious order." See also O'Connor (*Witness and Service*, 155) for a similar conclusion.

44. Markham ("The Decline of Vocations" in Felknor, 184) also mentions the lack of impact of the orders' mission statements.

45. Schnieders, "Reflections on the History," 71.

46. Several authors and researchers, notably Nygren and Ukeritis ("The Future of Religious Orders," 271) and O'Donnell ("Clerical Religious," 13) have noted that, by losing or relinquishing control of their institutions, religious orders have lost high-profile symbols of their group identity and mission.

47. Moran ("Death and Rebirth," 252) makes this argument. It is corroborated by Nygren and Ukeritis ("The Future of Religious Orders,"

264), who found in their survey that their respondents showed "little commitment" to working with the poor, in spite of the fact that this was, officially, a high priority for their communities. They also found that leaders of religious congregations were unable to formulate strategies to accomplish their congregation's purpose because they were no longer able to elicit a like response from the membership. ("Leadership Competencies," 390, 415) Often, the individual members' impulse to generosity was "eclipsed by self-preoccupation, psychological decompensation, stark individualism and a lessening of willingness to sacrifice ("Future of Religious Orders, 270). In such instances, the leadership had little authority to challenge the members to a prophetic role.

48. Moran, "Death and Rebirth," 280.

49. Markham, "Psychological Factors," 8, 10.

50. Chittister, "Religious Life Today: Response to Kerkhoffs I," 203. It is noteworthy that O'Shea ("Religious as Prophets," 112), after defining the prophetic role as *the* raison d'être for post-Vatican II religious communities, ends his article with a checklist of prophetic actions for *individuals*, not communities, to perform. Woodward (*Poets, Prophets*) is another author who, after defining religious life in prophetic terms, deals largely on the individual, or small-group interpersonal, level.

51. Wombacher, "Religious Life: 1965–1986," 64–65.

52. Ebaugh (*Women in the Vanishing Cloister,* 87) makes this argument. Munley ("Threads for the Loom," 200) states that the primary challenge for religious orders in the future will be to balance their members' strong tendencies toward indiviaualism with the communities' corporately discerned priorities. Merkle (*Committed by Choice,* 47) makes a similar point.

53. Leddy, *Reweaving Religious Life,* 70.

54. Moran ("Death and Rebirth," 253) and O'Murchu (*Religious Life,* 97) both make this point. Turcotte ("Le pluralisme," 35) notes the diminishment of a *group* interpretation of vocation in the Canadian community he studied, and a corresponding rise in *individual* interpretations.

55. Meenan, "On Dreaming Dreams," 553.

56. Neal, "Who They Are and What They Do" 165.

57. DeThomasis, *Imagination,* 22. See also Hennessey ("A Look at the Institution Itself," 35) and Turcotte ("Le pluralisme," 33; *Les chemins,* 140).

58. Nygren and Ukeritis, "The Future of Religious Orders," 263.

59. Leddy, *Reweaving Religious Life*, 62.

60. Wittberg, "Outward Orientation," 96.

61. Moran ("Death and Rebirth," 270–80) chronicles this for one religious order; Nygren and Ukeritis ("The Future of Religious Orders," 266) make a similar observation based on their national survey.

62. Meenan, "On Dreaming Dreams," 548. Turcotte ("Le recrutement," 422) makes a similar observation for Quebec: that young people interested in working in team or group ministry did not consider entering a religious order because the orders were no longer recognized for group works.

14. The Collapse of an Ideology, II

1. Larkin, "Scriptural-Theological Aspects," 1019.

2. See Kolmer (*Religious Women*, 31) and Fichter (*A Sociologist*, 106).

3. Leeming, "The Mysticism of Obedience."

4. Hagspiel, "Are You a Jellyfish?" 83.

5. See DeLetter ("Contemporary Depreciation of Religious Life"; "Keeping the Rules"). Many studies (for example, Becker, *The Re-Formed Jesuits*, 44, 76) note that the problems religious had with obedience began in the 1950s among their younger members.

6. McDonough (*Men Astutely Trained*, 157), Regan ("Superiors, Are They Outdated?"), and Tillard ("A Point of Departure," 432) all make these observations.

7. O'Connor ("Holy Obedience and Whole Obedience"), Vaughan ("Obedience and Psychologcial Maturity"), and S. Theresa Mary ("Religious Obedience and Critical Thinking") are all *Review* authors who make this point.

8. Schneider, "The Transformation," 23. Becker (*The Re-Formed Jesuits*, 171, 190, 251) notes that the influence of psychology on obedience was "the most potent of all," leading many to question whether religious life was in danger of being a psychologically deprived life because of this vow.

9. Quinonez and Turner, *The Transformation*, 116.

10. Neal, *From Nuns to Sisters*, 85. O'Hara ("Heralds of Hope," 43) makes a similar point.

11. Quoted in Fink, "Religious Obedience and the Holy Spirit," 64. Grindel and Peters note that "Vatican II stressed collegiality and subsidiarity, but did not treat the deeper issue of where authority ultimately resides in a religious community" ("Religious Life Issues" 270).

12. Quinonez amd Turner, *The Transformation*, 49.

13. Lackner, "Anomie and Religious Life," 629.

14. O'Murchu, *Religious Life*, 46.

15. See Ebaugh (*Women in the Vanishing Cloister*, 72), Merkle (*Committed by Chice*, 84), O'Murchu (*Religious Life*, 144), Neal (*From Nuns to Sisters*, 69), and Woodward (*Poets, Prophets*, 146) for these quotations. Similar is Kovat's renaming obedience "the vow of creativity" ("Reflections on the Vows," 3).

16. Casey, "Toward a Theology," 113–14.

17. Turcotte (*Les chemins*, 132; "Le pluralisme," 38).

18. Burns, *The Frontiers*, 142. See also Turcotte (*Les chemins*, 120, 123), and O'Connor (*Witness and Service*, 4), who describes how one religious order's new constitutions reduced the superior to being a chairperson who must implement the decisions of a board—a functionary, in other words: "She was to be subject to the board, not they to her."

19. See Dubay ("Changing Customs and Religious Obedience"), Regan ("Superiors: Are They Outdated?"), and Goggin and Knight ("Towards An Obedience of the Future").

20. Knight, "Spousal Commitment and Religious Life," 89. See also Schneiders (*New Wineskins*, 140, 164).

21. Aschenbrenner, "Assessing and Choosing," 42. See also Nygren and Ukeritis ("Religious Leadership Competencies," 414–15).

22. Clancey, "Three Problems," 848. See also Goggin and Knight ("Towards an Obedience"), Drennan ("Leadership in Change," 71), and McDonough ("Beyond the Liberal Model," 176) for this critique.

23. Nygren and Ukeritis, "The Future of Religious Orders," 267.

24. Knight, "Spousal Commitment," 89.

25. Kolmer (*Religious Women*, 55) makes this argument.

26. Neal, *Catholic Sisters in Transition*, 54.

27. Neal, "American Sisters, Organizational and Value Changes," 108.

28. Burns (*The Frontiers*, 141–42) makes this point. See Schweikert ("Toward the New Millennium," 43) for an example.

29. Moran, "Death and Rebirth," 214. In his study of a Canadian men's community, Turcotte (*Les chemins*, 63, 64, 80) notes that, by 1972, the supposedly binding decisions of the order's general chapter—its highest legislative authority—had little impact on the daily lives of the members, who either gave them lip service only or else interpreted them according to their own personal interests.

30. Moran, "Death and Rebirth," 216.

31. O'Connor, *Witness and Service*, 38, 40.

32. Moran, "Death and Rebirth," 225.

33. Ebaugh, *Women in the Vanishing Cloister*, 109. Neal (*From Nuns to Sisters*, 107) also notes instances of administrators being intimidated by members threatening to resign or withdraw their financial support from their congregation, which was increasingly dependent on their salaries. Turcotte (*Les chemins*, 116) notes that dependence on members' salaries could also lead to a "displacement of focus" within communities—from the ministerial value of the work to its financial remuneration.

34. Moran, "Death and Rebirth," 225.

35. Kolmer, *Religious Women*, 32.

36. See Garesche ("The Spirit of Poverty," 20) and Herbst ("Mindfulness," 180).

37. See Garesche ("The Spirit of Poverty") and Hagspiel ("Are You a Jellyfish?").

38. Hagspiel, "Are You a Jellyfish?"

39. Neal, *Catholic Sisters in Transition*. 45.

40. Aidan, "Poverty."

41. See S. Theresa Margaret ("The Territorial Imperative") and Casey ("Toward a Theology," 95–96).

42. See Barbieri ("The Young Religious and His Poverty"), Sikora ("Poverty Today"), Ayo ("Variance in the Religious Vows"), and Schneiders (*New Wineskins*, 91).

43. Barbieri, "The Young Religious and His Poverty."

44. Neal, "American Sisters, Organizational and Value Changes," 108.

45. See Orsy ("Poverty in Religious Life"), Sister Elaine Marie ("Religious Life and the Christian Life"), Sister Theresa Margaret ("The Territorial Imperative"), Conn ("Middle Class Poverty"), and Doyle ("Reflections on the Theology of Religious Life").

46. See Sister Elaine Marie ("Religious Life"), Greif ("The Vows"), DeMaria, "Non-Possessiveness"), Ridick ("Psychological Aspects of Religious Poverty"), Albrecht ("Evangelical Poverty"), Steidl-Meier ("Dynamic Aspects"), Genovesi ("The Faith of Christ"), Glavich ("The Paradox of Poverty"), Schineller ("Promises to Keep"), Fitz ("Religious Life as Acted Prophecy"), and Schneiders (*New Wineskins*, 186).

47. See O'Regan ("Unavailability"), MacDonald ("The Price of Poverty"), and Hogan ("The Poverty of Discipleship").

48. See Meiburger ("Toward a New Expression"), the Sisters of Mercy ("Meditative Description"), and Coulon and Nogosek ("Religious Vows as Commitment").

49. See Fichtner ("Religious Life in a Secularized Age"), Grosh ("Models of Poverty"), Faricy ("The Charism of Poverty"), and Ramsey ("The Center of Religious Poverty").

50. This argument is made by Orsy ("Poverty in Religious Life"), Tambasco ("The Vowed Life"), K. O'Shea ("A Christian"), Sikora ("Poverty Today"), Glowienka ("The Counsel of Poverty"), and Glavich ("The Paradox of Poverty").

51. See Fitzpatrick ("A Contemporary Understanding"), Law ("Poverty and the Space Around Us"), and Schneiders (*New Wineskins*, 91, 185).

52. Coulon and Nogosek, "Religious Vows as Commitment," 12.

53. Fichtner, "Religious Life in a Secularized Age."

54 King and Ferguson, *1992 CARA Formation Directory*. Munley ("An Exploratory Content Analysis," 186–87) found an even more prevalent mention of this theme in the thirty-five mission statements she studied. However, her sample may have been biased by being drawn only from LCWR member communities. Ebaugh (*Women in the Vanishing Cloister*, 118) notes that it took almost fifteen years before Vatican II's call for identifying with the materially poor was adopted by the order she observed.

55. See also Casey ("Toward a Theology", 94–123).

56. O'Murchu, *Religious Life*, 45, 160–161. Kovats ("Reflections on the Vows," 2) suggests renaming the vow of poverty "the vow of cosmic reverence."

57. Schneiders, *New Wineskins*, 53.

58. Lackner, "Anomie and Religious Life," 629. See also Grosh ("Models of Poverty"), Schneiders ("Reflections on the History," 70), and Turcotte (*Les chemins*, 110), who make this point.

59. S. Helen Marie, "Having Nothing," 704. See also Knight, ("Spousal Commitment," 88).

60. Markham, "Psychological Factors," 14.

61. Turcotte, *Les chemins*, 112.

62. Neal, "American Sisters: Organizational and Value Changes." 113.

63. Stahel, "Whither Religious Life?" See also Nygren and Ukeritis ("The Future of Religious Orders," 270).

64. White, "Poverty in Religious Life?" 147.

65. Donovan, "A More Limited Witness," 95.

66. Kolmer (*Religious Women*, 32) reports a similar finding in her wider survey of the literature of this period.

67. See Hagspiel ("Are You a Jellyfish?" 84), Herbst ("Mindfulness," 181), and Browning ("Friendship Among Religious"). Exclusivity, not homosexuality, appears to have been the reason for the suspicion of particular friendships.

68. See, for example, Hinnebusch ("Virgo Hostia"), Schleck ("The Meaning of the Religious Sisterhood"), Dubay ("Virginal Motherhood," "Virginal Temples"), Fink ("The Human Dimension"), Van Breeman ("Unmarriageable for God's Sake"), Rosetti ("The Celibacy Experience"), Casey ("Toward a Theology," 100), and O'Murchu (*Religious Life*, 131–32). The dates of these articles range from 1963 to 1991.

69. Schneiders, *New Wineskins*, 114.

70. It is worth noting that the *male* respondents to the survey said exactly the opposite: that the vow of chastity was the *least* meaningful and the *most* difficult for them. See Nygren and Ukeritis ("The Future of Religious Orders," 266).

71. See Schleck ("Sanctification Through Virginity," 829), Trundale ("Love and Perfect Chastity," 35), and Sikora ("Chastity and Love," 9) for these quotations.

72. Among them, see Burrell ("Complementarity"), Greif ("The Vows and Christian Life"), Wilson ("The Married and the Celibate"), and Steidl-Meier ("Dynamic Aspects").

73. This theme surfaces in articles by Vaughan ("Chastity and Psychosexual Development"), McCormick ("Psychosexual Development"), S. Elaine Marie ("Religious Life and Christian Life"), Wilson ("The Married and the Celibate"), and Fourez ("Christian Celibacy").

74. Quoted in DeThomasis (*Imagination*, 93). See also Woodward (*Poets, Prophets*, 231).

75. Neal, "American Sisters: Organizational and Value Changes," 109.

76. Ayo, "Variance in the Religious Vows," 36.

77. Genovesi, "The Faith of Christ," 191–92.

78. See Burrell ("Complementarity," 159), Faricy ("Reflection" 505), Orsy ("Chastity in Religious Life," 617), Fitz ("Religious Life as Acted Prophecy"), and Ramsey ("Christocentric Celibacy") for this argument.

79. Auw, "The Evangelical Counsels," 181.

80. See Knight ("Spousal Commitment") and Fichtner ("Religious Life in a Secularized Age"). Schneiders (*New Wineskins*, 116–17) also makes the distinction between chastity as a mystical sign and as a useful by-product. Kerkhofs ("The Synod Lineamenta," 287) reports an official statement by women's religious communities in Germany deploring "Lineamenta" terminology such as a "bridal relationship" with God as "outdated."

81. Englemeier ("The Celibate Struggles and Challenge") and Kneale ("TheSuperiority of the Religious Life"), both written in 1988, argue that celibacy is superior in some ways to marriage.

82. Among those making this argument, see Burns (*The Frontiers*, 25–46; "The Politics of Ideology," 1126–29), McDonough (*Men Astutely Trained*, 154–55, 374–78), Kurtz (*The Politics of Heresy*, 27), O'Connell ("Ultramonatanism," 205–07), and Coleman ("Catholic Integralism as Fundamentalism," 74–96).

83. O'Connor, *Witness and Service*, 153–54.

84. Langlois (*Le Catholicisme* 105, 148, 402–03) provides data for the recruitment of nineteenth century French congregations that support this

statement. One could also argue that nineteenth century Ireland and Bavaria were peripheral territories within the British and German states, that French Canadians were peripheral to the rest of Canada, and that the Catholic immigrants to the United States in this period were also a marginalized subculture.

85. The uses of these commitment mechanisms are described by Kanter (*Commitment and Community*, 79–112), Zablocki (*The Joyful Community*, 115–87), Robbins (*Cults, Converts and Charisma*, 82–83), and Hall ("Social Organization and Pathways of Commitment").

86. Schneiders, "Reflections on the History," 65.

87. Schneiders, *New Wineskins*, 97.

88. O'Connor, *Witness and Service*, 18–19. See also the Sacred Congregation for Religious, "Essential Elements," 135.

89. The comparison is made, for example, in Weaver (*New Catholic Women*, 90).

90. Quoted in Fichter ("Vanishing Church Professionals," 109). See Grindel and Peters ("Religious Life Issues," 271).

91. Kolmer (*Religious Women*, 53) notes this theme.

92. Markham, "Psychological Factors," 12.

93. Woodward (*Poets, Prophets and Pragmatists*, 51–52), Schneiders ("Reflections on the History," 70), and Schweickert ("Toward the New Millennium," 9) all make this claim.

94. Neal, *Catholic Sisters in Transition*, 43.

95. Neal, "A Report on the National Profile," appendix 19.

96. Wittberg, "Residence Stability and Decline," 78.

97. See Neal (*Catholic Sisters in Transition*, 29).

98. Becker (*The Re-Formed Jesuits*, 166) and Turcotte (*Les chemins*, 90) make this point.

99. E. McDonough, "Beyond the Liberal Model," 181. Merkle (*Committed by Choice*, 119) notes that individualism causes "a breakdown in community life. People seem to have little commitment to each other."

100. Schneiders, "Reflections on the History," 49.

101. DeThomasis, *Imagination*, 27–28.

102. Wittberg, "Residence Stability and Decline," 79–80.

103. Ibid., 80. See also Wittberg, ("Dyads and Triads") and Turcotte (*Les chemins*, 96) for the rising importance of individual personal relationships over a communal focus.

104. Nygren and Ukeritis, "The Future of Religious Orders," 271.

105. Neal, "The Sisters' Survey, 1980," 2.

106. See McDonough (*Men Astutely Trained*, 321) and Leddy (*Reweaving*, 57) for these quotations. Merkle (*Committed by Choice*, 122) makes a similar point. Becker (*The Re-Formed Jesuits*, 288) notes the decline in a common Jesuit spiritual formation, while Turcotte (*Les chemins*, 103) notes the rise in individual prayer and the decline in communal prayer in a Canadian men's order. In this, the religious communities may have been influenced by larger North American culture's "religion of self," in which each person "walks alone with Jesus." (Bloom, *The American Religion*, 37, 40)

107. Neal, "American Sisters: Organizational and Value Changes," 111.

108. See Casey ("Toward a Theology," 125), Merkle (*Committed by Choice*, 25, 36) and O'Murchu (*Religious Life*, 48) for examples. Schweickert ("Toward the New Millennium", 10) found that her respondents had an unclear vision of what the role of the vows would be in the future: Only 73 percent saw a role for obedience, and only 63 percent saw a role for celibacy.

109. Nygren and Ukeritis, "Future of Religious Orders," 268.

110. Bergant ("The Profound Changes," 78) and Nygren and Ukeritis ("The Future of Religious Orders," 271) make this point.

111. Markham ("The Decline of Vocations," in Felknor, 184) and Nygren and Ukeritis (*The Future of Religious Orders*, 141) both make this point. See, for example, Munley's upbeat interpretation of congregational documents. ("An Exploratory Content Analysis," 183–91), and Wittberg's ("Outward Orientation") critique.

112. Leddy, *Reweaving Religious Life*, 73. Nygren and Ukeritis (*The Future of Religious Orders*, 97) also make this point.

15. The Withdrawal of Resources

1. Ebaugh (*Women in the Vanishing Cloister*, 4) makes this point.

2. Ebaugh (*Women in the Vanishing Cloister*, 95) makes this point. See Heffernan ("Religious Vocations," 16–17), who quotes one sister's confes-

sion that, if the Peace Corps or VISTA had existed when she was a teenager, she would never have joined her community.

3. Fichter, "Vanishing Church Professionals," 107; Ebaugh, *Women in the Vanishing Cloister*, 91.

4. Turcotte ("Le recrutement," 416) makes this point for a Canadian men's order.

5. McDonough, *Men Astutely Trained*, 274, 467.

6. Johnson, "No Nunsense," makes this point. See also O'Hara ("Heralds of Hope," 40).

7. According to Markham ("Psychological Factors," 23; "The Decline of Vocations" in *New Catholic World*, 15 and in Felknor, 190), new entrants to male orders often do show evidence of psychological difficulties, whereas the women do not. Ebaugh (*Women in the Vanishing Cloister*, 101), on the other hand, mentions psychological deficiencies in the new women entrants as well.

8. See Markham ("Psychological Factors," 19; "The Decline of Vocations" in Felknor, 183; "The Decline of Vocations" in *New Catholic World*, 14).

9. Donovan ("A More Limited Witness," 94) makes this point.

10. This point is made by Ebaugh (*Women in the Vanishing Cloister*, 95–98), Johnson ("No Nunsense"), and Hennessey ("A Look at the Institution," 37).

11. O'Donoghue, "Women's Congregations," 119. Johnson ("No Nunsense"), Donovan ("A More Limited Witness" 92–93), Markham ("Psychological Factors," 15–16), and Sherman ("Fewer Vocations," 12–13) found similar parental reluctance in their studies. A recent *Newsweek* poll (*Newsweek*, August 16, 1993, 42–43) reported that only 44 percent of the Catholics surveyed would want their child to become a priest or a nun.

12. Markham, "Psychological Factors," 12; Ebaugh, *Women in the Vanishing Cloister*, 101; Grindel and Peters, "Religious Life Issues," 271.

13. National Opinion Research Center, *The Catholic Priest in the U.S.*, 270–271. See O'Neill ("St. Paul's Priests," 76) for an illustration of this process.

14. This is in contrast to the finding that clergy are now *more* likely to encourage young men to enter the *diocesan* priesthood than they were in the 1970s. See Hoge ("Changes in the Priesthood," 75).

15. See Padburg ("The Contexts," 26–27), Meenan ("On Dreaming Dreams," 548), Ebaugh (*Women in the Vanishing Cloister*, 100), and O'Donoghue ("Women's Congregations," 119), who report this argument.

16. See Falk ("Vocation: Identity and Commitment," 363) and King, *1991 CARA Formation Directory*, 9–10) for these two studies. See also Meenan ("On Dreaming Dreams," 548).

17. Colgan ("Nuns and the Women's Movement," 295), Wittberg ("Feminist Consciousness," 530–31), and Heslin ("In Transition," 121) all make this point.

18. Chafetz and Dworkin, *Female Revolt*, 79–80.

19. Kolbenschlag, "John Paul II," 259. See also Byrne ("In the Parish But Not Of It," 194), and Wittberg ("Job Satisfaction," 25–28).

20. Wittberg, "Feminist Consciousness," 235.

21. Munley, "An Exploratory Content Analysis," 235.

22. Wittberg, "Job Satisfaction," 24–28.

23. Quinonez and Turner, *The Transformation*, 108.

24. Ibid., 160–61. Padburg, ("The Contexts," 27), Neal (*Fron Nuns to Sisters*, 87), O'Connor (*Witness and Service*, 37–38), and Schweickert ("Toward the New Millennium" 77) report similar experiences.

25. Weaver (*New Catholic Women*, 83, 86, 88) discusses the repeated Vatican rebuffs LCWR officials experienced. Kolbenschlag ("John Paul II," 257) discusses the attempts to write a vow of obedience to the pope into the sisters' constitutions.

26. See Burns (*The Frontiers*, 58, 131) for the observations in this and the following sentence.

27. Nygren and Ukeritis, "The Future of Religious Orders," 271, 264. See also Merkle (*Committed by Choice*, 135).

28. See Leddy (*Reweaving Religious Life*, 309), Collins ("Sisters and the Eucharist," 97), and Chittister ("Religious Life Today," 203).

29. Schneiders ("Reflections on the History," 36), Schweickert ("Toward the New Millennium," 43, 77), and Donovan ("A More Limited Witness" 91) all mention the possibility of renouncing canonical status. O'Connor (*Witness and Service*, 38–39) details some of the liabilities of such a move.

30. Ebaugh, *Women in the Vanishing Cloister,* 107–08. See also Leddy (*Reweaving,* 71).

31. Nygren and Ukeritis, "The Future of Religious Orders," 271.

32. Neal, *Catholic Sisters in Transition,* 71. See Turcotte ("Sociologie et histoire," 71) for a similar process in Canada.

33. Neal, *Catholic Sisters in Transition,* 71.

34. Hennessey, "A Look at the Institution," 35. See Turcotte (*Les chemins,* 19–49) for a Canadian example of this.

35. Fichter, *A Sociologist,* 80.

36. Levine, *The Reconquest of Montreal,* 46–47. See also Turcotte ("Le pluralisme"). Dobbelaere and Voye ("Western European Catholicism," 213–14) make a similar point for Catholic institutions in Belgium and the Netherlands.

37. Ebaugh, *Women in the Vanishing Cloister,* 40.

38. Ibid., 41, 78. See also Nygren and Ukeritis (*The Future of Religious Orders,* 97).

39. Quoted in Quinonez and Turner, *The Transformation,* 107.

40. Quinonez and Turner, *The Transformation,* 107.

41. Ibid., 91.

42. Quoted in Osimo, "Women's Center," 10.

43. See Hirschman (*Exit, Voice and Loyalty,* 47) on the benefits that forcing its most vociferous members to exit has for the officials of an organization. See Kerkhofs ("European Religious Reply," 291) for a discussion of the endemic tension between the institutional Church and religious life.

44. Burns, *The Frontiers,* 152.

45. Quinonez and Turner, *The Transformation,* 123.

46. Davis, *City of Quartz,* 342. See also Reese (*Archbishop,* 310).

47. Reese, *Archbishop,* 35.

48. Quoted in Dosh ("Bishops Differ," 3).

16. Conclusions

1. See Coleman ("Catholic Integralism," 75–93) for a discussion of the issues mentioned in this paragraph.

2. Ammerman (*Baptist Battles*) and Warner (*New Wine in Old Wineskins*) recount such organizational takeovers, one on a denominational and the other on a congregational level.

3. Coleman, "Catholic Integralism," 93.

4. See Finke and Stark (*The Churching*, 18).

5. Manuel, *Utopias*, 70.

6. See the population figures for the churches studied by Ammerman (*Bible Believers*, 27–29) and Warner (*New Wine*, 21–27).

7. See Warner (*New Wine*, 284–88) for the theoretical development of the nascent/institutional dichotomy.

8. Coleman, "Catholic Integralism," 78.

9. See Greeley ("The Demography of American Catholics," 52–53) and Christiano ("The Church and the New Immigrants," 174–77). See also Marin and Gamba ("The Role of Expectations," 361) for evidence that religion plays a greater role in the lives of those who leave Catholicism than it does in the lives of those who remain.

10. To such an extent that Warner's respondents were unable even to articulate an identifying label for a virtuoso religiosity that *wasn't* fundamentalist (*New Wine*, 212).

11. See Luckmann ("Shrinking Transcendence," 135–36), Dobbelaere and Voye ("Western European Catholicism," 212), and Bloom (*The American Religion*, 37, 40) for discussion of this form of religious virtuosity.

12. Membership statistics from Monastic Fraternities of Jerusalem (*Jerusalem*) and an interview with S. Jane Burton, a former member, in May 1993.

13. O'Grady, "Helping", 6.

14. Gogan, "Lay Community" 180. According to O'Connor (*Witness and Service*, 160), one hundred priests have come from the Emmanuel community alone, and three-fourths of all recent French ordinations to the priesthood are from charismatic groups. Stuhlmueller ("Biblical Observations," 157), however, notes that charismatic seminarians are *less* likely than average to persevere in U.S. seminaries.

15. Gogan, "Lay Community," 179.

16. Ibid.

17. O'Murchu (*Religious Life*, 28) makes this point. See also DiIanni ("Religious Vocation: New Signs of the Times," 750–52).

18. According to Nygren and Ukeritis ("The Future of Religious Orders," 271), existing monastic orders that have reinstated a more specifically monastic lifestyle, are among the few established orders that are drawing new members.

19. Interview, Franciscan Sisters of the Renewal, January 1991.

20. The NCCB's current liaison with the new religious communities who are seeking canonical status is Cardinal Hickey of Washington, the same prelate who was appointed episcopal liaison for the newly formed, conservative Council of Major Superiors of Women Religious.

21. A novice of the new Franciscan sisters' community in Steubenville, Ohio, when asked what she thought about pre-Vatican II religious life laughed, and said, "I was born in 1967, so I don't know. In my total ignorance, my immediate reaction to the pre-Vatican II [model] is to reject it. . . . The only thing I know is that people give you the impression that people walked around like stiff boards. [demonstrates] It's good, I can see the tradition and everything, but I guess I picture it like those people didn't have feelings, that people weren't allowed to be individuals" (Interview, December 13, 1990).

22. Coleman, "Catholic Integralism," 80–81.

23. Opus Dei now has at least three times as many members as the Jesuits, the largest canonical religious order within Catholicism. See Riding, "Conservative Catholic Group"; and Walsh, *Opus Dei*, 6–10.

24. See Lehman (*Women Clergy*, 238–67) and Carroll et al. (*Women of the Cloth*, 113–38).

25. See Ammerman (*Baptist Battles*, 168–211).

26. See Walsh (*Opus Dei*, 53–54, 90) for the status of women in Opus Dei. See the Council of Major Superiors of Women Religious ("Statutes") and the surrounding editorial commentary in *Origins* 22:9, 160–161) for the subordination of this organization to the Church hierarchy.

27. Greeley ("The Demography of American Catholics," 55) applies this phrase to the defection of Latinos. See also Gannon ("A World Church and Christian Feminism," 134–36).

28. See March and Simon (*Organizations*, 136–61) for the tendency of organizations to rely on previous decision-making "programs" when facing new situations.

29. See Finke and Stark (*The Churching*, 86, 224) for these points.

30. See Nygren and Ukeritis (*The Future of Religious Orders*, 47, 56) for this quotation and the following sentence.

31. For example, O'Murchu (*Religious Life*, 94–95) doubts that simply rewriting an order's constitution can initiate a profound enough change to revitalize a community—and then suggests re-writing the order's vision statements instead. DeThomasis (*Imagination*, 35, 41, 77, 88) gives a cogent analysis of how *Lumen Gentium* has undermined the basic ideological paradigm that had distinguished religious life from the lay state—and then suggests that communities develop a new paradigm by transforming the *ministerial institutions* in which they operate, a tactic that appears not to relate to the problem he had originally described. Schweikert ("Toward the New Millennium," 10) notes the importance of a clear common vision and the present lack of such a vision among religious sisters—and yet recommends *further* encouragement of diversity by the orders. Woodward (*Poets, Prophets*, 51) defines community as the "fiery vision" that holds an order together—and then devotes the rest of her book to discussing individual personal relationships, rather than describing how a community might go about fostering its "fiery vision."

32. Nygren and Ukeritis, *The Future of Religious Orders*, 59.

33. Nygren, Ukeritis, McClelland et al., "Religious Leadership Competencies," 415.

34. See, for example, Whetten ("Organizational Growth," 338, 352), who makes this point.

35. See Finke and Stark (*The Churching*, 134) and Dolan (*Catholic Revivalism*).

Bibliography

Agnew, Francis H. 1980. "Obedience: A New Testament Reflection." *Review for Religious* 39: 404–18.

Aidala, Angela A. 1985. "Social Change, Gender Roles, and New Religious Movements." *Sociological Analysis* 46(3): 287–314.

Aidan, Father. 1963. "Poverty." *Review for Religious* 22: 402–6.

Albrecht, Barbara. 1977. "Evangelical Poverty." *Review for Religious* 36: 918–23.

———1982. "A Pope for Religious: John Paul II and the Consecrated Life." *Review for Religious* 41: 801–17.

Allen, Christine. 1983. "Women in Colonial French America," 80–100, in Rosemary R. Ruether and Rosemary S. Keller, eds., *Women and Religion in America*, vol. 2, *The Colonial and Revolutionary Periods*. San Francisco: Harper and Row.

Ammerman, Nancy T. 1988. *Bible Believers: Fundamantalists in the Modern World*. New Brunswick, N.J.: Rutgers University Press.

———1990. *Baptist Battles*. New Brunswick, N.J.: Rutgers University Press.

Arbuckle, Gerald A., S.M. 1988. *Out of Chaos: Refounding Religious Congregations*. New York: Paulist Press.

———1989. "Religious Life in the United States: Reflections of a Cultural Anthropologist," 197–209, in Laurie Felknor, ed., *The Crisis in Religious Vocations*. New York: Paulist Press.

———1993. "The Survival of Religious Life?" *Religious Life Review* 32(3): 131–37.

Aresto, Vito. 1989. "On Obedience and Mission." *Review for Religious* 48: 65–73.

Arthur Anderson & Co. 1990. *Retirement Needs Survey of U.S. Religious, III: Report to the Tri-Conference Retirement Office.* 3211 Fourth St., N.E., Washington, D.C.

————1992. *Retirement Needs Survey of U.S. Religious, IV: Report to the Tri-Conference Retirement Office.* 3211 Fourth St. N.E., Washington, D.C.

Aschenbrenner, George, S.J. 1984. "Assessing and Choosing Even as the Journey Continues." *Review for Religious* 43: 34–44.

Ashley, Benedict. 1990. *The Dominicans.* Collegeville, Minn.: The Liturgical Press.

Auw, Andre. 1969. "The Evangelical Counsels: Ways of Becoming Free." *Review for Religious* 28: 175–85.

Ayo, Nicholas. 1972. "Variance in the Religious Vows: What Poverty, Why Chaste, and Who Obey." *Review for Religious* 31: 32–40.

Balsam, Bonaventure. 1957. "God's Living Sermon and Mystery." *Review for Religious* 16: 257–64.

Barbieri, William M. 1966. "The Young Religious and His Poverty." *Review for Religious* 25: 288–93.

Barkun, Michael. 1974. *Disaster and the Millennium.* New Haven: Yale University Press.

————1985. "The Awakening Cycle Controversy." *Sociological Analysis* 46(4): 425–43.

————1986. *Crucible of the Millennium: The Burned-Over District of New York in the 1840's.* Syracuse, N.Y.: Syracuse University Press.

Bartholomeuz, Tessa. forthcoming. *Women Under the Bo Tree: Buddhist Nuns in Sri Lanka.* New York: Cambridge University Press.

Bates, Vernon L. 1991. "Lobbying for the Lord: The New Christian Right Home Schooling Movement and Grassroots Lobbying." *Review of Religious Research* 33(1): 3–17.

Becker, Joseph M. 1992. *The Re-Formed Jesuits,* Vol.1, *A History of Changes in Jesuit Formation During the Decade 1965–1975.* San Francisco: Ignatius Press.

Bellant, Russ. 1991. "Ohio Bishop May Blunt Sword of the Spirit Group," in *The National Catholic Reporter* 27(3): 5 (June 21, 1991).

Bergant, Dianne, C.S.A. 1989. "The Profound Changes in Religious Life Since Vatican II," 74–83, in Laurie Felknor, ed., *The Crisis in Religious Vocations.* New York: Paulist Press.

Berger, Alan L. 1981. "Hasidism and Moonism: Charisma in the Counter-culture." *Sociological Analysis* 41(4): 375–90.

Berger, Bennett M. 1981. *The Survival of a Counterculture.* Berkeley: University of California Press.

———1987. "Utopia and Its Environment," 419–30, in Yosef Gorni, Yaacov Oved and Idit Paz, eds., *Communal Life: An International Perspective.* New Brunswick: Transaction.

Berger, Peter. 1967. *The Sacred Canopy: Elements of a Sociological Theory of Religion.* Garden City, N.Y.: Doubleday.

Berger, Peter, and Thomas Luckmann. 1966. *The Social Construction of Reality.* New York: Doubleday.

Berry, Brian J. L. 1992. *America's Utopian Experiments: Communal Havens From Long-Wave Crises.* Hanover, N.H.: University Press of New England.

Biernatzki, William E. 1991. *Roots of Acceptance: The Intercultural Communication of Religious Meanings.* Rome: Gregorian Pontifical Institute.

Bilhartz, Terry D. 1986. *Urban Religion and the Second Great Awakening: Church and Society in Early National Baltimore.* Rutherford, N.J.: Fairleigh Dickinson University Press.

———1991. "Sex and the Second Great Awakening: The Feminization of American Religion Reconsidered," 117–35, in Philip R. Vandermeer and Robert P. Swirenga, eds., *Belief and Behavior: Essays in Religious History.* New Brunswick, N.J.: Rutgers University Press.

Bloom, Harold. 1992. *The American Religion.* New York: Simon and Schuster.

Boisvert, Lorenzo. 1965. "The Nature of Religious Authority." *Review for Religious* 24: 34–54.

Brezik, Victor B. 1989. "A Note from Underground to Fellow Religious." *Review for Religious* 48: 872–78.

Brinkman, Sister Marie, S.C.L. 1971. "Toward a Theology of Religious Life." *Review for Religious* 30: 563–77.

Briody, Elizabeth K., and Teresa A. Sullivan. 1988. "Sisters at Work: Career and Community Changes." *Work and Occupations* 15(3): 313–33.

Brock, Sebastian P., and Susan A. Harvey, eds., and trans. 1987. *Holy Women of the Syrian Orient.* Berkeley: University of California Press.

Bromley, David G., and Anson Shupe, Jr. 1980. "Financing the New Religions: A Resource Mobilization Approach." *Journal for the Scientific Study of Religion* 19(3): 227–39.

Brown, Peter. 1985. "The Notion of Virginity in the Early Church," 427–42, in Bernard McGinn and John Myendorff, eds., *Christian Spirituality I: Origins to the Twelfth Century*. New York: Crossroad.

————1988. *The Body and Society: Men, Women and Sexual Renunciation in Early Christianity*. New York: Columbia University Press.

Browning, Columban. 1959. "Friendship Among Religious." *Review for Religious* 18: 257–64.

Buckley, Michael J. 1989. "Seventeenth Century French Spirituality: Three Figures," 28–68, in Louis Dupre and Don E. Saliers, eds., *Christian Spirituality III: Protestant Reformation and Modern*. New York: Crossroad.

Bukowczyk, John J. 1988. "Mary the Messiah: Polish Immigrant Heresy and the Malleable Ideology of the Roman Catholic Church," 21–48, in Timothy J. Meagher, ed., *Urban American Catholicism*. New York: Garland.

Burns, Gene. 1990. "The Politics of Ideology: The Papal Struggle With Liberalism." *American Journal of Sociology* 95(5): 1123–52.

————1992. *The Frontiers of Catholicism: The Politics of Ideology in a Liberal World*. Berkeley: University of California Press.

Burrell, David B. 1967. "Complementarity: Man and Woman, Marriage and Virginity." *Review for Religious* 26: 141–60

Bynum, Caroline W. 1982. *Jesus as Mother: Studies in the Spirituality of the High Middle Ages*. Berkeley: University of California Press.

————1987a. *Holy Feast and Holy Fast*. Berkeley: University of California Press.

————1987b. "Religious Women in the Later Middle Ages," 121–39, in Jill Raitt, ed., *Christian Spirituality II: High Middle Ages and Reformation*. New York: Crossroad.

————1991. *Fragmentation and Redemption: Essays on Gender and the Human Body in Medieval Religion*. New York: Zone Books.

Byrne, Lavinia. 1993. "The Real Mary Ward," *Religious Life Review* 32(3): 138–42.

Byrne, Patricia. 1986. "Sisters of St. Joseph: The Americanization of a French Tradition." *U.S. Catholic Historian* 5(3–4): 241–72.

———1990. "In the Parish But Not of It: Sisters," 109–200, in Jay P. Dolan, ed., *Transforming Parish Ministry*. New York: Crossroad.

Cada, Lawrence, et al. 1979. *Shaping the Coming Age of Religious Life*. New York: Seabury Press.

Cain, James R. 1968. "Cloister and the Apostolate of Religious Women." *Review for Religious* 27: 916–35.

Callahan, Daniel. 1958. "The Perfect Pattern for Religious Life." *Review for Religious* 17: 91–96.

California Religious Support Fund. 1990. Informational Brochure.

Campbell, Debra. 1989. "Reformers and Activists," 152–81 in Karen Kennelly, ed., *American Catholic Women: A Historical Approach*. New York: Macmillan.

Carroll, Jackson W., Barbara Hargrove, and Adair Lummis. 1983. *Women of the Cloth*. San Francisco: Harper and Row.

Casey, Julianna, I.H.M. 1988. "Toward a Theology of the Vows," 78–126, in Carol Quigley, I.H.M., ed., *Turning Points in Religious Life*. Westminster, Md.: Christian Classics, Inc.

Casteras, Susan P. 1986. "Virgin Vows: The Early Victorian Artists' Portrayal of Nuns and Novices," 129–60, in Gail Malmgreen, ed., *Religion in the Lives of English Women, 1760–1930*. Bloomington: Indiana University Press.

Chafetz, Janet, and Anthony G. Dworkin. 1986. *Female Revolt: Women's Movements in World and Historical Perspective*. Totowa, N.J.: Rowman and Allanheld.

Charles-Edwards, Thomas. 1992. "The Pastoral Role of the Church in the Early Irish Laws," 63–80, in John Blair and Richard Sharpe, eds., *Pastoral Care Before the Parish*. Leicester: Leicester University Press.

Chittister, Joan. 1993. "Religious Life Today: Response to Kerkhofs." *Religious Life Review* 32(4): 202–07.

Chmielewski, Wendy, Louis J. Kern, and Marlyn Klee-Hartzell. 1993. *Women in Spiritual and Communitarian Societies in the U.S.* Syracuse: Syracuse University Press.

Christiano, Kevin J. 1991. "The Church and the New Immigrants," 169–86, in H. R. Ebaugh, ed., *Vatican II and U.S. Catholicism*. Greenwich Conn.: JAI Press.

Clancey, Thomas H., S.J. 1974. "Three Problems Concerning Obedience." *Review for Religious* 33: 844–60.

Clarke, Thomas. 1986. "Redeeming Conflict," 59–78, in Madonna Kohl-benschlag, ed., *Authority, Community and Conflict*. Kansas City: Sheed and Ward.

Clear, Caitriona. 1987. *Nuns in Nineteenth Century Ireland*. Dublin: Gill and Macmillan, Ltd.

Clifford, Anne. 1988. "Women Missioned in a Technological Culture," 37–56, in Nadine Foley, ed., *Claiming Our Truth: Reflections on Identity by U.S. Women Religious*. Washington, D.C.: Leadership Conference for Women Religious.

Clifford, Elizabeth Ann, O.L.V.M. 1981. *The Story of Victory Noll*. Fort Wayne, Id.: Keefer Printing Co.

Coakley, John. 1991. "Gender and the Authority of the Friars: The Significance of Holy Women for Thirteenth Century Franciscans and Dominicans." *Church History* 60(4): 445–60.

Cohn, Robert L. 1988. "Sainthood on the Periphery: The Case of Judaism," 43–68, in Richard Kieckhefer and George D. Bond, eds., *Sainthood: Its Manifestations in World Religions*. Berkeley: University of California Press.

Coleman, John. 1978. *The Evolution of Dutch Catholicism, 1958–1974*. Berkeley: University of California Press.

————1992. "Catholic Integralism as a Fundamentalism," 74–96 in Lawrence Kaplan, ed., *Fundamentalism in Comparative Perspective*. Amherst: University of Massachusetts Press.

Colgan, Mary. 1975. "Nuns and the Women's Movement." *Origins* 4(38): 593–96.

Collins, Mary. 1992. "Sisters and the Eucharist." *Religious Life Review* 31(6): 305–15.

Conference of Dutch Women Religious. 1993. "Comments on the Lineamenta." *Religious Life Review* 32(6): 348–58.

Conn, Marie, IHM. 1983. "Contractual Obedience: A View from the Other Side." *Review for Religious* 42: 530–33.

————1983. "Middle Class Poverty: A View From the Other Side." *Review for Religious* 42: 691–93.

Conover, Pamela J., and Stanley Feldman. 1984. "How People Organize the Political World: A Schematic Model." *American Journal of Political Science* 28(1): 95–126.

Converse, Philip E. 1964. "The Nature of Belief Systems in Mass Publics," 206–45, in David E. Apter, ed., *Ideology and Discontent.* New York: Free Press of Glencoe.

Coser, Lewis. 1974. *Greedy Institutions.* New York: Free Press.

Coulon, George, C.S.C., and Robert Nogosek, C.S.C. 1971. "Religious Vows as Commitment." *Review for Religious* 30: 9–18.

Council of Major Superiors of Women Religious. 1992. "Statutes." *Origins* 22(9): 160–63.

Coursey, Robert D., S.J. 1969. "Problems in the Theology of Religious Authority." *Review for Religious* 28: 452–57.

Courtenay, William J. 1987. "Spirituality and Late Scholasticism," 109–20, in Jill M. Raitt, ed., *Christian Spirituality II: High Middle Ages and Renaissance.* New York: Crossroad.

Cowburn, John, S.J. 1968. "The Analogy of Religious Authority and Obedience." *Review for Religious* 27: 604–12.

Cross, Whitney. 1950. *The Burned-Over District: The Social and Intellectual History of Enthusiastic Religion in Western New York, 1800–1850.* New York: Harper and Row.

Cubitt, Catherine. 1992. "Pastoral Care and Conciliar Canons," 193–211, in John Blair and Richard Sharpe, eds., *Pastoral Care Before the Parish.* Leicester: Leicester University Press.

Cunneen, Sally. 1968. *Sex, Female; Religion, Catholic.* London: Burns and Oats.

Curry, Catherine Ann. 1992. "Financial Sponsorship of Social and Religious Works by Sisters in San Francisco." Paper read at the annual Conference on the History of Women Religious, Tarrytown, N.Y., June 29, 1992.

D'Allaire, Micheline. 1971. *L'hopital general de Quebec, 1692–1764,* Montreal: Fides.

————1973. "Jeanne Mance." *Forces,* 23(1): 38–46.

Danielou, Jean, S.J. 1965. "The Place of Religious in the Structure of the Church." *Review for Religious* 24: 518–25.

Davis, Mike. 1990. *City of Quartz: Excavating the Future in Los Angeles.* London: Verso.

Deacon, Florence Jean. 1989. *Handmaids or Autonomous Women: The Charitable Activities, Institution-Building and Communal Relationships of*

Catholic Sisters in Nineteenth Century Wisconsin. Ph.D. diss., University of Wisconsin, Madison.

deBhaldraithe, Eoin. 1992. "The Eucharist in Religious Communities Since Vatican II." *Religious Life Review* 31(6): 296–304.

Deck, Allan Figueroa. 1992. "The Challenge of Evangelical/Pentecostal Christianity to Hispanic Catholicism in the United States." Working Paper Series 24, no. 1. Cushwa Center for the Study of American Catholicism. Notre Dame: Notre Dame University Press.

DeCock, Mary. 1989. "Turning Points in the Spirituality of an American Congregation: The Sisters of Charity of the Blessed Virgin Mary." *U.S.Catholic Historian* 10(1&2): 59–69.

DeLetter, P., S.J. 1951. "The Grace of Our Vocation." *Review for Religious* 10: 253–59.

———1952. "Contemporary Depreciation of Religious Life." *Review for Religious* 11: 34–41.

———1959. "Keeping the Rules." *Review for Religious* 18: 13–24.

DeMaria, Richard. 1975. "Non-Possessiveness and the Religious Vows." *Review for Religious* 34: 224–31.

———1978. *Communal Love at Oneida.* New York: The Edwin Mellen Press.

Denault, Bernard. 1975. "Sociographie generale des communautes religieuses au Quebec, 1837–1970," 17–117, in Bernard Denault and Benoit Levesque, eds., *Elements pour une sociologie des communautes religieuses au Quebec.* Montreal: Les Presses de l'Université de Montreal.

DeThomasis, Louis, F.S.C. 1992. *Imagination: A Future for Religious Life.* Winona, Minn.: The Metanoia Group.

Dews, D. Colin. 1986. "Ann Carr and the Female Revivalists of Leeds," 68–87, in Gail Malmgreen, ed., *Religion in the Lives of English Women, 1760–1930.* Bloomington: Indiana University Press.

Diamond, Sigmund. 1958. "From Organization to Society: Virginia in the Seventeenth Century." *American Journal of Sociology* 63(5): 457–75.

DiIanni, Albert. 1987. "Vocations and the Laicization of Religious Life." *America* 156(10): 207–11.

———1993. "Religious Vocations: New Signs of the Times." *Review for Religious* 52(5): 745–63.

Dobbeleare, Karel, and Liliane Voye. 1991. "Western European Catholicism Since Vatican II," 205–31, in H.R. Ebaugh, ed., *Vatican II and U.S. Catholicism*. Greenwich, Conn.: JAI Press.

Dodd, William H. 1964. "Attitudes of Religious Toward Laity." *Review For Religious* 23: 335–43.

Dolan, Jay P. 1978. *Catholic Revivalism: The American Experience, 1830–1900*. Notre Dame: University of Notre Dame Press.

————1985. *The American Catholic Experience: A History From Colonial Times to the Present*. New York: Doubleday.

Dolan, Jay P., ed. 1987. *The American Catholic Parish: A History from 1850 to the Present*. New York: Paulist.

Donovan, Mary A. 1984. "The Spectrum of Church Teaching on Religious Life," 212–28, in Robert J. Daly et al., *Religious Life in the U.S. Church: The New Dialog*. New York: Paulist.

————1989a. *Sisterhood as Power: The Past and Passion of Ecclesial Women*. New York: Crossroad.

————1989b. "Spirit to Structure: Historical Factors Affecting the Experiences of Charism in an American Religious Congregation." *U.S. Catholic Historian* 10(1–2): 1–12.

————1989c. "A More Limited Witness: A Historical Theologian Looks at the Signposts," 84–98, in Laurie Felknor, ed., *The Crisis in Religious Vocations*. New York: Paulist Press.

Doohan, Leonard. 1977. "Contemplation, Religious Authority and Obedience." *Review for Religious* 36: 565–75.

Dosh, Terry. 1992. "Bishops Differ on Exercise of power." *Bread Rising* 2(1): 3.

Doyle, Eric, O.F.M. 1973. "Reflections of the Theology for Religious Life." *Review for Religious* 32: 1238–43.

Drennan, Michael J. 1993. "Leadership in Change: A Reflection." *Religious Life Review* 32(2): 66–73.

Dries, Angelyn. 1989. "The Americanization of Religious Life: Women Religious, 1872–1922." *U.S. Catholic Historian* 10(1&2): 13–21.

Dubay, Thomas, S.M. 1963a. "Personal Integrity and Intellectual Obedience." *Review for Religious* 22: 493–501.

————1963b. "Understanding in a Superior." *Review for Religious* 22: 381–96.

———1965. "Virginal Motherhood." *Review for Religious* 24: 744–59.

———1968. "Virginal Temples." *Review for Religious* 27: 21–43.

———1973. "Changing Customs and Religious Obedience." *Review for Religious* 32: 316–23.

———1974. "A Dialog on Mediated Obedience." *Review for Religious* 33: 861–79.

Duncan, Glenn Ellen. 1991. "Where Do Nuns Come From?" *Catholic Digest* 55(3): 121–25.

Dumont-Johnson, Micheline. 1978. "Les communautes religieuses et la condition feminine." *Recherches sociographiques* 19(1): 79–102.

Durkheim, Emile. 1965. [1915] *Elementary Forms of the Religious Life.* Translated by J. W. Swain. New York: Free Press.

Ebaugh, Helen Rose F. 1977. *Out of the Cloister: A Study of Organizational Dilemmas.* Austin: University of Texas Press.

———1993. *Women in the Vanishing Cloister: Organizational Decline in Catholic Religious Orders in the United States.* New Brunswick, N.J.: Rutgers University Press.

Ebaugh, Helen Rose F., and Paul Ritterband. 1978. "Education and the Exodus From Convents." *Sociological Analysis* 39(4): 257–64.

Egan, Keith J. 1987. "The Spirituality of the Carmelites," 50–62, in Jill Raitt, ed., *Christian Spirituality II: High Middle Ages and Reformation.* New York: Crossroad.

Elaine Marie, Sister. 1964. "The Religious Profession as Covenant Action." *Review for Religious* 23: 207–15.

———1965. "Religious Life." *Review for Religious* 24: 430–43.

———1967. "Religious Life and the Christian Life." *Review for Religious* 26: 137–48.

Elkins, Sharon K. 1988. *Holy Women of Twelfth Century England.* Chapel Hill: University of North Carolina Press.

Engh, Michale E. 1992. *Frontier Faiths: Church, Temple and Synagogue in Los Angeles, 1846–1888.* Albuquerque: University of New Mexico Press.

Englemeier, Jaime. 1988. "The Celibate Struggle and Challenge." *Review for Religious* 47: 570–79.

Erikson, Kai. 1976. *Everything In Its Path.* New York: Simon and Schuster.

Etzioni, Amitai. 1961. *A Comparative Analysis of Complex Organizations.* New York: Free Press.

Ewen, Sister Mary Paul, S.S.C.J. 1984. "Theological Reflections on the Apostolic Religious Life." *Review for Religious* 43: 3–25.

Ewens, Mary. 1981. "The Leadership of Nuns in Immigrant Catholicism," 101–49 in Rosemary Ruether and Rosemary S. Keller, eds., *Women and Religion in America* vol. 1. New York: Harper and Row.

———1989a. "Women in the Convent," 17–47, in Karen Kennelly, ed., *American Catholic Women: A Historical Exploration.* New York: Macmillan.

———1989b. "The Vocation Decline of Women Religious: Some Historical Perspectives," 165–80, in Laurie Felknor, ed., *The Crisis in Religious Vocations.* New York: Paulist Press.

Eyerman, Ron, and Andrew Jamison. 1991. *Social Movements: A Cognitive Approach.* University Park, Pa.: The Pennsylvania State University Press.

Fagan, Sean. 1993. "The Identity of Religious." *Religious Life Review* 32(2): 74–79.

Faherty, William B. S.J. 1951. "The Destiny of Religious Women." *Review for Religious* 10: 47–50.

Falk, M. Marcelline. 1980. "Vocations: Identity and Commitment." *Review for Religious* 39: 357–65.

Faricy, Robert. 1967. "Reflections on Chastity and Consecration." *Review for Religious* 26: 503–06.

———1981. "The Charism of Poverty." *Review for Religious* 40: 841–45.

Farrell, Michael J. 1991. "New Generation of Seers Declares Mary is Back." *National Catholic Reporter* 27(36): 1–6.

Felknor, Laurie, ed., 1989. *The Crisis in Religious Vocations.* New York: Paulist Press.

Ferree, Myra M. 1992. "The Political Context of Rationality," 29–52, in Aldon D. Morris and Carol McClurg Mueller, eds., *Frontiers in Social Movement Theory.* New Haven: Yale University Press.

Ferree, Myra M., and Frederick D. Miller. 1985. "Mobilization and Meaning: Toward an Integration of Social Psychology and Resource Perspectives on Social Movements." *Sociological Inquiry* 55(1): 38–61.

Festinger, Leon, et al. 1956. *When Prophecy Fails.* Minneapolis: University of Minnesota Press.

Fialka, John J. 1986. "Sisters in Need: U.S. Nuns Face Crisis as More Grow Older with Meager Benefits." *Wall Street Journal* 207(97): 1. (May 19, 1986).

Fichter, Joseph, S.J. 1988. *A Sociologist Looks at Religion*. Wilmington, De.: Michael Glazier.

———1989a. *The Pastoral Provisions: Married Catholic Priests*. Kansas City: Sheed and Ward.

———1989b. "Vanishing Church Profesionals," 99–115, in Laurie Felknor, ed., *The Crisis in Religious Vocations*. New York: Paulist Press.

Fichtner, Joseph, O.S.C. 1966. "Metanoia or Conversion." *Review for Religious* 25: 18–31.

———1969. "Religious Life in a Secularized Age." *Review for Religious* 28: 21–34.

Fink, Peter E. 1968. "The Human Dimension of Religious Life." *Review for Religious* 27: 379–92.

———1971. "Religious Obedience and the Holy Spirit." *Review for Religious* 30: 64–79.

Finke, Roger, and Rodney Stark. 1989. "How the Upstart Sects Won America: 1776–1850." *Journal for the Scientific Study of Religion* 28(1): 27–44.

———1992. *The Churching of America, 1776–1990*. New Brunswick, N.J.: Rutgers University Press.

Fishman, Aryei. 1987. "Religious and Communal Life in an Evolutionary-Functional Perspective: The Orthodox Kibbutzim." *Comparative Studies in Society and History* 29(4): 763–86.

Fitz, James, S.M. 1982. "Religious Life as Acted Prophecy." *Review for Religious* 41: 923–30.

Fitzgerald, Kathryn. 1983. "By Obedience to the Truth." *Review for Religious* 42: 770–71.

Fitzgerald, Maureen. 1989. "The Perils of 'Passion and Poverty': Women Religious and the Care of Single Women in New York City, 1845–1890." *U.S. Catholic Historian* 10(1–2): 45–58.

Fitzpatrick, Maureen, F.M.S.C. 1980. "A Contemporary Understanding of the Vows." *Review for Religious* 39: 378–88.

Flannery, Austin, O.P. 1991. Editorial. *Religious Life Review* 30(2): 80–81.

————1992. Editorial. *Religious Life Review* 31 (1): 37–44.

————1992. Editorial. *Religious Life Review* 31 (4): 192–99.

————1992. Editorial. *Religious Life Review* 31 (5): 273–76.

————1992. Editorial. *Religious Life Review* 31 (6): 343–45.

————1993. Editorial. *Religious Life Review* 32 (1): 29–36.

Foley, Mary Ann. 1989. "Uncloistered Apostolic Life for Women: Marguerite Bourgeoys' Experiment in Ville Marie." *U.S. Catholic Historian* 10(1–2): 37–44.

————1991. *Uncloistered Apostolic Life for Women: Marguerite Bourgeoys' Experiment in Ville Marie.* Ph.D. diss., Yale University.

————1992. "Women as Evangelizers in Seventeenth Century New France" Paper read at the History of Christianity Conference, Notre Dame University, March 27, 1992.

Foley, Nadine, ed., 1988. *Claiming Our Truth: Reflections on Identity as U. S. Women Religious.* Washington, D.C.: Leadership Council of Women Religious.

Fontaine, Jacques. 1985. "The Practice of Christian Life: The Birth of the Laity," 453–91, in Bernard McGinn and John Meyendorff, eds., *Christian Spirituality I: Origins to the Twelfth Century.* New York: Crossroad.

Foot, Sarah. 1992. "Anglo-Saxon Minsters: A Review of Terminology," 212–25, in John Blair and Richard Sharpe, eds., *Pastoral Care Before the Parish.* Leicester: Leicester University Press.

Foster, Lawrence. 1991. *Women, Family and Utopia.* Syracuse: Syracuse University Press.

Fourez, Gerard M. 1972. "Christian Celibacy: A Mystery of Death and Resurrection." *Review for Religious* 31: 724–31.

Francis, E.K. 1950. "Toward a Typology of Religious Orders." *American Journal of Sociology* 55(5): 437–49.

Francis, M. Mary. 1970. "Creative Spiritual Leadership." *Review for Religious* 29: 497–505.

Frazee, Charles A. 1982. "Late Roman and Byzantine Legislation on the Monastic Life From the Fourth to the Eighth Centuries." *Church History* 51(3): 263–79.

————1988. "The Origins of Clerical Celibacy in the Western Church." *Church History* 57 (Supplement): 108–26.

Friedman, Debra, and Doug McAdam. 1992. "Collective Identity and Activism," 156–73, in Aldon D. Morris and Carol McClurg Mueller, eds., *Frontiers in Social Movement Theory.* New Haven: Yale University Press.

Froese, Walter. 1985. "On Reforming the Reformed: A Study of the Religious Changes and the Premonstratensians in Saxony." *Church History* 54(1): 20–28.

Futrell, John C., S.J. 1958. "Pius XII and the States of Perfection." *Review for Religious* 17: 321–25.

―――1969. "Some Reflections on Religious Life." *Review for Religious* 28: 705–18.

Gahan, Elizabeth M. 1992. "The Demographic Evolution of the Sisters of Charity of the Immaculate Conception as an Index of Canadian National Development." Paper presented at the annual Conference on the History of Women Religious, Tarrytown, N.Y., June 30, 1992.

Gallen, Joseph F., S.J. 1955. "Religious Clerical Formation and Sister Formation." *Review for Religious* 14: 205–15.

―――1955. "Renovation and Adaptation: What Can and Cannot be Changed.," *Review for Religious* 14: 293–318.

―――1959. "Examen on Renovation and Adaptation." *Review for Religious* 18: 353–59.

―――1965. "Contact and Spiritual Influence of the Superior." *Review for Religious* 24: 55–65.

―――1967. "Religious Obedience in Vatican Council II." *Review for Religious* 26: 242–60.

―――1982. "Chastity, Poverty and Obedience in the Proposed and Revised Canons." *Review for Religious* 43: 570–75.

Galot, Jean. 1965. "Why Religious Life?" *Review for Religious* 24: 505–17.

Gamson, William A. 1988. "Political Discourse and Collective Action," 219–44, in Bert Klandermans, Hanspeter Kriesi, and Sidney Tarrow, eds., *From Structure to Action: Comparing Social Movements Across Cultures* vol.1 in International Social Movement Research. Greenwich Conn.: JAI Press.

―――1991. "Commitment and Agency in Social Movements." *Sociological Forum* 6(1): 27–50.

————1993. "The Social Psychology of Collective Action," 53–76, in Aldon D. Morris and Carol McClurg Mueller, eds., *Frontiers in Social Movement Theory*. New Haven: Yale University Press.

Gannon, Margaret. 1988. "A World Church and Christian Feminism," 121–42, in Nadine Foley, ed., *Claiming Our Truth: Reflections on Identity by U.S. Women Religious*. Washington, D.C.: Leadership Conference of Women Religious.

Gannon, Thomas M. 1979. "Catholic Religious Orders in Sociological Perspective," 159–93, in Ross P. Scherer, ed., *American Denominational Organization: A Sociological View*. Pasadena: William Carey.

Garcia, Guillermo C. 1980. "Four Questions: One Reply." *Review for Religious* 39: 376–85.

Garesche, Edward, S.J. 1950. "The Spirit of Poverty and Modern Times." *Review for Religious* 9: 19–25.

Garvey, Thomas, C.S.J. 1972. "Religious Life: A Commitment to Men." *Review for Religious* 31: 40–43.

Gau, James V. 1973. "Discernment and the Vow of Obedience." *Review for Religious* 32: 569–74.

Geertz, Clifford. 1973. *The Interpretation of Cultures*. New York: Basic.

Genovesi, Vincent, S.J. 1979. "The Faith of Christ: Source of the Virtue of the Vows." *Review for Religious* 38: 186–96.

Gerber, Jurg. 1991. "From Bottles to Bombs: The Role of Success and Occupying a Unique Niche in Organizational Transformation." *Sociological Focus* 24(3): 225–43.

Gerlach, Luther P., and Virginia H. Hine. 1970. *People, Power and Change: Movements of Social Transformation*. Indianapolis: Bobbs-Merrill.

Glavitch, M. Kathleen. 1982. "The Paradox of Poverty." *Review for Religious* 41: 605–09.

Gleason, Philip, and David Salvaterra. 1988. "Ethnicity, Immigration and American Catholic History," 31–56, in Dolores Liptak, ed., *A Church of Many Cultures*. New York: Garland.

Glowienka, Emerine. 1975. "The Counsel of Poverty." *Review for Religious* 34: 248–55.

Goffman, Erving. 1961. *Asylums: Essays on the Social Situation of Mental Patients and Other Inmates*. Chicago: Aldine.

————1962. Personal correspondence reprinted in Kathleen Marie Cooney, *Reasons for Staying in a Religious Congregation From the Viewpoint of Women who Entered Between 1945 and 1975.* Ph.D. diss., Case Western Reserve University, 1988. 379.

Gogan, Brian. 1992. "Lay Community and Church Survival." *Religious Life Review* 31(4): 179–89.

Goggin, Ann, and David M. Knight. 1973. "Towards an Obedience of the Future." *Review for Religious* 32: 798–813.

Gold, Penny Schine. 1985. *The Lady and the Virgin: Image, Attitude and Experience in Twelfth Century France.* Chicago: University of Chicago Press.

Gordon-McCutchan, R.C. 1981. "The Irony of Evangelical History." *Journal for the Scientific Study of Religion* 20(4): 309–26.

Gray, Howard, S.J. 1989. "The Vocation Crisis: Reflections on an Approach to the Data," 40–51, in Laurie Felknor, ed., *The Crisis in Religious Vocations.* New York: Paulist Press.

Greeley, Andrew M. 1991. "The Demography of American Catholics, 1965–1990," 37–56, in H. R. Ebaugh, ed., *Vatican II and U.S. Catholicism* Greenwich, Conn.: JAI Press.

Greif, Gary, S.J. 1967. "The Vows and the Christian Life." *Review for Religious* 26: 805–33.

Grindel, John, and Sean Peters. 1992. "Religious Life Issues in a Time of Transition: A Report to the Lilly Endowment." *Review for Religious* 51: 267–75.

Griswold, Wendy. 1987. "A Methodological Approach for the Sociology of Culture." *Sociological Methodology* 17: 1–35.

Grosh, Gerald. R. 1975. "Models of Poverty." *Review for Religious* 34: 550–58.

Haas, Alois M. 1987. "Schools of Late Medieval Mysticism," 140–75, in Jill Raitt, ed., *Christian Spirituality II: High Middle Ages and Reformation.* New York: Crossroad.

Hagspiel, Bruno M. S.V.D. 1954. "Are You a Jellyfish?" *Review for Religious* 13: 79–85.

Hall, John R. 1988. "Social Organization and Pathways of Commitment: Types of Communal Groups, Rational Choice Theory, and the Kanter Thesis." *American Sociological Review* 53: 679–92.

Hannigan, John A. 1991. "Social Movement Theory and the Sociology of Religion: Toward a New Synthesis." *Sociological Analysis* 52(4): 311–31.

Haring, Bernard. 1963. "The Vocation of the Christian to Perfection." *Review for Religious* 22: 41–52.

Hart, Stephen. 1993. "Culture and Religion in Recent Social Movement Literature." Paper presented at the annual meeting of the Association for the Sociology of Religion.

Hatch, Nathan O. 1989. *The Democratization of American Christianity.* New Haven: Yale University Press.

Healy, Kathleen, ed., 1992. *Sisters of Mercy: Spirituality in America, 1843–1900.* New York: Paulist Press.

Heffernan, Esther. 1989. "Religious Vocations of American Women: Membership in a Socio-Historical Context." Paper presented at 1989 annual meeting of the Association for the Sociology of Religion, August 6–9, 1989, San Francisco.

Heft, James L. 1989. "From the Pope to the Bishops: Episcopal Authority From Vatican I to Vatican II," 55–78, in Bernard Cooke, ed., *The Papacy and the Church in the U.S.* New York: Paulist Press.

Heiling, George, and Barbara Heiling. 1990. "Coping with the Change of Generations in a Christian Commune." Paper given at the annual meeting of the American Sociological Association, Washington, D.C., August, 1990.

Helen Marie, Sister. 1966. "Having Nothing." *Review for Religious* 25: 703–13.

Hellman, J. A. Wayne. 1987. "The Spirituality of the Franciscans," 31–50, in Jill Raitt, ed., *Christian Spirituality II: High Middle Ages and Reformation.* New York: Crossroad.

Hendricks, Barbara, M.M. 1976. "Obedience to Mission." *Review for Religious* 35: 321–29.

Hennessey, James, S.J. 1989. "A Look At the Institution Itself," 32–39, in Laurie Felknor, ed., *The Crisis in Religious Vocations.* New York: Paulist Press.

Herbst, C. A. 1954. "Mindfulness." *Review for Religious* 13: 179–83.

Heschel, Abraham J. 1990. "The European Era in Jewish History," 1021 in Debroah Dash Moore, ed., *East European Jews in Two Worlds: Studies for the Yivo Annual.* Evanston, Il.: Northwestern University Press.

Heslin, Julia A. 1983. "In Transition: A Study of Women Religious Administrators in Non-Traditional Roles." Ph.D. Diss., Fordham University.

Hill, Michael. 1973. *The Religious Order: A Study of Virtuoso Religion and Its Legitimation in the Nineteenth Century Church of England.* London: Heinemann Educational Books.

Hillery, George A. 1983. "Monastic Occupations: A Study in Values," 191–210 in *Research in Sociology of Work: Peripheral Workers,* vol.2. Greenwich, Conn.: Jai Press.

————1992. *The Monastery: A Study in Freedom, Love and Community.* Westport, Conn.: Praeger.

Hinnebusch, Paul, O.P. 1963. "Virgo Hostia." *Review for Religious* 22: 668–73.

Hinnebusch, William, O.P. 1973. "How the Dominican Order Faced Its Crises." *Review for Religious* 32: 1307–21.

Hirschman, Albert O. 1970. *Exit, Voice and Loyalty: Responses to Decline in Firms, Organizations, and States.* Cambridge, Mass.: Harvard University Press.

Hogan, William F., O.P. 1963. "The Democratic Aspect of Religious Life." *Review for Religious* 22: 327–33.

————1983. "A Sense of Consecration." *Review for Religious* 42: 883–85.

————1986. "The Poverty of Discipleship." *Review for Religious* 45(2): 220–24.

Hoge, Dean R. 1987. *The Future of Catholic Leadership: Responses to the Priest Shortage.* Kansas City: Sheed and Ward.

————1991. "Changes in the Priesthood and Seminaries," 67–83, in H. R. Ebaugh, ed., *Vatican II and U.S. Catholicism.* Greenwich, Conn.: JAI Press.

Hoge, Dean R., Jackson W. Carroll, and Francis K. Scheets. 1988. *Patterns of Parish Leadership: Cost and Effectiveness in Four Denominations.* Kansas City: Sheed and Ward.

Hollermann, Ephrem. 1991. *The Reshaping of a Tradition: American Benedictine Women, 1852–1881.* Ph.D. diss., Marquette University.

Holstein, Henri, S.J. 1961. "The Mystery of Religious Life." *Review for Religious* 30: 317–29.

Hostie, Raymond. 1972. *La vie et mort des ordres religieux.* Paris: Desclee de Brouwer.

Hufton, Olwen H. 1974. *The Poor of Eighteenth Century France*. London: Oxford University Press.

"Imported Nuns." 1993. *Inside the Vatican* (December): 54–55.

Jean, Marguerite. 1977. *Evolution des communautes religieuses de femmes au Canada de 1639 à nos jours*. Montreal: Fides.

Jenkins, J. Craig. 1983. "Resource Mobilization Theory and the Study of Social Movements." *Annual Review of Sociology* 9: 527–53.

John Paul II. 1983. "Letter to U.S. Bishops on Religious Orders." *Origins* 13(8): 129–33. (July 7, 1983).

John, Sister Helen James, S.N.D. 1965. "Rahner on Roles in the Church." *Review for Religious* 24: 526–33.

Johnson, Mary, S.N.D. 1992. "No Nunsense: Attitudes of the New Generation of Catholic Women Religious in New England." Paper read at the November 1992 meeting of the Society for the Scientific Study of Religion, Washington, D.C.

Johnson, Penelope. 1991. *Equal in Monastic Profession*. Chicago: University of Chicago Press.

Johnston, William, S.J. 1969. "Religious Life: Contemplative Life." *Review for Religious* 28: 291–96.

Jones, Alan. 1978. "Obedience in the Contemporary World." *Review for Religious* 37: 333–41.

Jones, Arthur. 1993a. "Christian Brothers Search for Authenticity." *National Catholic Reporter* 29(16): 15. (February 19, 1993).

———1993b. "A Close Look at the Jesuit Orders." *National Catholic Reporter* 29(16): 21. (February 19, 1993).

Kanter, Rosabeth M. 1972. *Commitment and Community: Communes and Utopias in Sociological Perspective*. Cambridge, Mass.: Harvard University Press.

———1973. *Communes: Creating and Managing the Collective Life*. New York: Harper and Row.

Kantowicz, Edward R. 1983. *Corporation Sole: Cardinal Mundelein and Chicago Catholicism*. South Bend: Notre Dame University Press.

Kavanaugh, Kieran. 1989. "Spanish Sixteenth Century Carmel and Surrounding Movements," 69–92, in Louis Dupre, and Don E. Saliers, eds., *Christian Spirituality III: Post-Reformation and Modern*. New York: Crossroad.

Keating, Thomas. 1992. *Open Mind, Open Heart: The Contemplative Dimension of the Gospel.* Rockport Mass.: Element Press.

Kelleher, Sean, C.S.R. 1963. "Christian Liberty and the Rule." *Review for Religious* 22: 311–17.

Kenneally, James J. 1990. *The History of American Catholic Women.* New York: Crossroad.

Kennelly, Karen. 1984. "Historical Perspectives on the Experience of Religious Life in the American Church," 79–97, in Robert J. Daly et al., eds., *Religious Life in the U.S. Church: The New Dialog.* New York: Paulist.

Kephart, William M. 1987. *Extraordinary Groups.* 3d ed., New York: St. Martin's Press.

Kerkhofs, Jan. 1993a. "The Synod Lineamenta: European Religious Respond." *Religious Life Review* 32(5): 285–93.

———1993b. "Confidence in the Spirit of Jesus." *Religious Life Review* 32(5): 294–302.

Kern, Louis J. 1981. *An Ordered Love: Sex Roles and Sexuality in Victorian Utopias.* Chapel Hill: University of North Carolina Press.

Kieckhefer, Richard. 1984. *Unquiet Souls: Fourteenth Century Saints and Their Religious Milieu.* Chicago: University of Chicago Press.

———1987. "Major Currents in Late Medieval Devotion," 75–108, in Jill Raitt, ed., *Christian Spirituality II: High Middle Ages and Reformation.* New York: Crossroad.

———1988. "Imitators of Christ: Sainthood in the Christian Tradition," 1–42, in Richard Kieckhefer and George Bond, eds., *Sainthood: Its Manifestations in World Religions.* Berkeley: University of California Press.

Kiefer, Monica. n.d.a. *Log Cabin Days of the Kentucky Dominicans, 1822–1830.* Columbus, Ohio: Springs Press.
n.d.b. *In the Greenwood, Part II.* Columbus, Ohio: Springs Press.

Kiesling, Christopher. 1986. "Religious Life: God's Call and Our Response." *Review for Religious* 45: 493–501.

King, Eleace. 1991. *CARA Formation Directory for Men and Women Religious, 1991.* Washington, D.C.: Center for Applied Research in the Apostolate.

King, Eleace, and Thomas P. Ferguson. 1992. *CARA Formation Directory for Men and Women Religious, 1992*. Washington, D.C.: Center for Applied Research in the Apostolate.

Kitch, Sally L. 1989. *Chaste Liberation: Celibacy and Female Cultural Status*. Urbana: University of Illinois Press.

Klandermans, Bert. 1984. "Mobilization and Participation: Social-Psychological Expansion of Resource Mobilization Theory." *American Sociological Review* 49(5): 583–600.

———1988. "The Formation and Mobilization of Consensus," 173–96, in Bert Klandermans, Hanspeter Kriesi, and Sidney Tarrow, eds., *From Structure to Action: Comparing Social Movement Research Across Cultures*, vol. 1 in International Social Movement Research Series. Greenwich, Conn.: JAI Press.

———1992. "The Social Construction of Protest," 77–103, in Aldon D. Morris and Carol McClurg Mueller, eds., *Frontiers in Social Movement Theory*. New Haven: Yale University Press.

Kneale, Brendan. 1988. "The Superiority of Religious Life." *Review for Religious* 47: 505–10.

Knight, David, S.J. 1973. "Spousal Commitment and Religious Life." *Review for Religious* 32: 85–96.

Knoke, David. 1990. *Political Networks: the Structural Perspective*. New York: Cambridge University Press.

Knowles, David. 1976. *Bare Ruined Choirs: The Dissolution of English Monasticism*. New York: Cambridge University Press.

Kolbenschlag, Madonna. 1987. "John Paul II, U.S. Women Religious, and the Saturnian Complex," 250–61, in Hans Kung and Leonard Swidler, eds., *The Church in Anguish*. San Francisco: Harper and Row.

Kolmer, Elizabeth. 1984. *Religious Women in the United States: A Survey of the Influential Literature from 1950 to 1983*. Wilmington, Del.: Michael Glazier.

———1988. "Catholic Women Religious and Women's History," 1–13, in Joseph M. White, ed., *The American Catholic Religious Life*. New York: Garland.

Korczyk, Donna M. 1987. "Obedience, Authority and the Cross of Christ." *Review for Religious* 46: 371–76.

Kovats, Alexandra. 1992. "Reflections on the Vows From a Cosmic/Ecological Perspective." *Information* 146: 21–24.

Kraemer, Ross S. 1980. "The Conversion of Women to Ascetic Forms of Christianity." *Signs* 6(2): 298–306.

Kruse, Robert J. 1963a. "Authority in Religious Life." *Review for Religious* 22: 527–35.

———1963b. "Obedience in Religious Life." *Review for Religious* 22: 648–56.

Kurtz, Lester R. 1986. *The Politics of Heresy: The Modernist Crisis in Roman Catholicism.* Berkeley: University of California Press.

Lackner, Joseph H., S.M. 1969. "Anomie and Religious Life." *Review for Religious* 28: 628–36.

Langlois, Claude. 1984. *Le catholicisme au feminin.* Paris: Editions du Cerf.

Laporte, Jean Marc. 1967. "Religious Obedience: Interplay of the Charismatic and the Individual." *Review for Religious* 26: 844–59.

Larkin, Ernest E., O.Carm. 1968. "Scriptural-Theological Aspects of Religious Life." *Review for Religious* 27: 1013–26.

Lavrin, Asuncion. 1983. "Women and Religion in Spanish America," 43–65. in Rosemary R. Ruether and Rosemary S. Keller, eds., *Women and Religion in America: The Colonial and Revolutionary Periods.* San Francisco: Harper and Row.

Law, Charles A. 1978. "Poverty and the Space Around Us." *Review for Religious* 37: 365–70.

Lawrence, C. H. 1989. *Medieval Monasticism: Forms of Religious Life in Western Europe in the Middle Ages.* 2d edition. London: Longman.

Lawson, Ronald. 1991. "Religious Movements and Social Movement Theory." Paper read at the annual meeting of the Association for the Sociology of Religion, August 1991.

Leadership Conference of Women Religious. 1988. "Reflections Upon the Religious Life of U.S. Women Religious," 173–81, in Nadine Foley, ed., *Claiming Our Truth: Reflections on Identity By U.S. Women Religious.* Washington, D.C.: Leadership Conference of Women Religious.

———1992. "Statement on the Establishment of a New Council of Major Superiors of Women Religious." *Origins* 22(9): 159–60.

Leddy, Mary Jo. 1990. *Reweaving Religious Life: Beyond the Liberal Model.* Mystic, Conn.: Twenty-Third Publications.

Leeming, Bernard, S.J. 1956. "The Mysticism of Obedience." *Review for Religious* 15: 67–90.

Lehman, Edward C. 1985. *Women Clergy.* New Brunswick, N.J.: Transaction.

Leonard, Henry B. 1988. "Ethnic Tensions, Episcopal Leadership and the Emergence of the Twentieth Century American Catholic Church: The Cleveland Experience," 196–220, in Dolores Liptak, ed., *A Church of Many Cultures.* New York: Garland.

Lerner, Gerda. 1993. *The Creation of Feminist Consciousness.* New York: Oxford University Press.

Levesque, Benoit. 1975. "Les communautes religieuses francaises au Quebec: une emigration utopique?" 119–92, in Bernard Denault and Benoit Levesque, eds., *Elements pour une sociologie des communautes eeligieuses au Quebec.* Montreal: Les Presses de l'Université de Montreal.

Levine, Marc V. 1990. *The Reconquest of Montreal: Language Policy and Social Change in a Bilingual City.* Philadelphia: Temple University Press.

Levitas, Ruth. 1990. *The Concept of Utopia.* Syracuse: Syracuse University Press.

Light, Dale B. 1992. "Catholic Evangelism in Antebellum Philadelphia." Paper read at the Conference on the History of Christianity, Notre Dame University, March 27, 1992.

Little, Lester K. 1978. *Religious Poverty and the Profit Economy in Medieval Europe.* Ithaca: Cornell University Press.

Lofland, John. 1979. "White Hot Mobilization: Strategies of a Millenarian Movement," 157–66, in Mayer N. Zald and John D. McCarthy, eds., *The Dynamics of Social Movements.* Cambridge, Mass.: Winthrop.

Lozano, John M. 1983. *Foundresses, Founders, and Their Religious Families.* Chicago: Claret Center for Resources in Spirituality.

Lubich, Gino, and Piero Lazzarin. 1985. *Joan Antida Thouret: When God Hears the Voice of the Poor.* New York: New City Press.

Luckmann, Thomas. 1967. *The Invisible Religion: The Problem of Religion in Modern Society.* New York: Macmillan.

———1990. "Shrinking Transcendence, Expanding Religion?" *Sociological Analysis.* 50(2): 127–38.

Luddy, Marie. 1992. "Catholic Women and Philanthropy in Nineteenth Century Ireland." Paper read at the annual Conference on the History of Women Religious, Tarrytown, N.Y., July 1, 1992.

Luria, Keith P. 1989. "The Counter-Reformation and Popular Spirituality," 93–120, in Louis Dupre and Don E. Saliers, eds., *Christian Spirituality III: Post Reformation and Modern*. New York: Crossroad.

MacDonald, Donald. 1986. "The Price of Poverty." *Review for Religious* 45(1): 1–15.

MacQuarrie, Alan. 1992. "Early Christian Religious Houses in Scotland: Foundation and Function," 110–33, in John Blair and Richard Sharpe, eds., *Pastoral Care Before the Parish*. Leicester: Leicester University Press.

Macy, Michael W. 1991. "Chains of Co-Operation: Threshhold Effects in Collective Action." *American Sociological Review* 56: 730–47.

Manion, Patricia Jean. 1988. "One Perspective on Change," 57–66, in Nadine Foley, ed., *Claiming Our Truth: Reflections on Identity by U.S. Women Religious*. Washington, D.C.: Leadership Conference of Women Religious.

Mannard, Joseph G. 1986. "Maternity of the Spirit: Nuns and Domesticity in Antebellum America." *U.S. Catholic Historian* 5(3–4): 305–24.

Mannheim, Karl. 1952. "The Problem of Generations," 276–320, in *Essays on the Sociology of Knowledge*. New York: Oxford University Press.

Manuel, Frank E. 1966. *Utopias and Utopian Thought*. Boston: Houghton Mifflin.

March, James G., and Herbert A. Simon. 1958. *Organizations*. New York: John Wiley & Sons.

Maria, Sister. 1958. "Preliminary to Adaptation." *Review for Religious* 17: 339–50.

Marin, Gerardo, and Raymond J. Gamba. 1993. "The Role of Expectations in Religious Conversions: The Case of Hispanic Catholics." *Review of Religious Research* 34(4): 357–71.

Markham, Donna, O.P., n.d. "Psychological Factors Influencing the Decline of and Persistence in Religious Vocations." Unpublished Paper. Donna Markham, 1257 E. Siena Heights Drive, Adrian, Mich., 49221.

———1988. "The Decline of Vocations in the United States: Reflections from a Psychological Perspective." *New Catholic World* 231(1381): 13–17. (January/February 1988).

————1989. "The Decline of Vocations in the United States: Reflections From a Psychological Perspective," 181–96, in Laurie Felknor, ed., *The Crisis in Religious Vocations.* New York: Paulist Press.

Markham, Flannan. 1993a. "The Lineamenta." *Religious Life Review* 32(2): 103–06.

————1993b. "The 1994 Synod: Sprigs of Hope." *Religious Life Review* 32(6): 262–66.

Martelet, Gustave, S.J. 1965. "The Church's Holiness and Religious Life." *Review for Religious* 24: 882–913.

Martin, Dennis D. 1987. "Popular and Pastoral Issues in the Later Middle Ages." *Church History* 56(3): 320–30.

McAdam, Doug. 1982. *The Political Process and the Development of Black Insurgency.* Chicago: University of Chicago Press.

————1983. "The Decline of the Civil Rights Movement," 298–319, in Jo Freeman, ed., *Social Movements of the Sixties and Seventies.* New York: Longman.

McAdam, Doug, John D. McCarthy, and Mayer N. Zald. 1988. "Social Movements," 695–737, in Neil J. Smelser, ed., *Handbook of Sociology.* Newbury Park, Cal.: Sage.

McCarthy, John, and Mayer Zald. 1973. *The Trend of Social Movements in America: Professionalization and Resource Mobilization.* Morristown, N.J.: General Learning Press.

————1977. "Resource Mobilization and Social Movements: A Partial Theory." *American Journal of Sociology* 82: 1212–41.

McCarthy, Patricia. 1990. "The Vowed Life as a Peace Story to be Told." *Review for Religious* 49: 843–51.

McCormick, Richard A. 1964. "Psychosexual Development in Religious Life." *Review for Religious* 23: 724–40.

McDonnell, Ernest. 1969. *The Beguines and Beghards in Medieval Culture.* New York: Octagon Books.

McDonough, Elizabeth. 1991. "Beyond the Liberal Model: Quo Vadis?" 89–119, in J. Provost, and K. Walf, eds., *Ius Sequitur Vita: Law Follows Life* Leuven: University Press of Leuven.

————1993. "Charisms and Religious Life." *Review for Religious* 52(5): 646–59.

McDonough, Peter. 1992. *Men Astutely Trained: A History of the Jesuits in the American Century.* New York: Free Press.

McGuire, Meredith B. 1987. *Religion: The Social Context.* 2d edition. Belmont, Cal.: Wadsworth.

McKenna, Thomas. 1992. "Memories of the Future." *Review for Religious* 51: 241–59.

McLaughlin, Mary M. 1989. "Creating and Recreating Communities of Women: the Case of Corpus Domini, Ferrara, 1406–52." *Signs* 14(2): 293–320.

McNamara, Jo Ann. 1985. *A New Song: Celibate Women in the First Three Christian Centuries.* New York: Harrington Park Press.

McQuade, Rosalie. 1992. "My Dear Lord: Letters From Margaret Anna Cusack to Bishop Winand Michael Wigger." Paper read at the annual Conference on the History of Women Religious, Tarrytown, N.Y., June 30, 1992.

McRedmund, Louis. 1991. "The Jesuits in Ireland: Cromwell to the Restoration." *Religious Life Review* 30(2): 60–65.

Meenan, Daniel, S.J. 1984. "On Dreaming Dreams, Or the Making of a Revolution." *Review for Religious* 43: 547–57.

Meiburger, Anne. 1968. "Toward a New Expression of Poverty." *Review for Religious* 27: 113–19.

Melucci, Alberto. 1989. *Nomads of the Present: Social Movements and Individual Needs in Contemporary Society.* Philadelphia: Temple University Press.

Merkle, Judith A. 1992. *Commited by Chioce: Religious Life Today.* Collegeville, MN: The Liturgical Press.

Meyer, Daniel P. 1963. "Servility vs. Intelligent Obedience." *Review for Religious* 23: 203–06.

Miller, Frederick D. 1983. "The End of the SDS and the Emergence of the Weathermen: Demise Through Success," 279–97, in Jo Freeman, ed., *Social Movements of the Sixties and Seventies.* New York: Longman.

Miller, Timothy. 1991. "They Found a Formula: 450 Years of Hutterite Communitarianism," 79–91, in Timothy Miller, ed., *When Prophets Die: The Post-Charismatic Fate of New Religious Movements.* Albany, N.Y.: SUNY Press.

Misner, Barbara. 1988. *"Highly Respectable and Accomplished Ladies": Catholic Religious Women in America, 1790–1850.* New York: Garland.

———1989. "Women in the Convent," 17–47, in Karen Kennelly, ed., *American Catholic Women: A Historical Exploration.* New York: Macmillan.

Moaddel, Mansoor. 1992. "Ideology as Episodic Discourse: The Case of the Iranian Revolution." *American Sociological Review* 57(3): 353–79.

Modras, Ronald. 1992. "Materialism: A Code Word for Declining Seminary Enrollments." *Bread Rising* 2(7): 3.

Monastic Fraternities of Jerusalem. 1992. "Jerusalem." 32 Rue Geoffroy L'Asnier 75004. Paris, France.

Moran, Gerald F. 1991. "Sinners Are Turned Into Saints in Numbers: Puritanism and Revivalism in Colonial Connecticut," 38–62, in Philip R. Vandermeer, and Robert P. Swierenga, eds., *Belief and Behavior: Essays in the New Religious History*. New Brunswick: Rutgers University Press.

Moran, Robert E., C.S.P. 1972. "Death and Rebirth: A Case Study of Reform Efforts of a Roman Catholic Sisterhood." Ph.D. diss., University of California, Santa Barbara.

Moreno, Juan Ramon, S.J. 1992. "Religious Life in the Puebla Documents." *Review for Religious* 51: 707–15.

Morris, Joan. 1973. *The Lady Was a Bishop.* New York: Macmillan.

Mullahy, Bernard, C.S.C. 1955. "Community Life." *Review for Religious* 14: 141–50.

Munley, Anne. 1988. "An Exploratory Content Analysis of Major Themes Present in Selected Documents of U. S. Women Religious," 183–91, in Nadine Foley, ed., *Claiming Our Truth: Reflections on Identity by U.S. Women Religious*. Washington, D.C.: Leadership Conference of Women Religious.

————1992. *Threads for the Loom: LCWR Planning and Ministry Studies.* Silver Spring, Md.: Leadership Conference of Women Religious.

Murphy, Roseanne, and William T. Liu. 1966. "Organizational Stance and Change: A Comparative Study of Three Religious Congregations." *Review of Religious Research* 8(1): 37–50.

National Association of Treasurers of Religious Institutes. 1993. *Compensation Survey for 1992–1993.* NATRI, 8824 Cameron St., Silver Spring, Md., 20910.

National Opinion Research Center. 1972. *The Catholic Priest in the U.S.: Sociological Investigations.* Washington, D.C.: U.S. Catholic Conference.

Neal, M. Augusta. 1980. "The Sisters' Survey, 1980: A Report." *Probe* 10(5): 1–7.

————1884a. *Catholic Sisters in Transition: From the 1960s to the 1980s.* Wilmington, Del.: Michael Glazier.

————1984b. "Who They Are and What They Do," 152–70, in Robert J. Daly et al., eds., *Religious Life in the U.S. Church: The New Dialog.* New York: Paulist.

————1990. *From Nuns to Sisters: An Expanding Vocation.* Mystic, Conn.: Twenty-Third Publications.

————1991a. "American Sisters: Organizational and Value Changes," 105–21, in H. R. Ebaugh, ed., *Vatican II and U. S. Catholicism.* Greenwich, Conn.: JAI Press.

————1991b. *A Report on the National Profile of the Third Sisters' Survey.* Boston: Emmanuel College.

Neel, Carol. 1989. "The Origins of the Beguines," 240–60, in Judith M. Bennett et al., eds., *Sisters and Workers in the Middle Ages.* Chicago: University of Chicago Press.

Newman, Barbara. 1985. "Hildegard of Bingen: Visions and Validation." *Church History* 54(2): 163–75.

Nolan, Janet A. 1989. *Ourselves Alone: Women's Immigration from Ireland, 1885–1920.* Lexington, Ky.: University Presses of Kentucky.

Not With Silver or Gold. (anonymous) 1945. Paterson, N.J.: St. Anthony Guild Press.

Nygren, David, and Miriam Ukeritis. 1992. "The Future of Religious Orders in the United States." *Origins* 22(15): 258–72.

————1993. *The Future of Religious Orders in the United States: Transformation and Commitment.* Westport, Conn.: Praeger.

Nygren, David, Miriam Ukeritis, David McClelland et al. 1991. "Religious Leadership Competencies." *Review for Religious* 52: 390–417.

Oates, Mary J. 1983. "Organized Voluntarism: Catholic Sisters in Massachusetts, 1870–1940," 141–70, in Rosemary Ruether and Rosemary S. Keller, eds., *Women and Religion in America* vol.1. New York: Macmillan.

————1985. "The Good Sisters: The Work and Position of Catholic Churchwomen in Boston, 1870–1940," 171–99, in Robert E. Sullivan and James M. O'Toole, eds., *Catholic Boston: Studies in Religion and Community.* Boston: Archdiocese of Boston.

————1993. "Organizing for Service: Challenges to Community Life and Work in Catholic Sisterhoods, 1850–1940," 150–61, in Chmielewski et al., eds., *Women in Spiritual and Communitarian Societies in the U.S.* Syracuse: Syracuse University Press.

Oberschall, Anthony. 1973. *Social Conflict and Social Movement.* Englewood Cliffs: Prentice Hall.

O'Brien, David J. 1986. "A Historical Perspective," 108–23, in Madonna Kolbenschlag, ed., *Authority, Community and Conflict.* Kansas City: Sheed and Ward.

O'Brien, Kathleen. 1987. *Journeys: A Pre-amalgamation History of the Sisters of Mercy, Omaha Province.* Omaha, Neb.: Sisters of Mercy.

O'Connell, Marvin R. 1989. "John Ireland, the Vatican, and the French Connection," 99–117, in Bernard Cooke, ed., *The Papacy and the Church in the United States.* New York: Paulist Press.

————1984. "Ultramontanism and Dupanloup: the Compromise of 1865." *Church History* 53: 200–17.

O'Connor, David F. 1987. "The Public and Witness Dimensions of Religious Life." *Review for Religious* 46: 661–74.

————1990. *Witness and Service: Questions About Religious Life Today.* Mahwah, N.J.: Paulist Press.

O'Connor, Mother Margarita, I.B.V.M. n.d. *That Incomparable Woman.* Toronto: Palm Publishers.

O'Connor, Terence R. 1963. "Holy Obedience and Whole Obedience." *Review for Religious* 22: 634–47.

O'Donnell, Desmond. 1986. "The Vowed Life in a Secularized World." *Review for Religious* 45(2): 161–70.

————1993. "Clerical Religious: Taking Stock for the Synod." *Religious Life Review* 32(1): 5–14.

O'Donoghue, Helena. 1993a. "Women's Congregations Twenty-Five Years After Vatican II." *Religious Life Review* 30(3): 115–23.

————1993b. "What Hopes For the Synod?" *Religious Life Review* 32(4): 213–16.

Official Catholic Directory, 1993. Wilmette, Ill.: P. J. Kennedy & Sons.

O'Grady, Desmond. 1991. "Helping the Least of Their Brothers and Sisters." *Our Sunday Visitor* October 13, 1991, 6–7.

O'Hara, Mary L. 1990. "Heralds of Hope," 35–55, in Dolores Steinberg and Mary O'Hara, eds., *The Future of Religious Life.* Collegeville, MN: The Liturgical Press.

O'Leary, Brian. 1985. "Christian and Religious Obedience." *Review for Religious* 44: 513–20.

O'Malley, John. 1989. "Early Jesuit Spirituality: Spain and Italy," 3–27, in Louis Dupre and Don E. Saliers, eds., *Christian Spirituality III: Post Reformation and Modern*. New York: Crossroad.

O'Murchu, Diarmuid. 1992. *Religious Life: A Prophetic Vision*. Notre Dame: Ave Maria Press.

O'Neill, Daniel P. 1988. "St. Paul's Priests, 1850–1930: Recruitment, Ethnicity and Americanization," 70–77, in Dolores Liptak, ed., *A Church of Many Cultures*. New York: Garland.

O'Regan, John. 1981. "Unavailability as Poverty." *Review for Religious* 40: 540–46.

O'Reilly, James. 1968. "Lay and Religious States of Life: Their Distinction and Complementarity." *Review for Religious* 27: 1027–52.

O'Riordan, Sean. 1993. "Religious Life in a Time of Turbulence." *Religious Life Review* 32(3): 155–60.

O'Rourke, Kevin D. 1966. "Obedience and Subsidiarity in Religious Life." *Review for Religious* 25: 305–15.

Orsy, Ladislas. 1967. "Chastity in Religious Life." *Review for Religious* 26: 604–24.

———1967. "Poverty in Religious Life." *Review for Religious* 26: 60–82.

Osborne, Kenan. 1988. *Priesthood: A History of the Ordained Ministry in the Roman Catholic Church*. New York: Paulist.

O'Shea, Kevin. 1974. "A Christian is a Poor Man." *Review for Religious* 33: 1019–25.

O'Shea, Noirin. 1993. "Religious as Prophets." *Religious Life Review* 32(2): 107–12.

Osimo, Catherine. 1988. "Women's Center: Incarnational Spirituality," 9–36, in Nadine Foley, ed., *Claiming Our Truth: Reflections on Identity by U.S. Women Religious*. Washington, D.C.: Leadership Conference of Women Religious.

O'Toole, James M. 1992. *Militant and Triumphant: William Henry O'Connell and the Catholic Church in Boston, 1859–1944*. Notre Dame: Notre Dame University Press.

Padburg, John W. 1989. "The Contexts of Comings and Goings," 19–31, in Laurie Felknor, ed., *The Crisis in Religious Vocations: An Inside View*. New York: Paulist.

Pagels, Elaine H. 1976. "What Became of God the Mother? Conflicting Images of God in Early Christianity." *Signs* 2(2): 293–303.

———1988. *Adam, Eve and the Serpent.* New York: Random House.

Pennington, Basil. 1985. "The Cistercians," 205–17, in Bernard McGinn and John Myendorff, eds., *Christian Spirituality I: Origins to the Twelfth Century.* New York: Crossroad.

Peterson, Susan Carol, and Courtney Vaughn-Roberson. 1988. *Women With Vision: The Presentation Sisters of South Dakota: 1880–1985.* Urbana: University of Illinois Press.

Pontifical Commission. 1986. "U.S. Religious Life and the Decline of Vocations." *Origins* 16(25): 467–70. (December 4, 1986).

Popko, Kathleen. 1991. "Leadership in the 1990's: Designing for the Third Millenium." Presidential Address to the Leadership Conference of Women Religious, Annual Meeting, Albuquerque, N.M., August 27, 1991.

Portier, William L. 1989. "Church Unity and National Traditions: The Challenge to the Modern Papacy, 1682–1870," 25–54, in Bernard Cooke, ed., *The Papacy and the Church in the United States.* New York: Paulist Press.

Prelinger, Catherine M. 1986. "The Female Diaconate in the Anglican Church: What Kind of Ministry for Women," 161–92, in Gail Malmgreen, ed., *Religion in the Lives of English Women, 1760–1930.* Bloomington: Indiana University Press.

Provost, James H. 1989. "The Papacy: Power, Authority and Leadership," 189–215, in Bernard Cooke, ed., *The Papacy and the Church in the United States.* New York: Paulist Press.

Quigley, Carol. 1988. *Turning Points in Religious Life.* Westminster Md.: Christian Classics.

Quinn, John. 1983a. "Archbishop Quinn Discusses The Commission on Religious Life." *Origins* 13(8): 143–48. (July 7, 1983).

———1983b. "Religious Life: The Mystery and the Challenge." *Review for Religious* 42: 801–13.

———1992. "Statement on the Establishment of a New Council of Major Superiors of Women." *Origins* 22(9): 160.

Quinonez, Lora Ann, and Mary Daniel Turner. 1992. *The Transformation of American Catholic Sisters.* Philadelphia: Temple University Press.

Quintal, Claire. 1984. *Herald of Love: Father Marie Clement Staub, A.A., Apostle of the Sacred Heart and Founder of the Sisters of St. Joan of Arc, 1896–1936.* Privately Printed, Sisters of St. Joan of Arc, 1505 Rue de l'Assomption, Sillery, Quebec.

Ramsey, Boniface. 1983a. "The Center of Religious Poverty." *Review for Religious* 42: 534–44.

———1983b. "Christocentric Celibacy." *Review for Religious* 42: 217–24.

———1984. "Cruciform Obedience." *Review for Religious* 43: 664–71.

Rapley, Elizabeth. 1990. *The Devotes: Women and Church in Seventeenth Century France.* Montreal: McGill Queens University Press.

Ratigan, Mary T. C.S.J. "Ministry Rooted in the Vows." *Review for Religious* 37: 321–32.

Rausch, Thomas P. 1990. *Radical Christian Communities.* Collegeville, Minn.: Michael Glazier.

Raymond, Janice. 1972. "Nuns and Women's Liberation." *Andover Newton Quarterly* 12: 201–12.

Reck, Donald W. 1986. "Who Are We as Religious?" *Review for Religious* 45: 50–56.

Reese, Thomas. 1989. *Archbishop: Inside the Power Structure of the American Catholic Church.* New York: Harper and Row.

Regan, Columkille. 1976. "Superiors: Are They Outdated?" *Review for Religious* 35: 740–48.

Regan, David. 1993. "Religious Life in Brazil." *Religious Life Review* 32(2): 118–22.

Regan, M. Joanna, and Isabelle Keiss. 1988. *Tender Courage: A Reflection on the Life and Spirit of Catherine McAuley.* Chicago: Franciscan Herald Press.

Reinke, Darrel R. 1987. "Austin's Labor: Patterns of Governance in Medieval Augustinian Monasticism." *Church History* 56(2): 157–71.

Religion Watch. 1989. "Counting Jesuit Losses." *Religion Watch* 4(3): 4.

Ridick, Joyce. 1978. "Psychological Aspects of Religious Poverty." *Review for Religious* 37: 851–60.

Riding, Alan. 1989. "Conservative Catholic Group Casts Off its Cloak." *New York Times* October 25, 1989.

Robbins, Thomas. 1988. *Cults, Converts and Charisma: The Sociology of New Religious Movements.* Newberry Park: Sage.

Rodriguez, Edmundo. 1989. "Realities for Hispanics." *Company* 6(1): 8–11.

Roche, Maurice A., C.M. 1964. "The Male Religious in Past and Present." *Review for Religious* 25: 749–69.

Rosetti, Stephen. 1982. "The Celibacy Experience." *Review for Religious* 41: 659–77.

Rosser, Gervase. 1992. "The Cure of Souls in English Towns Before 1000," 267–84, in John Blair and Richard Sharpe, eds., *Pastoral Care Before the Parish.* Leicester: Leicester University Press.

Rubin, Miri. 1991. *Corpus Christi: The Eucharist in Late Medieval Culture.* New York: Cambridge University Press.

Sacred Congregation for Religious. 1983. "Essential Elements in Church Teaching on Religious Life." *Origins* 13(8): 133–42. (July 7, 1983).

Schineller, J. Peter, S.J. 1979. "Promises to Keep." *Review for Religious* 38: 35–39.

Schleck, Charles A., C.S.C. 1964. "The Meaning of the Religious Sisterhood." *Review for Religious* 23: 160–73.

———1965. "Sanctification Through Virginity." *Review for Religious* 24: 829–81.

———1966. "Sanctification Through Obedience." *Review for Religious* 25: 161–234.

———1969. "Reflections on the Theology of Religious Life." *Review for Religious* 28: 244–75.

Schneider, Mary L. 1986. "The Transformation of American Women Religious: The Sister Formation Conference as a Catalyst for Change, 1954–1964." Cushwa Center Working Paper Series. Series 17, no. 1. (Spring 1986) University of Notre Dame.

———1988. "American Sisters and the Roots of Change: The 1950's." *U.S. Catholic Historian* 7(1): 55–72.

Schneiders, Sandra Marie, I.H.M. 1986. *New Wineskins: Re-Imagining Religious Life Today.* New York: Paulist Press.

———1987. "Evangelical Equality: Religious Consecration, Mission and Witness, Part II." *Spirituality Today* 39: 56–61. (Spring 1987).

———1988. "Reflections on the History of Religious Life and Contemporary Developments," 13–17, in Carol Quigley, I.H.M., ed., *Turning Points in Religious Life.* Westminster, Md.: Christian Classics, Inc.

Schoenherr, Richard A., and Lawrence A. Young. 1990. *The Catholic Priest in the U.S.: Demographic Investigations.* Comparative Religious Organization Studies Publication, University of Wisconsin, Madison.

———1993. *Full Pews and Empty Altars.* Madison: University of Wisconsin Press.

Schulenburg, Jane. 1989. "Women's Monastic Communities, 500–1100: Patterns of Expansion and Decline," 208–39, in Judith M. Bennett et al., eds. *Sisters and Workers in the Middle Ages.* Chicago: University of Chicago Press.

Schweikert, Jeanne, S.S.S.F. 1992. "Toward the New Millennium: A National Vision of Religious Life." Chicago: Convergence, Inc.

Scott, Alan. 1990. *Ideology and the New Social Movements.* London: Unwin Hyman.

Sered, Susan Starr. 1991. "Conflict, Complement and Control: Family and Religion Among Eastern Jewish Women in Jerusalem." *Gender & Society* 5(1): 10–29.

Sewell, William H. 1988. "Ideologies and Social Revolution: Reflections on the French Case." *Journal of Modern History* 57(1): 57–85.

Sheets, John R., S.J. 1985. "The Primordial Mystery of Consecration." *Review for Religious* 44: 641–53.

———1992. "Address to the New Council of Major Superiors." *Origins* 22(24): 412–16.

Shenker, Barry. 1986. *Intentional Communities: Ideology and Alienation in Communal Societies.* London: Routledge and Kegan Paul.

Sherman, Sarah Marie, R.S.M. 1989. "Fewer Vocations: Crisis or Challenge?" 5–18, in Laurie Felknor, ed., *The Crisis in Religious Vocations.* New York: Paulist Press.

Shipps, Jan. 1985. *Mormonism: The Story of a New Religious Tradition.* Urbana: University of Illinois Press.

Signs. 1985. Special issue on communities of women. 10(4).

Sikora, Joseph. 1967. "Chastity and Love." *Review for Religious* 27: 5–20.

———1967. "Poverty Today." *Review for Religious* 26: 638–61.

Sills, David. 1957. *The Volunteers: Means and Ends in a National Organization.* Glencoe, Ill.: Free Press.

Sisters of Divine Providence. 1961. "Mother Maria de la Roche" Pamphlet. Techny, Ill.: Divine Word Publications.

Sisters of Mercy. 1970. "Meditative Description of the Gospel Counsels." *Review for Religious* 29: 143–49.

Sisters of Notre Dame de Namur. 1938. *Outline History of the Sisters of Notre Dame de Namur.* Washington, D.C.: Trinity College.

Skocpol, Theda. 1985. "Cultural Idioms and Political Ideologies in the Revolutionary Reconstruction of State Power: A Rejoinder to Sewell." *Journal of Modern History* 57(1): 86–96.

Snow, David A. and Robert D. Benford. 1988. "Ideology, Frame Resonance and Participant Mobilization," 197–215, in Bert Klandermans, Hanspeter Kriesi, and Sidney Tarrow, eds., *From Structure to Action: Comparing Social Movement Research Across Cultures,* vol. 1, in International Social Movement Research Series. Greenwich Conn.: JAI Press.

———1992. "Master Frames and Cycles of Protest," 133–55, in Aldon D. Morris and Carol McClurg Mueller, eds., *Frontiers in Social Movement Theory.* New Haven: Yale University Press.

Snow, David A., and Richard Machalek. 1984. "The Sociology of Conversion." *Annual Review of Sociology* 10: 167–80.

Snow, David A. et al. 1986. "Frame Alignment Processes, Micromobilization and Movement Participation." *American Sociological Review* 51(5): 464–81.

Stahel, Thomas. 1992. "Whither Religious Life?" *America* September 26, 180–81.

Steidl-Meier, Paul, S.J. 1978. "Dynamic Aspects of the Traditional Vows: Hearing, Sharing, Indwelling." *Review for Religious* 37: 288–93.

Stein, Stephen J. 1992. *The Shaker Experience in America.* New Haven: Yale University Press.

Steinberg, Dolores, and Mary L. O'Hara, eds. 1990. *The Future of Religious Life.* Collegeville, MN: The Liturgical Press.

Stepp, Laura Sessions. 1992. "Roman Catholic Orders in Decline, Author Says." *Washington Post* September 26, 1992, G11–12.

Storch, Neil T. 1985. "John Ireland and the Modernist Controversy." *Church History* 54(3): 353–65.

Strassberg, Barbara. 1988. "Polish Catholics in Transition," 184–202, in Thomas Gannon, ed., *World Catholicism in Transition.* New York: Macmillan.

Stuhlmueller, Carroll. 1989. "Biblical Observations on the Decline of Vocations to Religious Life," 152–64, in Laurie Felknor, ed., *The Crisis in Religious Vocations: An Inside View*. New York: Paulist.

Sullivan, Mary Louise. 1992. "Mother Cabrini, Italian Immigrant, and Immigrant Religious Today." Paper read at the annual Conference on the History of Women Religious, Tarrytown, N.Y., June 30, 1992.

Sullivan, Robert E. 1985. "Beneficial Relations: Toward a Social History of the Diocesan Priests of Boston, 1875–1944," 201–38, in Robert E. Sullivan, and James M. O'Toole, eds., *Catholic Boston: Studies in Religion and Community*. Boston: Catholic Archdiocese of Boston.

Surles, Eileen, R.C. 1970. *St. Therese Couderc: Foundress of the Cenacle*. Milan: Editrice Ancora Milan.

Swidler, Ann. 1986. "Culture in Action: Symbols and Strategies." *American Sociological Review* 51: 273–86.

Tambasco, Anthony, S.M. 1973. "The Vowed Life: Call, Response and Mission." *Review for Religious* 32: 675–72.

Tappert, Theodore G., trans. and ed., 1959. *The Book of Concord*. Philadelphia: Fortress Press.

Tarrow, Sidney. 1989. *Struggle, Politics and Reform: Collective Action, Social Movements and Cycles of Protest*. Western Societies Program, Occasional Paper no. 2. Ithaca: Cornell University Center for International Studies.

———1992. "Mentalities, Political Cultures, and Collective Action Frames," 174–202, in Aldon D. Morris and Carol McClurg Mueller, eds., *Frontiers in Social Movement Theory*. New Haven: Yale University Press.

Taves, Anne. 1986. *The Household of Faith: Roman Catholic Devotions in Mid-Nineteenth Century America*. Notre Dame: Notre Dame University Press.

Taylor, Judith D. 1980. *From Proselytizing to Social Reform: Three Generations of French Female Teaching Congregations, 1600–1720*. Ph.D. diss., History Department, Arizona State University.

Thacker, Alan. 1992. "Monks, Preaching and Pastoral Care in Early Anglo-Saxon England," 137–70, in John Blair and Richard Sharpe, eds., *Pastoral Care Before the Parish*. Leicester: Leicester University Press.

Theresa Margaret, Sister. 1968. "The Territorial Imperative." *Review for Religious* 27: 137–42.

Theresa Mary, C.S.C. 1963. "Religious Obedience and Critical Thinking." *Review for Religious* 22: 541–51.

Thompson, Margaret S. 1986. "Discovering Foremothers: Sisters, Society and the American Catholic Experience." *U.S. Catholic Historian* 5(3–4): 273–90.

————1989. "Sisterhood and Power: Class, Culture and Ethnicity in the American Convent." *Colby Library Quarterly* (Fall 1989): 149–75.

————1991. "Women, Feminism and the New Religious History: Catholic Sisters as a Case Study," 136–63, in Philip R. Vandermeer and Robert P. Swierenga, eds., *Belief and Behavior: Essays in the New Religious History.* New Brunswick: Rutgers University Press.

————1992. "Cultural Conundrum: Sisters, Ethnicity and the Adaptation of American Catholicism." *Mid America: An Historical Review.* 74(3): 205–30.

Tierney, Brian. 1989. "Pope and Bishops Before Trent: An Historical Survey," 11–24, in Bernard Cooke, ed., *The Papacy and the Church in the United States.* Mahwah, N.J.: Paulist Press.

Tillard, J. M. L., O.P. 1963. "Religious Life in the Mystery of the Church." *Review for Religious* 22: 613–33.

————1964a. "Religious Life: Sacrament of God's Presence." *Review for Religious* 23: 6–14.

————1964b. "Religious Life: Sign of the Eschatological Church." *Review for Religious* 23: 197–206.

————1965. "Religious Obedience: Mystery of Communion." *Review for Religious* 24: 66–86.

————1967. "A Point of Departure." *Review for Religious* 26: 424–40.

————1969. "Authority and Religious Life." *Review for Religious* 27: 80–103.

Tri-Conference Retirement Office. 1991. *Retirement Fund for Religious, 1990: Annual Report.* Washington, D.C.

Trundale, Charles B. 1962. "Love and Perfect Chastity." *Review for Religious* 21: 33–37.

Tugwell, Simon. 1987. "The Spirituality of the Dominicans," 15–31, in Jill Raitt, ed., *Christian Spirituality II: High Middle Ages and Reformation.* New York: Crossroad.

Turcotte, Paul-Andre. 1980. "Le recrutement dans les congregations religieuses Canadiennes." *Sciences religieuses* 9(4): 415–25.

———1982. "Le pluralisme dans les congregations religieuses quebecoises." *Sciences pastorales* 1(1): 27–40.

———1985. *Les chemins de la difference*. Montreal: Les editions Bellarmin.

———1987. "Les congregations masculines quebecoises." *Sciences religieuses* 16(3): 317–30.

———1989. "L'église, la secte, la mystique et l'ordre religieux." *Église et theologie* 20(1): 77–98.

———1990. "A l'intersection de l'église et de la secte: l'ordre religieux." *Sociologie et societes* 22(2): 65–80.

———1993a. "La recomposition identitaire dans les congregations enseignantes quebecoises," 521–30, in *Ethnologie des faits religieux en Europe*. Paris: Editions du C.T.H.S.

———1993b. "Sociologie et histoire." *Église et theologie* 24(1): 43–73.

Turner, Bryan S. 1991. *Religion and Social Theory*. 2d edition. Newbury Park, Cal.: Sage.

Vacher, Marguerite. 1991. *Des "regulieres" dans le siècle: Les soeurs de St. Joseph du Pere Medaille aux XVIIe et XVIIIe siècles*. Clermont-Ferrand Cedex: Editions Adosa.

Van Breeman, Peter G. 1975. "Unmarriageable For God's Sake." *Review for Religious* 34: 839–45.

Vatican Synod Secretariat. 1992. "Lineamenta: Consecrated Life in the Church and the World." *Origins* 22(26): 433–54.

Vaughan, Richard P., S.J. 1962. "Obedience and Psychological Maturity." *Review for Religious* 21: 203–06.

———1964. "Chastity and Psychosexual Development." *Review for Religious* 23: 715–23.

Veysey, Lawrence. 1973. *The Communal Experience*. Chicago: University of Chicago Press.

———1987. "Ideological Aspects of American Communal Movements," 28–36, in Yosef Gorni, Yaacov Oved, and Idit Paz, eds., *Communal Life: an International Perspective*. New Brunswick: Transaction.

Vida, M. Mary, O.S.F. 1966. "Freedom to Obey." *Review for Religious* 25: 104–13.

Vidulich, Dorothy A. 1990. *Peace Pays a Price: A Study of Margaret Anna Cusack*. Seattle: Windward Press.

Viola, M. Mary. 1966. "The Great Waste." *Review for Religious* 25: 114–24.

Wach, Joachim. 1944. *Sociology of Religion*. Chicago: University of Chicago Press.

Wagner, Jon. 1985. "Success in Intentional Communities: the Problem of Evaluation." *Communal Societies* 5: 89–100.

Wallace, Ruth A. 1991. "Women Administrators of Priestless Parishes: Constraints and Opportunities." *Review for Religious Research* 32(4):289–304.

———1992. *They Call Her Pastor: A New Role for Catholic Women*. Albany: State University of New York Press.

Walsh, Michael. 1991. *Opus Dei: An Investigation Into the Secret Society Struggling for Power Within the Roman Catholic Church*. San Francisco: Harper.

Ward, S. Mary Carl, RSM. 1966. "The Great Waste." *Review for Religious* 25: 114–24.

Warner, R. Stephen. 1988. *New Wine in Old Wineskins*. Berkeley: University of California Press.

Weaver, Mary Jo. 1985. *New Catholic Women: A Contemporary Challenge to Traditional Religious Authority*. New York: Harper and Row.

Weber, Max. 1958. *From Max Weber: Essays in Sociology*. Translated and edited by H. H. Garth and C. W. Mills. New York: Oxford University Press.

———1963. *The Sociology of Religion*. Translated by Ephraim Fischoff. Boston: Beacon Press.

Westerkamp, Marilyn J. 1991. "Enthusiastic Piety: From Scots-Irish Revivals to the Great Awakening," 63–87, in Philip R. Vandermeer and Robert P. Swierenga, eds., *Belief and Behavior: Essays in the New Religious History*. New Brunswick: Rutgers University Press.

Whetten, David A. 1987. "Organizational Growth and Decline Processes." *Annual Review of Sociology* 13: 335–58.

White, Teresa. 1991. "Poverty in Religious Life?" *Religious Life Review* 30(3): 144–53.

Whitehead, James D., and Evelyn Whitehead. 1990. "Obedience and Adult Faith." *Review for Religious* 49: 397–406.

Whitworth, John McKelvie. 1975. *God's Blueprints: A Sociological Study of Three Utopian Sects*. London: Routledge and Kegan Paul.

Wilson, George. 1969. "The Married and the Celibate: Mutual Signs in the One Great Sign." *Review for Religious* 28: 776–82.

Winstanley, Michael T. 1981. "The Pattern of Christ's Surrender and Freedom." *Review for Religious* 40: 866–81.

Wittberg, Patricia. 1988. "Outward Orientation in Declining Organizations," 89–105, in Nadine Foley, ed., *Claiming Our Truth: Reflections on Identity by U.S. Women Religious.* Washington, D.C.: Leadership Conference of Women Religious.

————1989a. "The Dual Labor Market in the Catholic Church: Expanding a Speculative Inquiry." *Review of Religious Research* 30(3): 287–90.

————1989b. "Feminist Consciousness among American Nuns: Patterns of Ideological Diffusion." *Women's Studies International Forum* 12(3): 529–37.

————1990. "Dyads and Triads: The Sociological Implications of Small-Group Living Arrangements." *Review for Religious* 49: 43–51.

————1993a. "Job Satisfaction among Lay, Clergy and Religious Order Workers for the Catholic Church: A Preliminary Investigation." *Review of Religious Research* 34(5): 19–33.

————1993b. "Residence Stability and Decline in Roman Catholic Religious Orders of Women: A Preliminary Investigation." *Journal for the Scientific Study of Religion* 32(1): 76–82.

Wombacher, Kristin, O.P. 1989. "Religious Life, 1965–85." 63–73, in Laurie Felknor, ed., *The Crisis in Religious Vocations.* New York: Paulist Press.

Woodward, Evelyn. 1987. *Poets, Prophets and Pragmatists: A New Challenge to Religious Life.* Notre Dame: Ave Maria Press.

Woodward, Kenneth L. 1990. *Making Saints.* New York: Simon and Schuster.

Woodward, Kenneth L. et al. 1990. "The Graying of the Convent." *Newsweek* (April 2, 1990), 50–51.

Woodward, Kenneth L. and Andrew Nagorski. 1991. "The Troubled Altar of Freedom." *Newsweek* (June 17, 1991), 43.

Wynne, Edward A. 1988. *Traditional Catholic Religious Orders: Living in Community.* New Brunswick, N.J.: Transaction.

Yinger, J. Milton. 1970. *The Scientific Study of Religion.* New York: Macmillan.

Zablocki, Benjamin. 1980a. *Alienation and Charisma: A Study of Contemporary American Communes*. New York: Free Press.

————1980b. *The Joyful Community*. Chicago: University of Chicago Press.

Zald, Mayer N. 1992. "Looking Backward to Look Forward," 326–48, in Aldon D. Morris and Carol McClurg Mueller, eds., *Frontiers of Social Movement Theory*. New Haven: Yale University Press.

Zimdars-Swartz, Sandra L. 1991. *Encountering Mary: From LaSalette to Medjugorje*. Princeton, N.J.: Princeton University Press.

Zinn, Grover A. 1985. "The Regular Canons," 218–28, in Bernard McGinn, and John Myendorff, eds., *Christian Spirituality I: Origins to the Twelfth Century*. New York: Crossroad.

Name Index

Subject Index